THE MODERN LIBRARY
OF THE WORLD'S BEST BOOKS

FOUR PLAYS BY

BERNARD SHAW

CANDIDA

CÆSAR AND CLEOPATRA

PYGMALION

HEARTBREAK HOUSE

FOUR PLAYS BY

BERNARD SHAW

CANDIDA

CÆSAR AND CLEOPATRA

PYGMALION

HEARTBREAK HOUSE

INTRODUCTION BY
LOUIS KRONENBERGER

THE MODERN LIBRARY · NEW YORK

Random House IS THE PUBLISHER OF *The Modern Library*

BENNETT A. CERF · DONALD S. KLOPFER · ROBERT K. HAAS

Manufactured in the United States of America
By H. Wolff

CONTENTS

Introduction

BY LOUIS KRONENBERGER

Among modern playwrights, Shaw was the only one with the variety, populousness, stature, dimensions of a great nation or continent: the career that stretches from *Arms and the Man* to *King Charles' Golden Days* is like something that extends from the Atlantic to the Pacific. But Shaw was no less, among modern playwrights, the only one with the torrential energy, the flood of wit and rhetoric, of a Niagara Falls. And if these two symbolic images help to express Shaw's tremendous virtues, they yet, in a sense, suggest his large limitations. I think it would be unwise to claim that Shaw, dramatically speaking, was anything much more than a continent in size and a cascading tumult in energy. I think it would be unwise to insist that he was also a great cathedral or holy place to worship in; or a mountaintop to survey the world from; or even entirely a human being like you and me.

His two virtues do help, of course, to compensate for what he was not. In terms of spaciousness, there are some two dozen plays still worth our attention; one or two novels deserving a glance; a collection of notable prefaces; the finest journalistic drama criticism and the finest journalistic music criticism known to me in English; some valuable literary criticism; a number of stimulating treatises; any number of fascinating letters; and even some pronouncements scribbled on postcards and paradoxes sent by cable. Out of all this, there emerge Bluntschli, Burgoyne, Mrs. Warren, Prossy, Cæsar, Broadbent, Keegan, John Tanner, Don Juan, Ann Whitefield, Andrew Undershaft, Higgins, Liza, Lavinia and how many other characters; "The more respectable a man is, the more things he has to be ashamed of" and how many other comments; the personal relations with Ellen Terry and Mrs. Patrick Campbell, the critical distinction between Bernhardt and Duse, the great defense of Verdi, the great declamations in Hell. All this quite lacks the dense homogeneous complexity of a Balzac's Paris or a Joyce's Dublin; it runs back to Methuselah and even before him; it leaps ahead into a world we can no more visualize than enter; it invents kingdoms and invades Heaven. There was never such diversity of setting nor range of scenery; there were never such deserts worth crossing for the sake of the oases; such dead cities worth visiting for the buried treasure; so many unattractive Irishmen worth knowing for their slaps at the English; so many bohemians worth tolerating for their sneers at the philistines; so many cads worth hobnobbing with for what they might whisper of the virtuous.

Still, the Shaw regarded as a continent ranks below the Shaw gazed upon as a waterfall. For the continent is not everywhere enjoyable in its diversity: it has sprawl along with size, lowlands along with eminences, Kansas Citys of the spirit, Kansas prairies of story-telling; there can be sameness of look despite change of air; and something so inconsistent about the countryside as to seem fraudulent. Has Shaw's Heaven a salubrious climate, or would one gasp there for air? And what of Don Juan's Life Force, when followed by praise for Undershaft's munitions? And of treating old ruins (like the philosophy of Lamarck) as though they were habitable houses? And what of the Fabian who all but swallowed the Führer? And of the mountain that, though it never went to Mahomet, did go to the Kremlin?

A continent is a thing of all weathers, and of varying and contradictory worlds. But a vast cataract, a Niagara Falls, is all one thing: is all rush, speed, tumult. It astounds, dazzles, overwhelms us as a marvel of Nature—and quite without reference to whether it enriches, enlightens, fortifies us as an object of wisdom. This staggering vitality, this endless flow of wit and rhetoric, has its own glorious self-justification. Where the wit happens also to show depth, or the language is channeled by thought and perception, we encounter something very close to greatness; but even where we do not, the performance is often as matchless as it is meaningless.

Shaw had, finally, the ability to catch and rivet attention; he had all of Niagara Falls' showmanship. Thus, when he turned playwright, he only needed to learn the routine ways and tricks of the theatre, which he quickly did, and eventually did without: for he had an instinctive sense of the theatrical, which is to say of the startling and the unexpected. He knew that success in a playwright doesn't rest on knowing how to make characters talk, but on how to make audiences do so. He had a fine natural gift for shocking people. He understood the value for a dramatist in being misunderstood; and, aware that even geniuses have their off days, he realized the importance of making skim milk masquerade as cream. *Candida*, for me, does that—along with making a three-sided relationship masquerade as sex.

Sex might very well be thought Shaw's tendon of Achilles; and not least because he seems to suggest that it's his forte. His trick, there, is to conceal the unconvincing beneath the unconventional. In *Candida*, the fiery young poet is madly in love with the glamorous older woman; and is not only dismissed at the end, but does little more than snarl at the husband throughout. In *Cæsar and Cleopatra*, the middle-aged conqueror is infatuated with the young enchantress; yet he resists her, not only in defiance of natural instinct, but in disobedience to historical truth. In *Pygmalion*, the rich bachelor raises the guttersnipe out of the gutter; feeds her, clothes her, makes a fine lady of her without making a dishonest woman—or even a wife. And in that Shavian Noah's Ark, *Heartbreak House*, the animals do virtually everything *except* pair off.

We should be immensely grateful to Shaw because he realizes that love-making, on the stage, can be a bore. But we must also be a little appalled for his not seeming aware that in real life it can be a pleasure. Despite all the varieties and vicissitudes

of love in Shaw, the theories and disquisitions, the gestures and
intrigues, the business of Ann-pursuing and John-pursued, the
chase in *Misalliance* through heather and hall, the countless
pages of *Getting Married,* the wheel of centuries in *Back to
Methuselah,* there is less in all this of honest sex than in a line
or two of passionate verse, a

> Christ! if my love were in my arms
> And I in my bed again.

Thus Shaw's Candida smacks for me of Portia, and of a curiously sexless Portia, for whom an ounce of devotion is worth
a pound of flesh. Yet, so classic is her situation, and so completely is she master of it, and so clever is the twist Shaw
introduces at the end, that this is not just perhaps Shaw's
biggest box-office play, but his one persuasively romantic
comedy.

With *Cæsar and Cleopatra,* however, I am all on Shaw's
side. For what Shaw did here, though untrue to Nature and
unfaithful to history, was I think in the interests of Art.
Cæsar's behavior toward Cleopatra in the play harmonizes
with Cæsar's behavior generally; harmonizes with Shaw's idea
of Cæsar and of Cæsar's rueful, well-nigh tragic, realizations.
In a way, of course, Shaw exalts here, and even idealizes, the
Strong Man, the dictator. But his Cæsar is the most humane
and philosophic of dictators; more Shaw than Cæsar; more
sad-eyed than sword-raising; one who seems to say that though
power indeed corrupts, without power Right cannot possibly
prevail. And he demonstrates that though bald and aging men
may rule the world, when it comes to losing their hearts to
young and youth-loving minxes, they risk having them broken.
So Cæsar does the prudent thing and goes away, promising to
send Marc Antony to Egypt. But the play, despite its title, is
not essentially about Cæsar and Cleopatra, about a man in
relation to a woman; and it is a larger and more distinguished

play for that very reason. The play concerns Cæsar, really; an idealized Cæsar who is differentiated here from Cæsarism; it is a political play, a philosophic one, and among the maturest and most durable Shaw ever wrote.

Sexlessness rears its ruddy beard again in *Pygmalion*, but there too we gain more than we lose. If Shaw balks at making Liza's relations to Higgins those of Cinderella to the Fairy Prince, neither does he make them Caliban's to Prospero:

> *You taught me language, and my profit of it*
> *Is, I know how to curse.*

Shaw permits *Pygmalion* all the trappings of romantic comedy; lets every one, even Liza, assume that Higgins will marry her; and in the theatre never flatly states that Higgins didn't. Shaw only says that Higgins didn't in the epilogue (which is written in pamphlet form). And he didn't for a very modern reason: because he had a mother fixation. But Higgins' lack of susceptibility is what, in the end, gives the play its freshness; and is equally what turns Liza into a hurt and indignant, and thus into a living woman.

Sex is, of course, not the issue in *Heartbreak House*: the issue, there, is hardly less than civilization itself. Shaw himself described the play as "cultured, leisured Europe before the war"—as, too, a kind of English *Cherry Orchard*. Here, as in Chekhov, we are meant to see in the outer life of a group the inner death of a society. Shaw uses a much larger stage, his people form a far more miscellaneous company, and the whole thing is orchestrated on a more grandiose and operatic scale. There are for me, here, few of the cello notes that abound in Chekhov, and a great many wind effects that Chekhov, far from striving after, might have smiled at: *Heartbreak House* is meant to be impressive, and it is. But along with vivid scenes and memorable characters and brilliant speeches, it has the garrulities and driftingness of Shaw's later period: it does not, for me, compare with that so much earlier large-scale work, *Cæsar and Cleopatra*.

In large or small scale, Shaw's plays orchestrate a mind whose atonalities are as effective as his well-tempered chords.

NEW YORK
JULY, 1953

Candida

1895

ACT I

A FINE morning in October 1894 in the north east quarter
of London, a vast district miles away from the London of May-
fair and St James's, and much less narrow, squalid, fetid and
airless in its slums. It is strong in unfashionable middle class
life: wide-streeted; myriad-populated; well served with ugly
iron urinals, Radical clubs, and tram lines carrying a perpetual
stream of yellow cars; enjoying in its main thoroughfares the
luxury of grass-grown "front gardens" untrodden by the foot
of man save as to the path from the gate to the hall door;
blighted by a callously endured monotony of miles and miles
of unlovely brick houses, black iron railings, stony pavements,
slated roofs, and respectably ill dressed or disreputably worse
dressed people, quite accustomed to the place, and mostly plod-
ding uninterestedly about somebody else's work. The little energy and eagerness that crop up shew themselves in cockney
cupidity and business "push." Even the policemen and the
chapels are not infrequent enough to break the monotony. The
sun is shining cheerfully: there is no fog; and though the smoke
effectually prevents anything, whether faces and hands or
bricks and mortar, from looking fresh and clean, it is not hanging heavily enough to trouble a Londoner.

This desert of unattractiveness has its oasis. Near the outer
end of the Hackney Road is a park of 217 acres, fenced in, not
by railings, but by a wooden paling, and containing plenty of
greensward, trees, a lake for bathers, flower beds which are
triumphs of the admired cockney art of carpet gardening, and a
sandpit, originally imported from the seaside for the delight of
children, but speedily deserted on its becoming a natural vermin preserve for all the petty fauna of Kingsland, Hackney,

3

and Hoxton. A bandstand, an unfurnished forum for religious, anti-religious, and political orators, cricket pitches, a gymnasium, and an old fashioned stone kiosk are among its attractions. Wherever the prospect is bounded by trees or rising green grounds, it is a pleasant place. Where the ground stretches flat to the grey palings, with bricks and mortar, sky signs, crowded chimneys and smoke beyond, the prospect makes it desolate and sordid.

The best view of Victoria Park is commanded by the front window of St Dominic's Parsonage, from which not a brick is visible. The parsonage is semi-detached, with a front garden and a porch. Visitors go up the flight of steps to the porch: tradespeople and members of the family go down by a door under the steps to the basement, with a breakfast room, used for all meals, in front, and the kitchen at the back. Upstairs, on the level of the hall door, is the drawingroom, with its large plate glass window looking out on the park. In this, the only sitting room that can be spared from the children and the family meals, the parson, the Reverend James Mavor Morell, does his work. He is sitting in a strong round backed revolving chair at the end of a long table, which stands across the window, so that he can cheer himself with a view of the park over his left shoulder. At the opposite end of the table, adjoining it, is a little table only half as wide as the other, with a typewriter on it. His typist is sitting at this machine, with her back to the window. The large table is littered with pamphlets, journals, letters, nests of drawers, an office diary, postage scales and the like. A spare chair for visitors having business with the parson is in the middle, turned to his end. Within reach of his hand is a stationery case, and a photograph in a frame. The wall behind him is fitted with bookshelves, on which an adept eye can measure the parson's casuistry and divinity by Maurice's Theological Essays and a complete set of Browning's poems, and the reformer's politics by a yellow backed Progress and Poverty, Fabian Essays, A Dream of John Ball, Marx's Capital, and half a dozen other literary landmarks in Socialism. Facing him on the other side of the room, near the typewriter, is the door. Further down opposite the fireplace, a bookcase stands on a cellaret, with a sofa near it. There is a generous fire burning; and the hearth, with a comfortable armchair and a black japanned flower-painted coal scuttle at one side, a miniature chair for children on the other, a varnished wooden mantelpiece, with neatly moulded shelves, tiny bits of mirror let into the panels, a travelling clock in a leather case (the inevitable wedding present), and on the wall above a large autotype of the chief figure in Titian's Assumption of the Virgin, is very inviting. Altogether the room is the room of a good housekeeper, vanquished, as far as the table is concerned, by an untidy man, but elsewhere mistress of the situation. The furniture, in its ornamental aspect, betrays the style of the advertised "drawingroom suite" of the pushing suburban furniture dealer; but there is nothing useless or pretentious in the room, money being too scarce in the house of an east end parson to be wasted on snobbish trimmings.

The Reverend James Mavor Morell is a Christian Socialist clergyman of the Church of England, and an active member of the Guild of St Matthew and the Christian Social Union. A vigorous, genial, popular man of forty, robust and goodlooking, full of energy, with pleasant, hearty, considerate manners, and a sound unaffected voice, which he uses with the clean athletic articulation of a practised orator, and with a wide range and perfect command of expression. He is a first rate clergyman, able to say what he likes to whom he likes, to lecture people without setting himself up against them, to impose his authority on them without humiliating them, and, on occasion, to interfere in their business without impertinence. His well-spring of enthusiasm and sympathetic emotion has never run dry for a moment: he still eats and sleeps heartily enough to win the daily battle between exhaustion and recuperation triumphantly. Withal, a great baby, pardonably vain of his powers and unconsciously pleased with himself. He has a healthy complexion:

*good forehead, with the brows somewhat blunt, and the eyes
bright and eager, mouth resolute but not particularly well cut,
and a substantial nose, with the mobile spreading nostrils of the
dramatic orator, void, like all his features, of subtlety.*

*The typist, Miss Proserpine Garnett, is a brisk little woman
of about 30, of the lower middle class, neatly but cheaply
dressed in a black merino skirt and a blouse, notably pert and
quick of speech, and not very civil in her manner, but sensitive
and affectionate. She is clattering away busily at her machine
whilst Morell opens the last of his morning's letters. He realizes
its contents with a comic groan of despair.*

Proserpine. Another lecture?

Morell. Yes. The Hoxton Freedom Group want me to ad-
dress them on Sunday morning (*he lays great emphasis on
Sunday, this being the unreasonable part of the business*).
What are they?

Proserpine. Communist Anarchists, I think.

Morell. Just like Anarchists not to know that they cant have
a parson on Sunday! Tell them to come to church if they want
to hear me: it will do them good. Say I can come on Mondays
and Thursdays only. Have you the diary there?

Proserpine (*taking up the diary*) Yes.

Morell. Have I any lecture on for next Monday?

Proserpine (*referring to diary*) Tower Hamlets Radical Club.

Morell. Well, Thursday then?

Proserpine. English Land Restoration League.

Morell. What next?

Proserpine. Guild of St Matthew on Monday. Independent
Labor Party, Greenwich Branch, on Thursday. Monday, So-
cial-Democratic Federation, Mile End Branch. Thursday, first
Confirmation class. (*Impatiently*) Oh, I'd better tell them you
cant come. Theyre only half a dozen ignorant and conceited
costermongers without five shillings between them.

Morell (*amused*) Ah; but you see theyre near relatives of mine.

Proserpine (*staring at him*) Relatives of yours!

Morell. Yes: we have the same father—in Heaven.

Proserpine (*relieved*) Oh, is that all?

Morell (*with a sadness which is a luxury to a man whose voice expresses it so finely*) Ah, you dont believe it. Everybody says it: nobody believes it: nobody. (*Briskly, getting back to business*) Well, well! Come, Miss Proserpine: cant you find a date for the costers? What about the 25th? That was vacant the day before yesterday.

Proserpine (*referring to diary*) Engaged. The Fabian Society.

Morell. Bother the Fabian Society! Is the 28th gone too?

Proserpine. City dinner. Youre invited to dine with the Founders' Company.

Morell. Thatll do: I'll go to the Hoxton Group of Freedom instead. (*She enters the engagement in silence, with impla-cable disparagement of the Hoxton Anarchists in every line of her face. Morell bursts open the cover of a copy of The Church Reformer, which has come by post, and glances through Mr Stewart Headlam's leader and the Guild of St Matthew news. These proceedings are presently enlivened by the appearance of Morell's curate, the Reverend Alexander Mill, a young gen-tleman gathered by Morell from the nearest University settle-ment, whither he had come from Oxford to give the east end of London the benefit of his university training. He is a con-ceitedly well intentioned, enthusiastic, immature novice, with nothing positively unbearable about him except a habit of speaking with his lips carefully closed a full half inch from each corner for the sake of a finicking articulation and a set of university vowels, this being his chief means so far of bringing his Oxford refinement (as he calls his habits) to bear on Hack-ney vulgarity. Morell, whom he has won over by a doglike devotion, looks up indulgently from The Church Reformer, and remarks*) Well, Lexy? Late again, as usual!

Lexy. I'm afraid so. I wish I could get up in the morning.

Morell (exulting in his own energy) Ha! Ha! *(Whimsically)* Watch and pray, Lexy: watch and pray.

Lexy. I know. *(Rising wittily to the occasion)* But how can I watch and pray when I am asleep? Isnt that so, Miss Prossy? *(He makes for the warmth of the fire).*

Proserpine (sharply) Miss Garnett, if you please.

Lexy. I beg your pardon. Miss Garnett.

Proserpine. Youve got to do all the work today.

Lexy (on the hearth) Why?

Proserpine. Never mind why. It will do you good to earn your supper before you eat it, for once in a way, as I do. Come! dont dawdle. You should have been off on your rounds half an hour ago.

Lexy (perplexed) Is she in earnest, Morell?

Morell (in the highest spirits: his eyes dancing) Yes. I am going to dawdle today.

Lexy. You! You dont know how.

Morell (rising) Ha! ha! Dont I? I'm going to have this morning all to myself. My wife's coming back: she's due here at 11.45.

Lexy (surprised) Coming back already! with the children? I thought they were to stay to the end of the month.

Morell. So they are: she's only coming up for two days, to get some flannel things for Jimmy, and to see how we're getting on without her.

Lexy (anxiously) But, my dear Morell, if what Jimmy and Fluffy had was scarlatina, do you think it wise—

Morell. Scarlatina! Rubbish! it was German measles. I brought it into the house myself from the Pycroft Street school. A parson is like a doctor, my boy: he must face infection as a soldier must face bullets. *(He claps Lexy manfully on the shoulders).* Catch the measles if you can, Lexy: she'll nurse you; and what a piece of luck that will be for you! Eh?

Lexy (*smiling uneasily*) It's so hard to understand you about Mrs Morell—

Morell (*tenderly*) Ah, my boy, get married: get married to a good woman; and then youll understand. Thats a foretaste of what will be best in the Kingdom of Heaven we are trying to establish on earth. That will cure you of dawdling. An honest man feels that he must pay Heaven for every hour of happiness with a good spell of hard unselfish work to make others happy. We have no more right to consume happiness without producing it than to consume wealth without producing it. Get a wife like my Candida; and youll always be in arrear with your repayment. (*He pats Lexy affectionately and moves to leave the room*).

Lexy. Oh, wait a bit: I forgot. (*Morell halts and turns with the door knob in his hand*). Your father-in-law is coming round to see you.

Morell, surprised and not pleased, shuts the door again, with a complete change of manner.

Morell. Mr Burgess?

Lexy. Yes. I passed him in the park, arguing with somebody. He asked me to let you know that he was coming.

Morell (*half incredulous*) But he hasnt called here for three years. Are you sure, Lexy? Youre not joking, are you?

Lexy (*earnestly*) No sir, really.

Morell (*thoughtfully*) Hm! Time for him to take another look at Candida before she grows out of his knowledge. (*He resigns himself to the inevitable, and goes out*).

Lexy looks after him with beaming worship. Miss Garnett, not being able to shake Lexy, relieves her feelings by worrying the typewriter.

Lexy. What a good man! What a thorough loving soul he is! (*He takes Morell's place at the table, making himself very comfortable as he takes out a cigaret*).

Proserpine (*impatiently, pulling the letter she has been working at off the typewriter and folding it*) Oh, a man ought to be able to be fond of his wife without making a fool of himself about her.

Lexy (*shocked*) Oh, Miss Prossy!

Proserpine (*snatching at the stationery case for an envelope, in which she encloses the letter as she speaks*) Candida here, and Candida there, and Candida everywhere! (*She licks the envelope*). It's enough to drive anyone out of their senses (*thumping the envelope to make it stick*) to hear a woman raved about in that absurd manner merely because she's got good hair and a tolerable figure.

Lexy (*with reproachful gravity*) I think her extremely beautiful, Miss Garnett. (*He takes the photograph up; looks at it; and adds, with even greater impressiveness*) e x t r e m e l y beautiful. How fine her eyes are!

Proserpine. Her eyes are not a bit better than mine: now! (*He puts down the photograph and stares austerely at her*). And you know very well you think me dowdy and second rate enough.

Lexy (*rising majestically*) Heaven forbid that I should think of any of God's creatures in such a way! (*He moves stiffly away from her across the room to the neighborhood of the bookcase*).

Proserpine (*sarcastically*) Thank you. Thats very nice and comforting.

Lexy (*saddened by her depravity*) I had no idea you had any feeling against Mrs Morell.

Proserpine (*indignantly*) I have no feeling against her. She's very nice, very good-hearted: I'm very fond of her, and can appreciate her real qualities far better than any man can. (*He shakes his head sadly. She rises and comes at him with intense pepperiness*). You dont believe me? You think I'm jealous? Oh, what a knowledge of the human heart you have, Mr Lexy Mill! How well you know the weaknesses of Woman, dont you? It must be so nice to be a man and have a fine penetrating intellect instead of mere emotions like us, and to know that the reason we dont share your amorous delusions is that we're all jealous of one another! (*She abandons him with a toss of her shoulders, and crosses to the fire to warm her hands*).

Lexy. Ah, if you women only had the same clue to Man's strength that you have to his weakness, Miss Prossy, there would be no Woman Question.

Proserpine (*over her shoulder, as she stoops, holding her hands to the blaze*) Where did you hear Morell say that? You didnt invent it yourself: youre not clever enough.

Lexy. Thats quite true. I am not ashamed of owing him that, as I owe him so many other spiritual truths. He said it at the annual conference of the Women's Liberal Federation. Allow me to add that though they didnt appreciate it, I, a mere man, did. (*He turns to the bookcase again, hoping that this may leave her crushed*).

Proserpine (*putting her hair straight at a panel of mirror in the mantelpiece*) Well, when you talk to me, give me your own ideas, such as they are, and not his. You never cut a poorer figure than when you are trying to imitate him.

Lexy (*stung*) I try to follow his example, not to imitate him.

Proserpine (*coming at him again on her way back to her work*) Yes, you do: you i m i t a t e him. Why do you tuck your umbrella under your left arm instead of carrying it in your hand like anyone else? Why do you walk with your chin stuck out before you, hurrying along with that eager look in your eyes? you! who never get up before half past nine in the morning. Why do you say "knoaledge" in church, though you always say "knolledge" in private conversation! Bah! do you think I dont know? (*She goes back to the typewriter*). Here! come and set about your work: weve wasted enough time for one morning. Here's a copy of the diary for today. (*She hands him a memorandum*).

Lexy (*deeply offended*) Thank you. (*He takes it and stands at the table with his back to her, reading it. She begins to transcribe her shorthand notes on the typewriter without troubling herself about his feelings*).

The door opens; and Mr Burgess enters unannounced. He is a man of sixty, made coarse and sordid by the compulsory self-ishness of petty commerce, and later on softened into sluggish bumptiousness by overfeeding and commercial success. A vulgar ignorant guzzling man, offensive and contemptuous to people whose labor is cheap, respectful to wealth and rank, and quite sincere and without rancor or envy in both attitudes. The world has offered him no decently paid work except that of a sweater; and he has become, in consequence, somewhat hoggish. But he has no suspicion of this himself, and honestly regards his commercial prosperity as the inevitable and socially wholesome triumph of the ability, industry, shrewdness, and experience in business of a man who in private is easygoing, affectionate, and humorously convivial to a fault. Corporeally he is podgy, with a snoutish nose in the centre of a flat square face, a dust colored beard with a patch of grey in the centre under his chin, and small watery blue eyes with a plaintively sentimental expres-sion, which he transfers easily to his voice by his habit of pomp-ously intoning his sentences.

Burgess (*stopping on the threshold, and looking round*) They told me Mr Morell was here.

Proserpine (*rising*) I'll fetch him for you.

Burgess (*staring disappointedly at her*) Youre not the same young lady as hused to typewrite for him?

Proserpine. No.

Burgess (*grumbling on his way to the hearth-rug*) No: she was young-er. (*Miss Garnett stares at him; then goes out, slam-ming the door*). Startin on your rounds, Mr Mill?

Lexy (*folding his memorandum and pocketing it*) Yes: I must be off presently.

Burgess (*momentously*) Dont let me detain you, Mr Mill. What I come about is private between me and Mr Morell.

Lexy (*huffily*) I have no intention of intruding, I am sure, Mr Burgess. G o o d morning.

Burgess (*patronizingly*) Oh, good morning to you.

Morell returns as Lexy is making for the door.

Morell (*to Lexy*) Off to work?

Lexy. Yes, sir.

Morell. Take my silk handkerchief and wrap your throat up. Theres a cold wind. Away with you.

Lexy, more than consoled for Burgess's rudeness, brightens up and goes out.

Burgess. Spoilin your korates as usu'l, James. Good mornin. When I pay a man, an' 'is livin depens on me, I keep him in 'is place.

Morell (*rather shortly*) I always keep my curates in their places as my helpers and comrades. If you get as much work out of your clerks and warehousemen as I do out of my curates, you must be getting rich pretty fast. Will you take your old chair.

He points with curt authority to the armchair beside the fireplace; then takes the spare chair from the table and sits down at an unfamiliar distance from his visitor.

Burgess (*without moving*) Just the same as hever, James!

Morell. When you last called—it was about three years ago, I think—you said the same thing a little more frankly. Your exact words then were "Just as big a fool as ever, James!"

Burgess (*soothingly*) Well, praps I did; but (*with conciliatory cheerfulness*) I meant no hoffence by it. A clorgyman is privileged to be a bit of a fool, you know: it's ony becomin in 'is profession that he should. Anyhow, I come here, not to rake up hold differences, but to let bygones be bygones. (*Suddenly becoming very solemn, and approaching Morell*). James: three years ago, you done me a hil turn. You done me hout of a contrac; an when I gev you arsh words in my natral disappointment, you turned my daughrter again me. Well, Ive come to hact the part of a Kerischin. (*Offering his hand*) I forgive you, James.

Morell (*starting up*) Confound your impudence!

Burgess (*retreating, with almost lachrymose deprecation of this treatment*) Is that becomin language for a clorgyman, James? And you so particlar, too!

Morell (*hotly*) No, sir: it is not becoming language for a clergyman. I used the wrong word. I should have said damn your impudence: thats what St Paul or any honest priest would have said to you. Do you think I have forgotten that tender of yours for the contract to supply clothing to the workhouse?

Burgess (*in a paroxysm of public spirit*) I hacted in the hinterest of the ratepayers, James. It was the lowest tender: you carnt deny that.

Morell. Yes, the lowest, because you paid worse wages than any other employer—starvation wages—aye, worse than starvation wages—to the women who made the clothing. Your wages would have driven them to the streets to keep body and soul together. (*Getting angrier and angrier*) Those women were my parishioners. I shamed the Guardians out of accepting your tender: I shamed the ratepayers out of letting them do it: I shamed everybody but you. (*Boiling over*) How dare you, sir, come here and offer to forgive me, and talk about your daughter, and—

Burgess. Heasy, James! heasy! heasy! Dont git hinto a fluster about nothink. Ive howned I was wrong.

Morell. Have you? I didnt hear you.

Burgess. Of course I did. I hown it now. Come: I harsk your pardon for the letter I wrote you. Is that enough?

Morell (*snapping his fingers*) Thats nothing. Have you raised the wages?

Burgess (*triumphantly*) Yes.

Morell. What!

Burgess (*unctuously*) Ive turned a moddle hemployer. I dont hemploy no women now: theyre all sacked; and the work is done by machinery. Not a man 'as less than sixpence a *hour*; and the skilled ands gits the Trade Union rate. (*Proudly*) What ave you to say to me now?

Morell (*overwhelmed*) Is it possible! Well, theres more joy in heaven over one sinner that repenteth!—(*Going to Burgess with an explosion of apologetic cordiality*) My dear Burgess: how splendid of you! I most heartily beg your pardon for my hard thoughts. (*Grasping his hand*) And now, dont you feel the better for the change? Come! confess! youre happier. You look happier.

Burgess (*ruefully*) Well, praps I do. I spose I must, since you notice it. At all events, I git my contrax assepted by the County Council. (*Savagely*) They dussent ave nothink to do with me unless I paid fair wages: curse em for a parcel o meddlin fools!

Morell (*dropping his hand, utterly discouraged*) So that was why you raised the wages! (*He sits down moodily*).

Burgess (*severely, in spreading, mounting tones*) Woy helse should I do it? What does it lead to but drink and huppishness in workin men? (*He seats himself magisterially in the easy chair*). It's hall very well for you, James: it gits you hinto the papers and makes a great man of you; but you never think of the arm you do, puttin money into the pockets of workin men that they dunno ow to spend, and takin it from people that might be makin a good huse on it.

Morell (*with a heavy sigh, speaking with cold politeness*) What is your business with me this morning? I shall not pretend to believe that you are here merely out of family sentiment.

Burgess (*obstinately*) Yes I ham: just family sentiment and nothink helse.

Morell (*with weary calm*) I dont believe you.

Burgess (*rising threateningly*) Dont say that to me again, James Mavor Morell.

Morell (*unmoved*) I'll say it just as often as may be necessary to convince you that it's true. I dont believe you.

Burgess (*collapsing into an abyss of wounded feeling*) Oh, well, if youre detormined to be hunfriendly, I spose I'd better go. (*He moves reluctantly towards the door. Morell makes no sign. He lingers*). I didnt hexpect to find a hunforgivin spirit in you, James. (*Morell still not responding, he takes a few more reluctant steps doorwards. Then he comes back, whining*). We huseter git on well enough, spite of our different hopinions. Woy are you so changed to me? I give you my word I come here in peeorr [pure] frenliness, not wishin to be hon bad terms with my hown daughrter's usban. Come, James: be a Kerischin, and shake ands. (*He puts his hand sentimentally on Morell's shoulder*).

Morell (*looking up at him thoughtfully*) Look here, Burgess. Do you want to be as welcome here as you were before you lost that contract?

Burgess. I do, James. I do—honest.

Morell. Then why dont you behave as you did then?

Burgess (*cautiously removing his hand*) Ow d'y' mean?

Morell. I'll tell you. You thought me a young fool then.

Burgess (*coaxingly*) No I didnt, James. I—

Morell (*cutting him short*) Yes, you did. And I thought you an old scoundrel.

Burgess (*most vehemently deprecating this gross self-accusation on Morell's part*) No you didnt, James. Now you do yourself a hinjustice.

Morell. Yes I did. Well, that did not prevent our getting on very well together. God made you what I call a scoundrel as He made me what you call a fool. (*The effect of this observation on Burgess is to remove the keystone of his moral arch. He becomes bodily weak, and, with his eyes fixed on Morell in a helpless stare, puts out his hand apprehensively to balance himself, as if the floor had suddenly sloped under him. Morell proceeds, in the same tone of quiet conviction*) It was not for me to quarrel with His handiwork in the one case more than in the other. So long as you come here honestly as a self-respecting, thorough, convinced scoundrel, justifying your scoundrelism and proud of it, you are welcome. But (*and now Morell's tone becomes formidable; and he rises and strikes the back of the chair for greater emphasis*) I wont have you here snivelling about being a model employer and a converted man when youre only an apostate with your coat turned for the sake of a County Council contract. (*He nods at him to enforce the point; then goes to the hearth-rug, where he takes up a comfortably commanding position with his back to the fire, and continues*) No: I like a man to be true to himself, even in wickedness. Come now: either take your hat and go; or else sit down and give me a good scoundrelly reason for wanting to be friends with me. (*Burgess, whose emotions have subsided sufficiently to be expressed by a dazed grin, is relieved by this concrete proposition. He ponders it for a moment, and then, slowly and very modestly, sits down in the chair Morell has just left*). Thats right. Now out with it.

Burgess (*chuckling in spite of himself*) Well, you orr a queer bird, James, and no mistake. But (*almost enthusiastically*) one carnt elp likin you: besides, as I said afore, of course one dont take hall a clorgyman says seriously, or the world couldnt go on. Could it now? (*He composes himself for graver discourse, and, turning his eyes on Morell, proceeds with dull seriousness*) Well, I dont mind tellin you, since it's your wish we should be free with one another, that I did think you a bit of a fool once; but I'm beginnin to think that praps I was be'ind the times a bit.

Morell (*exultant*) Aha! Youre finding that out at last, are you?

Burgess (*portentously*) Yes: times 'as changed mor'n I could a believed. Five yorr [year] ago, no sensible man would a thought o takin hup with your hidears. I hused to wonder you was let preach at all. Why, I know a clorgyman what 'as bin kep hout of his job for yorrs by the Bishop o London, although the pore feller's not a bit more religious than you are. But today, if hennyone was to horffer to bet me a thousan poud that youll hend by bein a bishop yourself, I dussent take the bet. (*Very impressively*) You and your crew are gittin hinfluential: I can see that. Theyll ave to give you somethink someday, if it's honly to stop your mouth. You ad the right instinc arter all, James: the line you took is the payin line in the long run for a man o your sort.

Morell (*offering his hand with thorough decision*) Shake hands, Burgess. Now youre talking honestly. I dont think theyll make me a bishop; but if they do, I'll introduce you to the biggest jobbers I can get to come to my dinner parties.

Burgess (*who has risen with a sheepish grin and accepted the hand of friendship*) You will ave your joke, James. Our quarrel's made up now, ain it?

A Woman's Voice. Say yes, James.

Startled, they turn quickly and find that Candida has just come in, and is looking at them with an amused maternal indulgence which is her characteristic expression. She is a woman of 33, well built, well nourished, likely, one guesses, to become matronly later on, but now quite at her best, with the double charm of youth and motherhood. Her ways are those of a woman who has found that she can always manage people by engaging their affection, and who does so frankly and instinctively without the smallest scruple. So far, she is like any other pretty woman who is just clever enough to make the most of her sexual attractions for trivially selfish ends; but Candida's serene brow, courageous eyes, and well set mouth and chin signify largeness of mind and dignity of character to ennoble her cunning in the affections. A wise-hearted observer, looking at her, would at once guess that whoever had placed the Virgin of the Assumption over her hearth did so because he fancied some spiritual resemblance between them, and yet would not suspect either her husband or herself of any such idea, or indeed of any concern with the art of Titian.

Just now she is in bonnet and mantle, carrying a strapped rug with her umbrella stuck through it, a handbag, and a supply of illustrated papers.

Morell (*shocked at his remissness*) Candida! Why— (*he

looks at his watch, and is horrified to find it so late). My darling! (*Hurrying to her and seizing the rug strap, pouring forth his remorseful regrets all the time*) I intended to meet you at the train. I let the time slip. (*Flinging the rug on the sofa*) I was so engrossed by— (*returning to her*) —I forgot—oh! (*He embraces her with penitent emotion*).

Burgess (*a little shamefaced and doubtful of his reception*) How orr you, Candy? (*She, still in Morell's arms, offers him her cheek, which he kisses*). James and me is come to a nunnerstannin. A honorable unnerstannin. Ain we, James?

Morell (*impetuously*) Oh bother your understanding! youve kept me late for Candida. (*With compassionate fervor*) My poor love: how did you manage about the luggage? How—

Candida (*stopping him and disengaging herself*) There! there! there! I wasnt alone. Eugene has been down with us; and we travelled together.

Morell (*pleased*) Eugene!

Candida. Yes: he's struggling with my luggage, poor boy. Go out, dear, at once; or he'll pay for the cab; and I dont want that. (*Morell hurries out. Candida puts down her handbag; then takes off her mantle and bonnet and puts them on the sofa with the rug, chatting meanwhile*). Well, papa: how are you getting on at home?

Burgess. The ouse aint worth livin in since you left it, Candy. I wish youd come round and give the gurl a talkin to. Who's this Eugene thats come with you?

Candida. Oh, Eugene's one of James's discoveries. He found him sleeping on the Embankment last June. Havnt you noticed our new picture (*pointing to the Virgin*)? He gave us that.

Burgess (*incredulously*) Garn! D'you mean to tell me— your hown father!—that cab touts or such like, orf the Embankment, buys pictures like that? (*Severely*) Dont deceive me, Candy: it's a 'Igh Church picture; and James chose it hisself.

Candida. Guess again. Eugene isnt a cab tout.

Burgess. Then what is he? (*Sarcastically*) A nobleman, I spose.

Candida (*nodding delightedly*) Yes. His uncle's a peer! A real live earl.

Burgess (*not daring to believe such good news*) No!

Candida. Yes. He had a seven day bill for £55 in his pocket when James found him on the Embankment. He thought he couldnt get any money for it until the seven days were up; and he was too shy to ask for credit. Oh, he's a dear boy! We are very fond of him.

Burgess (*pretending to belittle the aristocracy, but with his eyes gleaming*) Hm! I thort you wouldnt git a hearl's nevvy visitin in Victawriar Pawrk unless he were a bit of a flat. (*Looking again at the picture*) Of course I dont old with that picture, Candy; but still it's a 'igh class fust rate work of ort: I can see that. Be sure you hintrodooce me to im, Candy. (*He looks at his watch anxiously*). I can ony stay about two minutes.

Morell comes back with Eugene, whom Burgess contemplates moist-eyed with enthusiasm. He is a strange, shy youth of eighteen, slight, effeminate, with a delicate childish voice, and a hunted tormented expression and shrinking manner that shew the painful sensitiveness of very swift and acute apprehensiveness in youth, before the character has grown to its full strength. Miserably irresolute, he does not know where to stand or what to do. He is afraid of Burgess, and would run away into solitude if he dared; but the very intensity with which he feels a perfectly commonplace position comes from excessive nervous force; and his nostrils, mouth, and eyes betray a fiercely petulant wilfulness, as to the bent of which his brow, already lined with pity, is reassuring. He is so uncommon as to be almost unearthly; and to prosaic people there is something noxious in this unearthliness, just as to poetic people there is something angelic in it. His dress is anarchic. He wears an old blue serge jacket, unbuttoned, over a woollen lawn tennis shirt, with a silk handkerchief for a cravat, trousers matching the jacket, and brown canvas shoes. In these garments he has apparently lain in the heather and waded through the waters; and there is no evidence of his having ever brushed them.

As he catches sight of a stranger on entering, he stops, and edges along the wall on the opposite side of the room.

Morell (*as he enters*) Come along: you can spare us quarter of an hour at all events. This is my father-in-law. Mr Burgess—Mr Marchbanks.

Marchbanks (*nervously backing against the bookcase*) Glad to meet you, sir.

Burgess (*crossing to him with great heartiness, whilst Morell joins Candida at the fire*) Glad to meet you, I'm shore, Mr Morchbanks. (*Forcing him to shake hands*) Ow do you find yoreself this weather? Ope you aint lettin James put no foolish ideas into your ed?

Marchbanks. Foolish ideas? Oh, you mean Socialism? No.

Burgess. Thats right. (*Again looking at his watch*) Well, I must go now: theres no elp for it. Yore not comin my way, orr you, Mr Morchbanks?

Marchbanks. Which way is that?

Burgess. Victawriar Pawrk Station. Theres a city train at 12.25.

Morell. Nonsense. Eugene will stay to lunch with us, I expect.

Marchbanks (*anxiously excusing himself*) No—I—I—

Burgess. Well, well, I shornt press you: I bet youd rather lunch with Candy. Some night, I ope, youll come and dine with me at my club, the Freeman Founders in Nortn Folgit. Come: say you will!

Marchbanks. Thank you, Mr Burgess. Where is Norton Folgate? Down in Surrey, isnt it?

Burgess, inexpressibly tickled, begins to splutter with laughter.

Candida (coming to the rescue) Youll lose your train, papa, if you dont go at once. Come back in the afternoon and tell Mr Marchbanks where to find the club.

Burgess (roaring with glee) Down in Surrey! Har, har! thats not a bad one. Well, I never met a man as didnt know Nortn Folgit afore. *(Abashed at his own noisiness)* Goodbye, Mr Morchbanks: I know yore too ighbred to take my pleasantry in bad part. *(He again offers his hand).*

Marchbanks (taking it with a nervous jerk) Not at all.

Burgess. Bye, bye, Candy. I'll look in again later on. So long, James.

Morell. Must you go?

Burgess. Dont stir. *(He goes out with unabated heartiness).*

Morell. Oh, I'll see you off. *(He follows him).*

Eugene stares after them apprehensively, holding his breath until Burgess disappears.

Candida (laughing) Well, Eugene? *(He turns with a start, and comes eagerly towards her, but stops irresolutely as he meets her amused look).* What do you think of my father?

Marchbanks. I—I hardly know him yet. He seems to be a very nice old gentleman.

Candida (with gentle irony) And youll go to the Freeman Founders to dine with him, wont you?

Marchbanks (miserably, taking it quite seriously) Yes, if it will please you.

Candida (touched) Do you know, you are a very nice boy, Eugene, with all your queerness. If you had laughed at my father I shouldnt have minded; but I like you ever so much better for being nice to him.

Marchbanks. Ought I to have laughed? I noticed that he said something funny; but I am so ill at ease with strangers; and I never can see a joke. I'm very sorry. *(He sits down on the sofa, his elbows on his knees and his temples between his fists, with an expression of hopeless suffering).*

Candida (bustling him goodnaturedly) Oh come! You great baby, you! You are worse than usual this morning. Why were you so melancholy as we came along in the cab?

Marchbanks. Oh, that was nothing. I was wondering how much I ought to give the cabman. I know it's utterly silly; but you dont know how dreadful such things are to me—how I shrink from having to deal with strange people. *(Quickly and reassuringly)* But it's all right. He beamed all over and touched his hat when Morell gave him two shillings. I was on the point of offering him ten.

Morell comes back with a few letters and newspapers which have come by the midday post.

Candida. Oh, James dear, he was going to give the cabman ten shillings! ten shillings for a three minutes drive! Oh dear!

Morell (at the table, glancing through the letters) Never mind her, Marchbanks. The overpaying instinct is a generous one: better than the underpaying instinct, and not so common.

Marchbanks (relapsing into dejection) No: cowardice, incompetence. Mrs Morell's quite right.

Candida. Of course she is. *(She takes up her handbag).* And now I must leave you to James for the present. I suppose you are too much of a poet to know the state a woman finds her house in when she's been away for three weeks. Give me my rug. *(Eugene takes the strapped rug from the couch, and gives it to her. She takes it in her left hand, having the bag in her right).* Now hang my cloak across my arm. *(He obeys).* Now my hat. *(He puts it into the hand which has the bag).* Now open the door for me. *(He hurries before her and opens the door).* Thanks. *(She goes out; and Marchbanks shuts the door).*

Morell (still busy at the table) Youll stay to lunch, Marchbanks, of course.

Marchbanks (*scared*) I mustnt. (*He glances quickly at Morell, but at once avoids his frank look, and adds, with obvious disingenuousness*) I mean I cant.

Morell. You mean you wont.

Marchbanks (*earnestly*) No: I should like to, indeed. Thank you very much. But—but—

Morell. But—but—but—but—Bosh! If youd like to stay, stay. If youre shy, go and take a turn in the park and write poetry until half past one; and then come in and have a good feed.

Marchbanks. Thank you, I should like that very much. But I really mustnt. The truth is, Mrs Morell told me not to. She said she didnt think youd ask me to stay to lunch, but that I was to remember, if you did, that you didnt really want me to. (*Plaintively*) She said I'd understand; but I dont. Please dont tell her I told you.

Morell (*drolly*) Oh, is that all? Wont my suggestion that you should take a turn in the park meet the difficulty?

Marchbanks. How?

Morell (*exploding good-humoredly*) Why, you duffer— (*But this boisterousness jars himself as well as Eugene. He checks himself*). No. I wont put it in that way. (*He comes to Eugene with affectionate seriousness*). My dear lad: in a happy marriage like ours, there is something very sacred in the return of the wife to her home. (*Marchbanks looks quickly at him, half anticipating his meaning*). An old friend or a truly noble and sympathetic soul is not in the way on such occasions; but a chance visitor is. (*The hunted horror-stricken expression comes out with sudden vividness in Eugene's face as he understands. Morell, occupied with his own thoughts, goes on without noticing this*). Candida thought I would rather not have you here; but she was wrong. I'm very fond of you, my boy; and I should like you to see for yourself what a happy thing it is to be married as I am.

Marchbanks. Happy! Yo u r marriage! You think that! You believe that!

Morell (*buoyantly*) I know it, my lad. Larochefoucauld said that there are convenient marriages but no delightful ones. You dont know the comfort of seeing through and through a thundering liar and rotten cynic like that fellow. Ha! ha! Now, off with you to the park, and write your poem. Half past one, sharp, mind: we never wait for anybody.

Marchbanks (*wildly*) No: stop: you shant. I'll force it into the light.

Morell (*puzzled*) Eh? Force what?

Marchbanks. I must speak to you. There is something that must be settled between us.

Morell (*with a whimsical glance at his watch*) Now?

Marchbanks (*passionately*) Now. Before you leave this room. (*He retreats a few steps, and stands as if to bar Morell's way to the door*).

Morell (*without moving, and gravely, perceiving now that there is something serious the matter*) I'm not going to leave it, my dear boy: I thought you were. (*Eugene, baffled by his firm tone, turns his back on him, writhing with anger. Morell goes to him and puts his hand on his shoulder strongly and kindly, disregarding his attempt to shake it off*). Come: sit down quietly; and tell me what it is. And remember: we are friends, and need not fear that either of us will be anything but patient and kind to the other, whatever we may have to say.

Marchbanks (*twisting himself round on him*) Oh, I am not forgetting myself: I am only (*covering his face desperately with his hands*) full of horror. (*Then, dropping his hands, and thrusting his face forward fiercely at Morell, he goes on threateningly*) You shall see whether this is a time for patience and kindness. (*Morell, firm as a rock, looks indulgently at him*). Dont look at me in that self-complacent way. You think yourself stronger than I am; but I shall stagger you if you have a heart in your breast.

Morell (*powerfully confident*) Stagger me, my boy. Out with it.

Marchbanks. First—

Morell. First?

Marchbanks. I love your wife.

Morell recoils, and, after staring at him for a moment in utter amazement, bursts into uncontrollable laughter. Eugene is taken aback, but not disconcerted; and he soon becomes indignant and contemptuous.

Morell (*sitting down to have his laugh out*) Why, my dear child, of course you do. Everybody loves her: they cant help it. I like it. But (*looking up jocosely at him*) I say, Eugene: do you think yours is a case to be talked about? Youre under twenty: she's over thirty. Doesnt it look rather too like a case of calf love?

Marchbanks (*vehemently*) You dare say that of her! You think that way of the love she inspires! It is an insult to her!

Morell (*rising quickly, in an altered tone*) To her! Eugene: take care. I have been patient. I hope to remain patient. But there are some things I wont allow. Dont force me to shew you the indulgence I should shew to a child. Be a man.

Marchbanks (*with a gesture as if sweeping something behind him*) Oh, let us put aside all that cant. It horrifies me when I think of the doses of it she has had to endure in all the weary years during which you have selfishly and blindly sacrificed her to minister to your self-sufficiency: you! (*turning on him*) who have not one thought—one sense—in common with her.

Morell (*philosophically*) She seems to bear it pretty well. (*Looking him straight in the face*) Eugene, my boy: you are making a fool of yourself: a very great fool of yourself. Theres a piece of wholesome plain speaking for you. (*He knocks in the lesson with a nod in his old way, and posts himself on the hearth-rug, holding his hands behind him to warm them*).

Marchbanks. Oh, do you think I dont know all that? Do

you think that the things people make fools of themselves about are any less real and true than the things they behave sensibly about? (*Morell's gaze wavers for the first time. He forgets to warm his hands, and stands listening, startled and thoughtful*). They are more true: they are the only things that are true. You are very calm and sensible and moderate with me because you can see that I am a fool about your wife; just as no doubt that old man who was here just now is very wise over your Socialism, because he sees that y o u are a fool about it. (*Morell's perplexity deepens markedly. Eugene follows up his advantage, plying him fiercely with questions*). Does that prove you wrong? Does your complacent superiority to me prove that I am wrong?

Morell. Marchbanks: some devil is putting these words into your mouth. It is easy—terribly easy—to shake a man's faith in himself. To take advantage of that to break a man's spirit is devil's work. Take care of what you are doing. Take care.

Marchbanks (*ruthlessly*) I know. I'm doing it on purpose. I told you I should stagger you.

They confront one another threateningly for a moment. Then Morell recovers his dignity.

Morell (*with noble tenderness*) Eugene: listen to me. Some day, I hope and trust, you will be a happy man like me. (*Eugene chafes intolerantly, repudiating the worth of his happiness. Morell, deeply insulted, controls himself with fine forbearance, and continues steadily, with great artistic beauty of delivery*) You will be married; and you will be working with all your might and valor to make every spot on earth as happy as your own home. You will be one of the makers of the Kingdom of Heaven on earth; and—who knows?—you may be a master builder where I am only a humble journeyman; for dont think, my boy, that I cannot see in you, young as you are, promise of higher powers than I can ever pretend to. I well know that it is in the poet that the holy spirit of man—the god within him—is most godlike. It should make you tremble to think of that—to think that the heavy burthen and great gift of a poet may be laid upon you.

Marchbanks (*unimpressed and remorseless, his boyish crudity of assertion telling sharply against Morell's oratory*) It does not make me tremble. It is the want of it in others that makes me tremble.

Morell (*redoubling his force of style under the stimulus of his genuine feeling and Eugene's obduracy*) Then help to kindle it in them—in me—not to extinguish it. In the future, when you are as happy as I am, I will be your true brother in the faith. I will help you to believe that God has given us a world that nothing but our own folly keeps from being a paradise. I will help you to believe that every stroke of your work is sowing happiness for the great harvest that all—even the humblest—shall one day reap. And last, but trust me, not least, I will help you to believe that your wife loves you and is happy in her home. We need such help, Marchbanks: we need it greatly and always. There are so many things to make us doubt, if once we let our understanding be troubled. Even at home, we sit as if in camp, encompassed by a hostile army of doubts. Will you play the traitor and let them in on me?

Marchbanks (*looking round wildly*) Is it like this for her here always? A woman, with a great soul, craving for reality, truth, freedom; and being fed on metaphors, sermons, stale perorations, mere rhetoric. Do you think a woman's soul can live on your talent for preaching?

Morell (*stung*) Marchbanks: you make it hard for me to control myself. My talent is like yours insofar as it has any real worth at all. It is the gift of finding words for divine truth.

Marchbanks (*impetuously*) It's the gift of the gab, nothing more and nothing less. What has your knack of fine talking to do with the truth, any more than playing the organ has? Ive never been in your church; but Ive been to your political meetings; and Ive seen you do whats called rousing the meeting to enthusiasm: that is, you excited them until they be-

haved exactly as if they were drunk. And their wives looked
on and saw what fools they were. Oh, it's an old story: youll
find it in the Bible. I imagine King David, in his fits of enthusiasm, was very like you. (*Stabbing him with the words*)
"But his wife despised him in her heart."

Morell (*wrathfully*) Leave my house. Do you hear? (*He
advances on him threateningly*).

Marchbanks (*shrinking back against the couch*) Let me
alone. Dont touch me. (*Morell grasps him powerfully by the
lapell of his coat: he cowers down on the sofa and screams
passionately*) Stop, Morell: if you strike me, I'll kill myself: I
wont bear it. (*Almost in hysterics*) Let me go. Take your
hand away.

Morell (*with slow emphatic scorn*) You little snivelling
cowardly whelp. (*He releases him*). Go, before you frighten
yourself into a fit.

Marchbanks (*on the sofa, gasping, but relieved by the with-
drawal of Morell's hand*) I'm not afraid of you: it's you who
are afraid of me.

Morell (*quietly, as he stands over him*) It looks like it,
doesnt it?

Marchbanks (*with petulant vehemence*) Yes, it does.
(*Morell turns away contemptuously. Eugene scrambles to his
feet and follows him*). You think because I shrink from being
brutally handled—because (*with tears in his voice*) I can do
nothing but cry with rage when I am met with violence—
because I cant lift a heavy trunk down from the top of a cab
like you—because I cant fight you for your wife as a drunken
navvy would: all that makes you think I'm afraid of you. But
youre wrong. If I havnt got what you call British pluck, I
havnt British cowardice either: I'm not afraid of a clergyman's
ideas. I'll fight your ideas. I'll rescue her from her slavery to
them. I'll pit my own ideas against them. You are driving me
out of the house because you darent let her choose between
your ideas and mine. You are afraid to let me see her again.

(*Morell, angered, turns suddenly on him. He flies to the door in involuntary dread*). Let me alone, I say. I'm going.

Morell (*with cold scorn*) Wait a moment: I am not going to touch you: dont be afraid. When my wife comes back she will want to know why you have gone. And when she finds that you are never going to cross our threshold again, she will want to have that explained too. Now I dont wish to distress her by telling her that you have behaved like a blackguard.

Marchbanks (*coming back with renewed vehemence*) You shall. You must. If you give any explanation but the true one, you are a liar and a coward. Tell her what I said; and how you were strong and manly, and shook me as a terrier shakes a rat; and how I shrank and was terrified; and how you called me a snivelling little whelp and put me out of the house. If you dont tell her, I will: I'll write it to her.

Morell (*puzzled*) Why do you want her to know this?

Marchbanks (*with lyric rapture*) Because she will understand me, and know that I understand her. If you keep back one word of it from her—if you are not ready to lay the truth at her feet as I am—then you will know to the end of your days that she really belongs to me and not to you. Goodbye. (*Going*).

Morell (*terribly disquieted*) Stop: I will not tell her.

Marchbanks (*turning near the door*) Either the truth or a lie you must tell her, if I go.

Morell (*temporizing*) Marchbanks: it is sometimes justifiable—

Marchbanks (*cutting him short*) I know: to lie. It will be useless. Goodbye, Mr Clergyman.

As he turns finally to the door, it opens and Candida enters in her housekeeping dress.

Candida. Are you going, Eugene? (*Looking more observantly at him*) Well, dear me, just look at you, going out into the street in that state! You are a poet, certainly. Look at him, James! (*She takes him by the coat, and brings him forward, shewing him to Morell*). Look at his collar! look at his tie! look at his hair! One would think somebody had been throttling you. (*Eugene instinctively tries to look round at Morell; but she pulls him back*). Here! Stand still. (*She buttons his collar; ties his neckerchief in a bow; and arranges his hair*). There! Now you look so nice that I think youd better stay to lunch after all, though I told you you musnt. It will be ready in half an hour. (*She puts a final touch to the bow. He kisses her hand*). Dont be silly.

Marchbanks. I want to stay, of course; unless the reverend gentleman your husband has anything to advance to the contrary.

Candida. Shall he stay, James, if he promises to be a good boy and help me to lay the table?

Morell (shortly) Oh yes, certainly: he had better. (*He goes to the table and pretends to busy himself with his papers there*).

Marchbanks (offering his arm to Candida) Come and lay the table. (*She takes it. They go to the door together. As they pass out he adds*) I am the happiest of mortals.

Morell. So was I—an hour ago.

ACT II

THE SAME *day later in the afternoon. The same room. The chair for visitors has been replaced at the table. Marchbanks, alone and idle, is trying to find out how the typewriter works. Hearing someone at the door, he steals guiltily away to the window and pretends to be absorbed in the view. Miss Garnett, carrying the notebook in which she takes down Morell's letters in shorthand from his dictation, sits down at the typewriter and sets to work transcribing them, much too busy to notice Eugene. When she begins the second line she stops and stares at the machine. Something wrong evidently.*

Proserpine. Bother! Youve been meddling with my typewriter, Mr Marchbanks; and theres not the least use in your trying to look as if you hadnt.

Marchbanks (*timidly*) I'm very sorry, Miss Garnett. I only tried to make it write. (*Plaintively*) But it wouldnt.

Proserpine. Well, youve altered the spacing.

Marchbanks (*earnestly*) I assure you I didnt. I didnt indeed. I only turned a little wheel. It gave a sort of click.

Proserpine. Oh, now I understand. (*She restores the spacing, talking volubly all the time*). I suppose you thought it was a sort of barrel-organ. Nothing to do but turn the handle, and it would write a beautiful love letter for you straight off, eh?

Marchbanks (*seriously*) I suppose a machine c o u l d be made to write love letters. Theyre all the same, arnt they?

Proserpine (*somewhat indignantly: any such discussion, except by way of pleasantry, being outside her code of manners*) How do I know? Why do you ask me?

Marchbanks. I beg your pardon. I thought clever people —people who can do business and write letters and that

32

sort of thing—always had to have love affairs to keep them from going mad.

Proserpine (*rising, outraged*) Mr Marchbanks! (*She looks severely at him, and marches majestically to the bookcase*).

Marchbanks (*approaching her humbly*) I hope I havnt offended you. Perhaps I shouldnt have alluded to your love affairs.

Proserpine (*plucking a blue book from the shelf and turning sharply on him*) I havnt any love affairs. How dare you say such a thing? The idea! (*She tucks the book under her arm, and is flouncing back to her machine when he addresses her with awakened interest and sympathy*).

Marchbanks. Really! Oh, then you are shy, like me.

Proserpine. Certainly I am not shy. What do you mean?

Marchbanks (*secretly*) You must be: that is the reason there are so few love affairs in the world. We all go about longing for love: it is the first need of our natures, the first prayer of our hearts; but we dare not utter our longing: we are too shy. (*Very earnestly*) Oh, Miss Garnett, what would you not give to be without fear, without shame—

Proserpine (*scandalized*) Well, upon my word!

Marchbanks (*with petulant impatience*) Ah, dont say those stupid things to me: they dont deceive me: what use are they? Why are you afraid to be your real self with me? I am just like you.

Proserpine. Like m e! Pray are you flattering me or flattering yourself? I don't feel quite sure which. (*She again tries to get back to her work*).

Marchbanks (*stopping her mysteriously*) Hush! I go about in search of love; and I find it in unmeasured stores in the bosoms of others. But when I try to ask for it, this horrible shyness strangles me; and I stand dumb, or worse than dumb, saying meaningless things: foolish lies. And I see the affection I am longing for given to dogs and cats and pet birds, because they come and ask for it. (*Almost whispering*) It must be asked for: it is like a ghost: it cannot speak unless it is first spoken to. (*At his usual pitch, but with deep melancholy*) All the love in the world is longing to speak; only it dare not, because it is shy! shy! shy! That is the world's tragedy. (*With a deep sigh he sits in the visitors' chair and buries his face in his hands*).

Proserpine (*amazed, but keeping her wits about her: her point of honor in encounters with strange young men*) Wicked people get over that shyness occasionally, dont they?

Marchbanks (*scrambling up almost fiercely*) Wicked people means people who have no love: therefore they have no shame. They have the power to ask love because they dont need it: they have the power to offer it because they have none to give. (*He collapses into his seat, and adds, mournfully*) But we, who h a v e love, and long to mingle it with the love of others: we cannot utter a word. (*Timidly*) You find that, dont you?

Proserpine. Look here: if you dont stop talking like this, I'll leave the room, Mr Marchbanks: I really will. It's not proper.

She resumes her seat at the typewriter, opening the blue book and preparing to copy a passage from it.

Marchbanks (*hopelessly*) Nothing thats worth saying is proper. (*He rises, and wanders about the room in his lost way*). I cant understand you, Miss Garnett. What am I to talk about?

Proserpine (*snubbing him*) Talk about indifferent things. Talk about the weather.

Marchbanks. Would you talk about indifferent things if a child were by, crying bitterly with hunger?

Proserpine. I suppose not.

Marchbanks. Well: I cant talk about indifferent things with my heart crying out bitterly in i t s hunger.

Proserpine. Then hold your tongue.

Marchbanks. Yes: that is what it always comes to. We hold

our tongues. Does that stop the cry of your heart? for it does cry: doesnt it? It must, if you have a heart.

Proserpine (suddenly rising with her hand pressed on her heart) Oh, it's no use trying to work while you talk like that. *(She leaves her little table and sits on the sofa. Her feelings are keenly stirred).* It's no business of yours whether my heart cries or not; but I have a mind to tell you, for all that.

Marchbanks. You neednt. I know already that it must.

Proserpine. But mind! if you ever say I said so, I'll deny it.

Marchbanks (compassionately) Yes, I know. And so you havnt the courage to tell him?

Proserpine (bouncing up) H i m! Who?

Marchbanks. Whoever he is. The man you love. It might be anybody. The curate, Mr Mill, perhaps.

Proserpine (with disdain) Mr Mill!!! A fine man to break my heart about, indeed! I'd rather have you than Mr Mill.

Marchbanks (recoiling) No, really: I'm very sorry; but you mustnt think of that. I—

Proserpine (testily, going to the fireplace and standing at it with her back to him) Oh, dont be frightened: it's not you. It's not any one particular person.

Marchbanks. I know. You feel that you could love anybody that offered—

Proserpine (turning, exasperated) Anybody that offered! No, I do not. What do you take me for?

Marchbanks (discouraged) No use. You wont make me r e a l answers: only those things that everybody says. *(He strays to the sofa and sits down disconsolately).*

Proserpine (nettled at what she takes to be a disparagement of her manners by an aristocrat) Oh well, if you want original conversation, youd better go and talk to yourself.

Marchbanks. That is what all poets do: they talk to themselves out loud; and the world overhears them. But it's horribly lonely not to hear someone else talk sometimes.

Proserpine. Wait until Mr Morell comes. H e ' l l talk to you.

(*Marchbanks shudders*). Oh, you neednt make wry faces over him: he can talk better than you. (*With temper*) He'd talk your little head off. (*She is going back angrily to her place, when he, suddenly enlightened, springs up and stops her*).

Marchbanks. Ah! I understand now.

Proserpine (*reddening*) What do you understand?

Marchbanks. Your secret. Tell me: is it really and truly possible for a woman to love him?

Proserpine (*as if this were beyond all bounds*) Well!!

Marchbanks (*passionately*) No: answer me. I want to know: I m u s t know. *I* cant understand it. I can see nothing in him but words, pious resolutions, what people call goodness. You cant love that.

Proserpine (*attempting to snub him by an air of cool propriety*) I simply dont know what youre talking about. I dont understand you.

Marchbanks (*vehemently*) You do. You lie.

Proserpine. Oh!

Marchbanks. You d o understand; and you k n o w. (*Determined to have an answer*) Is it possible for a woman to love him?

Proserpine (*looking him straight in the face*) Yes. (*He covers his face with his hands*). Whatever is the matter with you! (*He takes down his hands. Frightened at the tragic mask presented to her, she hurries past him at the utmost possible distance, keeping her eyes on his face until he turns from her and goes to the child's chair beside the hearth, where he sits in the deepest dejection. As she approaches the door, it opens and Burgess enters. Seeing him, she ejaculates*) Praise heaven! here's somebody (*and feels safe enough to resume her place at her table. She puts a fresh sheet of paper into the typewriter as Burgess crosses to Eugene*).

Burgess (*bent on taking care of the distinguished visitor*) Well: so this is the way they leave you to yoreself, Mr Morchbanks. Ive come to keep you company. (*Marchbanks

looks up at him in consternation, which is quite lost on him).
James is receivin a deppitation in the dinin room; and Candy
is hupstairs heducating of a young stitcher gurl she's hin-
terested in. (*Condolingly*) You must find it lonesome here
with no one but the typist to talk to. (*He pulls round the easy
chair, and sits down*).

Proserpine (*highly incensed*) He'll be all right now that
he has the advantage of y o u r polished conversation: thats one
comfort, anyhow. (*She begins to typewrite with clattering
asperity*).

Burgess (*amazed at her audacity*) Hi was not addressin
myself to you, young woman, that I'm awerr of.

Proserpine. Did you ever see worse manners, Mr Marchbanks?

Burgess (*with pompous severity*) Mr Marchbanks is a
gentleman, and knows his place, which is more than some
people do.

Proserpine (*fretfully*) It's well you and I are not ladies
and gentlemen: I'd talk to you pretty straight if Mr Marchbanks wasnt here. (*She pulls the letter out of the machine so
crossly that it tears*). There! now I've spoiled this letter! have
to be done all over again! Oh, I cant contain myself: silly old
fathead!

Burgess (*rising, breathless with indignation*) Ho! I'm a
silly ole fat'ead, am I? Ho, indeed (*gasping*)! Hall right, my
gurl! Hall right. You just wait till I tell that to yore hemployer. Youll see. I'll teach you: see if I dont.

Proserpine (*conscious of having gone too far*) I—

Burgess (*cutting her short*) No: youve done it now. No
huse a-talkin to me. I'll let you know who I am. (*Proserpine
shifts her paper carriage with a defiant bang, and disdainfully goes on with her work*). Dont you take no notice of
her, Mr Morchbanks. She's beneath it. (*He loftily sits down
again*).

Marchbanks (*miserably nervous and disconcerted*) Hadnt

we better change the subject? I—I dont think Miss Garnett meant anything.

Proserpine (with intense conviction) Oh, didnt I though, just!

Burgess. I wouldnt demean myself to take notice on her.

An electric bell rings twice.

Proserpine (gathering up her notebook and papers) Thats for me. *(She hurries out).*

Burgess (calling after her) Oh, we can spare you. *(Somewhat relieved by the triumph of having the last word, and yet half inclined to try to improve on it, he looks after her for a moment; then subsides into his seat by Eugene, and addresses him very confidentially).* Now we're alone, Mr Morchbanks, let me give you a friendly int that I wouldnt give to heverybody. Ow long ave you known my son-in-law James ere?

Marchbanks. I dont know. I never can remember dates. A few months, perhaps.

Burgess. Ever notice hennythink queer about him?

Marchbanks. I dont think so.

Burgess (impressively) No more you wouldnt. Thats the danger on it. Well, he's mad.

Marchbanks. Mad!

Burgess. Mad as a Morch 'are. You take notice on him and youll see.

Marchbanks (uneasily) But surely that is only because his opinions—

Burgess (touching him on the knee with his forefinger, and pressing it to hold his attention) Thats the same what I hused to think, Mr Morchbanks. Hi thought long enough that it was ony his opinions; though, mind you, hopinions becomes vurry serious things when people takes to hactin on em as e does. But thats not what I go on. *(He looks round to make sure that they are alone, and bends over to Eugene's ear).* What do you think he sez to me this mornin in this very room?

—

Marchbanks. What?

Burgess. He sez to me—this is as sure as we're settin here now—he sez "I'm a fool," he sez; "and yore a scounderl." Me a scounderl, mind you! And then shook ands with me on it, as if it was to my credit! Do you mean to tell me as that man's sane?

Morell (*outside, calling to Proserpine as he opens the door*) Get all their names and addresses, Miss Garnett.

Proserpine (*in the distance*) Yes, Mr Morell.

Morell comes in, with the deputation's documents in his hands.

Burgess (*aside to Marchbanks*) Yorr he is. Just you keep your heye on im and see. (*Rising momentously*) I'm sorry, James, to ave to make a complaint to you. I dont want to do it; but I feel I oughter, as a matter o right and dooty.

Morell. Whats the matter?

Burgess. Mr Morchbanks will bear me hout: he was a witness. (*Very solemnly*) Yore young woman so far forgot herself as to call me a silly ole fat'ead.

Morell (*with tremendous heartiness*) Oh, now, isnt that e x a c t l y like Prossy? She's so frank: she cant contain herself! Poor Prossy! Ha! ha!

Burgess (*trembling with rage*) And do you hexpec me to put up with it from the like of er?

Morell. Pooh, nonsense! you cant take any notice of it. Never mind. (*He goes to the cellaret and puts the papers into one of the drawers*).

Burgess. Oh, Hi dont mind. Hi'm above it. But is it r i g h t? thats what I want to know. Is it right?

Morell. Thats a question for the Church, not for the laity. Has it done you any harm? thats the question for you, eh? Of course it hasnt. Think no more of it. (*He dismisses the subject by going to his place at the table and setting to work at his correspondence*).

Burgess (*aside to Marchbanks*) What did I tell you? Mad as a atter. (*He goes to the table and asks, with the sickly civility of a hungry man*) When's dinner, James?

Morell. Not for a couple of hours yet.

Burgess (*with plaintive resignation*) Gimme a nice book to read over the fire, will you, James: thur's a good chap.

Morell. What sort of book? A good one?

Burgess (*with almost a yell of remonstrance*) Nah-oo! Summat pleasant, just to pass the time. (*Morell takes an illustrated paper from the table and offers it. He accepts it humbly*). Thank yer, James. (*He goes back to the big chair at the fire, and sits there at his ease, reading*).

Morell (*as he writes*) Candida will come to entertain you presently. She has got rid of her pupil. She is filling the lamps.

Marchbanks (*starting up in the wildest consternation*) But that will soil her hands. I cant bear that, Morell: it's a shame. I'll go and fill them. (*He makes for the door*).

Morell. Youd better not. (*Marchbanks stops irresolutely*). She'd only set you to clean my boots, to save me the trouble of doing it myself in the morning.

Burgess (*with grave disapproval*) Dont you keep a servant now, James?

Morell. Yes; but she isnt a slave; and the house looks as if I kept three. That means that everyone has to lend a hand. It's not a bad plan: Prossy and I can talk business after breakfast while we're washing up. Washing up's no trouble when there are two people to do it.

Marchbanks (*tormentedly*) Do you think every woman is as coarse-grained as Miss Garnett?

Burgess (*emphatically*) Thats quite right, Mr Morchbanks: thats q u i t e right. She is corse-grained.

Morell (*quietly and significantly*) Marchbanks!

Marchbanks. Yes?

Morell. How many servants does your father keep?

Marchbanks (*pettishly*) Oh, I dont know. (*He moves to

the sofa, as if to get as far as possible from Morell's questioning, and sits down in great agony of spirit, thinking of the paraffin).

Morell (very gravely) So many that you dont know! *(More aggressively)* When theres anything coarse-grained to be done, you just ring the bell and throw it on to somebody else, eh?

Marchbanks. Oh, dont torture me. You dont even ring the bell. But your wife's beautiful fingers are dabbling in paraffin oil while you sit here comfortably preaching about it: ever-lasting preaching! preaching! words! words! words!

Burgess (intensely appreciating this retort) Har, har! Devil a better! *(Radiantly)* Ad you there, James, straight.

Candida comes in, well aproned, with a reading lamp trimmed, filled, and ready for lighting. She places it on the table near Morell, ready for use.

Candida (brushing her finger tips together with a slight twitch of her nose) If you stay with us, Eugene, I think I will hand over the lamps to you.

Marchbanks. I will stay on condition that you hand over all the rough work to me.

Candida. Thats very gallant; but I think I should like to see how you do it first. *(Turning to Morell)* James: youve not been looking after the house properly.

Morell. What have I done—or not done—my love?

Candida (with serious vexation) My own particular pet scrubbing brush has been used for blackleading. *(A heart-breaking wail bursts from Marchbanks. Burgess looks round, amazed. Candida hurries to the sofa).* Whats the matter? Are you ill, Eugene?

Marchbanks. No: not ill. Only horror! horror! horror! *(He bows his head on his hands).*

Burgess (shocked) What! Got the orrors, Mr Morchbanks! Oh, thats bad, at your age. You must leave it off grajally.

Candida (reassured) Nonsense, papa! It's only poetic horror, isnt it, Eugene *(petting him)*?

Burgess (abashed) Oh, poetic orror, is it? I beg your pordon, I'm shore. (*He turns to the fire again, deprecating his hasty conclusion*).

Candida. What is it, Eugene? the scrubbing brush? (*He shudders*). Well, there! never mind. (*She sits down beside him*). Wouldnt you like to present me with a nice new one, with an ivory back inlaid with mother-of-pearl?

Marchbanks (*softly and musically, but sadly and longingly*) No, not a scrubbing brush, but a boat: a tiny shallop to sail away in, far from the world, where the marble floors are washed by the rain and dried by the sun; where the south wind dusts the beautiful green and purple carpets. Or a chariot! to carry us up into the sky, where the lamps are stars, and dont need to be filled with paraffin oil every day.

Morell (*harshly*) And where there is nothing to do but to be idle, selfish, and useless.

Candida (*jarred*) Oh, James! how could you spoil it all?

Marchbanks (*firing up*) Yes, to be idle, selfish, and useless: that is, to be beautiful and free and happy: hasnt every man desired that with all his soul for the woman he loves? Thats my ideal: whats yours, and that of all the dreadful people who live in these hideous rows of houses? Sermons and scrubbing brushes! With you to preach the sermon and your wife to scrub.

Candida (*quaintly*) He cleans the boots, Eugene. You will have to clean them to-morrow for saying that about him.

Marchbanks. Oh, dont talk about boots! Your feet should be beautiful on the mountains.

Candida. My feet would not be beautiful on the Hackney Road without boots.

Burgess (*scandalized*) Come, Candy! dont be vulgar. Mr Morchbanks aint accustomed to it. Youre givin him the orrors again. I mean the poetic ones.

Morell is silent. Apparently he is busy with his letters: really he is puzzling with misgiving over his new and alarming ex-

*perience that the surer he is of his moral thrusts, the more
swiftly and effectively Eugene parries them. To find himself
beginning to fear a man whom he does not respect afflicts him
bitterly.*

Miss Garnett comes in with a telegram.

Proserpine (handing the telegram to Morell) Reply paid.
The boy's waiting. *(To Candida, coming back to her machine
and sitting down)* Maria is ready for you now in the kitchen,
Mrs Morell. *(Candida rises)*. The onions have come.

Marchbanks (convulsively) Onions!

Candida. Yes, onions. Not even Spanish ones: nasty little
red onions. You shall help me to slice them. Come along.

*She catches him by the wrist and runs out, pulling him
after her. Burgess rises in consternation, and stands aghast on
the hearth-rug, staring after them.*

Burgess. Candy didnt oughter andle a hearl's nevvy like
that. It's goin too fur with it. Lookee ere, James: do e often
git taken queer like that?

Morell (shortly, writing a telegram) I dont know.

Burgess (sentimentally) He talks very pretty. I awlus had
a turn for a bit of poetry. Candy takes arter me that-a-way.
Huseter make me tell er fairy stories when she was ony a little
kiddy not that igh *(indicating a stature of two feet or thereabouts)*.

Morell (preoccupied) Ah, indeed. *(He blots the telegram
and goes out)*.

Proserpine. Used you to make the fairy stories up out of
your own head?

*Burgess, not deigning to reply, strikes an attitude of the
haughtiest disdain on the hearth-rug.*

Proserpine (calmly) I should never have supposed you had
it in you. By the way, I'd better warn you, since youve taken
such a fancy to Mr Marchbanks. He's mad.

Burgess. Mad! What! Im too!!

Proserpine. Mad as a March hare. He did frighten me, I can tell you, just before you came in that time. Havent you noticed the queer things he says?

Burgess. So thats what the poetic orrors means. Blame me if it didnt come into my ed once or twyst that he was a bit horff 'is chump! (*He crosses the room to the door, lifting up his voice as he goes*). Well, this is a pretty sort of asylum for a man to be in, with no one but you to take care of him!

Proserpine (*as he passes her*) Yes, what a dreadful thing it would be if anything happened to y o u!

Burgess (*loftily*) Dont you haddress no remarks to me. Tell your hemployer that Ive gone into the gorden for a smoke.

Proserpine (*mocking*) Oh!

Before Burgess can retort, Morell comes back.

Burgess (*sentimentally*) Goin for a turn in the gording to smoke, James.

Morell (*brusquely*) Oh, all right, all right. (*Burgess goes out pathetically in the character of a weary old man. Morell stands at the table, turning over his papers, and adding, across to Proserpine, half humorously, half absently*) Well, Miss Prossy, why have you been calling my father-in-law names?

Proserpine (*blushing fiery red, and looking quickly up at him, half scared, half reproachful*) I—(*She bursts into tears*).

Morell (*with tender gaiety, leaning across the table towards her, and consoling her*) Oh, come! come! come! Never mind, Pross: he is a silly old fathead, isnt he?

With an explosive sob, she makes a dash at the door, and vanishes, banging it. Morell, shaking his head resignedly, sighs, and goes wearily to his chair, where he sits down and sets to work, looking old and careworn.

Candida comes in. She has finished her household work and taken off the apron. She at once notices his dejected appearance, and posts herself quietly at the visitors' chair, looking down at him attentively. She says nothing.

Morell (looking up, but with his pen raised ready to resume his work) Well? Where is Eugene?

Candida. Washing his hands in the scullery under the tap. He will make an excellent cook if he can only get over his dread of Maria.

Morell (shortly) Ha! No doubt. *(He begins writing again).*

Candida (going nearer, and putting her hand down softly on his to stop him as she says) Come here, dear. Let me look at you. *(He drops his pen and yields himself to her disposal. She makes him rise, and brings him a little away from the table, looking at him critically all the time).* Turn your face to the light. *(She places him facing the window).* My boy is not looking well. Has he been overworking?

Morell. Nothing more than usual.

Candida. He looks very pale, and grey, and wrinkled, and old. *(His melancholy deepens; and she attacks it with wilful gaiety)* Here: *(pulling him towards the easy chair)* youve done enough writing for to-day. Leave Prossy to finish it. Come and talk to me.

Morell. But—

Candida (insisting) Yes, I must be talked to. *(She makes him sit down, and seats herself on the carpet beside his knee).* Now *(patting his hand)* youre beginning to look better already. Why must you go out every night lecturing and talking? I hardly have one evening a week with you. Of course what you say is all very true; but it does no good: they dont mind what you say to them one little bit. They think they agree with you; but whats the use of their agreeing with you if they go and do just the opposite of what you tell them the moment your back is turned? Look at our congregation at St Dominic's! Why do they come to hear you talking about Christianity every Sunday? Why, just because theyve been so full of business and money-making for six days that they want to forget all about it and have a rest on the seventh; so that they can go back fresh and make money harder than ever! You positively help them at it instead of hindering them.

Morell (with energetic seriousness) You know very well, Candida, that I often blow them up soundly for that. And if there is nothing in their churchgoing but rest and diversion, why dont they try something more amusing? more self-indulgent? There must be some good in the fact that they prefer St Dominic's to worse places on Sundays.

Candida. Oh, the worse places arnt open; and even if they were, they darent be seen going to them. Besides, James dear, you preach so splendidly that it's as good as a play for them. Why do you think the women are so enthusiastic?

Morell (shocked) Candida!

Candida. Oh, I know. You silly boy: you think it's your Socialism and your religion; but if it were that, theyd do what you tell them instead of only coming to look at you. They all have Prossy's complaint.

Morell. Prossy's complaint! What do you mean, Candida?

Candida. Yes, Prossy, and all the other secretaries you ever had. Why does Prossy condescend to wash up the things, and to peel potatoes and abase herself in all manner of ways for six shillings a week less than she used to get in a city office? She's in love with you, James: thats the reason. Theyre all in love with you. And you are in love with preaching because you do it so beautifully. And you think it's all enthusiasm for the Kingdom of Heaven on earth; and so do they. You dear silly!

Morell. Candida: what dreadful! what soul-destroying cynicism! Are you jesting? Or—can it be?—are you jealous?

Candida (with curious thoughtfulness) Yes, I feel a little jealous sometimes.

Morell (incredulously) Of Prossy?

Candida (laughing) No, no, no, no. Not jealous of anybody. Jealous for somebody else, who is not loved as he ought to be.

Morell. Me?

Candida. You! Why, youre spoiled with love and worship: you get far more than is good for you. No: I mean Eugene.

Morell (*startled*) Eugene!

Candida. It seems unfair that all the love should go to you, and none to him; although he needs it so much more than you do. (*A convulsive movement shakes him in spite of himself*). Whats the matter? Am I worrying you?

Morell (*hastily*) Not at all. (*Looking at her with troubled intensity*) You know that I have perfect confidence in you, Candida.

Candida. You vain thing! Are you so sure of your irresistible attractions?

Morell. Candida; you are shocking me. I never thought of my attractions. I thought of your goodness, of your purity. That is what I confide in.

Candida. What a nasty uncomfortable thing to say to me! Oh, you a r e a clergyman, James: a thorough clergyman!

Morell (*turning away from her, heart-stricken*) So Eugene says.

Candida (*with lively interest, leaning over to him with her arms on his knee*) Eugene's always right. He's a wonderful boy: I have grown fonder and fonder of him all the time I was away. Do you know, James, that though he has not the least suspicion of it himself, he is ready to fall madly in love with me?

Morell (*grimly*) Oh, he has no suspicion of it himself, hasnt he?

Candida. Not a bit. (*She takes her arms from his knee, and turns thoughtfully, sinking into a more restful attitude with her hands in her lap*). Some day he will know: when he is grown up and experienced, like you. And he will know that I must have known. I wonder what he will think of me then.

Morell. No evil, Candida. I hope and trust, no evil.

Candida (*dubiously*) That will depend.

Morell (*bewildered*) Depend!

Candida (*looking at him*) Yes: it will depend on what happens to him. (*He looks vacantly at her*). Dont you see? It will depend on how he comes to learn what love really is. I mean on the sort of woman who will teach it to him.

Morell (*quite at a loss*) Yes. No. I dont know what you mean.

Candida (*explaining*) If he learns it from a good woman, then it will be all right: he will forgive me.

Morell. Forgive?

Candida. But suppose he learns it from a bad woman, as so many men do, especially poetic men, who imagine all women are angels! Suppose he only discovers the value of love when he has thrown it away and degraded himself in his ignorance! Will he forgive me then, do you think?

Morell. Forgive you for what?

Candida (*realizing how stupid he is, and a little disappointed, though quite tenderly so*) Dont you understand? (*He shakes his head. She turns to him again, so as to explain with the fondest intimacy*). I mean, will he forgive me for not teaching him myself? For abandoning him to the bad women for the sake of my goodness, of my purity, as you call it? Ah, James, how little you understand me, to talk of your confidence in my goodness and purity! I would give them both to poor Eugene as willingly as I would give my shawl to a beggar dying of cold, if there were nothing else to restrain me. Put your trust in my love for you, James; for if that went, I should care very little for your sermons: mere phrases that you cheat yourself and others with every day. (*She is about to rise*).

Morell. His words!

Candida (*checking herself quickly in the act of getting up*) Whose words?

Morell. Eugene's.

Candida (*delighted*) He is always right. He understands you; he understands me; he understands Prossy; and you, darling, you understand nothing. (*She laughs, and kisses him to console him. He recoils as if stabbed, and springs up*).

Morell. How can you bear to do that when—Oh, Candida (*with anguish in his voice*) I had rather you had plunged a grappling iron into my heart than given me that kiss.

Candida (*amazed*) My dear: whats the matter?

Morell (*frantically waving her off*) Dont touch me.

Candida. James!!!

They are interrupted by the entrance of Marchbanks with Burgess, who stop near the door, staring.

Marchbanks. Is anything the matter?

Morell (*deadly white, putting an iron constraint on himself*) Nothing but this: that either you were right this morning, or Candida is mad.

Burgess (*in loudest protest*) What! Candy mad too! Oh, come! come! come! (*He crosses the room to the fireplace, protesting as he goes, and knocks the ashes out of his pipe on the bars*).

Morell sits down at his table desperately, leaning forward to hide his face, and interlacing his fingers rigidly to keep them steady.

Candida (*to Morell, relieved and laughing*) Oh, youre only shocked! Is that all? How conventional all you unconventional people are! (*She sits gaily on the arm of the chair*).

Burgess. Come: be'ave yourself, Candy. Whatll Mr Morchbanks think of you?

Candida. This comes of James teaching me to think for myself, and never to hold back out of fear of what other people may think of me. It works beautifully as long as I think the same things as he does. But now! because I have just thought something different! look at him! Just look! (*She points to Morell, greatly amused*).

Eugene looks, and instantly presses his hand on his heart, as if some pain had shot through it. He sits down on the sofa like a man witnessing a tragedy.

Burgess (*on the hearth-rug*) Well, James, you certnly haint as himpressive lookin as usu'l.

Morell (*with a laugh which is half a sob*) I suppose not. I beg all your pardons: I was not conscious of making a fuss. (*Pulling himself together*) Well, well, well, well, well! (*He sets to work at his papers again with resolute cheerfulness*).

Candida (*going to the sofa and sitting beside Marchbanks, still in a bantering humor*) Well, Eugene: why are you so sad? Did the onions make you cry?

Marchbanks (*aside to her*) It is your cruelty. I hate cruelty. It is a horrible thing to see one person make another suffer.

Candida (*petting him ironically*) Poor boy! have I been cruel? Did I make it slice nasty little red onions?

Marchbanks (*earnestly*) Oh, stop, stop: I dont mean myself. You have made him suffer frightfully. I feel his pain in my own heart. I know that it is not your fault: it is something that must happen; but dont make light of it. I shudder when you torture him and laugh.

Candida (*incredulously*) I torture James! Nonsense, Eugene: how you exaggerate! Silly! (*She rises and goes to the table, a little troubled*). Dont work any more, dear. Come and talk to us.

Morell (*affectionately but bitterly*) Ah no: I cant talk. I can only preach.

Candida (*caressing his hand*) Well, come and preach.

Burgess (*strongly remonstrating*) Aw no, Candy. 'Ang it all!

Lexy Mill comes in, anxious and important.

Lexy (*hastening to shake hands with Candida*) How do you do, Mrs Morell? So glad to see you back again.

Candida. Thank you, Lexy. You know Eugene, dont you?

Lexy. Oh yes. How do you do, Marchbanks?

Marchbanks. Quite well, thanks.

Lexy (*to Morell*) Ive just come from the Guild of St

Matthew. They are in the greatest consternation about your telegram.

Candida. What did you telegraph about, James?

Lexy (*to Candida*) He was to have spoken for them to-night. Theyve taken the large hall in Mare Street and spent a lot of money on posters. Morell's telegram was to say he couldnt come. It came on them like a thunderbolt.

Candida (*surprised, and beginning to suspect something wrong*) Given up an engagement to speak!

Burgess. Fust time in his life, I'll bet. Ain it, Candy?

Lexy (*to Morell*) They decided to send an urgent telegram to you asking whether you could not change your mind. Have you received it?

Morell (*with restrained impatience*) Yes, yes: I got it.

Lexy. It was reply paid.

Morell. Yes, I know. I answered it. I cant go.

Candida. But why, James?

Morell (*almost fiercely*) Because I dont choose. These people forget that I am a man: they think I am a talking machine to be turned on for their pleasure every evening of my life. May I not have o n e night at home, with my wife, and my friends?

They are all amazed at this outburst, except Eugene. His expression remains unchanged.

Candida. Oh, James, you mustnt mind what I said about that. And if you dont go youll have an attack of bad conscience to-morrow.

Lexy (*intimidated, but urgent*) I know, of course, that they make the most unreasonable demands on you. But they have been telegraphing all over the place for another speaker; and they can get nobody but the President of the Agnostic League.

Morell (*promptly*) Well, an excellent man. What better do they want?

Lexy. But he always insists so powerfully on the divorce

of Socialism from Christianity. He will undo all the good we have been doing. Of course you know best; but—(*he shrugs his shoulders and wanders to the hearth beside Burgess*).

Candida (*coaxingly*) Oh, d o go, James. We'll all go.

Burgess (*grumblingly*) Look 'ere, Candy! I say! Let's stay at home by the fire, comfortable. He wont need to be more'n a couple-o-hour away.

Candida. Youll be just as comfortable at the meeting. We'll all sit on the platform and be great people.

Eugene (*terrified*) Oh please dont let us go on the platform. No: everyone will stare at us: I couldnt. I'll sit at the back of the room.

Candida. Dont be afraid. Theyll be too busy looking at James to notice you.

Morell. Prossy's complaint, Candida! Eh?

Candida (*gaily*) Yes: Prossy's complaint.

Burgess (*mystified*) Prossy's complaint! What are you talkin about, James?

Morell (*not heeding him, rises; goes to the door; and holds it open, calling in a commanding tone*) Miss Garnett.

Proserpine (*in the distance*) Yes, Mr Morell. Coming.

They all wait, except Burgess, who turns stealthily to Lexy.

Burgess. Listen ere, Mr Mill. Whats Prossy's complaint? Whats wrong with er?

Lexy (*confidentially*) Well, I dont exactly know; but she spoke very strangely to me this morning. I'm afraid she's a little out of her mind sometimes.

Burgess (*overwhelmed*) Why, it must be catchin! Four in the same ouse!

Proserpine (*appearing on the threshold*) What is it, Mr Morell?

Morell. Telegraph to the Guild of St Matthew that I am coming.

Proserpine (*surprised*) Dont they expect you?

Morell (*peremptorily*) Do as I tell you.

Proserpine, frightened, sits down at her typewriter, and obeys. Morell, now unaccountably resolute and forceful, goes across to Burgess. Candida watches his movements with growing wonder and misgiving.

Morell. Burgess: you dont want to come.

Burgess. Oh, dont put it like that, James. It's ony that it aint Sunday, you know.

Morell. I'm sorry. I thought you might like to be introduced to the chairman. He's on the Works Committee of the County Council, and has some influence in the matter of contracts. (*Burgess wakes up at once*). Youll come?

Burgess (*with enthusiasm*) Cawrse I'll come, James. Aint it awlus a pleasure to ear you!

Morell (*turning to Prossy*) I shall want you to take some notes at the meeting, Miss Garnett, if you have no other engagement. (*She nods, afraid to speak*). You are coming, Lexy, I suppose?

Lexy. Certainly.

Candida. We're all coming, James.

Morell. No: you are not coming; and Eugene is not coming. You will stay here and entertain him—to celebrate your return home. (*Eugene rises, breathless*).

Candida. But, James—

Morell (*authoritatively*) I insist. You do not want to come; and he does not want to come. (*Candida is about to protest*). Oh, dont concern yourselves: I shall have plenty of people without you: your chairs will be wanted by unconverted people who have never heard me before.

Candida (*troubled*) Eugene: wouldnt you like to come?

Morell. I should be afraid to let myself go before Eugene: he is so critical of sermons. (*Looking at him*) He knows I am afraid of him: he told me as much this morning. Well, I shall shew him how much afraid I am by leaving him here in your custody, Candida.

Marchbanks (*to himself, with vivid feeling*) Thats brave. Thats beautiful.

Candida (*with anxious misgiving*) But—but— Is anything the matter, James? (*Greatly troubled*) I cant understand—

Morell (*taking her tenderly in his arms and kissing her on the forehead*) Ah, I thought it was *I* who couldnt understand, dear.

ACT III

PAST TEN in the evening. The curtains are drawn, and the lamps lighted. The typewriter is in its case: the large table has been cleared and tidied: everything indicates that the day's work is over.

Candida and Marchbanks are sitting by the fire. The reading lamp is on the mantelshelf above Marchbanks, who is in the small chair, reading aloud. A little pile of manuscripts and a couple of volumes of poetry are on the carpet beside him. Candida is in the easy chair. The poker, a light brass one, is upright in her hand. Leaning back and looking intently at the point of it, with her feet stretched towards the blaze, she is in a waking dream, miles away from her surroundings and completely oblivious of Eugene.

Marchbanks (*breaking off in his recitation*) Every poet that ever lived has put that thought into a sonnet. He must: he cant help it. (*He looks to her for assent, and notices her absorption in the poker*). Havnt you been listening? (*No response*). Mrs Morell!

Candida (*starting*) Eh?

Marchbanks. Havnt you been listening?

Candida (*with a guilty excess of politeness*) Oh yes. It's very nice. Go on, Eugene. I'm longing to hear what happens to the angel.

Marchbanks (*letting the manuscript drop from his hand to the floor*) I beg your pardon for boring you.

Candida. But you are not boring me, I assure you. Please go on. Do, Eugene.

Marchbanks. I finished the poem about the angel quarter of an hour ago. Ive read you several things since.

55

Candida (*remorsefully*) I'm so sorry, Eugene. I think the poker must have hypnotized me. (*She puts it down*).

Marchbanks. It made me horribly uneasy.

Candida. Why didnt you tell me? I'd have put it down at once.

Marchbanks. I was afraid of making you uneasy too. It looked as if it were a weapon. If I were a hero of old I should have laid my drawn sword between us. If Morell had come in he would have thought you had taken up the poker because there was no sword between us.

Candida (*wondering*) What? (*With a puzzled glance at him*) I cant quite follow that. Those sonnets of yours have perfectly addled me. Why should there be a sword between us?

Marchbanks (*evasively*) Oh, never mind. (*He stoops to pick up the manuscript*).

Candida. Put that down again, Eugene. There are limits to my appetite for poetry: even your poetry. Youve been reading to me for more than two hours, ever since James went out. I want to talk.

Marchbanks (*rising, scared*) No: I mustnt talk. (*He looks round him in his lost way, and adds, suddenly*) I think I'll go out and take a walk in the park. (*He makes for the door*).

Candida. Nonsense: it's closed long ago. Come and sit down on the hearth-rug, and talk moonshine as you usually do. I want to be amused. Dont you want to?

Marchbanks (*half in terror, half enraptured*) Yes.

Candida. Then come along. (*She moves her chair back a little to make room*).

He hesitates; then timidly stretches himself on the hearth-rug, face upwards, and throws back his head across her knees, looking up at her.

Marchbanks. Oh, Ive been so miserable all the evening, because I was doing right. Now I'm doing wrong; and I'm happy.

Candida (tenderly amused at him) Yes: I'm sure you feel a great grown-up wicked deceiver. Quite proud of yourself, arnt you?

Marchbanks (raising his head quickly and turning a little to look round at her) Take care. I'm ever so much older than you, if you only knew. (*He turns quite over on his knees, with his hands clasped and his arms on her lap, and speaks with growing impulse, his blood beginning to stir*). May I say some wicked things to you?

Candida (without the least fear or coldness, and with perfect respect for his passion, but with a touch of her wise hearted maternal humor) No. But you may say anything you really and truly feel. Anything at all, no matter what it is. I am not afraid, so long as it is your real self that speaks, and not a mere attitude: a gallant attitude, or a wicked attitude, or even a poetic attitude. I put you on your honor and truth. Now say whatever you want to.

Marchbanks (the eager expression vanishing utterly from his lips and nostrils as his eyes light up with pathetic spirituality) Oh, now I cant say anything: all the words I know belong to some attitude or other—all except one.

Candida. What one is that?

Marchbanks (softly, losing himself in the music of the name) Candida, Candida, Candida, Candida, Candida. I must say that now, because you have put me on my honor and truth; and I never think or feel Mrs Morell: it is always Candida.

Candida. Of course. And what have you to say to Candida?

Marchbanks. Nothing but to repeat your name a thousand times. Dont you feel that every time is a prayer to you?

Candida. Doesnt it make you happy to be able to pray?

Marchbanks. Yes, very happy.

Candida. Well, that happiness is the answer to your prayer. Do you want anything more?

Marchbanks. No: I have come into heaven, where want is unknown.

Morell comes in. He halts on the threshold, and takes in the scene at a glance.

Morell (grave and self-contained) I hope I dont disturb you.

Candida starts up violently, but without the smallest embarrassment, laughing at herself. Eugene, capsized by her sudden movement, recovers himself without rising, and sits on the rug hugging his ankles, also quite unembarrassed.

Candida. Oh, James, how you startled me! I was so taken up with Eugene that I didnt hear your latchkey. How did the meeting go off? Did you speak well?

Morell. I have never spoken better in my life.

Candida. That was first rate! How much was the collection?

Morell. I forgot to ask.

Candida (to Eugene) He must have spoken splendidly, or he would never have forgotten that. *(To Morell)* Where are all the others?

Morell. They left long before I could get away: I thought I should never escape. I believe they are having supper somewhere.

Candida (in her domestic business tone) Oh, in that case, Maria may go to bed. I'll tell her. *(She goes out to the kitchen)*.

Morell (looking sternly down at Marchbanks) Well?

Marchbanks (squatting grotesquely on the hearth-rug, and actually at ease with Morell: even impishly humorous) Well?

Morell. Have you anything to tell me?

Marchbanks. Only that I have been making a fool of myself here in private whilst you have been making a fool of yourself in public.

Morell. Hardly in the same way, I think.

Marchbanks (eagerly, scrambling up) The very, very v e r y same way. I have been playing the Good Man. Just like you.

When you began your heroics about leaving me here with Candida—

Morell (*involuntarily*) Candida!

Marchbanks. Oh yes: Ive got that far. But dont be afraid. Heroics are infectious: I caught the disease from you. I swore not to say a word in your absence that I would not have said a month ago in your presence.

Morell. Did you keep your oath?

Marchbanks (*suddenly perching himself on the back of the easy chair*) It kept itself somehow until about ten minutes ago. Up to that moment I went on desperately reading to her—reading my own poems—anybody's poems—to stave off a conversation. I was standing outside the gate of Heaven, and refusing to go in. Oh, you cant think how heroic it was, and how uncomfortable! Then—

Morell (*steadily controlling his suspense*) Then?

Marchbanks (*prosaically slipping down into a quite ordinary attitude on the seat of the chair*) Then she couldnt bear being read to any longer.

Morell. And you approached the gate of Heaven at last?

Marchbanks. Yes.

Morell. Well? (*Fiercely*) Speak, man: have you no feeling for me?

Marchbanks (*softly and musically*) Then she became an angel; and there was a flaming sword that turned every way, so that I couldnt go in; for I saw that that gate was really the gate of Hell.

Morell (*triumphantly*) She repulsed you!

Marchbanks (*rising in wild scorn*) No, you fool: if she had done that I should never have seen that I was in Heaven already. Repulsed me! You think that would have saved us! virtuous indignation! Oh, you are not worthy to live in the same world with her. (*He turns away contemptuously to the other side of the room*).

Morell (*who has watched him quietly without changing his place*) Do you think you make yourself more worthy by reviling me, Eugene?

Marchbanks. Here endeth the thousand and first lesson. Morell: I dont think much of your preaching after all: I believe I could do it better myself. The man I want to meet is the man that Candida married.

Morell. The man that—? Do you mean me?

Marchbanks. I dont mean the Reverend James Mavor Morell, moralist and windbag. I mean the real man that the Reverend James must have hidden somewhere inside his black coat: the man that Candida loved. You cant make a woman like Candida love you by merely buttoning your collar at the back instead of in front.

Morell (*boldly and steadily*) When Candida promised to marry me, I was the same moralist and windbag you now see. I wore my black coat; and my collar was buttoned behind instead of in front. Do you think she would have loved me any the better for being insincere in my profession?

Marchbanks (*on the sofa, hugging his ankles*) Oh, she forgave you, just as she forgives me for being a coward, and a weakling, and what you call a snivelling little whelp and all the rest of it. (*Dreamily*) A woman like that has divine insight: she loves our souls, and not our follies and vanities and illusions, nor our collars and coats, nor any other of the rags and tatters we are rolled up in. (*He reflects on this for an instant; then turns intently to question Morell*). What I want to know is how you got past the flaming sword that stopped me.

Morell. Perhaps because I was not interrupted at the end of ten minutes.

Marchbanks (*taken aback*) What!

Morell. Man can climb to the highest summits; but he cannot dwell there long.

Marchbanks (*springing up*) It's false: there can he dwell for ever, and there only. It's in the other moments that he can find no rest, no sense of the silent glory of life. Where would you have me spend my moments, if not on the summits?

Morell. In the scullery, slicing onions and filling lamps.

Marchbanks. Or in the pulpit, scrubbing cheap earthenware souls?

Morell. Yes, that too. It was there that I earned my golden moment, and the right, in that moment, to ask her to love me. I did not take the moment on credit; nor did I use it to steal another man's happiness.

Marchbanks (*rather disgustedly, trotting back towards the fireplace*) I have no doubt you conducted the transaction as honestly as if you were buying a pound of cheese. (*He stops on the brink of the hearth-rug, and adds, thoughtfully, to himself, with his back turned to Morell*) I could only go to her as a beggar.

Morell (*starting*) A beggar dying of cold! asking for her shawl!

Marchbanks (*turning, surprised*) Thank you for touching up my poetry. Yes, if you like: a beggar dying of cold, asking for her shawl.

Morell (*excitedly*) And she refused. Shall I tell you why she refused? I can tell you, on her own authority. It was because of—

Marchbanks. She didnt refuse.

Morell. Not!

Marchbanks. She offered me all I chose to ask for: her shawl, her wings, the wreath of stars on her head, the lilies in her hand, the crescent moon beneath her feet—

Morell (*seizing him*) Out with the truth, man: my wife is my wife: I want no more of your poetic fripperies. I know well that if I have lost her love and you have gained it, no law will bind her.

Marchbanks (*quaintly, without fear or resistance*) Catch me by the shirt collar, Morell: she will arrange it for me afterwards as she did this morning. (*With quiet rapture*) I shall feel her hands touch me.

Morell. You young imp, do you know how dangerous it is to say that to me? Or (*with a sudden misgiving*) has something made you brave?

Marchbanks. I'm not afraid now. I disliked you before: that was why I shrank from your touch. But I saw to-day—when she tortured you—that you love her. Since then I have been your friend: you may strangle me if you like.

Morell (*releasing him*) Eugene: if that is not a heartless lie —if you have a spark of human feeling left in you—will you tell me what has happened during my absence?

Marchbanks. What happened! Why, the flaming sword (*Morell stamps with impatience*)—Well, in plain prose, I loved her so exquisitely that I wanted nothing more than the happiness of being in such love. And before I had time to come down from the highest summits, y o u came in.

Morell (*suffering deeply*) So it is still unsettled. Still the misery of doubt.

Marchbanks. Misery! I am the happiest of men. I desire nothing now but her happiness. (*In a passion of sentiment*) Oh, Morell, let us both give her up. Why should she have to choose between a wretched little nervous disease like me, and a pig-headed parson like you? Let us go on a pilgrimage, you to the east and I to the west, in search of a worthy lover for her: some beautiful archangel with purple wings—

Morell. Some fiddlestick! Oh, if she is mad enough to leave me for you, who will protect her? who will help her? who will work for her? who will be a father to her children? (*He sits down distractedly on the sofa, with his elbows on his knees and his head propped on his clenched fists*).

Marchbanks (*snapping his fingers wildly*) She does not ask those silly questions. It is she who wants somebody to protect, to help, to work for: somebody to give her children to protect, to help and to work for. Some grown-up man who has become as a little child again. Oh, you fool, you fool, you triple fool! I am the man, Morell: I am the man. (*He dances about excitedly, crying*) You dont understand what a woman is. Send for her, Morell: send for her and let her choose between— (*The door opens and Candida enters. He stops as if petrified*).

Candida (*amazed, on the threshold*) What on earth are you at, Eugene?

Marchbanks (*oddly*) James and I are having a preaching match; and he is getting the worst of it.

Candida looks quickly round at Morell. Seeing that he is distressed, she hurries down to him, greatly vexed.

Candida. You have been annoying him. Now I wont have it, Eugene: do you hear? (*She puts her hand on Morell's shoulder, and quite forgets her wifely tact in her anger*). My boy shall not be worried: I will protect him.

Morell (*rising proudly*) Protect!

Candida (*not heeding him: to Eugene*) What have you been saying?

Marchbanks (*appalled*) Nothing. I—

Candida. Eugene! Nothing?

Marchbanks (*piteously*) I mean—I—I'm very sorry. I wont do it again: indeed I wont. I'll let him alone.

Morell (*indignantly, with an aggressive movement towards Eugene*) Let me alone! You young—

Candida (*stopping him*) Sh!—no: let me deal with him, James.

Marchbanks. Oh, youre not angry with me, are you?

Candida (*severely*) Yes I am: very angry. I have a good mind to pack you out of the house.

Morell (*taken aback by Candida's vigor, and by no means relishing the position of being rescued by her from another man*) Gently, Candida, gently. I am able to take care of myself.

Candida (*petting him*) Yes, dear: of course you are. But you mustnt be annoyed and made miserable.

Marchbanks (*almost in tears, turning to the door*) I'll go.

Candida. Oh, you neednt go: I cant turn you out at this time of night. (*Vehemently*) Shame on you! For shame!

Marchbanks (*desperately*) But what have I done?

Candida. I know what you have done: as well as if I had been here all the time. Oh, it was unworthy! You are like a child: you cannot hold your tongue.

Marchbanks. I would die ten times over sooner than give you a moment's pain.

Candida (*with infinite contempt for this puerility*) Much good your dying would do me!

Morell. Candida, my dear: this altercation is hardly quite seemly. It is a matter between two men; and I am the right person to settle it.

Candida. Two men! Do you call that a man? (*To Eugene*) You bad boy!

Marchbanks (*gathering a whimsically affectionate courage from the scolding*) If I am to be scolded like a boy, I must make a boy's excuse. He began it. And he's bigger than I am.

Candida (*losing confidence a little as her concern for Morell's dignity takes the alarm*) That cant be true. (*To Morell*) You didnt begin it, James, did you?

Morell (*contemptuously*) No.

Marchbanks (*indignant*) Oh!

Morell (*to Eugene*) You began it: this morning. (*Candida, instantly connecting this with his mysterious allusion in the afternoon to something told him by Eugene in the morning, looks at him with quick suspicion. Morell proceeds, with the emphasis of offended superiority*) But your other point is true. I am certainly the bigger of the two, and, I hope, the stronger, Candida. So you had better leave the matter in my hands.

Candida (*again soothing him*) Yes, dear; but—(*troubled*) I dont understand about this morning.

Morell (*gently snubbing her*) You need not understand, my dear.

Candida. But James, I (*the street bell rings*)—Oh bother! Here they all come. (*She goes out to let them in*).

Marchbanks (*running to Morell*) Oh, Morell, isnt it dreadful? She's angry with us: she hates me. What shall I do?

Morell (*with quaint desperation, walking up and down the middle of the room*) Eugene: my head is spinning round. I shall begin to laugh presently.

Marchbanks (*following him anxiously*) No, no: she'll think Ive thrown you into hysterics. Dont laugh.

Boisterous voices and laughter are heard approaching. Lexy Mill, his eyes sparkling, and his bearing denoting unwonted elevation of spirit, enters with Burgess, who is greasy and self-complacent, but has all his wits about him. Miss Garnett, with her smartest hat and jacket on, follows them; but though her eyes are brighter than before, she is evidently a prey to misgiving. She places herself with her back to her typewriting table, with one hand on it to steady herself, passing the other across her forehead as if she were a little tired and giddy. Marchbanks relapses into shyness and edges away into the corner near the window, where Morell's books are.

Lexy (*exhilarated*) Morell: I m u s t congratulate you. (*Grasping his hand*) What a noble, splendid, inspired address you gave us! You surpassed yourself.

Burgess. So you did, James. It fair kep me awake to the lars' word. Didnt it, Miss Garnett?

Proserpine (*worriedly*) Oh, I wasnt minding you: I was trying to make notes. (*She takes out her notebook, and looks at her stenography, which nearly makes her cry*).

Morell. Did I go too fast, Pross?

Proserpine. Much too fast. You know I cant do more than ninety words a minute. (*She relieves her feelings by throwing her notebook angrily beside her machine, ready for use next morning*).

Morell (*soothingly*) Oh well, well, never mind, never mind, never mind. Have you all had supper?

Lexy. Mr Burgess has been kind enough to give us a really splendid supper at the Belgrave.

Burgess (with effusive magnanimity) Dont mention it, Mr Mill. (*Modestly*) Youre arty welcome to my little treat.

Proserpine. We had champagne. I never tasted it before. I feel quite giddy.

Morell (surprised) A champagne supper! That was very handsome. Was it my eloquence that produced all this extravagance?

Lexy (rhetorically) Your eloquence, and Mr Burgess's goodness of heart. (*With a fresh burst of exhilaration*) And what a very fine fellow the chairman is, Morell! He came to supper with us.

Morell (with long drawn significance, looking at Burgess) O-o-o-h! the chairman. N o w I understand.

Burgess covers with a deprecatory cough a lively satisfaction with his own diplomatic cunning. Lexy folds his arms and leans against the head of the sofa in a high-spirited attitude after nearly losing his balance. Candida comes in with glasses, lemons, and a jug of hot water on a tray.

Candida. Who will have some lemonade? You know our rules: total abstinence. (*She puts the tray on the table, and takes up the lemon squeezer, looking enquiringly round at them*).

Morell. No use, dear. Theyve all had champagne. Pross has broken her pledge.

Candida (to Proserpine) You dont mean to say youve been drinking champagne!

Proserpine (stubbornly) Yes I do. I'm only a beer teetotaller, not a champagne teetotaller. I dont like beer. Are there any letters for me to answer, Mr Morell?

Morell. No more to-night.

Proserpine. Very well. Goodnight, everybody.

Lexy (gallantly) Had I not better see you home, Miss Garnett?

Proserpine. No thank you. I shant trust myself with any-body to-night. I wish I hadnt taken any of that stuff. (*She takes uncertain aim at the door; dashes at it; and barely escapes without disaster*).

Burgess (*indignantly*) Stuff indeed! That gurl dunno what champagne is! Pommery and Greeno at twelve and six a bottle. She took two glasses amost straight horff.

Morell (*anxious about her*) Go and look after her, Lexy.

Lexy (*alarmed*) But if she should really be— Suppose she began to sing in the street, or anything of that sort.

Morell. Just so: she may. Thats why youd better see her safely home.

Candida. Do, Lexy: theres a good fellow. (*She shakes his hand and pushes him gently to the door*).

Lexy. It's evidently my duty to go. I hope it may not be necessary. Goodnight, Mrs Morell. (*To the rest*) Goodnight. (*He goes. Candida shuts the door*).

Burgess. He was gushin with hextra piety hisself arter two sips. People carnt drink like they huseter. (*Bustling across to the hearth*) Well, James: it's time to lock up. Mr Morchbanks: shall I ave the pleasure of your company for a bit o the way ome?

Marchbanks (*affrightedly*) Yes: I'd better go. (*He hurries towards the door; but Candida places herself before it, barring his way*).

Candida (*with quiet authority*) You sit down. Youre not going yet.

Marchbanks (*quailing*) No: I—I didnt mean to. (*He sits down abjectly on the sofa*).

Candida. Mr Marchbanks will stay the night with us, papa.

Burgess. Oh well, I'll say goodnight. So long, James. (*He shakes hands with Morell, and goes over to Eugene*). Make em give you a nightlight by your bed, Mr Morchbanks: itll comfort you if you wake up in the night with a touch of that complaint of yores. Goodnight.

Marchbanks. Thank you: I will. Goodnight, Mr Burgess. (*They shake hands. Burgess goes to the door*).

Candida (intercepting Morell, who is following Burgess) Stay here, dear: I'll put on papa's coat for him. (*She goes out with Burgess*).

Marchbanks (rising and stealing over to Morell) Morell: theres going to be a terrible scene. Arnt you afraid?

Morell. Not in the least.

Marchbanks. I never envied you your courage before. (*He puts his hand appealingly on Morell's forearm*). Stand by me, wont you?

Morell (casting him off resolutely) Each for himself, Eugene. She must choose between us now.

Candida returns. Eugene creeps back to the sofa like a guilty schoolboy.

Candida (between them, addressing Eugene) Are you sorry?

Marchbanks (earnestly) Yes. Heartbroken.

Candida. Well then, you are forgiven. Now go off to bed like a good little boy: I want to talk to James about you.

Marchbanks (rising in great consternation) Oh, I cant do that, Morell. I must be here. I'll not go away. Tell her.

Candida (her suspicions confirmed) Tell me what? (*His eyes avoid hers furtively. She turns and mutely transfers the question to Morell*).

Morell (bracing himself for the catastrophe) I have nothing to tell her, except (*here his voice deepens to a measured and mournful tenderness*) that she is my greatest treasure on earth —if she is really mine.

Candida (coldly, offended by his yielding to his orator's instinct and treating her as if she were the audience at the Guild of St Matthew) I am sure Eugene can say no less, if that is all.

Marchbanks (discouraged) Morell: she's laughing at us.

Morell (with a quick touch of temper) There is nothing to laugh at. Are you laughing at us, Candida?

Candida (with quiet anger) Eugene is very quick-witted,

James. I hope I am going to laugh; but I am not sure that I am not going to be very angry. (*She goes to the fireplace, and stands there leaning with her arms on the mantelpiece, and her foot on the fender, whilst Eugene steals to Morell and plucks him by the sleeve*).

Marchbanks (*whispering*) Stop, Morell. Dont let us say anything.

Morell (*pushing Eugene away without deigning to look at him*) I hope you dont mean that as a threat, Candida.

Candida (*with emphatic warning*) Take care, James. Eugene: I asked you to go. Are you going?

Morell (*putting his foot down*) He shall not go. I wish him to remain.

Marchbanks. I'll go. I'll do whatever you want. (*He turns to the door*).

Candida. Stop! (*He obeys*). Didnt you hear James say he wished you to stay? James is master here. Dont you know that?

Marchbanks (*flushing with a young poet's rage against tyranny*) By what right is he master?

Candida (*quietly*) Tell him, James.

Morell (*taken aback*) My dear: I dont know of any right that makes me master. I assert no such right.

Candida (*with infinite reproach*) You dont know! Oh, James! James! (*To Eugene, musingly*) I wonder do you understand, Eugene! (*He shakes his head helplessly, not daring to look at her*). No: youre too young. Well, I give you leave to stay: to stay and learn. (*She comes away from the hearth and places herself between them*). Now, James! whats the matter? Come: tell me.

Marchbanks (*whispering tremulously across to him*) Dont.

Candida. Come. Out with it!

Morell (*slowly*) I meant to prepare your mind carefully, Candida, so as to prevent misunderstanding.

Candida. Yes, dear: I am sure you did. But never mind: I shant misunderstand.

Morell. Well—er— (*he hesitates, unable to find the long explanation which he supposed to be available*).

Candida. Well?

Morell (*blurting it out baldly*) Eugene declares that you are in love with him.

Marchbanks (*frantically*) No, no, no, no, never. I did not, Mrs Morell: it's not true. I said I loved you. I said I understood you, and that he couldnt. And it was not after what passed there before the fire that I spoke: it was not, on my word. It was this morning.

Candida (*enlightened*) This morning!

Marchbanks. Yes. (*He looks at her, pleading for credence, and then adds simply*) That was what was the matter with my collar.

Candida. Your collar? (*Suddenly taking in his meaning she turns to Morell, shocked*). Oh, James: did you— (*she stops*)?

Morell (*ashamed*) You know, Candida, that I have a temper to struggle with. And he said (*shuddering*) that you despised me in your heart.

Candida (*turning quickly on Eugene*) Did you say that?

Marchbanks (*terrified*) No.

Candida (*almost fiercely*) Then James has just told me a falsehood. Is that what you mean?

Marchbanks. No, no: I—I—(*desperately*) it was David's wife. And it wasnt at home: it was when she saw him dancing before all the people.

Morell (*taking the cue with a debater's adroitness*) Dancing before all the people, Candida; and thinking he was moving their hearts by his mission when they were only suffering from —Prossy's complaint. (*She is about to protest: he raises his hand to silence her*). Dont try to look indignant, Candida—

Candida. Try!

Morell (*continuing*) Eugene was right. As you told me a few hours after, he is always right. He said nothing that you did not say far better yourself. He is the poet, who sees everything; and I am the poor parson, who understands nothing.

Candida (*remorsefully*) Do you mind what is said by a foolish boy, because I said something like it in jest?

Morell. That foolish boy can speak with the inspiration of a child and the cunning of a serpent. He has claimed that you belong to him and not to me; and, rightly or wrongly, I have come to fear that it may be true. I will not go about tortured with doubts and suspicions. I will not live with you and keep a secret from you. I will not suffer the intolerable degradation of jealousy. We have agreed—he and I—that you shall choose between us now. I await your decision.

Candida (*slowly recoiling a step, her heart hardened by his rhetoric in spite of the sincere feeling behind it*) Oh! I am to choose, am I? I suppose it is quite settled that I must belong to one or the other.

Morell (*firmly*) Quite. You must choose definitely.

Marchbanks (*anxiously*) Morell: you dont understand. She means that she belongs to herself.

Candida (*turning on him*) I mean that, and a good deal more, Master Eugene, as you will both find out presently. And pray, my lords and masters, what have you to offer for my choice? I am up for auction, it seems. What do you bid, James?

Morell (*reproachfully*) Cand— (*He breaks down: his eyes and throat fill with tears: the orator becomes a wounded animal*). I cant speak—

Candida (*impulsively going to him*) Ah, dearest—

Marchbanks (*in wild alarm*) Stop: it's not fair. You musnt shew her that you suffer, Morell. I am on the rack too; but I am not crying.

Morell (*rallying all his forces*) Yes: you are right. It is not for pity that I am bidding. (*He disengages himself from Candida*).

Candida (*retreating, chilled*) I beg your pardon, James: I did not mean to touch you. I am waiting to hear your bid.

Morell (*with proud humility*) I have nothing to offer you but my strength for your defence, my honesty for your surety, my ability and industry for your livelihood, and my authority and position for your dignity. That is all it becomes a man to offer to a woman.

Candida (*quite quietly*) And you, Eugene? What do you offer?

Marchbanks. My weakness. My desolation. My heart's need.

Candida (*impressed*) Thats a good bid, Eugene. Now I know how to make my choice.

She pauses and looks curiously from one to the other, as if weighing them. Morell, whose lofty confidence has changed into heartbreaking dread at Eugene's bid, loses all power of concealing his anxiety. Eugene, strung to the highest tension, does not move a muscle.

Morell (*in a suffocated voice: the appeal bursting from the depths of his anguish*) Candida!

Marchbanks (*aside, in a flash of contempt*) Coward!

Candida (*significantly*) I give myself to the weaker of the two.

Eugene divines her meaning at once: his face whitens like steel in a furnace.

Morell (*bowing his head with the calm of collapse*) I accept your sentence, Candida.

Candida. Do y o u understand, Eugene?

Marchbanks. Oh, I feel I'm lost. He cannot bear the burden.

Morell (*incredulously, raising his head and voice with comic abruptness*) Do you mean m e , Candida?

Candida (*smiling a little*) Let us sit and talk comfortably over it like three friends. (*To Morell*) Sit down, dear. (*Morell, quite lost, takes the chair from the fireside: the children's chair*). Bring me that chair, Eugene. (*She indicates the easy chair. He fetches it silently, even with something like cold strength, and places it next Morell, a little behind him. She sits down. He takes the visitor's chair himself, and sits, inscru-*

table. When they are all settled she begins, throwing a spell of quietness on them by her calm, sane, tender tone). You remember what you told me about yourself, Eugene: how nobody has cared for you since your old nurse died: how those clever fashionable sisters and successful brothers of yours were your mother's and father's pets: how miserable you were at Eton: how your father is trying to starve you into returning to Oxford: how you have had to live without comfort or welcome or refuge: always lonely, and nearly always disliked and misunderstood, poor boy!

Marchbanks (faithful to the nobility of his lot) I had my books. I had Nature. And at last I met you.

Candida. Never mind that just at present. Now I want you to look at this other boy here: my boy! spoiled from his cradle. We go once a fortnight to see his parents. You should come with us, Eugene, to see the pictures of the hero of that household. James as a baby! the most wonderful of all babies. James holding his first school prize, won at the ripe age of eight! James as the captain of his eleven! James in his first frock coat! James under all sorts of glorious circumstances! You know how strong he is (I hope he didnt hurt you): how clever he is: how happy. *(With deepening gravity)* Ask James's mother and his three sisters what it cost to save James the trouble of doing anything but be strong and clever and happy. Ask me what it costs to be James's mother and three sisters and wife and mother to his children all in one. Ask Prossy and Maria how troublesome the house is even when we have no visitors to help us to slice the onions. Ask the tradesmen who want to worry James and spoil his beautiful sermons who it is that puts them off. When there is money to give, he gives it: when there is money to refuse, I refuse it. I build a castle of comfort and indulgence and love for him, and stand sentinel always to keep little vulgar cares out. I make him master here, though he does not know it, and could not tell you a moment ago how it came to be so. *(With sweet irony)* And when he thought I might go away with you, his only anxiety was—what should become of m e ! And to tempt me to stay he offered me (*leaning forward to stroke his hair caressingly at each phrase*) h i s strength for m y defence! his industry for my livelihood! his dignity for my position! his—(*relenting*) ah, I am mixing up your beautiful cadences and spoiling them, am I not, darling? (*She lays her cheek fondly against his*).

Morell (*quite overcome, kneeling beside her chair and embracing her with boyish ingenuousness*) It's all true, every word. What I am you have made me with the labor of your hands and the love of your heart. You are my wife, my mother, my sisters: you are the sum of all loving care ro me.

Candida (*in his arms, smiling, to Eugene*) Am I y o u r mother and sisters to you, Eugene?

Marchbanks (*rising with a fierce gesture of disgust*) Ah, never. Out, then, into the night with me!

Candida (*rising quickly*) You are not going like that, Eugene?

Marchbanks (*with the ring of a man's voice—no longer a boy's—in the words*) I know the hour when it strikes. I am impatient to do what must be done.

Morell (*who has also risen*) Candida: dont let him do anything rash.

Candida (*confident, smiling at Eugene*) Oh, there is no fear. He has learnt to live without happiness.

Marchbanks. I no longer desire happiness: life is nobler than that. Parson James: I give you my happiness with both hands: I love you because you have filled the heart of the woman I loved. Goodbye. (*He goes towards the door*).

Candida. One last word. (*He stops, but without turning to her. She goes to him*). How old are you, Eugene?

Marchbanks. As old as the world now. This morning I was eighteen.

Candida. Eighteen! Will you, for my sake, make a little poem out of the two sentences I am going to say to you? And will you promise to repeat it to yourself whenever you think of me?

Marchbanks (*without moving*) Say the sentences.

Candida. When I am thirty, she will be forty-five. When I am sixty, she will be seventy-five.

Marchbanks (*turning to her*) In a hundred years, we shall be the same age. But I have a better secret than that in my heart. Let me go now. The night outside grows impatient.

Candida. Goodbye. (*She takes his face in her hands; and as he divines her intention and falls on his knees, she kisses his forehead. Then he flies out into the night. She turns to Morell, holding out her arms to him*). Ah, James!

They embrace. But they do not know the secret in the poet's heart.

will you promise to repeat it to yourself whenever you think of me?

Marchbanks (will out moving). Say the sentences.

Candida. When I am thirty, she will be forty-five. When I am sixty, she will be seventy-five.

Marchbanks (turning to her). In a hundred years, we shall be the same age. But I have a better secret than that in my heart. Let me go now. The night outside grows impatient.

Candida. Good-bye. (She takes his face in her hands; and as he divines her intention and falls on his knees, she kisses his forehead. Then he flies out into the night. She turns to Morell, holding out her arms to him.) Ah, James!

They embrace. But they do not know the secret in the poet's heart.

Cæsar and Cleopatra

A HISTORY

1898

PROLOGUE

IN THE DOORWAY of the temple of Ra in Memphis. Deep gloom. An august personage with a hawk's head is mysteriously visible by his own light in the darkness within the temple. He surveys the modern audience with great contempt; and finally speaks the following words to them.

Peace! Be silent and hearken unto me, ye quaint little islanders. Give ear, ye men with white paper on your breasts and nothing written thereon (to signify the innocence of your minds). Hear me, ye women who adorn yourselves alluringly and conceal your thoughts from your men, leading them to believe that ye deem them wondrous strong and masterful whilst in truth ye hold them in your hearts as children without judgment. Look upon my hawk's head; and know that I am Ra, who was once in Egypt a mighty god. Ye cannot kneel nor prostrate yourselves; for ye are packed in rows without freedom to move, obstructing one another's vision; neither do any of ye regard it as seemly to do ought until ye see all the rest do so too; wherefore it commonly happens that in great emergencies ye do nothing though each telleth his fellow that something must be done. I ask you not for worship, but for silence. Let not your men speak nor your women cough; for I am come to draw you back two thousand years over the graves of sixty generations. Ye poor posterity, think not that ye are the first. Other fools before ye have seen the sun rise and set, and the moon change her shape and her hour. As they were so ye are; and yet not so great; for the pyramids my people built stand to this day; whilst the dustheaps on which ye slave, and

which ye call empires, scatter in the wind even as ye pile your
dead sons' bodies on them to make yet more dust.

Hearken to me then, oh ye compulsorily educated ones.
Know that even as there is an old England and a new, and ye
stand perplexed between the twain; so in the days when I was
worshipped was there an old Rome and a new, and men standing perplexed between them. And the old Rome was poor and
little, and greedy and fierce, and evil in many ways; but because its mind was little and its work was simple, it knew its
own mind and did its own work; and the gods pitied it and
helped it and strengthened it and shielded it; for the gods are
patient with littleness. Then the old Rome, like the beggar on
horseback, presumed on the favor of the gods, and said, "Lo!
there is neither riches nor greatness in our littleness: the road
to riches and greatness is through robbery of the poor and
slaughter of the weak." So they robbed their own poor until
they became great masters of that art, and knew by what laws
it could be made to appear seemly and honest. And when they
had squeezed their own poor dry, they robbed the poor of
other lands, and added those lands to Rome until there came
a new Rome, rich and huge. And I, Ra, laughed; for the minds
of the Romans remained the same size whilst their dominion
spread over the earth.

Now mark me, that ye may understand what ye are presently to see. Whilst the Romans still stood between the old
Rome and the new, there arose among them a mighty soldier:
Pompey the Great. And the way of the soldier is the way of
death; but the way of the gods is the way of life; and so it
comes that a god at the end of his way is wise and a soldier at
the end of his way is a fool. So Pompey held by the old Rome,
in which only soldiers could become great; but the gods turned
to the new Rome, in which any man with wit enough could
become what he would. And Pompey's friend Julius Cæsar was
on the side of the gods; for he saw that Rome had passed beyond the control of the little old Romans. This Cæsar was a

great talker and a politician: he bought men with words and with gold, even as ye are bought. And when they would not be satisfied with words and gold, and demanded also the glories of war, Cæsar in his middle age turned his hand to that trade; and they that were against him when he sought their welfare, bowed down before him when he became a slayer and a conqueror; for such is the nature of you mortals. And as for Pompey, the gods grew tired of his triumphs and his airs of being himself a god; for he talked of law and duty and other matters that concerned not a mere human worm. And the gods smiled on Cæsar; for he lived the life they had given him boldly, and was not forever rebuking us for our indecent ways of creation, and hiding our handiwork as a shameful thing. Ye know well what I mean; for this is one of your own sins.

And thus it fell out between the old Rome and the new, that Cæsar said, "Unless I break the law of old Rome, I cannot take my share in ruling her; and the gift of ruling that the gods gave me will perish without fruit." But Pompey said, "The law is above all; and if thou break it thou shalt die." Then said Cæsar, "I will break it: kill me who can." And he broke it. And Pompey went for him, as ye say, with a great army to slay him and uphold the old Rome. So Cæsar fled across the Adriatic sea; for the high gods had a lesson to teach him, which lesson they shall also teach you in due time if ye continue to forget them and to worship that cad among gods, Mammon. Therefore before they raised Cæsar to be master of the world, they were minded to throw him down into the dust, even beneath the feet of Pompey, and blacken his face before the nations. And Pompey they raised higher than ever, he and his laws and his high mind that aped the gods, so that his fall might be the more terrible. And Pompey followed Cæsar, and overcame him with all the majesty of old Rome, and stood over him and over the whole world even as ye stand over it with your fleet that covers thirty miles of the sea. And when Cæsar was brought down to utter nothingness, he made a last stand to die honorably, and did not despair; for he said, "Against me there is Pompey, and the old Rome, and the law and the legions: all all against me; but high above these are the gods; and Pompey is a fool." And the gods laughed and approved; and on the field of Pharsalia the impossible came to pass; the blood and iron ye pin your faith on fell before the spirit of man; for the spirit of man is the will of the gods; and Pompey's power crumbled in his hand, even as the power of imperial Spain crumbled when it was set against your fathers in the days when England was little, and knew her own mind, and had a mind to know instead of a circulation of newspapers. Wherefore look to it, lest some little people whom ye would enslave rise up and become in the hand of God the scourge of your boastings and your injustices and your lusts and stupidities.

And now, would ye know the end of Pompey, or will ye sleep while a god speaks? Heed my words well; for Pompey went where ye have gone, even to Egypt, where there was a Roman occupation even as there was but now a British one. And Cæsar pursued Pompey to Egypt; a Roman fleeing, and a Roman pursuing: dog eating dog. And the Egyptians said, "Lo: these Romans which have lent money to our kings and levied a distraint upon us with their arms, call for ever upon us to be loyal to them by betraying our own country to them. But now behold two Romes! Pompey's Rome and Cæsar's Rome! To which of the twain shall we pretend to be loyal?" So they turned in their perplexity to a soldier that had once served Pompey, and that knew the ways of Rome and was full of her lusts. And they said to him, "Lo: in thy country dog eats dog; and both dogs are coming to eat us: what counsel hast thou to give us?" And this soldier, whose name was Lucius Septimius, and whom ye shall presently see before ye, replied, "Ye shall diligently consider which is the bigger dog of the two; and ye shall kill the other dog for his sake and thereby earn his favor." And the Egyptians said, "Thy counsel is expedient; but if we kill a man outside the law we set ourselves in the place of the gods; and this we dare not do. But thou, being a Roman, art accustomed to this kind of killing; for thou hast imperial instincts. Wilt thou therefore kill the lesser dog for us?" And he said, "I will; for I have made my home in Egypt; and I desire consideration and influence among you." And they said, "We knew well thou wouldst not do it for nothing: thou shalt have thy reward." Now when Pompey came, he came alone in a little galley, putting his trust in the law and the constitution. And it was plain to the people of Egypt that Pompey was now but a very small dog. So when he set his foot on the shore he was greeted by his old comrade Lucius Septimius, who welcomed him with one hand and with the other smote off his head, and kept it as it were a pickled cabbage to make a present to Cæsar. And mankind shuddered; but the gods laughed; for Septimius was but a knife that Pompey had sharpened; and when it turned against his own throat they said that Pompey had better have made Septimius a ploughman than so brave and readyhanded a slayer. Therefore again I bid you beware, ye who would all be Pompeys if ye dared; for war is a wolf that may come to your own door.

Are ye impatient with me? Do ye crave for a story of an unchaste woman? Hath the name of Cleopatra tempted ye hither? Ye foolish ones; Cleopatra is as yet but a child that is whipped by her nurse. And what I am about to shew you for the good of your souls is how Cæsar, seeking Pompey in Egypt, found Cleopatra; and how he received that present of a pickled cabbage that was once the head of Pompey; and what things happened between the old Cæsar and the child queen before he left Egypt and battled his way back to Rome to be slain there as Pompey was slain, by men in whom the spirit of Pompey still lived. All this ye shall see; and ye shall marvel, after your ignorant manner, that men twenty centuries ago were already just such as you, and spoke and lived as ye speak and live, no worse and no better, no wiser and no sillier. And the two thousand years that have past are to me, the god Ra, but a moment;

nor is this day any other than the day in which Cæsar set foot
in the land of my people. And now I leave you; for ye are a
dull folk, and instruction is wasted on you; and I had not
spoken so much but that it is in the nature of a god to struggle
for ever with the dust and the darkness, and to drag from them,
by the force of his longing for the divine, more life and more
light. Settle ye therefore in your seats and keep silent; for ye
are about to hear a man speak, and a great man he was, as ye
count greatness. And fear not that I shall speak to you again:
the rest of the story must ye learn from them that lived it.
Farewell; and do not presume to applaud me. (*The temple
vanishes in utter darkness*).

[1912].

AN ALTERNATIVE TO THE PROLOGUE

AN OCTOBER night on the Syrian border of Egypt towards the end of the XXXIII Dynasty, in the year 706 by Roman computation, afterwards reckoned by Christian computation as 48 B.C. A great radiance of silver fire, the dawn of a moonlit night, is rising in the east. The stars and the cloudless sky are our own contemporaries, nineteen and a half centuries younger than we know them; but you would not guess that from their appearance. Below them are two notable drawbacks of civilization: a palace, and soldiers. The palace, an old, low, Syrian building of whitened mud, is not so ugly as Buckingham Palace; and the officers in the courtyard are more highly civilized than modern English officers: for example, they do not dig up the corpses of their dead enemies and mutilate them, as we dug up Cromwell and the Mahdi. They are in two groups: one intent on the gambling of their captain Belzanor, a warrior of fifty, who, with his spear on the ground beside his knee, is stooping to throw dice with a sly-looking young Persian recruit; the other gathered about a guardsman who has just finished telling a naughty story (still current in English barracks) at which they are laughing uproariously. They are about a dozen in number, all highly aristocratic young Egyptian guardsmen, handsomely equipped with weapons and armor, very unEnglish in point of not being ashamed of and uncomfortable in their professional dress; on the contrary, rather ostentatiously and arrogantly warlike, as valuing themselves on their military caste.

Belzanor is a typical veteran, tough and wilful; prompt, capable and crafty where brute force will serve; helpless and boyish when it will not: an effective sergeant, an incompetent general, a deplorable dictator. Would, if influentially connected, be employed in the two last capacities by a modern

*European State on the strength of his success in the first. Is
rather to be pitied just now in view of the fact that Julius
Cæsar is invading his country. Not knowing this, is intent on
his game with the Persian, whom, as a foreigner, he considers
quite capable of cheating him.*

*His subalterns are mostly handsome young fellows whose
interest in the game and the story symbolize with tolerable
completeness the main interests in life of which they are conscious. Their spears are leaning against the walls, or lying on
the ground ready to their hands. The corner of the courtyard
forms a triangle of which one side is the front of the palace,
with a doorway, the other a wall with a gateway. The story-
tellers are on the palace side: the gamblers, on the gateway
side. Close to the gateway, against the wall, is a stone block
high enough to enable a Nubian sentinel, standing on it, to
look over the wall. The yard is lighted by a torch stuck in the
wall. As the laughter from the group round the storyteller dies
away, the kneeling Persian, winning the throw, snatches up the
stake from the ground.*

Belzanor. By Apis, Persian, thy gods are good to thee.

The Persian. Try yet again, O captain. Double or quits!

Belzanor. No more. I am not in the vein.

The Sentinel (*poising his javelin as he peers over the wall*)
Stand. Who goes there?

*They all start, listening. A strange voice replies from with-
out.*

Voice. The bearer of evil tidings.

Belzanor (*calling to the sentry*) Pass him.

The Sentinel (*grounding his javelin*) Draw near, O bearer
of evil tidings.

Belzanor (*pocketing the dice and picking up his spear*) Let
us receive this man with honor. He bears evil tidings.

*The guardsmen seize their spears and gather about the gate,
leaving a way through for the new comer.*

Persian (*rising from his knee*) Are evil tidings, then, so honorable?

Belzanor. O barbarous Persian, hear my instruction. In Egypt the bearer of good tidings is sacrificed to the gods as a thank offering; but no god will accept the blood of the messenger of evil. When we have good tidings, we are careful to send them in the mouth of the cheapest slave we can find. Evil tidings are borne by young noblemen who desire to bring themselves into notice. (*They join the rest at the gate*).

The Sentinel. Pass, O young captain; and bow the head in the House of the Queen.

Voice. Go anoint thy javelin with fat of swine, O Blackamoor; for before morning the Romans will make thee eat it to the very butt.

The owner of the voice, a fairhaired dandy, dressed in a different fashion from that affected by the guardsmen, but no less extravagantly, comes through the gateway laughing. He is somewhat battlestained; and his left forearm, bandaged, comes through a torn sleeve. In his right hand he carries a Roman sword in its sheath. He swaggers down the courtyard, the Persian on his right, Belzanor on his left, and the guardsmen crowding down behind him.

Belzanor. Who are thou that laughest in the House of Cleopatra the Queen, and in the teeth of Belzanor, the captain of her guard?

The New Comer. I am Bel Affris, descended from the gods.

Belzanor (*ceremoniously*) Hail, cousin!

All (*except the Persian*) Hail, cousin!

Persian. All the Queen's guards are descended from the gods, O stranger, save myself. I am Persian, and descended from many kings.

Bel Affris (*to the guardsmen*) Hail, cousins! (*To the Persian, condescendingly*) Hail, mortal!

Belzanor. You have been in battle, Bel Affris; and you are

a soldier among soldiers. You will not let the Queen's women
have the first of your tidings.

Bel Affris. I have no tidings, except that we shall have our
throats cut presently, women, soldiers, and all.

Persian (*to Belzanor*) I told you so.

The Sentinel (*who has been listening*) Woe, alas!

Bel Affris (*calling to him*) Peace, peace, poor Ethiop: destiny
is with the gods who painted thee black. (*To Belzanor*) What
has this mortal (*indicating the Persian*) told you?

Belzanor. He says that the Roman Julius Cæsar, who has
landed on our shores with a handful of followers, will make
himself master of Egypt. He is afraid of the Roman soldiers.
(*The guardsmen laugh with boisterous scorn*). Peasants,
brought up to scare crows and follow the plough! Sons of
smiths and millers and tanners! And we nobles, consecrated
to arms, descended from the gods!

Persian. Belzanor: the gods are not always good to their
poor relations.

Belzanor (*hotly, to the Persian*) Man to man, are we worse
than the slaves of Cæsar?

Bel Affris (*stepping between them*) Listen, cousin. Man
to man, we Egyptians are as gods above the Romans.

The Guardsmen (*exultantly*) Aha!

Bel Affris. But this Cæsar does not pit man against man: he
throws a legion at you where you are weakest as he throws
a stone from a catapult; and that legion is as a man with one
head, a thousand arms, and no religion. I have fought against
them; and I know.

Belzanor (*derisively*) Were you frightened, cousin?

*The guardsmen roar with laughter, their eyes sparkling at
the wit of their captain.*

Bel Affris. No, cousin; but I was beaten. They were frightened (perhaps); but they scattered us like chaff.

*The guardsmen, much damped, utter a growl of contemptu-
ous disgust.*

Belzanor. Could you not die?

Bel Affris. No: that was too easy to be worthy of a descendant of the gods. Besides, there was no time: all was over in a moment. The attack came just where we least expected it.

Belzanor. That shews that the Romans are cowards.

Bel Affris. They care nothing about cowardice, these Romans: they fight to win. The pride and honor of war are nothing to them.

Persian. Tell us the tale of the battle. What befell?

The Guardsmen (*gathering eagerly round Bel Affris*) Ay: the tale of the battle.

Bel Affris. Know then, that I am a novice in the guard of the temple of Ra in Memphis, serving neither Cleopatra nor her brother Ptolemy, but only the high gods. We went a journey to inquire of Ptolemy why he had driven Cleopatra into Syria, and how we of Egypt should deal with the Roman Pompey, newly come to our shores after his defeat by Cæsar at Pharsalia. What, think ye, did we learn? Even that Cæsar is coming also in hot pursuit of his foe, and that Ptolemy has slain Pompey, whose severed head he holds in readiness to present to the conqueror. (*Sensation among the guardsmen*). Nay, more: we found that Cæsar is already come; for we had not made half a day's journey on our way back when we came upon a city rabble flying from his legions, whose landing they had gone out to withstand.

Belzanor. And ye, the temple guard! did ye not withstand these legions?

Bel Affris. What man could, that we did. But there came the sound of a trumpet whose voice was as the cursing of a black mountain. Then saw we a moving wall of shields coming towards us. You know how the heart burns when you charge a fortified wall; but how if the fortified wall were to charge you?

The Persian (*exulting in having told them so*) Did I not say it?

Bel Affris. When the wall came nigh, it changed into a line of men—common fellows enough, with helmets, leather tunics, and breastplates. Every man of them flung his javelin: the one that came my way drove through my shield as through a papyrus—lo there! (*he points to the bandage on his left arm*) and would have gone through my neck had I not stooped. They were charging at the double then, and were upon us with short swords almost as soon as their javelins. When a man is close to you with such a sword, you can do nothing with our weapons: they are all too long.

The Persian. What did you do?

Bel Affris. Doubled my fist and smote my Roman on the sharpness of his jaw. He was but mortal after all: he lay down in a stupor; and I took his sword and laid it on. (*Drawing the sword*) Lo! a Roman sword with Roman blood on it!

The Guardsmen (*approvingly*) Good! (*They take the sword and hand it round, examining it curiously*).

The Persian. And your men?

Bel Affris. Fled. Scattered like sheep.

Belzanor (*furiously*) The cowardly slaves! Leaving the descendants of the gods to be butchered!

Bel Affris (*with acid coolness*) The descendants of the gods did not stay to be butchered, cousin. The battle was not to the strong; but the race was to the swift. The Romans, who have no chariots, sent a cloud of horsemen in pursuit, and slew multitudes. Then our high priest's captain rallied a dozen descendants of the gods and exhorted us to die fighting. I said to myself: surely it is safer to stand than to lose my breath and be stabbed in the back; so I joined our captain and stood. Then the Romans treated us with respect; for no man attacks a lion when the field is full of sheep, except for the pride and honor of war, of which these Romans know nothing. So we escaped with our lives; and I am come to warn you that you must open your gates to Cæsar; for his advance guard is scarce an hour behind me; and not an Egyptian warrior is left standing between you and his legions.

The Sentinel. Woe, alas! (*He throws down his javelin and flies into the palace*).

Belzanor. Nail him to the door, quick! (*The guardsmen rush for him with their spears; but he is too quick for them*). Now this news will run through the palace like fire through stubble.

Bel Affris. What shall we do to save the women from the Romans?

Belzanor. Why not kill them?

Persian. Because we should have to pay blood money for some of them. Better let the Romans kill them: it is cheaper.

Belzanor (*awestruck at his brain power*) O subtle one! O serpent!

Bel Affris. But your Queen?

Belzanor. True: we must carry off Cleopatra.

Bel Affris. Will ye not await her command?

Belzanor. Command! a girl of sixteen! Not we. At Memphis ye deem her a Queen: here we know better. I will take her on the crupper of my horse. When we soldiers have carried her out of Cæsar's reach, then the priests and the nurses and the rest of them can pretend she is a queen again, and put their commands into her mouth.

Persian. Listen to me, Belzanor.

Belzanor. Speak, O subtle beyond thy years.

The Persian. Cleopatra's brother Ptolemy is at war with her. Let us sell her to him.

The Guardsmen. O subtle one! O serpent!

Belzanor. We dare not. We are descended from the gods; but Cleopatra is descended from the river Nile; and the lands of our fathers will grow no grain if the Nile rises not to water them. Without our father's gifts we should live the lives of dogs.

Persian. It is true: the Queen's guard cannot live on its pay. But hear me further, O ye kinsmen of Osiris.

The Guardsmen. Speak, O subtle one. Hear the serpent begotten!

Persian. Have I heretofore spoken truly to you of Cæsar, when you thought I mocked you?

Guardsmen. Truly, truly.

Belzanor (*reluctantly admitting it*) So Bel Affris says.

Persian. Hear more of him, then. This Cæsar is a great lover of women: he makes them his friends and counsellors.

Belzanor. Faugh! This rule of women will be the ruin of Egypt!

The Persian. Let it rather be the ruin of Rome! Cæsar grows old now: he is past fifty and full of labors and battles. He is too old for the young women; and the old women are too wise to worship him.

Bel Affris. Take heed, Persian. Cæsar is by this time almost within earshot.

Persian. Cleopatra is not yet a woman: neither is she wise. But she already troubles men's wisdom.

Belzanor. Ay: that is because she is descended from the river Nile and a black kitten of the sacred White Cat. What then?

Persian. Why, sell her secretly to Ptolemy, and then offer ourselves to Cæsar as volunteers to fight for the overthrow of her brother and the rescue of our Queen, the Great Grand-daughter of the Nile.

The Guardsmen. O serpent!

Persian. He will listen to us if we come with her picture in our mouths. He will conquer and kill her brother, and reign in Egypt with Cleopatra for his Queen. And we shall be her guard.

Guardsmen. O subtlest of all the serpents! O admiration! O wisdom!

Bel Affris. He will also have arrived before you have done talking, O word spinner.

Belzanor. That is true. (*An affrighted uproar in the palace interrupts him*). Quick: the flight has begun: guard the door. (*They rush to the door and form a cordon before it with their spears. A mob of women-servants and nurses surges out. Those in front recoil from the spears, screaming to those behind to keep back. Belzanor's voice dominates the disturbance as he shouts*) Back there. In again, unprofitable cattle.

The Guardsmen. Back, unprofitable cattle.

Belzanor. Send us out Ftatateeta, the Queen's chief nurse.

The Women (*calling into the palace*) Ftatateeta, Ftatateeta. Come, come. Speak to Belzanor.

A Woman. Oh, keep back. You are thrusting me on the spearheads.

A huge grim woman, her face covered with a network of tiny wrinkles, and her eyes old, large, and wise; sinewy handed, very tall, very strong; with the mouth of a bloodhound and the jaws of a bulldog, appears on the threshold. She is dressed like a person of consequence in the palace, and confronts the guardsmen insolently.

Ftatateeta. Make way for the Queen's chief nurse.

Belzanor (*with solemn arrogance*) Ftatateeta: I am Belzanor, the captain of the Queen's guard, descended from the gods.

Ftatateeta (*retorting his arrogance with interest*) Belzanor: I am Ftatateeta, the Queen's chief nurse; and your divine ancestors were proud to be painted on the wall in the pyramids of the kings whom my fathers served.

The women laugh triumphantly.

Belzanor (*with grim humor*) Ftatateeta: daughter of a long-tongued, swivel-eyed chameleon, the Romans are at hand. (*A cry of terror from the women: they would fly but for the spears*). Not even the descendants of the gods can resist them; for they have each man seven arms, each carrying seven spears. The blood in their veins is boiling quicksilver; and their wives become mothers in three hours, and are slain and eaten the next day.

A shudder of horror from the women. Ftatateeta, despising them and scorning the soldiers, pushes her way through the crowd and confronts the spear points undismayed.

Ftatateeta. Then fly and save yourselves, O cowardly sons of the cheap clay gods that are sold to fish porters; and leave us to shift for ourselves.

Belzanor. Not until you have first done our bidding, O terror of manhood. Bring out Cleopatra the Queen to us; and then go whither you will.

Ftatateeta (*with a derisive laugh*) Now I know why the gods have taken her out of our hands. (*The guardsmen start and look at one another*). Know, thou foolish soldier, that the Queen has been missing since an hour past sundown.

Belzanor (*furiously*) Hag: you have hidden her to sell to Cæsar or her brother. (*He grasps her by the left wrist, and drags her, helped by a few of the guard, to the middle of the courtyard, where, as they fling her on her knees, he draws a murderous looking knife*). Where is she? Where is she? or— (*he threatens to cut her throat*).

Ftatateeta (*savagely*) Touch me, dog; and the Nile will not rise on your fields for seven times seven years of famine.

Belzanor (*frightened, but desperate*) I will sacrifice: I will pay. Or stay. (*To the Persian*) You, O subtle one: your father's lands lie far from the Nile. Slay her.

Persian (*threatening her with his knife*) Persia has but one god; yet he loves the blood of old women. Where is Cleopatra?

Ftatateeta. Persian: as Osiris lives, I do not know. I chid her for bringing evil days upon us by talking to the sacred cats of the priests, and carrying them in her arms. I told her she would be left alone here when the Romans came as a punishment for her disobedience. And now she is gone—run away—hidden. I speak the truth. I call Osiris to witness—

The Women (*protesting officiously*) She speaks the truth, Belzanor.

Belzanor. You have frightened the child: she is hiding. Search—quick—into the palace—search every corner.

The guards, led by Belzanor, shoulder their way into the palace through the flying crowd of women, who escape through the courtyard gate.

Ftatateeta (screaming) Sacrilege! Men in the Queen's chambers! Sa—(*her voice dies away as the Persian puts his knife to her throat*).

Bel Affris (laying a hand on Ftatateeta's left shoulder) Forbear her yet a moment, Persian. (*To Ftatateeta, very significantly*) Mother: your gods are asleep or away hunting; and the sword is at your throat. Bring us to where the Queen is hid, and you shall live.

Ftatateeta (contemptuously) Who shall stay the sword in the hand of a fool, if the high gods put it there? Listen to me, ye young men without understanding. Cleopatra fears me; but she fears the Romans more. There is but one power greater in her eyes than the wrath of the Queen's nurse and the cruelty of Cæsar; and that is the power of the Sphinx that sits in the desert watching the way to the sea. What she would have it know, she tells into the ears of the sacred cats; and on her birthday she sacrifices to it and decks it with poppies. Go ye therefore into the desert and seek Cleopatra in the shadow of the Sphinx; and on your heads see to it that no harm comes to her.

Bel Affris (to the Persian) May we believe this, O subtle one?

Persian. Which way come the Romans?

Bel Affris. Over the desert, from the sea, by this very Sphinx.

Persian (to Ftatateeta) O mother of guile! O aspic's tongue! You have made up this tale so that we two may go into the desert and perish on the spears of the Romans. (*Lifting his knife*) Taste death.

Ftatateeta. Not from thee, baby. (*She snatches his ankle*

*from under him and flies stooping along the palace wall,
vanishing in the darkness within its precinct. Bel Affris roars
with laughter as the Persian tumbles. The guardsmen rush out
of the palace with Belzanor and a mob of fugitives, mostly
carrying bundles).*

Persian. Have you found Cleopatra?

Belzanor. She is gone. We have searched every corner.

The Nubian Sentinel *(appearing at the door of the palace)*
Woe! Alas! Fly, fly!

Belzanor. What is the matter now?

The Nubian Sentinel. The sacred white cat has been stolen.

All. Woe! woe! *(General panic. They all fly with cries of
consternation. The torch is thrown down and extinguished in
the rush. The noise of the fugitives dies away. Darkness and
dead silence).*

ACT I

THE SAME darkness into which the temple of Ra and the Syrian palace vanished. The same silence. Suspense. Then the blackness and stillness break softly into silver mist and strange airs as the windswept harp of Memnon plays at the dawning of the moon. It rises full over the desert; and a vast horizon comes into relief, broken by a huge shape which soon reveals itself in the spreading radiance as a Sphinx pedestalled on the sands. The light still clears, until the upraised eyes of the image are distinguished looking straight forward and upward in infinite fearless vigil, and a mass of color between its great paws defines itself as a heap of red poppies on which a girl lies motionless, her silken vest heaving gently and regularly with the breathing of a dreamless sleeper, and her braided hair glittering in a shaft of moonlight like a bird's wing.

Suddenly there comes from afar a vaguely fearful sound (it might be the bellow of a Minotaur softened by great distance) and Memnon's music stops. Silence: then a few faint high-ringing trumpet notes. Then silence again. Then a man comes from the south with stealing steps, ravished by the mystery of the night, all wonder, and halts, lost in contemplation, opposite the left flank of the Sphinx, whose bosom, with its burden, is hidden from him by its massive shoulder.

The Man. Hail, Sphinx: salutation from Julius Cæsar! I have wandered in many lands, seeking the lost regions from which my birth into this world exiled me, and the company of creatures such as I myself. I have found flocks and pastures, men and cities, but no other Cæsar, no air native to me, no man kindred to me, none who can do my day's deed, and think my night's thought. In the little world yonder, Sphinx, my place is as high as yours in this great desert; only I wander, and you sit still; I conquer, and you endure; I work and wonder, you watch and wait; I look up and am dazzled, look down and am darkened, look round and am puzzled, whilst your eyes never turn from looking out—out of the world—to the lost region—the home from which we have strayed. Sphinx, you and I, strangers to the race of men, are no strangers to one another: have I not been conscious of you and of this place since I was born? Rome is a madman's dream: this is my Reality. These starry lamps of yours I have seen from afar in Gaul, in Britain, in Spain, in Thessaly, signalling great secrets to some eternal sentinel below, whose post I never could find. And here at last is their sentinel—an image of the constant and immortal part of my life, silent, full of thoughts, alone in the silver desert. Sphinx, Sphinx: I have climbed mountains at night to hear in the distance the stealthy footfall of the winds that chase your sands in forbidden play—our invisible children, O Sphinx, laughing in whispers. My way hither was the way of destiny; for I am he of whose genius you are the symbol: part brute, part woman, and part god—nothing of man in me at all. Have I read your riddle, Sphinx?

The Girl (*who has wakened, and peeped cautiously from her nest to see who is speaking*) Old gentleman.

Cæsar (*starting violently, and clutching his sword*) Immortal gods!

The Girl. Old gentleman: dont run away.

Cæsar (*stupefied*) "Old gentleman: dont run away"!!! This to Julius Cæsar!

The Girl (*urgently*) Old gentleman.

Cæsar. Sphinx: you presume on your centuries. I am younger than you, though your voice is but a girl's voice as yet.

The Girl. Climb up here, quickly; or the Romans will come and eat you.

Cæsar (*running forward past the Sphinx's shoulder, and seeing her*) A child at its breast! a divine child!

The Girl. Come up quickly. You must get up at its side and creep round.

Cæsar (*amazed*) Who are you?

The Girl. Cleopatra, Queen of Egypt.

Cæsar. Queen of the Gypsies, you mean.

Cleopatra. You must not be disrespectful to me, or the Sphinx will let the Romans eat you. Come up. It is quite cosy here.

Cæsar (*to himself*) What a dream! What a magnificent dream! Only let me not wake, and I will conquer ten conti-nents to pay for dreaming it out to the end. (*He climbs to the Sphinx's flank, and presently reappears to her on the pedestal, stepping round its right shoulder*).

Cleopatra. Take care. Thats right. Now sit down: you may have its other paw. (*She seats herself comfortably on its left paw*). It is very powerful and will protect us; but (*shivering, and with plaintive loneliness*) it would not take any notice of me or keep me company. I am glad you have come: I was very lonely. Did you happen to see a white cat anywhere?

Cæsar (*sitting slowly down on the right paw in extreme wonderment*) Have you lost one?

Cleopatra. Yes: the sacred white cat: is it not dreadful? I brought him here to sacrifice him to the Sphinx; but when we got a little way from the city a black cat called him, and he jumped out of my arms and ran away to it. Do you think that the black cat can have been my great-great-great-grand-mother?

Cæsar (*staring at her*) Your great-great-great-grandmother! Well, why not? Nothing would surprise me on this night of nights.

Cleopatra. I think it must have been. My great-grand-mother's great-grandmother was a black kitten of the sacred white cat; and the river Nile made her his seventh wife. That is why my hair is so wavy. And I always want to be let do as I like, no matter whether it is the will of the gods or not: that is because my blood is made with Nile water.

Cæsar. What are you doing here at this time of night? Do you live here?

Cleopatra. Of course not: I am the Queen; and I shall live in the palace at Alexandria when I have killed my brother, who drove me out of it. When I am old enough I shall do just what I like. I shall be able to poison the slaves and see them wriggle, and pretend to Ftatateeta that she is going to be put into the fiery furnace.

Cæsar. Hm! Meanwhile why are you not at home and in bed?

Cleopatra. Because the Romans are coming to eat us all. You are not at home and in bed either.

Cæsar (with conviction) Yes I am. I live in a tent; and I am now in that tent, fast asleep and dreaming. Do you suppose that I believe you are real, you impossible little dream witch?

Cleopatra (giggling and leaning trustfully towards him) You are a funny old gentleman. I like you.

Cæsar. Ah, that spoils the dream. Why dont you dream that I am young?

Cleopatra. I wish you were; only I think I should be more afraid of you. I like men, especially young men with round strong arms; but I am afraid of them. You are old and rather thin and stringy; but you have a nice voice; and I like to have somebody to talk to, though I think you are a little mad. It is the moon that makes you talk to yourself in that silly way.

Cæsar. What! you heard that, did you? I was saying my prayers to the great Sphinx.

Cleopatra. But this isnt the great Sphinx.

Cæsar (much disappointed, looking up at the statue) What!

Cleopatra. This is only a dear little kitten of a Sphinx. Why, the great Sphinx is so big that it has a temple between its paws. This is my pet Sphinx. Tell me: do you think the Romans have any sorcerers who could take us away from the Sphinx by magic?

Cæsar. Why? Are you afraid of the Romans?

Cleopatra (very seriously) Oh, they would eat us if they caught us. They are barbarians. Their chief is called Julius Cæsar. His father was a tiger and his mother a burning mountain; and his nose is like an elephant's trunk. (*Cæsar involuntarily rubs his nose*). They all have long noses, and ivory tusks, and little tails, and seven arms with a hundred arrows in each; and they live on human flesh.

Cæsar. Would you like me to shew you a real Roman?

Cleopatra (terrified) No. You are frightening me.

Cæsar. No matter: this is only a dream—

Cleopatra (excitedly) It is not a dream: it is not a dream. See, see. (*She plucks a pin from her hair and jabs it repeatedly into his arm*).

Cæsar. Ffff—Stop. (*Wrathfully*) How dare you?

Cleopatra (abashed) You said you were dreaming. (*Whimpering*) I only wanted to shew you—

Cæsar (gently) Come, come: dont cry. A queen mustnt cry. (*He rubs his arm, wondering at the reality of the smart*). Am I awake? (*He strikes his hand against the Sphinx to test its solidity. It feels so real that he begins to be alarmed, and says perplexedly*) Yes, I— (*quite panicstricken*) no: impossible: madness, madness! (*Desperately*) Back to camp—to camp. (*He rises to spring down from the pedestal*).

Cleopatra (flinging her arms in terror round him) No: you shant leave me. No, no, no: dont go. I'm afraid—afraid of the Romans.

Cæsar (as the conviction that he is really awake forces itself on him) Cleopatra: can you see my face well?

Cleopatra. Yes. It is so white in the moonlight.

Cæsar. Are you sure it is the moonlight that makes me look whiter than an Egyptian? (*Grimly*) Do you notice that I have a rather long nose?

Cleopatra (*recoiling, paralysed by a terrible suspicion*) Oh!

Cæsar. It is a Roman nose, Cleopatra.

Cleopatra. Ah! (*With a piercing scream she springs up; darts round the left shoulder of the Sphinx; scrambles down to the sand; and falls on her knees in frantic supplication, shrieking*) Bite him in two, Sphinx: bite him in two. I meant to sacrifice the white cat—I did indeed—I (*Cæsar, who has slipped down from the pedestal, touches her on the shoulder*)—Ah! (*She buries her head in her arms*).

Cæsar. Cleopatra: shall I teach you a way to prevent Cæsar from eating you?

Cleopatra (*clinging to him piteously*) Oh do, do, do. I will steal Ftatateeta's jewels and give them to you. I will make the river Nile water your lands twice a year.

Cæsar. Peace, peace, my child. Your gods are afraid of the Romans: you see the Sphinx dare not bite me, nor prevent me carrying you off to Julius Cæsar.

Cleopatra (*in pleading murmurings*) You wont, you wont. You said you wouldnt.

Cæsar. Cæsar never eats women.

Cleopatra (*springing up full of hope*) What!

Cæsar (*impressively*) But he eats girls (*she relapses*) and cats. Now you are a silly little girl; and you are descended from the black kitten. You are both a girl and a cat.

Cleopatra (*trembling*) And will he eat me?

Cæsar. Yes; unless you make him believe that you are a woman.

Cleopatra. Oh, you must get a sorcerer to make a woman of me. Are you a sorcerer?

Cæsar. Perhaps. But it will take a long time; and this very night you must stand face to face with Cæsar in the palace of your fathers.

Cleopatra. No, no. I darent.

Cæsar. Whatever dread may be in your soul—however terrible Cæsar may be to you—you must confront him as a brave

woman and a great queen; and you must feel no fear. If
your hand shakes: if your voice quavers; then—night and
death! (*She moans*). But if he thinks you worthy to rule, he
will set you on the throne by his side and make you the
real ruler of Egypt.

Cleopatra (*despairingly*) No: he will find me out: he will
find me out.

Cæsar (*rather mournfully*) He is easily deceived by women.
Their eyes dazzle him; and he sees them not as they are, but
as he wishes them to appear to him.

Cleopatra (*hopefully*) Then we will cheat him. I will put
on Ftatateeta's head-dress; and he will think me quite an old
woman.

Cæsar. If you do that he will eat you at one mouthful.

Cleopatra. But I will give him a cake with my magic opal
and seven hairs of the white cat baked in it; and—

Cæsar (*abruptly*) Pah! you are a little fool. He will eat
your cake and you too. (*He turns contemptuously from her*).

Cleopatra (*running after him and clinging to him*) Oh
please, p l e a s e! I will do whatever you tell me. I will be good.
I will be your slave. (*Again the terrible bellowing note sounds
across the desert, now closer at hand. It is the bucina, the
Roman war trumpet*).

Cæsar. Hark!

Cleopatra (*trembling*) What was that?

Cæsar. Cæsar's voice.

Cleopatra (*pulling at his hand*) Let us run away. Come.
Oh, come.

Cæsar. You are safe with me until you stand on your throne
to receive Cæsar. Now lead me thither.

Cleopatra (*only too glad to get away*) I will, I will. (*Again
the buccina*). Oh come, come, come: the gods are angry. Do
you feel the earth shaking?

Cæsar. It is the tread of Cæsar's legions.

Cleopatra (*drawing him away*) This way, quickly. And let

us look for the white cat as we go. It is he that has turned
you into a Roman.

Cæsar. Incorrigible, oh, incorrigible! Away! (*He follows
her, the buccina sounding louder as they steal across the desert.
The moonlight wanes: the horizon again shows black against the
sky, broken only by the fantastic silhouette of the Sphinx. The
sky itself vanishes in darkness, from which there is no relief
until the gleam of a distant torch falls on great Egyptian pillars
supporting the roof of a majestic corridor. At the further end
of this corridor a Nubian slave appears carrying the torch.
Cæsar, still led by Cleopatra, follows him. They come down the
corridor, Cæsar peering keenly about at the strange architecture, and at the pillar shadows between which, as the passing
torch makes them hurry noiselessly backwards, figures of men
with wings and hawks' heads, and vast black marble cats, seem
to flit in and out of ambush. Further along, the wall turns a
corner and makes a spacious transept in which Cæsar sees, on
his right, a throne, and behind the throne a door. On each side
of the throne is a slender pillar with a lamp on it.*

Cæsar. What place is this?

Cleopatra. This is where I sit on the throne when I am
allowed to wear my crown and robes. (*The slave holds his
torch to shew the throne*).

Cæsar. Order the slave to light the lamps.

Cleopatra (*shyly*) Do you think I may?

Cæsar. Of course. You are the Queen. (*She hesitates*). Go
on.

Cleopatra (*timidly, to the slave*) Light all the lamps.

Ftatateeta (*suddenly coming from behind the throne*) Stop.
(*The slave stops. She turns sternly to Cleopatra, who quails
like a naughty child*). Who is this you have with you; and
how dare you order the lamps to be lighted without my per-
mission? (*Cleopatra is dumb with apprehension*).

Cæsar. Who is she?

Cleopatra. Ftatateeta.

Ftatateeta (*arrogantly*) Chief nurse to—

Cæsar (*cutting her short*) I speak to the Queen. Be silent. (*To Cleopatra*) Is this how your servants know their places? Send her away; and do you (*to the slave*) do as the Queen has bidden. (*The slave lights the lamps. Meanwhile Cleopatra stands hesitating, afraid of Ftatateeta*). You are the Queen: send her away.

Cleopatra (*cajoling*) Ftatateeta, dear: you must go away— just for a little.

Cæsar. You are not commanding her to go away: you are begging her. You are no Queen. You will be eaten. Farewell. (*He turns to go*).

Cleopatra (*clutching him*) No, no, no. Dont leave me.

Cæsar. A Roman does not stay with queens who are afraid of their slaves.

Cleopatra. I am not afraid. Indeed I am not afraid.

Ftatateeta. We shall see who is afraid here. (*Menacingly*) Cleopatra—

Cæsar. On your knees, woman: am I also a child that you dare trifle with me? (*He points to the floor at Cleopatra's feet. Ftatateeta, half cowed, half savage, hesitates. Cæsar calls to the Nubian*) Slave. (*The Nubian comes to him*) Can you cut off a head? (*The Nubian nods and grins ecstatically, showing all his teeth. Cæsar takes his sword by the scabbard, ready to offer the hilt to the Nubian, and turns again to Ftatateeta, repeating his gesture*). Have you remembered yourself, mistress?

Ftatateeta, crushed, kneels before Cleopatra, who can hardly believe her eyes.

Ftatateeta (*hoarsely*) O Queen, forget not thy servant in the days of thy greatness.

Cleopatra (*blazing with excitement*) Go. Begone. Go away. (*Ftatateeta rises with stooped head, and moves backwards towards the door. Cleopatra watches her submission eagerly, almost clapping her hands, which are trembling. Suddenly she cries*) Give me something to beat her with. (*She snatches a*

snake-skin from the throne and dashes after Ftatateeta, whirl-
ing it like a scourge in the air. Cæsar makes a bound and
manages to catch her and hold her while Ftatateeta escapes).

Cæsar. You scratch, kitten, do you?

Cleopatra (*breaking from him*) I will beat somebody. I
will beat him. (*She attacks the slave*). There, there, there!
(*The slave flies for his life up the corridor and vanishes. She
throws the snake-skin away and jumps on the step of the throne
with her arms waving, crying*) I am a real Queen at last—a
real, real Queen! Cleopatra the Queen! (*Cæsar shakes his head
dubiously, the advantage of the change seeming open to question from the point of view of the general welfare of Egypt. She
turns and looks at him exultantly. Then she jumps down from
the steps, runs to him, and flings her arms round him rapturously, crying*) Oh, I love you for making me a Queen.

Cæsar. But queens love only kings.

Cleopatra. I will make all the men I love kings. I will make
you a king. I will have many young kings, with round, strong
arms; and when I am tired of them I will whip them to death;
but you shall always be my king: my nice, kind, wise, good
old king.

Cæsar. Oh, my wrinkles, my wrinkles! And my child's heart!
You will be the most dangerous of all Cæsar's conquests.

Cleopatra (*appalled*) Cæsar! I forgot Cæsar. (*Anxiously*)
You will tell him that I am a Queen, will you not?—a real
Queen. Listen! (*stealthily coaxing him*): let us run away and
hide until Cæsar is gone.

Cæsar. If you fear Cæsar, you are no true queen; and though
you were to hide beneath a pyramid, he would go straight to
it and lift it with one hand. And then—! (*he chops his teeth
together*).

Cleopatra (*trembling*) Oh!

Cæsar. Be afraid if you dare. (*The note of the buccina re-
sounds again in the distance. She moans with fear. Cæsar
exults in it, exclaiming*) Aha! Cæsar approaches the throne of

Cleopatra. Come: take your place. (*He takes her hand and leads her to the throne. She is too downcast to speak*). Ho, there. Teetatota. How do you call your slaves?

Cleopatra (*spiritlessly, as she sinks on the throne and cowers there, shaking*). Clap your hands.

He claps his hands. Ftatateeta returns.

Cæsar. Bring the Queen's robes, and her crown, and her women; and prepare her.

Cleopatra (*eagerly—recovering herself a little*) Yes, the crown, Ftatateeta: I shall wear the crown.

Ftatateeta. For whom must the Queen put on her state?

Cæsar. For a citizen of Rome. A king of kings, Totateeta.

Cleopatra (*stamping at her*) How dare you ask questions? Go and do as you are told. (*Ftatateeta goes out with a grim smile. Cleopatra goes on eagerly, to Cæsar*) Cæsar will know that I am a Queen when he sees my crown and robes, will he not?

Cæsar. No. How shall he know that you are not a slave dressed up in the Queen's ornaments?

Cleopatra. You must tell him.

Cæsar. He will not ask me. He will know Cleopatra by her pride, her courage, her majesty, and her beauty. (*She looks very doubtful*). Are you trembling?

Cleopatra (*shivering with dread*) No, I—I—(*in a very sickly voice*) No.

Ftatateeta and three women come in with the regalia.

Ftatateeta. Of all the Queen's women, these three alone are left. The rest are fled. (*They begin to deck Cleopatra, who submits, pale and motionless*).

Cæsar. Good, good. Three are enough. Poor Cæsar generally has to dress himself.

Ftatateeta (*contemptuously*) The queen of Egypt is not a Roman barbarian. (*To Cleopatra*) Be brave, my nursling. Hold up your head before this stranger.

Cæsar (*admiring Cleopatra, and placing the crown on her head*) Is it sweet or bitter to be a Queen, Cleopatra?

Cleopatra. Bitter.

Cæsar. Cast out fear; and you will conquer Cæsar. Tota: are the Romans at hand?

Ftatateeta. They are at hand; and the guard has fled.

The Women (*wailing subduedly*) Woe to us!

The Nubian comes running down the hall.

Nubian. The Romans are in the courtyard. (*He bolts through the door. With a shriek, the women fly after him. Ftatateeta's jaw expresses savage resolution: she does not budge. Cleopatra can hardly restrain herself from following them. Cæsar grips her wrist, and looks steadfastly at her. She stands like a martyr*).

Cæsar. The Queen must face Cæsar alone. Answer "So be it."

Cleopatra (*white*) So be it.

Cæsar (*releasing her*) Good.

A tramp and tumult of armed men is heard. Cleopatra's terror increases. The buccina sounds close at hand, followed by a formidable clangor of trumpets. This is too much for Cleopatra: she utters a cry and darts towards the door. Ftatateeta stops her ruthlessly.

Ftatateeta. You are my nursling. You have said "So be it"; and if you die for it, you must make the Queen's word good. (*She hands Cleopatra to Cæsar, who takes her back, almost beside herself with apprehension, to the throne*).

Cæsar. Now, if you quail—! (*He seats himself on the throne*).

She stands on the step, all but unconscious, waiting for death. The Roman soldiers troop in tumultuously through the corridor, headed by their ensign with his eagle, and their buccinator, a burly fellow with his instrument coiled round his body, its brazen bell shaped like the head of a howling wolf. When they reach the transept, they stare in amazement at the throne; dress into ordered rank opposite it; draw their swords and lift them in the air with a shout of Hail, Cæsar. Cleopatra turns and stares wildly at Cæsar; grasps the situation; and, with a great sob of relief, falls into his arms.

ACT II

ALEXANDRIA. A hall on the first floor of the Palace, ending in a loggia approached by two steps. Through the arches of the loggia the Mediterranean can be seen, bright in the morning sun. The clean lofty walls, painted with a procession of the Egyptian theocracy, presented in profile as flat ornament, and the absence of mirrors, sham perspectives, stuffy upholstery and textiles, make the place handsome, wholesome, simple and cool, or, as a rich English manufacturer would express it, poor, bare, ridiculous and unhomely. For Tottenham Court Road civilization is to this Egyptian civilization as glass bead and tattoo civilization is to Tottenham Court Road.

The young king Ptolemy Dionysus (aged ten) is at the top of the steps, on his way in through the loggia, led by his guardian Pothinus, who has him by the hand. The court is assembled to receive him. It is made up of men and women (some of the women being officials) of various complexions and races, mostly Egyptian; some of them, comparatively fair, from lower Egypt, some, much darker, from upper Egypt; with a few Greeks and Jews. Prominent in a group on Ptolemy's right hand is Theodotus, Ptolemy's tutor. Another group, on Ptolemy's left, is headed by Achillas, the general of Ptolemy's troops. Theodotus is a little old man, whose features are as cramped and wizened as his limbs, except his tall straight forehead, which occupies more space than all the rest of his face. He maintains an air of magpie keenness and profundity, listening to what the others say with the sarcastic vigilance of a philosopher listening to the exercises of his disciples. Achillas is a tall handsome man of thirty-five, with a fine black beard curled like the coat of a poodle. Apparently not a clever man, but distinguished and dignified. Pothinus is a vigorous man of fifty, a eunuch, passionate, energetic and quick witted, but of common mind and

*character; impatient and unable to control his temper. He has
fine tawny hair, like fur. Ptolemy, the King, looks much older
than an English boy of ten; but he has the childish air, the
habit of being in leading strings, the mixture of impotence and
petulance, the appearance of being excessively washed, combed
and dressed by other hands, which is exhibited by court-bred
princes of all ages.*

*All receive the King with reverences. He comes down the
steps to a chair of state which stands a little to his right, the
only seat in the hall. Taking his place before it, he looks
nervously for instructions to Pothinus, who places himself at
his left hand.*

Pothinus. The King of Egypt has a word to speak.

Theodotus (*in a squeak which he makes impressive by
sheer self-opinionativeness*) Peace for the King's word!

Ptolemy (*without any vocal inflexions: he is evidently repeating a lesson*) Take notice of this all of you. I am the firstborn son of Auletes the Flute Blower who was your King.
My sister Berenice drove him from his throne and reigned
in his stead but—but—(*he hesitates*)—

Pothinus (*stealthily prompting*)—but the gods would not
suffer—

Ptolemy. Yes—the gods would not suffer—not suffer— (*He
stops; then, crestfallen*) I forget what the gods would not
suffer.

Theodotus. Let Pothinus, the King's guardian, speak for the
King.

Pothinus (*suppressing his impatience with difficulty*) The
King wished to say that the gods would not suffer the im-
piety of his sister to go unpunished.

Ptolemy (*hastily*) Yes: I remember the rest of it. (*He resumes his monotone*). Therefore the gods sent a stranger one
Mark Antony a Roman captain of horsemen across the sands
of the desert and he set my father again upon the throne

And my father took Berenice my sister and struck her head off. And now that my father is dead yet another of his daughters my sister Cleopatra would snatch the kingdom from me and reign in my place. But the gods would not suffer— (*Pothinus coughs admonitorily*)—the gods—the gods would not suffer—

Pothinus (*prompting*)—will not maintain—

Ptolemy. Oh yes—will not maintain such iniquity they will give her head to the axe even as her sister's. But with the help of the witch Ftatateeta she hath cast a spell on the Roman Julius Cæsar to make him uphold her false pretence to rule in Egypt. Take notice then that I will not suffer—that I will not suffer—(*pettishly, to Pothinus*) What is that I will not suffer?

Pothinus (*suddenly exploding with all the force and emphasis of political passion*) The King will not suffer a foreigner to take from him the throne of our Egypt. (*A shout of applause*). Tell the King, Achillas, how many soldiers and horsemen follow the Roman?

Theodotus. Let the King's general speak!

Achillas. But two Roman legions, O King. Three thousand soldiers and scarce a thousand horsemen.

The court breaks into derisive laughter; and a great chattering begins, amid which Rufio, a Roman officer, appears in the loggia. He is a burly, black-bearded man of middle age, very blunt, prompt and rough, with small clear eyes, and plump nose and cheeks, which, however, like the rest of his flesh, are in iron-hard condition.

Rufio (*from the steps*) Peace, ho! (*The laughter and chatter cease abruptly*). Cæsar approaches.

Theodotus (*with much presence of mind*) The King permits the Roman commander to enter!

Cæsar, plainly dressed, but wearing an oak wreath to conceal his baldness, enters from the loggia, attended by Britannus, his secretary, a Briton, about forty, tall, solemn, and already slightly bald, with a heavy, drooping, hazel-colored moustache trained so as to lose its ends in a pair of trim whiskers. He is carefully dressed in blue, with portfolio, inkhorn, and reed pen at his girdle. His serious air and sense of the importance of the business in hand is in marked contrast to the kindly interest of Cæsar, who looks at the scene, which is new to him, with the frank curiosity of a child, and then turns to the king's chair: Britannus and Rufio posting themselves near the steps at the other side.

Cæsar (*looking at Pothinus and Ptolemy*) Which is the King? the man or the boy?

Pothinus. I am Pothinus, the guardian of my lord the King

Cæsar (*patting Ptolemy kindly on the shoulder*) So you are the King. Dull work at your age, eh? (*To Pothinus*) Your servant, Pothinus. (*He turns away unconcernedly and comes slowly along the middle of the hall, looking from side to side at the courtiers until he reaches Achillas*). And this gentleman?

Theodotus. Achillas, the King's general.

Cæsar (*to Achillas, very friendly*) A general, eh? I am a general myself. But I began too old, too old. Health and many victories, Achillas!

Achillas. As the gods will, Cæsar.

Cæsar (*turning to Theodotus*) And you, sir, are—?

Theodotus. Theodotus, the King's tutor.

Cæsar. You teach men how to be kings, Theodotus. That is very clever of you. (*Looking at the gods on the walls as he turns away from Theodotus and goes up again to Pothinus*) And this place?

Pothinus. The council chamber of the chancellors of the King's treasury, Cæsar.

Cæsar. Ah! that reminds me. I want some money.

Pothinus. The King's treasury is poor, Cæsar.

Cæsar. Yes: I notice that there is but one chair in it.

Rufio (shouting gruffly) Bring a chair there, some of you, for Cæsar.

Ptolemy (rising shyly to offer his chair) Cæsar—

Cæsar (kindly) No, no, my boy: that is your chair of state. Sit down.

He makes Ptolemy sit down again. Meanwhile Rufio, looking about him, sees in the nearest corner an image of the god Ra, represented as a seated man with the head of a hawk. Before the image is a bronze tripod, about as large as a three-legged stool, with a stick of incense burning on it. Rufio, with Roman resourcefulness and indifference to foreign superstitions, promptly seizes the tripod; shakes off the incense; blows away the ash; and dumps it down behind Cæsar, nearly in the middle of the hall.

Rufio. Sit on that, Cæsar.

A shiver runs through the court, followed by a hissing whisper of Sacrilege!

Cæsar (seating himself) Now, Pothinus, to business. I am badly in want of money.

Britannus (disapproving of these informal expressions) My master would say that there is a lawful debt due to Rome by Egypt, contracted by the King's deceased father to the Triumvirate; and that it is Cæsar's duty to his country to require immediate payment.

Cæsar (blandly) Ah, I forgot. I have not made my companions known here. Pothinus: this is Britannus, my secretary. He is an islander from the western end of the world, a day's voyage from Gaul. (*Britannus bows stiffly*). This gentleman is Rufio, my comrade in arms. (*Rufio nods*). Pothinus: I want 1,600 talents.

The courtiers, appalled, murmur loudly, and Theodotus and Achillas appeal mutely to one another against so monstrous a demand.

Pothinus (*aghast*) Forty million sesterces! Impossible. There is not so much money in the King's treasury.

Cæsar (*encouragingly*) O n l y sixteen hundred talents, Pothinus. Why count it in sesterces? A sestertius is only worth a loaf of bread.

Pothinus. And a talent is worth a racehorse. I say it is impossible. We have been at strife here, because the King's sister Cleopatra falsely claims his throne. The King's taxes have not been collected for a whole year.

Cæsar. Yes they have, Pothinus. My officers have been collecting them all morning. (*Renewed whisper and sensation, not without some stifled laughter, among the courtiers*).

Rufio (*bluntly*) You must pay, Pothinus. Why waste words? You are getting off cheaply enough.

Pothinus (*bitterly*) Is it possible that Cæsar, the conqueror of the world, has time to occupy himself with such a trifle as our taxes?

Cæsar. My friend: taxes are the chief business of a conqueror of the world.

Pothinus. Then take warning, Cæsar. This day, the treasures of the temple and the gold of the King's treasury shall be sent to the mint to be melted down for our ransom in the sight of the people. They shall see us sitting under bare walls and drinking from wooden cups. And their wrath be on your head, Cæsar, if you force us to this sacrilege!

Cæsar. Do not fear, Pothinus: the people know how well wine tastes in wooden cups. In return for your bounty, I will settle this dispute about the throne for you, if you will. What say you?

Pothinus. If I say no, will that hinder you?

Rufio (*defiantly*) No.

Cæsar. You say the matter has been at issue for a year, Pothinus. May I have ten minutes at it?

Pothinus. You will do your pleasure, doubtless.

Cæsar. Good! But first, let us have Cleopatra here.

Theodotus. She is not in Alexandria: she is fled into Syria.

Cæsar. I think not. (*To Rufio*) Call Totateeta.

Rufio (*calling*) Ho there, Teetatota.

*Ftatateeta enters the loggia, and stands arrogantly at the top
of the steps.*

Ftatateeta. Who pronounces the name of Ftatateeta, the
Queen's chief nurse?

Cæsar. Nobody can pronounce it, Tota, except yourself.
Where is your mistress?

*Cleopatra, who is hiding behind Ftatateeta, peeps out at
them laughing. Cæsar rises.*

Cæsar. Will the Queen favor us with her presence for a
moment?

Cleopatra (*pushing Ftatateeta aside and standing haughtily
on the brink of the steps*) Am I to behave like a Queen?

Cæsar. Yes.

*Cleopatra immediately comes down to the chair of state;
seizes Ptolemy; drags him out of his seat; then takes his place
in the chair. Ftatateeta seats herself on the step of the loggia,
and sits there, watching the scene with sibylline intensity.*

Ptolemy (*mortified, and struggling with his tears*) Cæsar:
this is how she treats me always. If I am a king why is she
allowed to take everything from me?

Cleopatra. You are not to be King, you little cry-baby. You
are to be eaten by the Romans.

Cæsar (*touched by Ptolemy's distress*) Come here, my boy,
and stand by me.

*Ptolemy goes over to Cæsar, who, resuming his seat on the
tripod, takes the boy's hand to encourage him. Cleopatra, furiously jealous, rises and glares at them.*

Cleopatra (*with flaming cheeks*) Take your throne: I dont
want it. (*She flings away from the chair, and approaches
Ptolemy, who shrinks from her*). Go this instant and sit down
in your place.

Cæsar. Go, Ptolemy. Always take a throne when it is offered to you.

Rufio. I hope you will have the good sense to follow your own advice when we return to Rome, Cæsar.

Ptolemy slowly goes back to the throne, giving Cleopatra a wide berth, in evident fear of her hands. She takes his place beside Cæsar.

Cæsar. Pothinus—

Cleopatra (interrupting him) Are you not going to speak to me?

Cæsar. Be quiet. Open your mouth again before I give you leave, and you shall be eaten.

Cleopatra. I am not afraid. A queen must not be afraid. Eat my husband there, if you like: he is afraid.

Cæsar (starting) Your husband! What do you mean?

Cleopatra (pointing to Ptolemy) That little thing.

The two Romans and the Briton stare at one another in amazement.

Theodotus. Cæsar: you are a stranger here, and not conversant with our laws. The kings and queens of Egypt may not marry except with their own royal blood. Ptolemy and Cleopatra are born king and consort just as they are born brother and sister.

Britannus (shocked) Cæsar: this is not proper.

Theodotus (outraged) How!

Cæsar (recovering his self-possession) Pardon him, Theodotus: he is a barbarian, and thinks that the customs of his tribe and island are the laws of nature.

Britannus. On the contrary, Cæsar, it is these Egyptians who are barbarians; and you do wrong to encourage them. I say it is a scandal.

Cæsar. Scandal or not, my friend, it opens the gate of peace. *(He addresses Pothinus seriously).* Pothinus: hear what I propose.

Rufio. Hear Cæsar there.

Cæsar. Ptolemy and Cleopatra shall reign jointly in Egypt.

Achillas. What of the King's younger brother and Cleopatra's younger sister?

Rufio (explaining) There is another little Ptolemy, Cæsar: so they tell me.

Cæsar. Well, the little Ptolemy can marry the other sister; and we will make them both a present of Cyprus.

Pothinus (impatiently) Cyprus is of no use to anybody.

Cæsar. No matter: you shall have it for the sake of peace.

Britannus (unconsciously anticipating a later statesman) Peace with honor, Pothinus.

Pothinus (mutinously) Cæsar: be honest. The money you demand is the price of our freedom. Take it; and leave us to settle our own affairs.

The Bolder Courtiers (encouraged by Pothinus's tone and Cæsar's quietness) Yes, yes. Egypt for the Egyptians!

The conference now becomes an altercation, the Egyptians becoming more and more heated. Cæsar remains unruffled; but Rufio grows fiercer and doggeder, and Britannus haughtily indignant.

Rufio (contemptuously) Egypt for the Egyptians! Do you forget that there is a Roman army of occupation here, left by Aulus Gabinius when he set up your toy king for you?

Achillas (suddenly asserting himself) And now under my command. I am the Roman general here, Cæsar.

Cæsar (tickled by the humor of the situation) And also the Egyptian general, eh?

Pothinus (triumphantly) That is so, Cæsar.

Cæsar (to Achillas) So you can make war on the Egyptians in the name of Rome, and on the Romans—on me, if necessary—in the name of Egypt?

Achillas. That is so, Cæsar.

Cæsar. And which side are you on at present, if I may presume to ask, general?

Achillas. On the side of the right and of the gods.

Cæsar. Hm! How many men have you?

Achillas. That will appear when I take the field.

Rufio (*truculently*) Are your men Romans? If not, it matters not how many there are, provided you are no stronger than 500 to ten.

Pothinus. It is useless to try to bluff us, Rufio. Cæsar has been defeated before and may be defeated again. A few weeks ago Cæsar was flying for his life before Pompey: a few months hence he may be flying for his life before Cato and Juba of Numidia, the African King.

Achillas (*following up Pothinus's speech menacingly*) What can you do with 4,000 men?

Theodotus (*following up Achillas's speech with a raucous squeak*) And without money? Away with you.

All the Courtiers (*shouting fiercely and crowding towards Cæsar*) Away with you. Egypt for the Egyptians! Begone.

Rufio bites his beard, too angry to speak. Cæsar sits as comfortably as if he were at breakfast, and the cat were clamoring for a piece of Finnan-haddie.

Cleopatra. Why do you let them talk to you like that, Cæsar? Are you afraid?

Cæsar. Why, my dear, what they say is quite true.

Cleopatra. But if you go away, I shall not be Queen.

Cæsar. I shall not go away until you are Queen.

Pothinus. Achillas: if you are not a fool, you will take that girl whilst she is under your hand.

Rufio (*daring them*) Why not take Cæsar as well, Achillas?

Pothinus (*retorting the defiance with interest*) Well said, Rufio. Why not?

Rufio. Try, Achillas. (*Calling*) Guard there.

The loggia immediately fills with Cæsar's soldiers, who stand, sword in hand, at the top of the steps, waiting the word to charge from their centurion, who carries a cudgel. For a moment the Egyptians face them proudly: then they retire sullenly to their former places.

Britannus. You are Cæsar's prisoners, all of you.

Cæsar (*benevolently*) Oh no, no, no. By no means. Cæsar's guests, gentlemen.

Cleopatra. Wont you cut their heads off?

Cæsar. What! Cut off your brother's head?

Cleopatra. Why not? He would cut off mine, if he got the chance. Wouldnt you, Ptolemy?

Ptolemy (*pale and obstinate*) I would. I will, too, when I grow up.

Cleopatra is rent by a struggle between her newly-acquired dignity as a queen, and a strong impulse to put out her tongue at him. She takes no part in the scene which follows, but watches it with curiosity and wonder, fidgeting with the restlessness of a child, and sitting down on Cæsar's tripod when he rises.

Pothinus. Cæsar: if you attempt to detain us—

Rufio. He will succeed, Egyptian: make up your mind to that. We hold the palace, the beach, and the eastern harbor. The road to Rome is open; and you shall travel it if Cæsar chooses.

Cæsar (*courteously*) I could do no less, Pothinus, to secure the retreat of my own soldiers. I am accountable for every life among them. But you are free to go. So are all here, and in the palace.

Rufio (*aghast at this clemency*) What! Renegades and all?

Cæsar (*softening the expression*) Roman army of occupation and all, Rufio.

Pothinus (*bewildered*) But—but—but—

Cæsar. Well, my friend?

Pothinus. You are turning us out of our own palace into the streets; and you tell us with a grand air that we are free to go! It is for you to go.

Cæsar. Your friends are in the street, Pothinus. You will be safer there.

Pothinus. This is a trick. I am the King's guardian: I refuse to stir. I stand on my right here. Where is your right?

Cæsar. It is in Rufio's scabbard, Pothinus. I may not be able to keep it there if you wait too long.

Sensation.

Pothinus (*bitterly*) And this is Roman justice!

Theodotus. But not Roman gratitude, I hope.

Cæsar. Gratitude! Am I in your debt for any service, gentlemen?

Theodotus. Is Cæsar's life of so little account to him that he forgets that we have saved it?

Cæsar. My life! Is that all?

Theodotus. Your life. Your laurels. Your future.

Pothinus. It is true. I can call a witness to prove that but for us, the Roman army of occupation, led by the greatest soldier in the world, would now have Cæsar at its mercy. (*Calling through the loggia*) Ho, there, Lucius Septimius (*Cæsar starts, deeply moved*): if my voice can reach you, come forth and testify before Cæsar.

Cæsar (*shrinking*) No, no.

Theodotus. Yes, I say. Let the military tribune bear witness.

Lucius Septimius, a clean shaven, trim athlete of about 40, with symmetrical features, resolute mouth, and handsome, thin Roman nose, in the dress of a Roman officer, comes in through the loggia and confronts Cæsar, who hides his face with his robe for a moment; then, mastering himself, drops it, and confronts the tribune with dignity.

Pothinus. Bear witness, Lucius Septimius. Cæsar came hither in pursuit of his foe. Did we shelter his foe?

Lucius. As Pompey's foot touched the Egyptian shore, his head fell by the stroke of my sword.

Theodotus (*with viperish relish*) Under the eyes of his wife and child! Remember that, Cæsar! They saw it from the ship he had just left. We have given you a full and sweet measure of vengeance.

Cæsar (*with horror*) Vengeance!

Pothinus. Our first gift to you, as your galley came into the roadstead, was the head of your rival for the empire of the world. Bear witness, Lucius Septimius: is it not so?

Lucius. It is so. With this hand, that slew Pompey, I placed his head at the feet of Cæsar.

Cæsar. Murderer! So would you have slain Cæsar, had Pompey been victorious at Pharsalia.

Lucius. Woe to the vanquished, Cæsar! When I served Pompey, I slew as good men as he, only because he conquered them. His turn came at last.

Theodotus (*flatteringly*) The deed was not yours, Cæsar, but ours—nay, mine; for it was done by my counsel. Thanks to us, you keep your reputation for clemency, and have your vengeance too.

Cæsar. Vengeance! Vengeance!! Oh, if I could stoop to vengeance, what would I not exact from you as the price of this murdered man's blood? (*They shrink back, appalled and disconcerted*). Was he not my son-in-law, my ancient friend, for 20 years the master of great Rome, for 30 years the compeller of victory? Did not I, as a Roman, share his glory? Was the Fate that forced us to fight for the mastery of the world, of our making? Am I Julius Cæsar, or am I a wolf, that you fling to me the grey head of the old soldier, the laurelled conqueror, the mighty Roman, treacherously struck down by this callous ruffian, and then claim my gratitude for it! (*To Lucius Septimius*) Begone: you fill me with horror.

Lucius (*cold and undaunted*) Pshaw! You have seen severed heads before, Cæsar, and severed right hands too, I think; some thousands of them, in Gaul, after you vanquished Vercingetorix. Did you spare him, with all your clemency? Was that vengeance?

Cæsar. No, by the gods! would that it had been! Vengeance at least is human. No, I say: those severed right hands, and the brave Vercingetorix basely strangled in a vault beneath the

Capitol, were (*with shuddering satire*) a wise severity, a necessary protection to the commonwealth, a duty of statesmanship
—follies and fictions ten times bloodier than honest vengeance!
What a fool was I then! To think that men's lives should be
at the mercy of such fools! (*Humbly*) Lucius Septimius, pardon me: why should the slayer of Vercingetorix rebuke the
slayer of Pompey? You are free to go with the rest. Or stay if
you will: I will find a place for you in my service.

Lucius. The odds are against you, Cæsar. I go. (*He turns to
go out through the loggia*).

Rufio (*full of wrath at seeing his prey escaping*) That means
that he is a Republican.

Lucius (*turning defiantly on the loggia steps*) And what are
you?

Rufio. A Cæsarian, like all Cæsar's soldiers.

Cæsar (*courteously*) Lucius: believe me, Cæsar is no Cæsarian. Were Rome a true republic, then were Cæsar the first of
Republicans. But you have made your choice. Farewell.

Lucius. Farewell. Come. Achillas, whilst there is yet time.

*Cæsar, seeing that Rufio's temper threatens to get the worse
of him, puts his hand on his shoulder and brings him down the
hall out of harm's way, Britannus accompanying them and
posting himself on Cæsar's right hand. This movement brings
the three in a little group to the place occupied by Achillas,
who moves haughtily away and joins Theodotus on the other
side. Lucius Septimius goes out through the soldiers in the
loggia. Pothinus, Theodotus and Achillas follow him with the
courtiers, very mistrustful of the soldiers, who close up in their
rear and go out after them, keeping them moving without
much ceremony. The King is left in his chair, piteous, obstinate, with twitching face and fingers. During these movements
Rufio maintains an energetic grumbling, as follows:*—

Rufio (*as Lucius departs*) Do you suppose he would let us
go if he had our heads in his hands?

Cæsar. I have no right to suppose that his ways are any baser than mine.

Rufio. Psha!

Cæsar. Rufio: if I take Lucius Septimius for my model, and become exactly like him, ceasing to be Cæsar, will you serve me still?

Britannus. Cæsar: this is not good sense. Your duty to Rome demands that her enemies should be prevented from doing further mischief (*Cæsar, whose delight in the moral eye-to-business of his British secretary is inexhaustible, smiles indulgently*).

Rufio. It is no use talking to him, Britannus: you may save your breath to cool your porridge. But mark this, Cæsar. Clemency is very well for you; but what is it for your soldiers, who have to fight to-morrow the men you spared yesterday? You may give what orders you please; but I tell you that your next victory will be a massacre, thanks to your clemency. I, for one, will take no prisoners. I will kill my enemies in the field; and then you can preach as much clemency as you please: I shall never have to fight them again. And now, with your leave, I will see these gentry off the premises. (*He turns to go*).

Cæsar (*turning also and seeing Ptolemy*) What! have they left the boy alone! Oh shame, shame!

Rufio (*taking Ptolemy's hand and making him rise*) Come, your majesty!

Ptolemy (*to Cæsar, drawing away his hand from Rufio*) Is he turning me out of my palace?

Rufio (*grimly*) You are welcome to stay if you wish.

Cæsar (*kindly*) Go, my boy. I will not harm you but you will be safer away, among your friends. Here you are in the lion's mouth.

Ptolemy (*turning to go*) It is not the lion I fear, but (*looking at Rufio*) the jackal. (*He goes out through the loggia*).

Cæsar (*laughing approvingly*) Brave boy!

Cleopatra (jealous of Cæsar's approbation, calling after Ptolemy) Little silly. You think that very clever.

Cæsar. Britannus: attend the King. Give him in charge to that Pothinus fellow. *(Britannus goes out after Ptolemy).*

Rufio (pointing to Cleopatra) And this piece of goods? What is to be done with h e r ? However, I suppose I may leave that to you. *(He goes out through the loggia).*

Cleopatra (flushing suddenly and turning on Cæsar) Did you mean me to go with the rest?

Cæsar (a little preoccupied, goes with a sigh to Ptolemy's chair, whilst she waits for his answer with red cheeks and clenched fist) You are free to do just as you please, Cleopatra.

Cleopatra. Then you do not care whether I stay or not?

Cæsar (smiling) Of course I had rather you stayed.

Cleopatra. Much, m u c h rather?

Cæsar (nodding) Much, much rather.

Cleopatra. Then I consent to stay, because I am asked. But I do not want to, mind.

Cæsar. That is quite understood. *(Calling)* Totateeta.

Ftatateeta, still seated, turns her eyes on him with a sinister expression, but does not move.

Cleopatra (with a splutter of laughter) Her name is not Totateeta: it is Ftatateeta. *(Calling)* Ftatateeta. *(Ftatateeta instantly rises and comes to Cleopatra).*

Cæsar (stumbling over the name) Tfatafeeta will forgive the erring tongue of a Roman. Tota: the Queen will hold her state here in Alexandria. Engage women to attend upon her; and do all that is needful.

Ftatateeta. Am I then the mistress of the Queen's household?

Cleopatra (sharply) No: I am the mistress of the Queen's household. Go and do as you are told, or I will have you thrown into the Nile this very afternoon, to poison the poor crocodiles.

Cæsar (shocked) Oh no, no.

Cleopatra. Oh yes, yes. You are very sentimental, Cæsar; but you are clever; and if you do as I tell you, you will soon learn to govern.

Cæsar, quite dumbfounded by this impertinence, turns in his chair and stares at her.

Ftatateeta, smiling grimly, and showing a splendid set of teeth, goes, leaving them alone together.

Cæsar. Cleopatra: I really think I must eat you, after all.

Cleopatra (kneeling beside him and looking at him with eager interest, half real, half affected to shew how intelligent she is) You must not talk to me now as if I were a child.

Cæsar. You have been growing up since the Sphinx introduced us the other night; and you think you know more than I do already.

Cleopatra (taken down, and anxious to justify herself) No: that would be very silly of me: of course I know that. But— (*suddenly*) are you angry with me?

Cæsar. No.

Cleopatra (only half believing him) Then why are you so thoughtful?

Cæsar (rising) I have work to do, Cleopatra.

Cleopatra (drawing back) Work! (*Offended*) You are tired of talking to me; and that is your excuse to get away from me.

Cæsar (sitting down again to appease her) Well, well: another minute. But then—work!

Cleopatra. Work! what nonsense! You must remember that you are a king now: I have made you one. Kings dont work.

Cæsar. Oh! Who told you that, little kitten? Eh?

Cleopatra. My father was King of Egypt; and he never worked. But he was a great king, and cut off my sister's head because she rebelled against him and took the throne from him.

Cæsar. Well; and how did he get his throne back again?

Cleopatra (eagerly, her eyes lighting up) I will tell you.

A beautiful young man, with strong round arms, came over the desert with many horsemen, and slew my sister's husband and gave my father back his throne. (*Wistfully*) I was only twelve then. Oh, I wish he would come again, now that I am a queen. I would make him my husband.

Cæsar. It might be managed, perhaps; for it was I who sent that beautiful young man to help your father.

Cleopatra (*enraptured*) You know him!

Cæsar (*nodding*) I do.

Cleopatra. Has he come with you? (*Cæsar shakes his head: she is cruelly disappointed*). Oh, I wish he had, I wish he had. If only I were a little older; so that he might not think me a mere kitten, as you do! But perhaps that is because you are old. He is many many years younger than you, is he not?

Cæsar (*as if swallowing a pill*) He is somewhat younger.

Cleopatra. Would he be my husband, do you think, if I asked him?

Cæsar. Very likely.

Cleopatra. But I should not like to ask him. Could you not persuade him to ask me—without knowing that I wanted him to?

Cæsar (*touched by her innocence of the beautiful young man's character*) My poor child!

Cleopatra. Why do you say that as if you were sorry for me? Does he love anyone else?

Cæsar. I am afraid so.

Cleopatra (*tearfully*) Then I shall not be his first love.

Cæsar. Not quite the first. He is greatly admired by women.

Cleopatra. I wish I could be the first. But if he loves me, I will make him kill all the rest. Tell me: is he still beautiful? Do his strong round arms shine in the sun like marble?

Cæsar. He is in excellent condition—considering how much he eats and drinks.

Cleopatra. Oh, you must not say common, earthly things about him; for I love him. He is a god.

Cæsar. He is a great captain of horsemen, and swifter of foot than any other Roman.

Cleopatra. What is his real name?

Cæsar (puzzled) His r e a l name?

Cleopatra. Yes. I always call him Horus, because Horus is the most beautiful of our gods. But I want to know his real name.

Cæsar. His name is Mark Antony.

Cleopatra (musically) Mark Antony, Mark Antony, Mark Antony! What a beautiful name! (*She throws her arms round Cæsar's neck*). Oh, how I love you for sending him to help my father! Did you love my father very much?

Cæsar. No, my child; but your father, as you say, never worked. I always work. So when he lost his crown he had to promise me 16,000 talents to get it back for him.

Cleopatra. Did he ever pay you?

Cæsar. Not in full.

Cleopatra. He was quite right: it was too dear. The whole world is not worth 16,000 talents.

Cæsar. That is perhaps true, Cleopatra. Those Egyptians who work paid as much of it as he could drag from them. The rest is still due. But as I most likely shall not get it, I must go back to my work. So you must run away for a little and send my secretary to me.

Cleopatra (coaxing) No: I want to stay and hear you talk about Mark Antony.

Cæsar. But if I do not get to work, Pothinus and the rest of them will cut us off from the harbor; and then the way from Rome will be blocked.

Cleopatra. No matter: I dont want you to go back to Rome.

Cæsar. But you want Mark Antony to come from it.

Cleopatra (springing up) Oh yes, yes, yes: I forgot. Go quickly and work, Cæsar; and keep the way over the sea open for my Mark Antony. (*She runs out through the loggia, kissing her hand to Mark Antony across the sea*).

Cæsar (going briskly up the middle of the hall to the loggia steps) Ho, Brittanus. *(He is startled by the entry of a wounded Roman soldier, who confronts him from the upper step).* What now?

Soldier (pointing to his bandaged head) This, Cæsar; and two of my comrades killed in the market place.

Cæsar (quiet, but attending) Ay. Why?

Soldier. There is an army come to Alexandria, calling itself the Roman army.

Cæsar. The Roman army of occupation. Ay?

Soldier. Commanded by one Achillas.

Cæsar. Well?

Soldier. The citizens rose against us when the army entered the gates. I was with two others in the market place when the news came. They set upon us. I cut my way out; and here I am.

Cæsar. Good. I am glad to see you alive. *(Rufio enters the loggia hastily, passing behind the soldier to look out through one of the arches at the quay beneath).* Rufio: we are besieged.

Rufio. What! Already?

Cæsar. Now or to-morrow: what does it matter? We shall be besieged.

Britannus runs in.

Britannus. Cæsar—

Cæsar (anticipating him) Yes: I know. *(Rufio and Britannus come down the hall from the loggia at opposite sides, past Cæsar, who waits for a moment near the step to say to the soldier)* Comrade: give the word to turn out on the beach and stand by the boats. Get your wound attended to. Go. *(The soldier hurries out. Cæsar comes down the hall between Rufio and Britannus)* Rufio: we have some ships in the west harbor. Burn them.

Rufio (staring) Burn them!!

Cæsar. Take every boat we have in the east harbor, and

seize the Pharos—that island with the lighthouse. Leave half our men behind to hold the beach and the quay outside this palace: that is the way home.

Rufio (*disapproving strongly*) Are we to give up the city?

Cæsar. We have not got it, Rufio. This palace we have; and—what is that building next door?

Rufio. The theatre.

Cæsar. We will have that too: it commands the strand. For the rest, Egypt for the Egyptians!

Rufio. Well, you know best, I suppose. Is that all?

Cæsar. That is all. Are those ships burnt yet?

Rufio. Be easy: I shall waste no more time. (*He runs out*).

Britannus. Cæsar: Pothinus demands speech of you. In my opinion he needs a lesson. His manner is most insolent.

Cæsar. Where is he?

Britannus. He waits without.

Cæsar. Ho there! admit Pothinus.

Pothinus appears in the loggia, and comes down the hall very haughtily to Cæsar's left hand.

Cæsar. Well, Pothinus?

Pothinus. I have brought you our ultimatum, Cæsar.

Cæsar. Ultimatum! The door was open: you should have gone out through it before you declared war. You are my prisoner now. (*He goes to the chair and loosens his toga*).

Pothinus (*scornfully*) I your prisoner! Do you know that you are in Alexandria, and that King Ptolemy, with an army outnumbering your little troop a hundred to one, is in possession of Alexandria?

Cæsar (*unconcernedly taking off his toga and throwing it on the chair*) Well, my friend, get out if you can. And tell your friends not to kill any more Romans in the market place. Otherwise my soldiers, who do not share my celebrated clemency, will probably kill you. Britannus: pass the word to the guard; and fetch my armor. (*Britannus runs out. Rufio returns*). Well?

Rufio (pointing from the loggia to a cloud of smoke drifting over the harbor) See there! *(Pothinus runs eagerly up the steps to look out).*

Cæsar. What, ablaze already! Impossible!

Rufio. Yes, five good ships, and a barge laden with oil grappled to each. But it is not my doing: the Egyptians have saved me the trouble. They have captured the west harbor.

Cæsar (anxiously) And the east harbor? The lighthouse, Rufio?

Rufio (with a sudden splutter of raging ill usage, coming down to Cæsar and scolding him) Can I embark a legion in five minutes? The first cohort is already on the beach. We can do no more. If you want faster work, come and do it yourself.

Cæsar (soothing him) Good, good. Patience, Rufio, patience.

Rufio. Patience! Who is impatient here, you or I? Would I be here, if I could not oversee them from that balcony?

Cæsar. Forgive me, Rufio; and *(anxiously)* hurry them as much as—

He is interrupted by an outcry as of an old man in the extremity of misfortune. It draws near rapidly; and Theodotus rushes in, tearing his hair, and squeaking the most lamentable exclamations. Rufio steps back to stare at him, amazed at his frantic condition. Pothinus turns to listen.

Theodotus (on the steps, with uplifted arms) Horror unspeakable! Woe, alas! Help!

Rufio. What now?

Cæsar (frowning) Who is slain?

Theodotus. Slain! Oh, worse than the death of ten thousand men! Loss irreparable to mankind!

Rufio. What has happened, man?

Theodotus (rushing down the hall between them) The fire has spread from your ships. The first of the seven wonders of the world perishes. The library of Alexandria is in flames.

Rufio. Psha! *(Quite relieved, he goes up to the loggia and watches the preparations of the troops on the beach).*

Cæsar. Is that all?

Theodotus (unable to believe his senses) All! Cæsar: will you go down to posterity as a barbarous soldier too ignorant to know the value of books?

Cæsar. Theodotus: I am an author myself; and I tell you it is better that the Egyptians should live their lives than dream them away with the help of books.

Theodotus (kneeling, with genuine literary emotion: the passion of the pedant) Cæsar: once in ten generations of men, the world gains an immortal book.

Cæsar (inflexible) If it did not flatter mankind, the common executioner would burn it.

Theodotus. Without history, death will lay you beside your meanest soldier.

Cæsar. Death will do that in any case. I ask no better grave.

Theodotus. What is burning there is the memory of mankind.

Cæsar. A shameful memory. Let it burn.

Theodotus (wildly) Will you destroy the past?

Cæsar. Ay, and build the future with its ruins. (*Theodotus, in despair, strikes himself on the temples with his fists*). But harken, Theodotus, teacher of kings: you who valued Pompey's head no more than a shepherd values an onion, and who now kneel to me, with tears in your old eyes, to plead for a few sheepskins scrawled with errors. I cannot spare you a man or a bucket of water just now; but you shall pass freely out of the palace. Now, away with you to Achillas; and borrow his legions to put out the fire. (*He hurries him to the steps*).

Pothinus (significantly) You understand, Theodotus: I remain a prisoner.

Theodotus. A prisoner!

Cæsar. Will you stay to talk whilst the memory of mankind is burning? (*Calling through the loggia*) Ho there! Pass Theodotus out. (*To Theodotus*) Away with you.

Theodotus (*To Pothinus*) I must go to save the library. (*He hurries out*).

Cæsar. Follow him to the gate, Pothinus. Bid him urge your people to kill no more of my soldiers, for your sake.

Pothinus. My life will cost you dear if you take it, Cæsar. (*He goes out after Theodotus*).

Rufio, absorbed in watching the embarkation, does not notice the departure of the two Egyptians.

Rufio (*shouting from the loggia to the beach*) All ready, there?

A Centurion (*from below*) All ready. We wait for Cæsar.

Cæsar. Tell them Cæsar is coming—the rogues! (*Calling*) Britannicus. (*This magniloquent version of his secretary's name is one of Cæsar's jokes. In later years it would have meant, quite seriously and officially, Conqueror of Britain*).

Rufio (*calling down*) Push off, all except the longboat. Stand by it to embark, Cæsar's guard there. (*He leaves the balcony and comes down into the hall*). Where are those Egyptians? Is this more clemency? Have you let them go?

Cæsar (*chuckling*) I have let Theodotus go to save the library. We must respect literature, Rufio.

Rufio (*raging*) Folly on folly's head! I believe if you could bring back all the dead of Spain, Gaul, and Thessaly to life, you would do it that we might have the trouble of fighting them over again.

Cæsar. Might not the gods destroy the world if their only thought were to be at peace next year? (*Rufio, out of all patience, turns away in anger. Cæsar suddenly grips his sleeve, and adds slyly in his ear*) Besides, my friend: every Egyptian we imprison means imprisoning two Roman soldiers to guard him. Eh?

Rufio. Agh! I might have known there was some fox's trick behind your fine talking. (*He gets away from Cæsar with an ill-humored shrug, and goes to the balcony for another look at the preparations; finally goes out*).

Cæsar. Is Britannus asleep? I sent him for my armor an hour ago. (*Calling*) Britannicus, thou British islander. Britannicus!

Cleopatra runs in through the loggia with Cæsar's helmet and sword, snatched from Britannus, who follows her with a cuirass and greaves. They come down to Cæsar, she to his left hand, Britannus to his right.

Cleopatra. I am going to dress you, Cæsar. Sit down. (*He obeys*). These Roman helmets are so becoming! (*She takes off his wreath*). Oh! (*She bursts out laughing at him*).

Cæsar. What are you laughing at?

Cleopatra. Youre bald (*beginning with a big B, and ending with a splutter*).

Cæsar (*almost annoyed*) Cleopatra! (*He rises, for the convenience of Britannus, who puts the cuirass on him*).

Cleopatra. So that is why you wear the wreath—to hide it.

Britannus. Peace, Egyptian: they are the bays of the conqueror. (*He buckles the cuirass*).

Cleopatra. Peace, thou: islander! (*To Cæsar*) You should rub your head with strong spirits of sugar, Cæsar. That will make it grow.

Cæsar (*with a wry face*) Cleopatra: do you like to be reminded that you are very young?

Cleopatra (*pouting*) No.

Cæsar (*sitting down again, and setting out his leg for Britannus, who kneels to put on his greaves*) Neither do I like to be reminded that I am—middle aged. Let me give you ten of my superfluous years. That will make you 26, and leave me only—no matter. Is it a bargain?

Cleopatra. Agreed. 26, mind. (*She puts the helmet on him*). Oh! How nice! You look only about 50 in it!

Britannus (*looking up severely at Cleopatra*) You must not speak in this manner to Cæsar.

Cleopatra. Is it true that when Cæsar caught you on that island, you were painted all over blue?

Britannus. Blue is the color worn by all Britons of good standing. In war we stain our bodies blue; so that though our enemies may strip us of our clothes and our lives, they cannot strip us of our respectability. (*He rises*).

Cleopatra (*with Cæsar's sword*) Let me hang this on. Now you look splendid. Have they made any statues of you in Rome?

Cæsar. Yes, many statues.

Cleopatra. You must send for one and give it to me.

Rufio (*coming back into the loggia, more impatient than ever*) Now Cæsar: have you done talking? The moment your foot is aboard there will be no holding our men back: the boats will race one another for the lighthouse.

Cæsar (*drawing his sword and trying the edge*) Is this well set today, Britannicus? At Pharsalia it was as blunt as a barrel-hoop.

Britannus. It will split one of the Egyptian's hairs today, Cæsar. I have set it myself.

Cleopatra (*suddenly throwing her arms in terror round Cæsar*) Oh, you are not really going into battle to be killed?

Cæsar. No, Cleopatra. No man goes to battle to be killed.

Cleopatra. But they do get killed. My sister's husband was killed in battle. You must not go. Let him go (*pointing to Rufio. They all laugh at her*). Oh please, please dont go. What will happen to me if you never come back?

Cæsar (*gravely*) Are you afraid?

Cleopatra (*shrinking*) No.

Cæsar (*with quiet authority*) Go to the balcony; and you shall see us take the Pharos. You must learn to look on battles. Go. (*She goes, downcast, and looks out from the balcony*). That is well. Now, Rufio. March.

Cleopatra (*suddenly clapping her hands*) Oh, you will not be able to go!

Cæsar. Why? What now?

Cleopatra. They are drying up the harbor with buckets—

a multitude of soldiers—over there (*pointing out across the
sea to her left*)—they are dipping up the water.

Rufio (*hastening to look*) It is true. The Egyptian army!
Crawling over the edge of the west harbor like locusts. (*With
sudden anger he strides down to Cæsar*). This is your accursed
clemency, Cæsar. Theodotus has brought them.

Cæsar (*delighted at his own cleverness*) I meant him to,
Rufio. They have come to put out the fire. The library will
keep them busy whilst we seize the lighthouse. Eh? (*He
rushes out buoyantly through the loggia, followed by Britannus*).

Rufio (*disgustedly*) More foxing! Agh! (*He rushes off. A
shout from the soldiers announces the appearance of Cæsar
below*).

Centurion (*below*) All aboard. Give way there. (*Another
shout*).

Cleopatra (*waving her scarf through the loggia arch*) Goodbye, goodbye, dear Cæsar. Come back safe. Goodbye!

ACT III

THE EDGE of the quay in front of the palace, looking out west over the east harbor of Alexandria to Pharos island, just off the end of which, and connected with it by a narrow mole, is the famous lighthouse, a gigantic square tower of white marble diminishing in size storey by storey to the top, on which stands a cresset beacon. The island is joined to the main land by the Heptastadium, a great mole or causeway five miles long bounding the harbor on the south.

In the middle of the quay a Roman sentinel stands on guard pilum in hand, looking out to the lighthouse with strained attention, his left hand shading his eyes. The pilum is a stout wooden shaft 4½ feet long, with an iron spit about three feet long fixed in it. The sentinel is so absorbed that he does not notice the approach from the north end of the quay of four Egyptian market porters carrying rolls of carpet, preceded by Ftatateeta and Apollodorus the Sicilian. Apollodorus is a dashing young man of about 24, handsome and debonair, dressed with deliberate æstheticism in the most delicate purples and dove greys, with ornaments of bronze, oxydized silver, and stones of jade and agate. His sword, designed as carefully as a medieval cross, has a blued blade showing through an openwork scabbard of purple leather and filagree. The porters, conducted by Ftatateeta, pass along the quay behind the sentinel to the steps of the palace, where they put down their bales and squat on the ground. Apollodorus does not pass along with them: he halts, amused by the preoccupation of the sentinel.

Apollodorus (calling to the sentinel) Who goes there, eh?
Sentinel (starting violently and turning with his pilum at the charge, revealing himself as a small, wiry, sandy-haired,

137

conscientious young man with an elderly face) Whats this? Stand. Who are you?

Apollodorus. I am Apollodorus the Sicilian. Why, man, what are you dreaming of? Since I came through the lines beyond the theatre there, I have brought my caravan past three sentinels, all so busy staring at the lighthouse that not one of them challenged me. Is this Roman discipline?

Sentinel. We are not here to watch the land but the sea. Cæsar has just landed on the Pharos. (*Looking at Ftatateeta*) What have you here? Who is this piece of Egyptian crockery?

Ftatateeta. Apollodorus: rebuke this Roman dog; and bid him bridle his tongue in the presence of Ftatateeta, the mistress of the Queen's household.

Apollodorus. My friend: this is a great lady, who stands high with Cæsar.

Sentinel (*not at all impressed, pointing to the carpets*) And what is all this truck?

Apollodorus. Carpets for the furnishing of the Queen's apartments in the palace. I have picked them from the best carpets in the world; and the Queen shall choose the best of my choosing.

Sentinel. So you are the carpet merchant?

Apollodorus (*hurt*) My friend: I am a patrician.

Sentinel. A patrician! A patrician keeping a shop instead of following arms!

Apollodorus. I do not keep a shop. Mine is a temple of the arts. I am a worshipper of beauty. My calling is to choose beautiful things for beautiful queens. My motto is Art for Art's sake.

Sentinel. That is not the password.

Apollodorus. It is a universal password.

Sentinel. I know nothing about universal passwords. Either give me the password for the day or get back to your shop.

Ftatateeta, roused by his hostile tone, steals towards the edge of the quay with the step of a panther, and gets behind him

Apollodorus. How if I do neither?

Sentinel. Then I will drive this pilum through you.

Apollodorus. At your service, my friend. (*He draws his sword, and springs to his guard with unruffled grace*).

Ftatateeta (*suddenly seizing the sentinel's arms from behind*) Thrust your knife into the dog's throat, Apollodorus. (*The chivalrous Apollodorus laughingly shakes his head; breaks ground away from the sentinel towards the palace; and lowers his point*).

Sentinel (*struggling vainly*) Curse on you! Let me go. Help ho!

Ftatateeta (*lifting him from the ground*) Stab the little Roman reptile. Spit him on your sword.

A couple of Roman soldiers, with a centurion, come running along the edge of the quay from the north end. They rescue their comrade, and throw off Ftatateeta, who is sent reeling away on the left hand of the sentinel.

Centurion (*an unattractive man of fifty, short in his speech and manners, with a vinewood cudgel in his hand*) How now? What is all this?

Ftatateeta (*to Apollodorus*) Why did you not stab him? There was time!

Apollodorus. Centurion: I am here by order of the Queen to—

Centurion (*interrupting him*) The Queen! Yes, yes: (*to the sentinel*) pass him in. Pass all these bazaar people in to the Queen, with their goods. But mind you pass no one out that you have not passed in—not even the Queen herself.

Sentinel. This old woman is dangerous: she is as strong as three men. She wanted the merchant to stab me.

Apollodorus. Centurion: I am not a merchant. I am a patrician and a votary of art.

Centurion. Is the woman your wife?

Apollodorus (*horrified*) No, no! (*Correcting himself po-*

litely) Not that the lady is not a striking figure in her own way. But (*emphatically*) she is n o t my wife.

Ftatateeta (*to the centurion*) Roman: I am Ftatateeta, the mistress of the Queen's household.

Centurion. Keep your hands off our men, mistress; or I will have you pitched into the harbor, though you were as strong as ten men. (*To his men*) To your posts: march! (*He returns with his men the way they came*).

Ftatateeta (*looking malignantly after him*) We shall see whom Isis loves best: her servant Ftatateeta or a dog of a Roman.

Sentinel (*to Apollodorus, with a wave of his pilum towards the palace*) Pass in there; and keep your distance. (*Turning to Ftatateeta*) Come within a yard of me, you old crocodile; and I will give you this (*the pilum*) in your jaws.

Cleopatra (*calling from the palace*) Ftatateeta, Ftatateeta.

Ftatateeta (*looking up, scandalized*) Go from the window, go from the window. There are men here.

Cleopatra. I am coming down.

Ftatateeta (*distracted*) No, no. What are you dreaming of? O ye gods, ye gods! Apollodorus: bid your men pick up your bales; and in with me quickly.

Apollodorus. Obey the mistress of the Queen's household.

Ftatateeta (*impatiently, as the porters stoop to lift the bales*) Quick, quick: she will be out upon us. (*Cleopatra comes from the palace and runs across the quay to Ftatateeta*). Oh that ever I was born!

Cleopatra (*eagerly*) Ftatateeta: I have thought of something. I want a boat—at once.

Ftatateeta. A boat! No, no: you cannot. Apollodorus: speak to the Queen.

Apollodorus (*gallantly*) Beautiful queen: I am Apollodorus the Sicilian, your servant, from the bazaar. I have brought you the three most beautiful Persian carpets in the world to choose from.

Cleopatra. I have no time for carpets to-day. Get me a boat.

Ftatateeta. What whim is this? You cannot go on the water except in the royal barge.

Apollodorus. Royalty, Ftatateeta, lies not in the barge but in the Queen. (*To Cleopatra*) The touch of your majesty's foot on the gunwale of the meanest boat in the harbor will make it royal. (*He turns to the harbor and calls seaward*) Ho there, boatman! Pull in to the steps.

Cleopatra. Apollodorus: you are my perfect knight; and I will always buy my carpets through you. (*Apollodorus bows joyously. An oar appears above the quay; and the boatman, a bullet-headed, vivacious, grinning fellow, burnt almost black by the sun, comes up a flight of steps from the water on the sentinel's right, oar in hand, and waits at the top*). Can you row, Apollodorus?

Apollodorus. My oars shall be your majesty's wings. Whither shall I row my Queen?

Cleopatra. To the lighthouse. Come. (*She makes for the steps*).

Sentinel (*opposing her with his pilum at the charge*) Stand. You cannot pass.

Cleopatra (*flushing angrily*) How dare you? Do you know that I am the Queen?

Sentinel. I have my orders. You cannot pass.

Cleopatra. I will make Cæsar have you killed if you do not obey me.

Sentinel. He will do worse to me if I disobey my officer. Stand back.

Cleopatra. Ftatateeta: strangle him.

Sentinel (*alarmed—looking apprehensively at Ftatateeta, and brandishing his pilum*) Keep off, there.

Cleopatra (*running to Apollodorus*) Apollodorus: make your slaves help us.

Apollodorus. I shall not need their help, lady. (*He draws his sword*). Now, soldier: choose which weapon you will defend yourself with. Shall it be sword against pilum, or sword against sword?

Sentinel. Roman against Sicilian, curse you. Take that. (*He hurls his pilum at Apollodorus, who drops expertly on one knee. The pilum passes whizzing over his head and falls harmless. Apollodorus, with a cry of triumph, springs up and attacks the sentinel, who draws his sword and defends himself, crying*) Ho there, guard. Help!

Cleopatra, half frightened, half delighted, takes refuge near the palace, where the porters are squatting among the bales. The boatman, alarmed, hurries down the steps out of harm's way, but stops, with his head just visible above the edge of the quay, to watch the fight. The sentinel is handicapped by his fear of an attack in the rear from Ftatateeta. His swordsmanship, which is of a rough and ready sort, is heavily taxed, as he has occasionally to strike at her to keep her off between a blow and a guard with Apollodorus. The centurion returns with several soldiers. Apollodorus springs back towards Cleopatra as this reinforcement confronts him.

Centurion (*coming to the sentinel's right hand*) What is this? What now?

Sentinel (*panting*) I could do well enough by myself if it werent for the old woman. Keep her off me: that is all the help I need.

Centurion. Make your report, soldier. What has happened?

Ftatateeta. Centurion: he would have slain the Queen.

Sentinel (*bluntly*) I would, sooner than let her pass. She wanted to take boat, and go—so she said—to the lighthouse. I stopped her, as I was ordered to; and she set this fellow on me. (*He goes to pick up his pilum and returns to his place with it*).

Centurion (*turning to Cleopatra*) Cleopatra: I am loth to offend you; but without Cæsar's express order we dare not let you pass beyond the Roman lines.

Apollodorus. Well, Centurion; and has not the lighthouse been within the Roman lines since Cæsar landed there?

Cleopatra. Yes, yes. Answer that, if you can.

Centurion (to Apollodorus) As for you, Apollodorus, you may thank the gods that you are not nailed to the palace door with a pilum for your meddling.

Apollodorus (urbanely) My military friend, I was not born to be slain by so ugly a weapon. When I fall, it will be (*holding up his sword*) by this white queen of arms, the only weapon fit for an artist. And now that you are convinced that we do not want to go beyond the lines, let me finish killing your sentinel and depart with the Queen.

Centurion (as the sentinel makes an angry demonstration) Peace there, Cleopatra: I must abide by my orders, and not by the subtleties of this Sicilian. You must withdraw into the palace and examine your carpets there.

Cleopatra (pouting) I will not: I am the Queen. Cæsar does not speak to me as you do. Have Cæsar's centurions changed manners with his scullions?

Centurion (sulkily) I do my duty. That is enough for me.

Apollodorus. Majesty: when a stupid man is doing something he is ashamed of, he always declares that it is his duty.

Centurion (angry) Apollodorus—

Apollodorus (interrupting him with defiant elegance) I will make amends for that insult with my sword at fitting time and place. Who says artist, says duellist. (*To Cleopatra*) Hear my counsel, star of the east. Until word comes to these soldiers from Cæsar himself, you are a prisoner. Let me go to him with a message from you, and a present; and before the sun has stooped half way to the arms of the sea, I will bring you back Cæsar's order of release.

Centurion (sneering at him) And you will sell the Queen the present, no doubt.

Apollodorus. Centurion: the Queen shall have from me, without payment, as the unforced tribute of Sicilian taste to

Egyptian beauty, the richest of these carpets for her present to Cæsar.

Cleopatra (*exultantly, to the centurion*) Now you see what an ignorant common creature you are!

Centurion (*curtly*) Well, a fool and his wares are soon parted. (*He turns to his men*). Two more men to this post here; and see that no one leaves the palace but this man and his merchandise. If he draws his sword again inside the lines, kill him. To your posts. March.

He goes out, leaving two auxiliary sentinels with the other.

Apollodorus (*with polite goodfellowship*) My friends: will you not enter the palace and bury our quarrel in a bowl of wine? (*He takes out his purse, jingling the coins in it*). The Queen has presents for you all.

Sentinel (*very sulky*) You heard our orders. Get about your business.

First Auxiliary. Yes: you ought to know better. Off with you.

Second Auxiliary (*looking longingly at the purse—this sentinel is a hooknosed man, unlike his comrade, who is squab faced*) Do not tantalize a poor man.

Apollodorus (*to Cleopatra*) Pearl of Queens: the centurion is at hand; and the Roman soldier is incorruptible when his officer is looking. I must carry your word to Cæsar.

Cleopatra (*who has been meditating among the carpets*) Are these carpets very heavy?

Apollodorus. It matters not how heavy. There are plenty of porters.

Cleopatra. How do they put the carpets into boats? Do they throw them down?

Apollodorus. Not into small boats, majesty. It would sink them.

Cleopatra. Not into that man's boat, for instance? (*pointing to the boatman*).

Apollodorus. No. Too small.

Cleopatra. But you can take a carpet to Cæsar in it if I send one?

Apollodorus. Assuredly.

Cleopatra. And you will have it carried gently down the steps and take great care of it?

Apollodorus. Depend on me.

Cleopatra. Great, g r e a t care?

Apollodorus. More than of my own body.

Cleopatra. You will promise me not to let the porters drop it or throw it about?

Apollodorus. Place the most delicate glass goblet in the palace in the heart of the roll, Queen; and if it be broken, my head shall pay for it.

Cleopatra. Good. Come, Ftatateeta. (*Ftatateeta comes to her. Apollodorus offers to squire them into the palace*). No, Apollodorus, you must not come. I will choose a carpet for myself. You must wait here. (*She runs into the palace*).

Apollodorus (*to the porters*) Follow this lady (*indicating Ftatateeta*); and obey her.

The porters rise and take up their bales.

Ftatateeta (*addressing the porters as if they were vermin*) This way. And take your shoes off before you put your feet on those stairs.

She goes in, followed by the porters with the carpets. Meanwhile Apollodorus goes to the edge of the quay and looks out over the harbor. The sentinels keep their eyes on him malignantly.

Apollodorus (*addressing the sentinel*) My friend—

Sentinel (*rudely*) Silence there.

First Auxiliary. Shut your muzzle, you.

Second Auxiliary (*in a half whisper, glancing apprehensively towards the north end of the quay*) Cant you wait a bit?

Apollodorus. Patience, worthy three-headed donkey. (*They mutter ferociously; but he is not at all intimidated*). Listen: were you set here to watch me, or to watch the Egyptians?

Sentinel. We know our duty.

Apollodorus. Then why dont you do it? There is something going on over there (*pointing southwestward to the mole*).

Sentinel (*sulkily*) I do not need to be told what to do by the like of you.

Apollodorus. Blockhead. (*He begins shouting*) Ho there, Centurion, Hoiho!

Sentinel. Curse your meddling. (*Shouting*) Hoiho! Alarm! Alarm!

First and Second Auxiliaries. Alarm! alarm! Hoiho!

The Centurion comes running in with his guard.

Centurion. What now? Has the old woman attacked you again? (*Seeing Apollodorus*) Are you here still?

Apollodorus (*pointing as before*) See there. The Egyptians are moving. They are going to recapture the Pharos. They will attack by sea and land: by land along the great mole; by sea from the west harbor. Stir yourselves, my military friends: the hunt is up. (*A clangor of trumpets from several points along the quay*). Aha! I told you so.

Centurion (*quickly*) The two extra men pass the alarm to the south posts. One man keep guard here. The rest with me —quick.

The two auxiliary sentinels run off to the south. The centurion and his guard run off northward; and immediately afterwards the buccina sounds. The four porters come from the palace carrying a carpet, followed by Ftatateeta.

Sentinel (*handling his pilum apprehensively*) You again! (*The porters stop*).

Ftatateeta. Peace, Roman fellow: you are now single-handed. Apollodorus: this carpet is Cleopatra's present to Cæsar. It has rolled up in it ten precious goblets of the thinnest Iberian crystal, and a hundred eggs of the sacred blue pigeon. On your honor, let not one of them be broken.

Apollodorus. On my head be it! (*To the porters*) Into the boat with them carefully.

The porters carry the carpet to the steps.

First Porter (*looking down at the boat*) Beware what you do, sir. Those eggs of which the lady speaks must weigh more than a pound apiece. This boat is too small for such a load.

Boatman (*excitedly rushing up the steps*) Oh thou injurious porter! Oh thou unnatural son of a she-camel! (*To Apollodorus*) My boat, sir, hath often carried five men. Shall it not carry your lordship and a bale of pigeons' eggs? (*To the porter*) Thou mangey dromedary, the gods shall punish thee for this envious wickedness.

First Porter (*stolidly*) I cannot quit this bale now to beat thee; but another day I will lie in wait for thee.

Apollodorus (*going between them*) Peace there. If the boat were but a single plank, I would get to Cæsar on it.

Ftatateeta (*anxiously*) In the name of the gods, Apollodorus, run no risks with that bale.

Apollodorus. Fear not, thou venerable grotesque: I guess its great worth. (*To the porters*) Down with it, I say; and gently; or ye shall eat nothing but stick for ten days.

The boatman goes down the steps, followed by the porters with the bale: Ftatateeta and Apollodorus watching from the edge.

Apollodorus. Gently, my sons, my children—(*with sudden alarm*) gently, ye dogs. Lay it level in the stern—so—tis well.

Ftatateeta (*screaming down at one of the porters*) Do not step on it, do not step on it. Oh thou brute beast!

First Porter (*ascending*) Be not excited, mistress: all is well.

Ftatateeta (*panting*) All well! Oh, thou hast given my heart a turn! (*She clutches her side, gasping*).

The four porters have now come up and are waiting at the stairhead to be paid.

Apollodorus. Here, ye hungry ones. (*He gives money to the first porter, who holds it in his hand to shew to the others.*

They crowd greedily to see how much it is, quite prepared, after the Eastern fashion, to protest to heaven against their patron's stinginess. But his liberality overpowers them).

First Porter. O bounteous prince!

Second Porter. O lord of the bazaar!

Third Porter. O favored of the gods!

Fourth Porter. O father to all the porters of the market!

Sentinel (enviously, threatening them fiercely with his pilum) Hence, dogs: off. Out of this. *(They fly before him northward along the quay).*

Apollodorus. Farewell, Ftatateeta. I shall be at the lighthouse before the Egyptians. *(He descends the steps).*

Ftatateeta. The gods speed thee and protect my nursling!

The sentry returns from chasing the porters and looks down at the boat, standing near the stairhead lest Ftatateeta should attempt to escape.

Apollodorus (from beneath, as the boat moves off) Farewell, valiant pilum pitcher.

Sentinel. Farewell, shopkeeper.

Apollodorus. Ha, ha! Pull, thou brave boatman, pull. Soho-o-o-o-o! *(He begins to sing in barcarolle measure to the rhythm of the oars)*

> My heart, my heart, spread out thy wings:
> Shake off thy heavy load of love—

Give me the oars, O son of a snail.

Sentinel (threatening Ftatateeta) Now mistress: back to your henhouse. In with you.

Ftatateeta (falling on her knees and stretching her hands over the waters) Gods of the seas, bear her safely to the shore!

Sentinel. Bear who safely? What do you mean?

Ftatateeta (looking darkly at him) Gods of Egypt and of Vengeance, let this Roman fool be beaten like a dog by his captain for suffering her to be taken over the waters.

Sentinel. Accursed one: is she then in the boat? (*He calls over the sea*) Hoiho, there, boatman! Hoiho!

Apollodorus (*singing in the distance*)

> My heart, my heart, be whole and free:
> Love is thine only enemy.

Meanwhile Rufio, the morning's fighting done, sits munching dates on a faggot of brushwood outside the door of the lighthouse, which towers gigantic to the clouds on his left. His helmet, full of dates, is between his knees; and a leathern bottle of wine is by his side. Behind him the great stone pedestal of the lighthouse is shut in from the open sea by a low stone parapet, with a couple of steps in the middle to the broad coping. A huge chain with a hook hangs down from the lighthouse crane above his head. Faggots like the one he sits on lie beneath it ready to be drawn up to feed the beacon.

Cæsar is standing on the step at the parapet looking out anxiously, evidently ill at ease. Britannus comes out of the lighthouse door.

Rufio. Well, my British islander. Have you been up to the top?

Britannus. I have. I reckon it at 200 feet high.

Rufio. Anybody up there?

Britannus. One elderly Tyrian to work the crane; and his son, a well conducted youth of 14.

Rufio (*looking at the chain*) What! An old man and a boy work that! Twenty men, you mean.

Britannus. Two only, I assure you. They have counterweights, and a machine with boiling water in it which I do not understand: it is not of British design. They use it to haul up barrels of oil and faggots to burn in the brazier on the roof.

Rufio. But—

Britannus. Excuse me: I came down because there are messengers coming along the mole to us from the island. I must see what their business is. (*He hurries out past the light-house*).

Cæsar (*coming away from the parapet, shivering and out of sorts*) Rufio: this has been a mad expedition. We shall be beaten. I wish I knew how our men are getting on with that barricade across the great mole.

Rufio (*angrily*) Must I leave my food and go starving to bring you a report?

Cæsar (*soothing him nervously*) No, Rufio, no. Eat, my son, eat. (*He takes another turn, Rufio chewing dates meanwhile*). The Egyptians cannot be such fools as not to storm the barricade and swoop down on us here before it is finished. It is the first time I have ever run an avoidable risk. I should not have come to Egypt.

Rufio. An hour ago you were all for victory.

Cæsar (*apologetically*) Yes: I was a fool—rash, Rufio—boyish.

Rufio. Boyish! Not a bit of it. Here (*offering him a handful of dates*).

Cæsar. What are these for?

Rufio. To eat. Thats whats the matter with you. When a man comes to your age, he runs down before his midday meal. Eat and drink; and then have another look at our chances.

Cæsar (*taking the dates*) My age! (*He shakes his head and bites a date*). Yes, Rufio: I am an old man—worn out now—true, quite true. (*He gives way to melancholy contemplation, and eats another date*). Achillas is still in his prime: Ptolemy is a boy. (*He eats another date, and plucks up a little*). Well, every dog has his day; and I have had mine: I cannot complain. (*With sudden cheerfulness*) These dates are not bad, Rufio. (*Britannus returns, greatly excited, with a leathern bag. Cæsar is himself again in a moment*). What now?

Britannus (*triumphantly*) Our brave Rhodian mariners have captured a treasure. There! (*He throws the bag down at Cæsar's feet*). Our enemies are delivered into our hands.

Cæsar. In that bag?

Britannus. Wait till you hear, Cæsar. This bag contains all the letters which have passed between Pompey's party and the army of occupation here.

Cæsar. Well?

Britannus (*impatient of Cæsar's slowness to grasp the situation*) Well, we shall now know who your foes are. The name of every man who has plotted against you since you crossed the Rubicon may be in these papers, for all we know.

Cæsar. Put them in the fire.

Britannus. Put them—(*he gasps*)!!!!

Cæsar. In the fire. Would you have me waste the next three years of my life in proscribing and condemning men who will be my friends when I have proved that my friendship is worth more than Pompey's was—than Cato's is. O incorrigible British islander: am I a bull dog, to seek quarrels merely to shew how stubborn my jaws are?

Britannus. But your honor—the honor of Rome—

Cæsar. I do not make human sacrifices to my honor, as your Druids do. Since you will not burn these, at least I can drown them. (*He picks up the bag and throws it over the parapet into the sea*).

Britannus. Cæsar: this is mere eccentricity. Are traitors to be allowed to go free for the sake of a paradox?

Rufio (*rising*) Cæsar: when the islander has finished preaching, call me again. I am going to have a look at the boiling water machine. (*He goes into the lighthouse*).

Britannus (*with genuine feeling*) O Cæsar, my great master, if I could but persuade you to regard life seriously, as men do in my country!

Cæsar. Do they truly do so, Britannus?

Britannus. Have you not been there? Have you not seen them? What Briton speaks as you do in your moments of levity? What Briton neglects to attend the services at the sacred grove? What Briton wears clothes of many colors as you do, instead of plain blue, as all solid, well esteemed men should? These are moral questions with us.

Cæsar. Well, well, my friend: some day I shall settle down and have a blue toga, perhaps. Meanwhile, I must get on as best I can in my flippant Roman way. (*Apollodorus comes past the lighthouse*). What now?

Britannus (*turning quickly, and challenging the stranger with official haughtiness*) What is this? Who are you? How did you come here?

Apollodorus. Calm yourself, my friend: I am not going to eat you. I have come by boat, from Alexandria, with precious gifts for Cæsar.

Cæsar. From Alexandria!

Britannus (*severely*) That is Cæsar, sir.

Rufio (*appearing at the lighthouse door*) Whats the matter now?

Apollodorus. Hail, great Cæsar! I am Apollodorus the Sicilian, an artist.

Britannus. An artist! Why have they admitted this vagabond?

Cæsar. Peace, man. Apollodorus is a famous patrician amateur.

Britannus (*disconcerted*) I crave the gentleman's pardon. (*To Cæsar*) I understood him to say that he was a professional. (*Somewhat out of countenance, he allows Apollodorus to approach Cæsar, changing places with him. Rufio, after looking Apollodorus up and down with marked disparagement, goes to the other side of the platform*).

Cæsar. You are welcome, Apollodorus. What is your business?

Apollodorus. First, to deliver to you a present from the Queen of Queens.

Cæsar. Who is that?

Apollodorus. Cleopatra of Egypt.

Cæsar (*taking him into his confidence in his most winning manner*) Apollodorus: this is no time for playing with presents. Pray you, go back to the Queen, and tell her that if all goes well I shall return to the palace this evening.

Apollodorus. Cæsar: I cannot return. As I approached the lighthouse, some fool threw a great leathern bag into the sea. It broke the nose of my boat; and I had hardly time to get myself and my charge to the shore before the poor little cockleshell sank.

Cæsar. I am sorry, Apollodorus. The fool shall be rebuked. Well, well: what have you brought me? The Queen will be hurt if I do not look at it.

Rufio. Have we time to waste on this trumpery? The Queen is only a child.

Cæsar. Just so: that is why we must not disappoint her. What is the present, Apollodorus?

Apollodorus. Cæsar: it is a Persian carpet—a beauty! And in it are—so I am told—pigeons' eggs and crystal goblets and fragile precious things. I dare not for my head have it carried up that narrow ladder from the causeway.

Rufio. Swing it up by the crane, then. We will send the eggs to the cook, drink our wine from the goblets; and the carpet will make a bed for Cæsar.

Apollodorus. The crane! Cæsar: I have sworn to tender this bale of carpets as I tender my own life.

Cæsar (*cheerfully*) Then let them swing you up at the same time; and if the chain breaks, you and the pigeons' eggs will perish together. (*He goes to the chain and looks up along it, examining it curiously*).

Apollodorus (*to Britannus*) Is Cæsar serious?

Britannus. His manner is frivolous because he is an Italian; but he means what he says.

Apollodorus. Serious or not, he spake well. Give me a squad of soldiers to work the crane.

Britannus. Leave the crane to me. Go and await the descent of the chain.

Apollodorus. Good. You will presently see me there (*turning to them all and pointing with an eloquent gesture to the sky above the parapet*) rising like the sun with my treasure.

He goes back the way he came. Britannus goes into the lighthouse.

Rufio (*ill-humoredly*) Are you really going to wait here for this foolery, Cæsar?

Cæsar (*backing away from the crane as it gives signs of working*) Why not?

Rufio. The Egyptians will let you know why not if they have the sense to make a rush from the shore end of the mole before our barricade is finished. And here we are waiting like children to see a carpet full of pigeons' eggs.

The chain rattles, and is drawn up high enough to clear the parapet. It then swings round out of sight behind the lighthouse.

Cæsar. Fear not, my son Rufio. When the first Egyptian takes his first step along the mole, the alarm will sound; and we two will reach the barricade from our end before the Egyptians reach it from their end—we two, Rufio: I, the old man, and you, his biggest boy. And the old man will be there first. So peace; and give me some more dates.

Apollodorus (*from the causeway below*) Soho, haul away. So-ho-o-o-o! (*The chain is drawn up and comes round again from behind the lighthouse. Apollodorus is swinging in the air with his bale of carpet at the end of it. He breaks into song as he soars above the parapet*)

> Aloft, aloft, behold the blue
> That never shone in woman's eyes—

Easy there: stop her. (*He ceases to rise*). Further round! (*The chain comes forward above the platform*).

Rufio (*calling up*) Lower away there. (*The chain and its load begin to descend*).

Apollodorus (*calling up*) Gently—slowly—mind the eggs.

Rufio (calling up) Easy there—slowly—slowly.

Apollodorus and the bale are deposited safely on the flags in the middle of the platform. Rufio and Cæsar help Apollodorus to cast off the chain from the bale.

Rufio. Haul up.

The chain rises clear of their heads with a rattle. Britannus comes from the lighthouse and helps them to uncord the carpet.

Apollodorus (when the cords are loose) Stand off, my friends: let Cæsar see. *(He throws the carpet open).*

Rufio. Nothing but a heap of shawls. Where are the pigeons' eggs?

Apollodorus. Approach, Cæsar; and search for them among the shawls.

Rufio (drawing his sword) Ha, treachery! Keep back, Cæsar: I saw the shawl move: there is something alive there.

Britannus (drawing his sword) It is a serpent.

Apollodorus. Dares Cæsar thrust his hand into the sack where the serpent moves?

Rufio (turning on him) Treacherous dog—

Cæsar. Peace. Put up your swords. Apollodorus: your serpent seems to breathe very regularly. *(He thrusts his hand under the shawls and draws out a bare arm).* This is a pretty little snake.

Rufio (drawing out the other arm) Let us have the rest of you.

They pull Cleopatra up by the wrists into a sitting position. Britannus, scandalized, sheathes his sword with a drive of protest.

Cleopatra (gasping) Oh, I'm smothered. Oh, Cæsar, a man stood on me in the boat; and a great sack of something fell upon me out of the sky; and then the boat sank; and then I was swung up into the air and bumped down.

Cæsar (petting her as she rises and takes refuge on his breast) Well, never mind: here you are safe and sound at last.

Rufio. Ay; and now that she is here, what are we to do with her?

Britannus. She cannot stay here, Cæsar, without the companionship of some matron.

Cleopatra (*jealously, to Cæsar, who is obviously perplexed*) Arnt you glad to see me?

Cæsar. Yes, yes; I am very glad. But Rufio is very angry; and Britannus is shocked.

Cleopatra (*contemptuously*) You can have their heads cut off, can you not?

Cæsar. They would not be so useful with their heads cut off as they are now, my sea bird.

Rufio (*to Cleopatra*) We shall have to go away presently and cut some of your Egyptians' heads off. How will you like being left here with the chance of being captured by that little brother of yours if we are beaten?

Cleopatra. But you mustnt leave me alone. Cæsar: you will not leave me alone, will you?

Rufio. What! not when the trumpet sounds and all our lives depend on Cæsar's being at the barricade before the Egyptians reach it? Eh?

Cleopatra. Let them lose their lives: they are only soldiers.

Cæsar (*gravely*) Cleopatra: when that trumpet sounds, we must take every man his life in his hand, and throw it in the face of Death. And of my soldiers who have trusted me there is not one whose hand I shall not hold more sacred than your head. (*Cleopatra is overwhelmed. Her eyes fill with tears*). Apollodorus: you must take her back to the palace.

Apollodorus. Am I a dolphin, Cæsar, to cross the seas with young ladies on my back? My boat is sunk: all yours are either at the barricade or have returned to the city. I will hail one if I can: that is all I can do. (*He goes back to the causeway*).

Cleopatra (*struggling with her tears*) It does not matter. I will not go back. Nobody cares for me.

Cæsar. Cleopatra—

Cleopatra. You want me to be killed.

Cæsar (still more gravely) My poor child: your life matters little here to anyone but yourself. (*She gives way altogether at this, casting herself down on the faggots weeping. Suddenly a great tumult is heard in the distance, buccinas and trumpets sounding through a storm of shouting. Britannus rushes to the parapet and looks along the mole. Cæsar and Rufio turn to one another with quick intelligence*).

Cæsar. Come, Rufio.

Cleopatra (scrambling to her knees and clinging to him) No no. Do not leave me, Cæsar. (*He snatches his skirt from her clutch*). Oh!

Britannus (from the parapet) Cæsar: we are cut off. The Egyptians have landed from the west harbor between us and the barricade!!!

Rufio (running to see) Curses! It is true. We are caught like rats in a trap.

Cæsar (ruthfully) Rufio, Rufio: my men at the barricade are between the sea party and the shore party. I have murdered them.

Rufio (coming back from the parapet to Cæsar's right hand) Ay: that comes of fooling with this girl here.

Apollodorus (coming up quickly from the causeway) Look over the parapet, Cæsar.

Cæsar. We have looked, my friend. We must defend ourselves here.

Apollodorus. I have thrown the ladder into the sea. They cannot get in without it.

Rufio. Ay; and we cannot get out. Have you thought of that?

Apollodorus. Not get out! Why not? You have ships in the east harbor.

Britannus (hopefully, at the parapet) The Rhodian galleys

are standing in towards us already. (*Cæsar quickly joins Britannus at the parapet*).

Rufio (*to Apollodorus, impatiently*) And by what road are we to walk to the galleys, pray?

Apollodorus (*with gay, defiant rhetoric*) By the road that leads everywhere—the diamond path of the sun and moon. Have you never seen the child's shadow play of The Broken Bridge? "Ducks and geese with ease get over"—eh? (*He throws away his cloak and cap, and binds his sword on his back*).

Rufio. What are you talking about?

Apollodorus. I will shew you. (*Calling to Britannus*) How far off is the nearest galley?

Britannus. Fifty fathom.

Cæsar. No, no: they are further off than they seem in this clear air to your British eyes. Nearly quarter of a mile, Apollodorus.

Apollodorus. Good. Defend yourselves here until I send you a boat from that galley.

Rufio. Have you wings, perhaps?

Apollodorus. Water wings, soldier. Behold!

He runs up the steps between Cæsar and Britannus to the coping of the parapet; springs into the air; and plunges head foremost into the sea.

Cæsar (*like a schoolboy—wildly excited*) Bravo, bravo! (*Throwing off his cloak*) By Jupiter, I will do that too.

Rufio (*seizing him*) You are mad. You shall not.

Cæsar. Why not? Can I not swim as well as he?

Rufio (*frantic*) Can an old fool dive and swim like a young one? He is twenty-five and you are fifty.

Cæsar (*breaking loose from Rufio*) Old!!!

Britannus (*shocked*) Rufio: you forget yourself.

Cæsar. I will race you to the galley for a week's pay, father Rufio.

Cleopatra. But me! me!!! me!!! what is to become of me?

Cæsar. I will carry you on my back to the galley like a

dolphin. Rufio: when you see me rise to the surface, throw her in: I will answer for her. And then in with you after her, both of you.

Cleopatra. No, no, NO. I shall be drowned.

Britannus. Cæsar: I am a man and a Briton, not a fish. I must have a boat. I cannot swim.

Cleopatra. Neither can I.

Cæsar (to Britannus) Stay here, then, alone, until I recapture the lighthouse: I will not forget you. Now, Rufio.

Rufio. You have made up your mind to this folly?

Cæsar. The Egyptians have made it up for me. What else is there to do? And mind where you jump: I do not want to get your fourteen stone in the small of my back as I come up. (He runs up the steps and stands on the coping).

Britannus (anxiously) One last word, Cæsar. Do not let yourself be seen in the fashionable part of Alexandria until you have changed your clothes.

Cæsar (calling over the sea) Ho, Apollodorus: (he points skyward and quotes the barcarolle)

The white upon the blue above—

Apollodorus (swimming in the distance)

Is purple on the green below—

Cæsar (exultantly) Aha! (He plunges into the sea).

Cleopatra (running excitedly to the steps) Oh, let me see. He will be drowned (Rufio seizes her)—Ah—ah—ah—ah! (He pitches her screaming into the sea. Rufio and Britannus roar with laughter).

Rufio (looking down after her) He has got her. (To Britannus) Hold the fort, Briton. Cæsar will not forget you. (He springs off).

Britannus (running to the steps to watch them as they swim) All safe, Rufio?

Rufio (swimming) All safe.

Cæsar (*swimming further off*) Take refuge up there by the beacon; and pile the fuel on the trap door, Britannus.

Britannus (*calling in reply*) I will first do so, and then commend myself to my country's gods. (*A sound of cheering from the sea. Britannus gives full vent to his excitement*). The boat has reached him: Hip, hip, hip, hurrah!

ACT IV

CLEOPATRA'S *sousing in the east harbor of Alexandria was in October 48 B.C. In March 47 she is passing the afternoon in her boudoir in the palace, among a bevy of her ladies, listening to a slave girl who is playing the harp in the middle of the room. The harpist's master, an old musician, with a lined face, prominent brows, white beard, moustache and eyebrows twisted and horned at the ends, and a consciously keen and pretentious expression, is squatting on the floor close to her on her right, watching her performance. Ftatateeta is in attendance near the door, in front of a group of female slaves. Except the harp player all are seated: Cleopatra in a chair opposite the door on the other side of the room; the rest on the ground. Cleopatra's ladies are all young, the most conspicuous being Charmian and Iras, her favorites. Charmian is a hatchet faced, terra cotta colored little goblin, swift in her movements, and neatly finished at the hands and feet. Iras is a plump, good-natured creature, rather fatuous, with a profusion of red hair, and a tendency to giggle on the slightest provocation.*

Cleopatra. Can I—

Ftatateeta (insolently, to the player) Peace, thou! The Queen speaks. (*The player stops*).

Cleopatra (to the old musician) I want to learn to play the harp with my own hands. Cæsar loves music. Can you teach me?

Musician. Assuredly I and no one else can teach the queen. Have I not discovered the lost method of the ancient Egyptians, who could make a pyramid tremble by touching a bass string? All the other teachers are quacks: I have exposed them repeatedly.

Cleopatra. Good: you shall teach me. How long will it take?

Musician. Not very long: only four years. Your Majesty must first become proficient in the philosophy of Pythagoras.

Cleopatra. Has she (*indicating the slave*) become proficient in the philosophy of Pythagoras?

Musician. Oh, she is but a slave. She learns as a dog learns.

Cleopatra. Well, then, I will learn as a dog learns; for she plays better than you. You shall give me a lesson every day for a fortnight. (*The musician hastily scrambles to his feet and bows profoundly*). After that, whenever I strike a false note you shall be flogged; and if I strike so many that there is not time to flog you, you shall be thrown into the Nile to feed the crocodiles. Give the girl a piece of gold; and send them away.

Musician (*much taken aback*) But true art will not be thus forced.

Ftatateeta (*pushing him out*) What is this? Answering the Queen, forsooth. Out with you.

He is pushed out by Ftatateeta, the girl following with her harp, amid the laughter of the ladies and slaves.

Cleopatra. Now, can any of you amuse me? Have you any stories or any news?

Iras. Ftatateeta—

Cleopatra. Oh, Ftatateeta, Ftatateeta, always Ftatateeta. Some new tale to set me against her.

Iras. No: this time Ftatateeta has been virtuous. (*All the ladies laugh—not the slaves*). Pothinus has been trying to bribe her to let him speak with you.

Cleopatra (*wrathfully*) Ha! you all sell audiences with me, as if I saw whom you please, and not whom I please. I should like to know how much of her gold piece that harp girl will have to give up before she leaves the palace.

Iras. We can easily find out that for you.

The ladies laugh.

Cleopatra (*frowning*) You laugh; but take care, take care. I will find out some day how to make myself served as Cæsar is served.

Charmian. Old hooknose! (*They laugh again*).

Cleopatra (*revolted*) Silence. Charmian: do not you be a silly little Egyptian fool. Do you know why I allow you all to chatter impertinently just as you please, instead of treating you as Ftatateeta would treat you if she were Queen?

Charmian. Because you try to imitate Cæsar in everything; and he lets everybody say what they please to him.

Cleopatra. No; but because I asked him one day why he did so; and he said "Let your women talk; and you will learn something from them." What have I to learn from them? I said. "What they are," said he; and oh! you should have seen his eye as he said it. You would have curled up, you shallow things. (*They laugh. She turns fiercely on Iras*). At whom are you laughing—at me or at Cæsar?

Iras. At Cæsar.

Cleopatra. If you were not a fool, you would laugh at me; and if you were not a coward you would not be afraid to tell me so. (*Ftatateeta returns*). Ftatateeta: they tell me that Pothinus has offered you a bribe to admit him to my presence.

Ftatateeta (*protesting*) Now by my father's gods—

Cleopatra (*cutting her short despotically*) Have I not told you not to deny things? You would spend the day calling your father's gods to witness to your virtues if I let you. Go take the bribe; and bring in Pothinus. (*Ftatateeta is about to reply*). Dont answer me. Go.

Ftatateeta goes out; and Cleopatra rises and begins to prowl to and fro between her chair and the door, meditating. All rise and stand.

Iras (*as she reluctantly rises*) Heigho! I wish Cæsar were back in Rome.

Cleopatra (*threateningly*) It will be a bad day for you all when he goes. Oh, if I were not ashamed to let him see that

I am as cruel at heart as my father, I would make you repent that speech! Why do you wish him away?

Charmian. He makes you so terribly prosy and serious and learned and philosophical. It is worse than being religious, at o u r ages. (*The ladies laugh*).

Cleopatra. Cease that endless cackling, will you. Hold your tongues.

Charmian (*with mock resignation*) Well, well: we must try to live up to Cæsar.

They laugh again. Cleopatra rages silently as she continues to prowl to and fro. Ftatateeta comes back with Pothinus, who halts on the threshold.

Ftatateeta (*at the door*) Pothinus craves the ear of the—

Cleopatra. There, there: that will do: let him come in. (*She resumes her seat. All sit down except Pothinus, who advances to the middle of the room. Ftatateeta takes her former place*). Well, Pothinus: what is the latest news from your rebel friends?

Pothinus (*haughtily*) I am no friend of rebellion. And a prisoner does not receive news.

Cleopatra. You are no more a prisoner than I am—than Cæsar is. These six months we have been besieged in this palace by my subjects. You are allowed to walk on the beach among the soldiers. Can I go further myself, or can Cæsar?

Pothinus. You are but a child, Cleopatra, and do not understand these matters.

The ladies laugh. Cleopatra looks inscrutably at him.

Charmian. I see you do not know the latest news, Pothinus.

Pothinus. What is that?

Charmian. That Cleopatra is no longer a child. Shall I tell you how to grow much older, and much, m u c h wiser in one day?

Pothinus. I should prefer to grow wiser without growing older.

Charmian. Well, go up to the top of the lighthouse; and

get somebody to take you by the hair and throw you into the sea. (*The ladies laugh*).

Cleopatra. She is right, Pothinus: you will come to the shore with much conceit washed out of you. (*The ladies laugh. Cleopatra rises impatiently*). Begone, all of you. I will speak with Pothinus alone. Drive them out, Ftatateeta. (*They run out laughing. Ftatateeta shuts the door on them*). What are you waiting for?

Ftatateeta. It is not meet that the Queen remain alone with—

Cleopatra (*interrupting her*) Ftatateeta: must I sacrifice you to your father's gods to teach you that I am Queen of Egypt, and not you?

Ftatateeta (*indignantly*) You are like the rest of them. You want to be what these Romans call a New Woman. (*She goes out, banging the door*).

Cleopatra (*sitting down again*) Now, Pothinus: why did you bribe Ftatateeta to bring you hither?

Pothinus (*studying her gravely*) Cleopatra: what they tell me is true. You are changed.

Cleopatra. Do you speak with Cæsar every day for six months: and you will be changed.

Pothinus. It is the common talk that you are infatuated with this old man.

Cleopatra. Infatuated? What does that mean? Made foolish, is it not? Oh no: I wish I were.

Pothinus. You wish you were made foolish! How so?

Cleopatra. When I was foolish, I did what I liked, except when Ftatateeta beat me; and even then I cheated her and did it by stealth. Now that Cæsar has made me wise, it is no use my liking or disliking: I do what must be done, and have no time to attend to myself. That is not happiness; but it is greatness. If Cæsar were gone, I think I could govern the Egyptians; for what Cæsar is to me, I am to the fools around me.

Pothinus (*looking hard at her*) Cleopatra: this may be the vanity of youth.

Cleopatra. No, no: it is not that I am so clever, but that the others are so stupid.

Pothinus (*musingly*) Truly, that is the great secret.

Cleopatra. Well, now tell me what you came to say?

Pothinus (*embarrassed*) I! Nothing.

Cleopatra. Nothing!

Pothinus. At least—to beg for my liberty: that is all.

Cleopatra. For that you would have knelt to Cæsar. No, Pothinus: you came with some plan that depended on Cleopatra being a little nursery kitten. Now that Cleopatra is a Queen, the plan is upset.

Pothinus (*bowing his head submissively*) It is so.

Cleopatra (*exultant*) Aha!

Pothinus (*raising his eyes keenly to hers*) Is Cleopatra then indeed a Queen, and no longer Cæsar's prisoner and slave?

Cleopatra. Pothinus: we are all Cæsar's slaves—all we in this land of Egypt—whether we will or no. And she who is wise enough to know this will reign when Cæsar departs.

Pothinus. You harp on Cæsar's departure.

Cleopatra. What if I do?

Pothinus. Does he not love you?

Cleopatra. Love me! Pothinus: Cæsar loves no one. Who are those we love? Only those whom we do not hate: all people are strangers and enemies to us except those we love. But it is not so with Cæsar. He has no hatred in him: he makes friends with everyone as he does with dogs and children. His kindness to me is a wonder: neither mother, father, nor nurse have ever taken so much care for me, or thrown open their thoughts to me so freely.

Pothinus. Well: is not this love?

Cleopatra. What! when he will do as much for the first girl he meets on his way back to Rome? Ask his slave, Britannus: he has been just as good to him. Nay, ask his very horse!

His kindness is not for anything in me: it is in his own nature.

Pothinus. But how can you be sure that he does not love you as men love women?

Cleopatra. Because I cannot make him jealous. I have tried.

Pothinus. Hm! Perhaps I should have asked, then, do y o u love h i m?

Cleopatra. Can one love a god? Besides, I love another Roman: one whom I saw long before Cæsar—no god, but a man —one who can love and hate—one whom I can hurt and who would hurt me.

Pothinus. Does Cæsar know this?

Cleopatra. Yes.

Pothinus. And he is not angry?

Cleopatra. He promises to send him to Egypt to please me!

Pothinus. I do not understand this man.

Cleopatra (with superb contempt) Y o u understand Cæsar! How could you? (*Proudly*) I do—by instinct.

Pothinus (deferentially, after a moment's thought) Your Majesty caused me to be admitted to-day. What message has the Queen for me?

Cleopatra. This. You think that by making my brother king, you will rule in Egypt, because you are his guardian and he is a little silly.

Pothinus. The Queen is pleased to say so.

Cleopatra. The Queen is pleased to say this also. That Cæsar will eat up you, and Achillas, and my brother, as a cat eats up mice; and that he will put on this land of Egypt as a shepherd puts on his garment. And when he has done that, he will return to Rome, and leave Cleopatra here as his viceroy.

Pothinus (breaking out wrathfully) That he shall never do. We have a thousand men to his ten; and we will drive him and his beggarly legions into the sea.

Cleopatra (with scorn, getting up to go) You rant like any common fellow. Go, then, and marshal your thousands; and make haste; for Mithridates of Pergamos is at hand with re inforcements for Cæsar. Cæsar has held you at bay with two legions: we shall see what he will do with twenty.

Pothinus. Cleopatra—

Cleopatra. Enough, enough: Cæsar has spoiled me for talking to weak things like you. (*She goes out. Pothinus, with a gesture of rage, is following, when Ftatateeta enters and stops him*).

Pothinus. Let me go forth from this hateful place.

Ftatateeta. What angers you?

Pothinus. The curse of all the gods of Egypt be upon her! She has sold her country to the Roman, that she may buy it back from him with her kisses.

Ftatateeta. Fool: did she not tell you that she would have Cæsar gone?

Pothinus. You listened?

Ftatateeta. I took care that some honest woman should be at hand whilst you were with her.

Pothinus. Now by the gods—

Ftatateeta. Enough of your gods! Cæsar's gods are all powerful here. It is no use y o u coming to Cleopatra: you are only an Egyptian. She will not listen to any of her own race: she treats us all as children.

Pothinus. May she perish for it!

Ftatateeta (*balefully*) May your tongue wither for that wish! Go! send for Lucius Septimius, the slayer of Pompey. He is a Roman: may be she will listen to him. Begone!

Pothinus (*darkly*) I know to whom I must go now.

Ftatateeta (*suspiciously*) To whom, then?

Pothinus. To a greater Roman than Lucius. And mark this, mistress. You thought, before Cæsar came, that Egypt should presently be ruled by you and your crew in the name of Cleopatra. I set myself against it—

Ftatateeta (*interrupting him—wrangling*) Ay; that it might be ruled by you and y o u r crew in the name of Ptolemy.

Pothinus. Better me, or even you, than a woman with a Roman heart; and that is what Cleopatra is now become. Whilst I live, she shall never rule. So guide yourself accordingly. (*He goes out*).

It is by this time drawing on to dinner time. The table is laid on the roof of the palace; and thither Rufio is now climbing, ushered by a majestic palace official, wand of office in hand, and followed by a slave carrying an inlaid stool. After many stairs they emerge at last into a massive colonnade on the roof. Light curtains are drawn between the columns on the north and east to soften the westering sun. The official leads Rufio to one of these shaded sections. A cord for pulling the curtains apart hangs down between the pillars.

The Official (*bowing*) The Roman commander will await Cæsar here.

The slave sets down the stool near the southernmost column, and slips out through the curtains.

Rufio (*sitting down, a little blown*) Pouf! That was a climb. How high have we come?

The Official. We are on the palace roof, O Beloved of Victory!

Rufio. Good! the Beloved of Victory has no more stairs to get up.

A second official enters from the opposite end, walking backwards.

The Second Official. Cæsar approaches.

Cæsar, fresh from the bath, clad in a new tunic of purple silk, comes in, beaming and festive, followed by two slaves carrying a light couch, which is hardly more than an elaborately designed bench. They place it near the northmost of the two curtained columns. When this is done they slip out through the curtains; and the two officials, formally bowing, follow them. Rufio rises to receive Cæsar.

Cæsar (*coming over to him*) Why, Rufio! (*Surveying his dress with an air of admiring astonishment*) A new baldrick! A new golden pommel to your sword! And you have had your hair cut. But not your beard—? impossible! (*He sniffs at Rufio's beard*). Yes, perfumed, by Jupiter Olympus!

Rufio (*growling*) Well: is it to please myself?

Cæsar (*affectionately*) No, my son Rufio, but to please me -to celebrate my birthday.

Rufio (*contemptuously*) Your birthday! You always have a birthday when there is a pretty girl to be flattered or an ambassador to be conciliated. We had seven of them in ten months last year.

Cæsar (*contritely*) It is true, Rufio! I shall never break myself of these petty deceits.

Rufio. Who is to dine with us—besides Cleopatra?

Cæsar. Apollodorus the Sicilian.

Rufio. That popinjay!

Cæsar. Come! the popinjay is an amusing dog—tells a story; sings a song; and saves us the trouble of flattering the Queen. What does she care for old politicians and camp-fed bears like us? No: Apollodorus is good company, Rufio, good company.

Rufio. Well, he can swim a bit and fence a bit: he might be worse, if he only knew how to hold his tongue.

Cæsar. The gods forbid he should ever learn! Oh, this military life! this tedious, brutal life of action! That is the worst of us Romans: we are mere doers and drudgers: a swarm of bees turned into men. Give me a good talker—one with wit and imagination enough to live without continually doing something!

Rufio. Ay! a nice time he would have of it with you when dinner was over! Have you noticed that I am before my time?

Cæsar. Aha! I thought that meant something. What is it?

Rufio. Can we be overheard here?

Cæsar. Our privacy invites eavesdropping. I can remedy that. (*He claps his hands twice. The curtains are drawn, revealing the roof garden with a banqueting table set across in the middle for four persons, one at each end, and two side by* side. The side next Cæsar and Rufio is blocked with golden wine vessels and basins. A gorgeous major-domo is superintending the laying of the table by a staff of slaves. The colonnade goes round the garden at both sides to the further end, where a gap in it, like a great gateway, leaves the view open to the sky beyond the western edge of the roof, except in the middle, where a life size image of Ra, seated on a huge plinth, towers up, with hawk head and crown of asp and disk. His altar, which stands at his feet, is a single white stone). Now everybody can see us, nobody will think of listening to us. (He sits down on the bench left by the two slaves).

Rufio (sitting down on his stool) Pothinus wants to speak to you. I advise you to see him: there is some plotting going on here among the women.

Cæsar. Who is Pothinus?

Rufio. The fellow with hair like squirrel's fur—the little King's bear leader, whom you kept prisoner.

Cæsar (annoyed) And has he not escaped?

Rufio. No.

Cæsar (rising imperiously) Why not? You have been guarding this man instead of watching the enemy. Have I not told you always to let prisoners escape unless there are special orders to the contrary? Are there not enough mouths to be fed without him?

Rufio. Yes; and if you would have a little sense and let me cut his throat, you would save his rations. Anyhow, he w o n t escape. Three sentries have told him they would put a pilum through him if they saw him again. What more can they do? He prefers to stay and spy on us. So would I if I had to do with generals subject to fits of clemency.

Cæsar (resuming his seat, argued down) Hm! And so he wants to see me.

Rufio. Ay. I have brought him with me. He is waiting there (jerking his thumb over his shoulder) under guard.

Cæsar. And you want me to see him?

Rufio (*obstinately*) I dont want anything. I daresay you will do what you like. Dont put it on to me.

Cæsar (*with an air of doing it expressly to indulge Rufio*) Well, well: let us have him.

Rufio (*calling*) Ho there, guard! Release your man and send him up. (*Beckoning*). Come along!

Pothinus enters and stops mistrustfully between the two, looking from one to the other.

Cæsar (*graciously*) Ah, Pothinus! You are welcome. And what is the news this afternoon?

Pothinus. Cæsar: I come to warn you of a danger, and to make you an offer.

Cæsar. Never mind the danger. Make the offer.

Rufio. Never mind the offer. Whats the danger?

Pothinus. Cæsar: you think that Cleopatra is devoted to you.

Cæsar (*gravely*) My friend: I already know what I think. Come to your offer.

Pothinus. I will deal plainly. I know not by what strange gods you have been enabled to defend a palace and a few yards of beach against a city and an army. Since we cut you off from Lake Mareotis, and you dug wells in the salt sea sand and brought up buckets of fresh water from them, we have known that your gods are irresistible, and that you are a worker of miracles. I no longer threaten you—

Rufio (*sarcastically*) Very handsome of you, indeed.

Pothinus. So be it: you are the master. Our gods sent the north west winds to keep you in our hands; but you have been too strong for them.

Cæsar (*gently urging him to come to the point*) Yes, yes, my friend. But what then?

Rufio. Spit it out, man. What have you to say?

Pothinus. I have to say that you have a traitress in your camp. Cleopatra—

The Major-Domo (at the table, announcing) The Queen!
(Cæsar and Rufio rise).

Rufio (aside to Pothinus) You should have spat it out sooner,
you fool. Now it is too late.

*Cleopatra, in gorgeous raiment, enters in state through the
gap in the colonnade, and comes down past the image of Ra
and past the table to Cæsar. Her retinue, headed by Ftatateeta,
joins the staff at the table. Cæsar gives Cleopatra his seat,
which she takes.*

Cleopatra (quickly, seeing Pothinus) What is h e doing
here?

*Cæsar (seating himself beside her, in the most amiable of
tempers)* Just going to tell me something about you. You
shall hear it. Proceed, Pothinus.

Pothinus (disconcerted) Cæsar—(*he stammers*).

Cæsar. Well, out with it.

Pothinus. What I have to say is for your ear, not for the
Queen's.

Cleopatra (with subdued ferocity) There are means of
making you speak. Take care.

Pothinus (defiantly) Cæsar does not employ those means.

Cæsar. My friend: when a man has anything to tell in
this world, the difficulty is not to make him tell it, but to
prevent him from telling it too often. Let me celebrate my
birthday by setting you free. Farewell: we shall not meet again.

Cleopatra (angrily) Cæsar: this mercy is foolish.

Pothinus (to Cæsar) Will you not give me a private audience? Your life may depend on it. *(Cæsar rises loftily).*

Rufio (aside to Pothinus) Ass! Now we shall have some
heroics.

Cæsar (oratorically) Pothinus—

Rufio (interrupting him) Cæsar: the dinner will spoil if
you begin preaching your favorite sermon about life and death.

Cleopatra (priggishly) Peace, Rufio. I desire to hear Cæsar.

Rufio (*bluntly*) Your Majesty has heard it before. You repeated it to Apollodorus last week; and he thought it was all your own. (*Cæsar's dignity collapses. Much tickled, he sits down again and looks roguishly at Cleopatra, who is furious. Rufio calls as before*) Ho there, guard! Pass the prisoner out. He is released. (*To Pothinus*) Now off with you. You have lost your chance.

Pothinus (*his temper overcoming his prudence*) I will speak.

Cæsar (*to Cleopatra*) You see. Torture would not have wrung a word from him.

Pothinus. Cæsar: you have taught Cleopatra the arts by which the Romans govern the world.

Cæsar. Alas! they cannot even govern themselves. What then?

Pothinus. What then? Are you so besotted with her beauty that you do not see that she is impatient to reign in Egypt alone, and that her heart is set on your departure?

Cleopatra (*rising*) Liar!

Cæsar (*shocked*) What! Protestations! Contradictions!

Cleopatra (*ashamed, but trembling with suppressed rage*) No. I do not deign to contradict. Let him talk. (*She sits down again*).

Pothinus. From her own lips I have heard it. You are to be her catspaw: you are to tear the crown from her brother's head and set it on her own, delivering us all into her hand—delivering yourself also. And then Cæsar can return to Rome, or depart through the gate of death, which is nearer and surer.

Cæsar (*calmly*) Well, my friend; and is not this very natural?

Pothinus (*astonished*) Natural! Then you do not resent treachery?

Cæsar. Resent! O thou foolish Egyptian, what have I to do with resentment? Do I resent the wind when it chills me, or the night when it makes me stumble in the darkness? Shall

I resent youth when it turns from age, and ambition when it turns from servitude? To tell me such a story as this is but to tell me that the sun will rise to-morrow.

Cleopatra (*unable to contain herself*) But it is false—false. I swear it.

Cæsar. It is true, though you swore it a thousand times, and believed all you swore. (*She is convulsed with emotion. To screen her, he rises and takes Pothinus to Rufio, saying*) Come, Rufio: let us see Pothinus past the guard. I have a word to say to him. (*Aside to them*) We must give the Queen a moment to recover herself. (*Aloud*) Come. (*He takes Pothinus and Rufio out with him, conversing with them meanwhile*). Tell your friends, Pothinus, that they must not think I am opposed to a reasonable settlement of the country's affairs— (*They pass out of hearing*).

Cleopatra (*in a stifled whisper*) Ftatateeta, Ftatateeta.

Ftatateeta (*hurrying to her from the table and petting her*) Peace, child: be comforted—

Cleopatra (*interrupting her*) Can they hear us?

Ftatateeta. No, dear heart, no.

Cleopatra. Listen to me. If he leaves the Palace alive, never see my face again.

Ftatateeta. He? Poth—

Cleopatra (*striking her on the mouth*) Strike his life out as I strike his name from your lips. Dash him down from the wall. Break him on the stones. Kill, kill, kill him.

Ftatateeta (*shewing all her teeth*) The dog shall perish.

Cleopatra. Fail in this, and you go out from before me for ever.

Ftatateeta (*resolutely*) So be it. You shall not see my face until his eyes are darkened.

Cæsar comes back, with Apollodorus, exquisitely dressed, and Rufio.

Cleopatra (*to Ftatateeta*) Come soon—soon. (*Ftatateeta turns her meaning eyes for a moment on her mistress; then goes grimly away past Ra and out. Cleopatra runs like a gazelle to Cæsar)* So you have come back to me, Cæsar. *(Caressingly)* I thought you were angry. Welcome, Apollodorus. *(She gives him her hand to kiss, with her other arm about Cæsar).*

Apollodorus. Cleopatra grows more womanly beautiful from week to week.

Cleopatra. Truth, Apollodorus?

Apollodorus. Far, far short of the truth! Friend Rufio threw a pearl into the sea: Cæsar fished up a diamond.

Cæsar. Cæsar fished up a touch of rheumatism, my friend. Come: to dinner! to dinner! *(They move towards the table).*

Cleopatra (skipping like a young fawn) Yes, to dinner. I have ordered s u c h a dinner for you, Cæsar!

Cæsar. Ay? What are we to have?

Cleopatra. Peacocks' brains.

Cæsar (as if his mouth watered) Peacocks' brains, Apollodorus!

Apollodorus. Not for me. I prefer nightingales' tongues. *(He goes to one of the two covers set side by side).*

Cleopatra. Roast boar, Rufio!

Rufio (gluttonously) Good! *(He goes to the seat next Apollodorus, on his left).*

Cæsar (looking at his seat, which is at the end of the table, to Ra's left hand) What has become of my leathern cushion?

Cleopatra (at the opposite end) I have got new ones for you.

The Major-Domo. These cushions, Cæsar, are of Maltese gauze, stuffed with rose leaves.

Cæsar. Rose leaves! Am I a caterpillar? *(He throws the cushions away and seats himself on the leather mattress underneath).*

Cleopatra. What a shame! My new cushions!

The Major-Domo (at Cæsar's elbow) What shall we serve to whet Cæsar's appetite?

Cæsar. What have you got?

The Major-Domo. Sea hedgehogs, black and white sea acorns, sea nettles, beccaficoes, purple shellfish—

Cæsar. Any oysters?

The Major-Domo. Assuredly.

Cæsar. B r i t i s h oysters?

The Major-Domo (assenting) British oysters, Cæsar.

Cæsar. Oysters, then. (*The Major-Domo signs to a slave at each order; and the slave goes out to execute it*). I have been in Britain—that western land of romance—the last piece of earth on the edge of the ocean that surrounds the world. I went there in search of its famous pearls. The British pearl was a fable; but in searching for it I found the British oyster.

Apollodorus. All posterity will bless you for it. (*To the Major-Domo*) Sea hedgehogs for me.

Rufio. Is there nothing solid to begin with?

The Major-Domo. Fieldfares with asparagus—

Cleopatra (interrupting) Fattened fowls! have some fattened fowls, Rufio.

Rufio. Ay, that will do.

Cleopatra (greedily) Fieldfares for me.

The Major-Domo. Cæsar will deign to choose his wine? Sicilian, Lesbian, Chian—

Rufio (contemptuously) All Greek.

Apollodorus. Who would drink Roman wine when he could get Greek? Try the Lesbian, Cæsar.

Cæsar. Bring me my barley water.

Rufio (with intense disgust) Ugh! Bring me my Falernian (*The Falernian is presently brought to him*).

Cleopatra (pouting) It is waste of time giving you dinners, Cæsar. My scullions would not condescend to your diet.

Cæsar (relenting) Well, well: let us try the Lesbian. (*The Major-Domo fills Cæsar's goblet; then Cleopatra's and Apollodorus's*). But when I return to Rome, I will make laws against these extravagances. I will even get the laws carried out.

Cleopatra (*coaxingly*) Never mind. To-day you are to be like other people: idle, luxurious, and kind. (*She stretches her hand to him along the table*).

Cæsar. Well, for once I will sacrifice my comfort—(*kissing her hand*) there! (*He takes a draught of wine*). Now are you satisfied?

Cleopatra. And you no longer believe that I long for your departure for Rome?

Cæsar. I no longer believe anything. My brains are asleep. Besides, who knows whether I shall return to Rome?

Rufio (*alarmed*) How? Eh? What?

Cæsar. What has Rome to shew me that I have not seen already? One year of Rome is like another, except that I grow older, whilst the crowd in the Appian Way is always the same age.

Apollodorus. It is no better here in Egypt. The old men, when they are tired of life, say "We have seen everything except the source of the Nile."

Cæsar (*his imagination catching fire*) And why not see that? Cleopatra: will you come with me and track the flood to its cradle in the heart of the regions of mystery? Shall we leave Rome behind us—Rome, that has achieved greatness only to learn how greatness destroys nations of men who are not great! Shall I make you a new kingdom, and build you a holy city there in the great unknown?

Cleopatra (*rapturously*) Yes, yes. You shall.

Rufio. Ay: now he will conquer Africa with two legions before we come to the roast boar.

Apollodorus. Come: no scoffing. This is a noble scheme: in it Cæsar is no longer merely the conquering soldier, but the creative poet-artist. Let us name the holy city, and consecrate it with Lesbian wine.

Cæsar. Cleopatra shall name it herself.

Cleopatra. It shall be called Cæsar's Gift to his Beloved.

Apollodorus. No, no. Something vaster than that—something universal, like the starry firmament.

Cæsar (*prosaically*) Why not simply The Cradle of the Nile?

Cleopatra. No: the Nile is my ancestor; and he is a god. Oh! I have thought of something. The Nile shall name it himself. Let us call upon him. (*To the Major-Domo*) Send for him. (*The three men stare at one another; but the Major-Domo goes out as if he had received the most matter-of-fact order*). And (*to the retinue*) away with you all.

The retinue withdraws, making obeisance.

A priest enters, carrying a miniature sphinx with a tiny tripod before it. A morsel of incense is smoking in the tripod. The priest comes to the table and places the image in the middle of it. The light begins to change to the magenta purple of the Egyptian sunset, as if the god had brought a strange colored shadow with him. The three men are determined not to be impressed; but they feel curious in spite of themselves.

Cæsar. What hocus-pocus is this?

Cleopatra. You shall see. And it is n o t hocus-pocus. To do it properly, we should kill something to please him; but perhaps he will answer Cæsar without that if we spill some wine to him.

Apollodorus (*turning his head to look up over his shoulder at Ra*) Why not appeal to our hawkheaded friend here?

Cleopatra (*nervously*) Sh! He will hear you and be angry.

Rufio (*phlegmatically*) The source of the Nile is out of his district, I expect.

Cleopatra. No: I will have my city named by nobody but my dear little sphinx, because it was in its arms that Cæsar found me asleep. (*She languishes at Cæsar then turns curtly to the priest*). Go. I am a priestess, and have power to take your charge from you. (*The priest makes a reverence and goes out*). Now let us call on the Nile all together. Perhaps he will rap on the table.

Cæsar. What! table rapping! Are such superstitions still believed in this year 707 of the Republic?

Cleopatra. It is no superstition: our priests learn lots of things from the tables. Is it not so, Apollodorus?

Apollodorus. Yes: I profess myself a converted man. When Cleopatra is priestess, Apollodorus is devotee. Propose the conjuration.

Cleopatra. You must say with me "Send us thy voice, Father Nile."

All Four (*holding their glasses together before the idol*) Send us thy voice, Father Nile.

The death cry of a man in mortal terror and agony answers them. Appalled, the men set down their glasses, and listen. Silence. The purple deepens in the sky. Cæsar, glancing at Cleopatra, catches her pouring out her wine before the god, with gleaming eyes, and mute assurances of gratitude and worship. Apollodorus springs up and runs to the edge of the roof to peer down and listen.

Cæsar (*looking piercingly at Cleopatra*) What was that?

Cleopatra (*petulantly*) Nothing. They are beating some slave.

Cæsar. Nothing.

Rufio. A man with a knife in him, I'll swear.

Cæsar (*rising*) A murder!

Apollodorus (*at the back, waving his hand for silence*) S-sh! Silence. Did you hear that?

Cæsar. Another cry?

Apollodorus (*returning to the table*) No, a thud. Something fell on the beach, I think.

Rufio (*grimly, as he rises*) Something with bones in it, eh?

Cæsar (*shuddering*) Hush, hush, Rufio. (*He leaves the table and returns to the colonnade: Rufio following at his left elbow, and Apollodorus at the other side*).

Cleopatra (*still in her place at the table*) Will you leave me, Cæsar? Apollodorus: are you going?

Apollodorus. Faith, dearest Queen, my appetite is gone.

Cæsar. Go down to the courtyard, Apollodorus; and find out what has happened.

Apollodorus nods and goes out, making for the staircase by which Rufio ascended.

Cleopatra. Your soldiers have killed somebody, perhaps. What does it matter?

The murmur of a crowd rises from the beach below. Cæsar and Rufio look at one another.

Cæsar. This must be seen to. (*He is about to follow Apollodorus when Rufio stops him with a hand on his arm as Ftatateeta comes back by the far end of the roof, with dragging steps, a drowsy satiety in her eyes and in the corners of the bloodhound lips. For a moment Cæsar suspects that she is drunk with wine. Not so Rufio: he knows well the red vintage that has inebriated her*).

Rufio (*in a low tone*) There is some mischief between those two.

Ftatateeta. The Queen looks again on the face of her servant.

Cleopatra looks at her for a moment with an exultant reflection of her murderous expression. Then she flings her arms round her; kisses her repeatedly and savagely; and tears off her jewels and heaps them on her. The two men turn from the spectacle to look at one another. Ftatateeta drags herself sleepily to the altar; kneels before Ra; and remains there in prayer. Cæsar goes to Cleopatra, leaving Rufio in the colonnade.

Cæsar (*with searching earnestness*) Cleopatra: what has happened?

Cleopatra (*in mortal dread of him, but with her utmost cajolery*) Nothing, dearest Cæsar. (*With sickly sweetness, her voice almost failing*) Nothing. I am innocent. (*She approaches him affectionately*). Dear Cæsar: are you angry with me?

Why do you look at me so? I have been here with you all the time. How can I know what has happened?

Cæsar (reflectively) That is true.

Cleopatra (greatly relieved, trying to caress him) Of course it is true. (*He does not respond to the caress*) You know it is true, Rufio.

The murmur without suddenly swells to a roar and subsides.

Rufio. I shall know presently (*He makes for the altar in the burly trot that serves him for a stride, and touches Ftatateeta on the shoulder*). Now, mistress: I shall want you. (*He orders her, with a gesture, to go before him*).

Ftatateeta (rising and glowering at him) My place is with the Queen.

Cleopatra. She has done no harm, Rufio.

Cæsar (to Rufio) Let her stay.

Rufio (sitting down on the altar) Very well. Then my place is here too; and you can see what is the matter for yourself. The city is in a pretty uproar, it seems.

Cæsar (with grave displeasure) Rufio: there is a time for obedience.

Rufio. And there is a time for obstinacy. (*He folds his arms doggedly*).

Cæsar (to Cleopatra) Send her away.

Cleopatra (whining in her eagerness to propitiate him) Yes, I will. I will do whatever you ask me, Cæsar, always, because I love you. Ftatateeta: go away.

Ftatateeta. The Queen's word is my will. I shall be at hand for the Queen's call. (*She goes out past Ra, as she came*).

Rufio (following her) Remember, Cæsar, your bodyguard also is within call. (*He follows her out*).

Cleopatra, presuming upon Cæsar's submission to Rufio, leaves the table and sits down on the bench in the colonnade.

Cleopatra. Why do you allow Rufio to treat you so? You should teach him his place.

Cæsar. Teach him to be my enemy, and to hide his thoughts from me as you are now hiding yours.

Cleopatra (*her fears returning*) Why do you say that, Cæsar? Indeed, indeed, I am not hiding anything. You are wrong to treat me like this. (*She stifles a sob*). I am only a child; and you turn into stone because you think some one has been killed. I cannot bear it. (*She purposely breaks down and weeps. He looks at her with profound sadness and complete coldness. She looks up to see what effect she is producing. Seeing that he is unmoved, she sits up, pretending to struggle with her emotion and to put it bravely away*). But there: I know you hate tears: you shall not be troubled with them. I know you are not angry, but only sad; only I am so silly, I cannot help being hurt when you speak coldly. Of course you are quite right: it is dreadful to think of anyone being killed or even hurt; and I hope nothing really serious has—(*her voice dies away under his contemptuous penetration*).

Cæsar. What has frightened you into this? What have you done? (*A trumpet sounds on the beach below*). Aha! that sounds like the answer.

Cleopatra (*sinking back trembling on the bench and covering her face with her hands*) I have not betrayed you, Cæsar: I swear it.

Cæsar. I know that. I have not trusted you. (*He turns from her, and is about to go out when Apollodorus and Britannus drag in Lucius Septimius to him. Rufio follows. Cæsar shudders*). Again, Pompey's murderer!

Rufio. The town has gone mad, I think. They are for tearing the palace down and driving us into the sea straight away. We laid hold of this renegade in clearing them out of the courtyard.

Cæsar. Release him. (*They let go his arms*). What has offended the citizens, Lucius Septimius?

Lucius. What did you expect, Cæsar? Pothinus was a favorite of theirs.

Cæsar. What has happened to Pothinus? I set him free, here, not half an hour ago. Did they not pass him out?

Lucius. Ay, through the gallery arch sixty feet above ground, with three inches of steel in his ribs. He is as dead as Pompey. We are quits now, as to killing—you and I.

Cæsar (shocked) Assassinated!—our prisoner, our guest! (*He turns reproachfully on Rufio*) Rufio—

Rufio (emphatically—anticipating the question) Whoever did it was a wise man and a friend of yours (*Cleopatra is greatly emboldened*); but none of u s had a hand in it. So it is no use to frown at me. (*Cæsar turns and looks at Cleopatra*).

Cleopatra (violently—rising) He was slain by order of the Queen of Egypt. I am not Julius Cæsar the dreamer, who allows every slave to insult him. Rufio has said I did well: now the others shall judge me too. (*She turns to the others*). This Pothinus sought to make me conspire with him to betray Cæsar to Achillas and Ptolemy. I refused; and he cursed me and came privily to Cæsar to accuse me of his own treachery. I caught him in the act; and he insulted me—m e , the Queen! to my face. Cæsar would not avenge me: he spoke him fair and set him free. Was I right to avenge myself? Speak, Lucius.

Lucius. I do not gainsay it. But you will get little thanks from Cæsar for it.

Cleopatra. Speak, Apollodorus. Was I wrong?

Apollodorus. I have only one word of blame, most beautiful. You should have called upon me, your knight; and in fair duel I should have slain the slanderer.

Cleopatra (passionately) I will be judged by your very slave, Cæsar. Britannus: speak. Was I wrong?

Britannus. Were treachery, falsehood, and disloyalty left unpunished, society must become like an arena full of wild beasts, tearing one another to pieces. Cæsar is in the wrong.

Cæsar (with quiet bitterness) And so the verdict is against me, it seems.

Cleopatra (*vehemently*) Listen to me, Cæsar. If one man in all Alexandria can be found to say that I did wrong, I swear to have myself crucified on the door of the palace by my own slaves.

Cæsar. If one man in all the world can be found, now or forever, to k n o w that you did wrong, that man will have either to conquer the world as I have, or be crucified by it. (*The uproar in the streets again reaches them*). Do you hear? These knockers at your gate are also believers in vengeance and in stabbing. You have slain their leader: it is right that they shall slay you. If you doubt it, ask your four counsellors here. And then in the name of that right (*he emphasizes the word with great scorn*) shall I not slay them for murdering their Queen, and be slain in my turn by their countrymen as the invader of their fatherland? Can Rome do less then than slay these slayers, too, to shew the world how Rome avenges her sons and her honor? And so, to the end of history, murder shall breed murder, always in the name of right and honor and peace, until the gods are tired of blood and create a race that can understand. (*Fierce uproar. Cleopatra becomes white with terror*). Hearken, you who must not be insulted. Go near enough to catch their words: you will find them bitterer than the tongue of Pothinus. (*Loftily, wrapping himself up in an impenetrable dignity*) Let the Queen of Egypt now give her orders for vengeance, and take her measures for defence; for she has renounced Cæsar. (*He turns to go*).

Cleopatra (*terrified, running to him and falling on her knees*) You will not desert me, Cæsar. You will defend the palace.

Cæsar. You have taken the powers of life and death upon you. I am only a dreamer.

Cleopatra. But they will kill me.

Cæsar. And why not?

Cleopatra. In pity—

Cæsar. Pity! What! has it come to this so suddenly, that nothing can save you now but pity? Did it save Pothinus?

She rises, wringing her hands, and goes back to the bench in despair. Apollodorus shews his sympathy with her by quietly posting himself behind the bench. The sky has by this time become the most vivid purple, and soon begins to change to a glowing pale orange, against which the colonnade and the great image shew darklier and darklier.

Rufio. Cæsar: enough of preaching. The enemy is at the gate.

Cæsar (turning on him and giving way to his wrath) Ay; and what has held him baffled at the gate all these months? Was it my folly, as you deem it, or your wisdom? In this Egyptian Red Sea of blood, whose hand has held all your heads above the waves? *(Turning on Cleopatra)* And yet, when Cæsar says to such an one, "Friend, go free," you, clinging for your little life to my sword, dare steal out and stab him in the back? And you, soldiers and gentlemen, and honest servants as you forget that you are, applaud this assassination, and say "Cæsar is in the wrong." By the gods, I am tempted to open my hand and let you all sink into the flood.

Cleopatra (with a ray of cunning hope) But, Cæsar, if you do, you will perish yourself.

Cæsar's eyes blaze.

Rufio (greatly alarmed) Now, by great Jove, you filthy little Egyptian rat, that is the very word to make him walk out alone into the city and leave us here to be cut to pieces. *(Desperately, to Cæsar)* Will you desert us because we are a parcel of fools? I mean no harm by killing: I do it as a dog kills a cat, by instinct. We are all dogs at your heels; but we have served you faithfully.

Cæsar (relenting) Alas, Rufio, my son, my son: as dogs we are like to perish now in the streets.

Apollodorus (at his post behind Cleopatra's seat) Cæsar: what you say has an Olympian ring in it: it must be right; for it is fine art. But I am still on the side of Cleopatra. If we must die, she shall not want the devotion of a man's heart nor the strength of a man's arm.

Cleopatra (*sobbing*) But I dont want to die.

Cæsar (*sadly*) Oh, ignoble, ignoble!

Lucius (*coming forward between Cæsar and Cleopatra*) Hearken to me, Cæsar. It may be ignoble; but I also mean to live as long as I can.

Cæsar. Well, my friend, you are likely to outlive Cæsar. Is it any magic of mine, think you, that has kept your army and this whole city at bay for so long? Yesterday, what quarrel had they with me that they should risk their lives against me? But today we have flung them down their hero, murdered; and now every man of them is set upon clearing out this nest of assassins—for such we are and no more. Take courage then; and sharpen your sword. Pompey's head has fallen; and Cæsar's head is ripe.

Apollodorus. Does Cæsar despair?

Cæsar (*with infinite pride*) He who has never hoped can never despair. Cæsar, in good or bad fortune, looks his fate in the face.

Lucius. Look it in the face, then; and it will smile as it always has on Cæsar.

Cæsar (*with involuntary haughtiness*) Do you presume to encourage me?

Lucius. I offer you my services. I will change sides if you will have me.

Cæsar (*suddenly coming down to earth again, and looking sharply at him, divining that there is something behind the offer*) What! At this point?

Lucius (*firmly*) At this point.

Rufio. Do you suppose Cæsar is mad, to trust you?

Lucius. I do not ask him to trust me until he is victorious. I ask for my life, and for a command in Cæsar's army. And since Cæsar is a fair dealer, I will pay in advance.

Cæsar. Pay! How?

Lucius. With a piece of good news for you.

Cæsar divines the news in a flash.

Rufio. What news?

Cæsar (with an elate and buoyant energy which makes Cleopatra sit up and stare) What news! What news, did you say, my son Rufio? The relief has arrived: what other news remains for us? Is it not so, Lucius Septimius? Mithridates of Pergamos is on the march.

Lucius. He has taken Pelusium.

Cæsar (delighted) Lucius Septimius: you are henceforth my officer. Rufio: the Egyptians must have sent every soldier from the city to prevent Mithridates crossing the Nile. There is nothing in the streets now but mob—mob!

Lucius. It is so. Mithridates is marching by the great road to Memphis to cross above the Delta. Achillas will fight him there.

Cæsar (all audacity) Achillas shall fight Cæsar there. See, Rufio. (*He runs to the table; snatches a napkin; and draws a plan on it with his finger dipped in wine, whilst Rufio and Lucius Septimius crowd about him to watch, all looking closely, for the light is now almost gone*). Here is the palace (*pointing to his plan*): here is the theatre. You (*to Rufio*) take twenty men and pretend to go by t h a t street (*pointing it out*); and whilst they are stoning you, out go the cohorts by this and this. My streets are right, are they, Lucius?

Lucius. Ay, that is the fig market—

Cæsar (too much excited to listen to him) I saw them the day we arrived. Good! (*He throws the napkin on the table, and comes down again into the colonnade*). Away, Britannus: tell Petronius that within an hour half our forces must take ship for the western lake. See to my horse and armor. (*Britannus runs out*). With the rest, I shall march round the lake and up the Nile to meet Mithridates. Away, Lucius; and give the word. (*Lucius hurries out after Britannus*). Apollodorus: lend me your sword and your right arm for this campaign.

Apollodorus. Ay, and my heart and life to boot.

Cæsar (*grasping his hand*) I accept both. (*Mighty handshake*). Are you ready for work?

Apollodorus. Ready for Art—the Art of War (*he rushes out after Lucius, totally forgetting Cleopatra*).

Rufio. Come! this is something like business.

Cæsar (*buoyantly*) Is it not, my only son? (*He claps his hands. The slaves hurry in to the table*). No more of this mawkish revelling: away with all this stuff: shut it out of my sight and be off with you. (*The slaves begin to remove the table; and the curtains are drawn, shutting in the colonnade*). You understand about the streets, Rufio?

Rufio. Ay, I think I do. I will get through them, at all events.

The buccina sounds busily in the courtyard beneath.

Cæsar. Come, then: we must talk to the troops and hearten them. You down to the beach: I to the courtyard. (*He makes for the staircase*).

Cleopatra (*rising from her seat, where she has been quite neglected all this time, and stretching out her hands timidly to him*) Cæsar.

Cæsar (*turning*) Eh?

Cleopatra. Have you forgotten me?

Cæsar (*indulgently*) I am busy now, my child, busy. When I return your affairs shall be settled. Farewell; and be good and patient.

He goes, preoccupied and quite indifferent. She stands with clenched fists, in speechless rage and humiliation.

Rufio. That game is played and lost, Cleopatra. The woman always gets the worst of it.

Cleopatra (*haughtily*) Go. Follow your master.

Rufio (*in her ear, with rough familiarity*) A word first. Tell

your executioner that if Pothinus had been properly killed—
in the throat—he would not have called out. Your man
bungled his work.

Cleopatra (enigmatically) How do you know it was a man?

Rufio (startled, and puzzled) It was not you: you were with
us when it happened. (*She turns her back scornfully on him.
He shakes his head, and draws the curtains to go out. It is now
a magnificent moonlit night. The table has been removed.
Ftatateeta is seen in the light of the moon and stars, again in
prayer before the white altar-stone of Ra. Rufio starts; closes
the curtains again softly; and says in a low voice to Cleopatra*)
Was it she? with her own hand?

Cleopatra (threateningly) Whoever it was, let my enemies
beware of her. Look to it, Rufio, you who dare make the
Queen of Egypt a fool before Cæsar.

Rufio (looking grimly at her) I will look to it, Cleopatra.
(*He nods in confirmation of the promise, and slips out through
the curtains, loosening his sword in its sheath as he goes*).

Roman Soldiers (in the courtyard below) Hail, Cæsar! Hail,
hail!

*Cleopatra listens. The buccina sounds again, followed by sev-
eral trumpets.*

Cleopatra (wringing her hands and calling) Ftatateeta.
Ftatateeta. It is dark; and I am alone. Come to me. (*Silence*)
Ftatateeta. (*Louder*) Ftatateeta. (*Silence. In a panic she
snatches the cord and pulls the curtains apart*).

*Ftatateeta is lying dead on the altar of Ra, with her throat
cut. Her blood deluges the white stone.*

ACT V

HIGH NOON. *Festival and military pageant on the esplanade before the palace. In the east harbor Cæsar's galley, so gorgeously decorated that it seems to be rigged with flowers, is alongside the quay, close to the steps Apollodorus descended when he embarked with the carpet. A Roman guard is posted there in charge of a gangway, whence a red floorcloth is laid down the middle of the esplanade, turning off to the north opposite the central gate in the palace front, which shuts in the esplanade on the south side. The broad steps of the gate, crowded with Cleopatra's ladies, all in their gayest attire, are like a flower garden. The façade is lined by her guard, officered by the same gallants to whom Bel Affris announced the coming of Cæsar six months before in the old palace on the Syrian border. The north side is lined by Roman soldiers, with the townsfolk on tiptoe behind them, peering over their heads at the cleared esplanade, in which the officers stroll about, chatting. Among these are Belzanor and the Persian; also the centurion, vinewood cudgel in hand, battle worn, thick-booted, and much outshone, both socially and decoratively, by the Egyptian officers.*

Apollodorus makes his way through the townsfolk and calls to the officers from behind the Roman line.

Apollodorus. Hullo! May I pass?

Centurion. Pass Apollodorus the Sicilian there! (*The sol-diers let him through*).

Belzanor. Is Cæsar at hand?

Apollodorus. Not yet. He is still in the market place. I could not stand any more of the roaring of the soldiers! After half an hour of the enthusiasm of an army, one feels the need of a little sea air.

Persian. Tell us the news. Hath he slain the priests?

Apollodorus. Not he. They met him in the market place with ashes on their heads and their gods in their hands. They placed the gods at his feet. The only one that was worth looking at was Apis: a miracle of gold and ivory work. By my advice he offered the chief priest two talents for it.

Belzanor (appalled) Apis the all-knowing for two talents! What said the Priest?

Apollodorus. He invoked the mercy of Apis, and asked for five.

Belzanor. There will be famine and tempest in the land for this.

Persian. Pooh! Why did not Apis cause Cæsar to be vanquished by Achillas? Any fresh news from the war, Apollodorus?

Apollodorus. The little King Ptolemy was drowned.

Belzanor. Drowned! How?

Apollodorus. With the rest of them. Cæsar attacked them from three sides at once and swept them into the Nile. Ptolemy's barge sank.

Belzanor. A marvellous man, this Cæsar! Will he come soon, think you?

Apollodorus. He was settling the Jewish question when I left.

A flourish of trumpets from the north, and commotion among the townsfolk, announces the approach of Cæsar.

Persian. He has made short work of them. Here he comes. (*He hurries to his post in front of the Egyptian lines*).

Belzanor (following him) Ho there! Cæsar comes.

The soldiers stand at attention, and dress their lines. Apollodorus goes to the Egyptian line.

Centurion (hurrying to the gangway guard) Attention there! Cæsar comes.

Cæsar arrives in state with Rufio: Britannus following. The soldiers receive him with enthusiastic shouting.

Cæsar. I see my ship awaits me. The hour of Cæsar's fare-well to Egypt has arrived. And now, Rufio, what remains to be done before I go?

Rufio (at his left hand) You have not yet appointed a Roman governor for this province.

Cæsar (looking whimsically at him, but speaking with per-fect gravity) What say you to Mithridates of Pergamos, my reliever and rescuer, the great son of Eupator?

Rufio. Why, that you will want him elsewhere. Do you forget that you have some three or four armies to conquer on your way home?

Cæsar. Indeed! Well, what say you to yourself?

Rufio (incredulously) I! I a governor! What are you dream-ing of? Do you not know that I am only the son of a freedman?

Cæsar (affectionately) Has not Cæsar called you his son? *(Calling to the whole assembly)* Peace awhile there; and hear me.

The Roman Soldiers. Hear Cæsar.

Cæsar. Hear the service, quality, rank and name of the Roman governor. By service, Cæsar's shield; by quality, Cæsar's friend; by rank, a Roman soldier. *(The Roman soldiers give a triumphant shout).* By name, Rufio. *(They shout again).*

Rufio (kissing Cæsar's hand) Ay: I am Cæsar's shield; but of what use shall I be when I am no longer on Cæsar's arm? Well, no matter—*(He becomes husky, and turns away to recover himself).*

Cæsar. Where is that British Islander of mine?

Britannus (coming forward on Cæsar's right hand) Here, Cæsar.

Cæsar. Who bade you, pray, thrust yourself into the battle of the Delta, uttering the barbarous cries of your native land, and affirming yourself a match for any four of the Egyptians, to whom you applied unseemly epithets?

Britannus. Cæsar: I ask you to excuse the language that escaped me in the heat of the moment.

Cæsar. And how did you, who cannot swim, cross the canal with us when we stormed the camp?

Britannus. Cæsar: I clung to the tail of your horse.

Cæsar. These are not the deeds of a slave, Britannicus, but of a free man.

Britannus. Cæsar: I was born free.

Cæsar. But they call you Cæsar's slave.

Britannus. Only as Cæsar's slave have I found real freedom.

Cæsar (moved) Well said. Ungrateful that I am, I was about to set you free; but now I will not part from you for a million talents. (*He claps him friendly on the shoulder. Britannus, gratified, but a trifle shamefaced, takes his hand and kisses it sheepishly*).

Belzanor (to the Persian) This Roman knows how to make men serve him.

Persian. Ay: men too humble to become dangerous rivals to him.

Belzanor. O subtle one! O cynic!

Cæsar (seeing Apollodorus in the Egyptian corner, and calling to him) Apollodorus: I leave the art of Egypt in your charge. Remember: Rome loves art and will encourage it ungrudgingly.

Apollodorus. I understand, Cæsar. Rome will produce no art itself; but it will buy up and take away whatever the other nations produce.

Cæsar. What! Rome produce no art! Is peace not an art? is war not an art? is government not an art? is civilization not an art? All these we give you in exchange for a few ornaments. You will have the best of the bargain. (*Turning to Rufio*) And now, what else have I to do before I embark? (*Trying to recollect*) There is something I cannot remember: what c a n it be? Well, well: it must remain undone: we must not waste this favorable wind. Farewell, Rufio.

Rufio. Cæsar: I am loth to let you go to Rome without your shield. There are too many daggers there.

Cæsar. It matters not: I shall finish my life's work on my way back; and then I shall have lived long enough. Besides: I have always disliked the idea of dying: I had rather be killed. Farewell.

Rufio (*with a sigh, raising his hands and giving Cæsar up as incorrigible*) Farewell. (*They shake hands*).

Cæsar (*waving his hand to Apollodorus*) Farewell, Apollodorus, and my friends, all of you. Aboard!

The gangway is run out from the quay to the ship. As Cæsar moves towards it, Cleopatra, cold and tragic, cunningly dressed in black, without ornaments or decoration of any kind, and thus making a striking figure among the brilliantly dressed bevy of ladies as she passes through it, comes from the palace and stands on the steps. Cæsar does not see her until she speaks.

Cleopatra. Has Cleopatra no part in this leavetaking?

Cæsar (*enlightened*) Ah, I k n e w there was something. (*To Rufio*) How could you let me forget her, Rufio? (*Hastening to her*) Had I gone without seeing you, I should never have forgiven myself. (*He takes her hands, and brings her into the middle of the esplanade. She submits stonily*). Is this mourning for me?

Cleopatra. No.

Cæsar (*remorsefully*) Ah, that was thoughtless of me! It is for your brother.

Cleopatra. No.

Cæsar. For whom, then?

Cleopatra. Ask the Roman governor whom you have left us.

Cæsar. Rufio?

Cleopatra. Yes: Rufio. (*She points at him with deadly scorn*). He who is to rule here in Cæsar's name, in Cæsar's way, according to Cæsar's boasted laws of life.

Cæsar (*dubiously*) He is to rule as he can, Cleopatra. He has taken the work upon him, and will do it in his own way.

Cleopatra. Not in your way, then?

Cæsar (*puzzled*) What do you mean by my way?

Cleopatra. Without punishment. Without revenge. Without judgment.

Cæsar (*approvingly*) Ay: that is the right way, the great way, the only possible way in the end. (*To Rufio*) Believe it, Rufio, if you can.

Rufio. Why, I believe it, Cæsar. You have convinced me of it long ago. But look you. You are sailing for Numidia to-day. Now tell me: if you meet a hungry lion there, you will not punish it for wanting to eat you?

Cæsar (*wondering what he is driving at*) No.

Rufio. Nor revenge upon it the blood of those it has already eaten.

Cæsar. No.

Rufio. Nor judge it for its guiltiness.

Cæsar. No.

Rufio. What, then, will you do to save your life from it?

Cæsar (*promptly*) Kill it, man, without malice, just as it would kill me. What does this parable of the lion mean?

Rufio. Why, Cleopatra had a tigress that killed men at her bidding. I thought she might bid it kill you some day. Well, had I not been Cæsar's pupil, what pious things might I not have done to that tigress! I might have punished it. I might have revenged Pothinus on it.

Cæsar (*interjects*) Pothinus!

Rufio (*continuing*) I might have judged it. But I put all these follies behind me; and, without malice, only cut its throat. And that is why Cleopatra comes to you in mourning.

Cleopatra (*vehemently*) He has shed the blood of my servant Ftatateeta. On your head be it as upon his, Cæsar, if you hold him free of it.

Cæsar (*energetically*) On my head be it, then; for it was well done. Rufio: had you set yourself in the seat of the judge, and with hateful ceremonies and appeals to the gods handed that woman over to some hired executioner to be slain before the people in the name of justice, never again would I have touched your hand without a shudder. But this was natural slaying: I feel no horror at it.

Rufio, satisfied, nods at Cleopatra, mutely inviting her to mark that.

Cleopatra (*pettish and childish in her impotence*) No: not when a Roman slays an Egyptian. All the world will now see how unjust and corrupt Cæsar is.

Cæsar (*taking her hands coaxingly*) Come: do not be angry with me. I am sorry for that poor Totateeta. (*She laughs in spite of herself*). Aha! you are laughing. Does that mean reconciliation?

Cleopatra (*angry with herself for laughing*) No, no, NO!! But it is so ridiculous to hear you call her Totateeta.

Cæsar. What! As much a child as ever, Cleopatra! Have I not made a woman of you after all?

Cleopatra. Oh, it is you who are a great baby: you make me seem silly because you will not behave seriously. But you have treated me badly; and I do not forgive you.

Cæsar. Bid me farewell.

Cleopatra. I will not.

Cæsar (*coaxing*) I will send you a beautiful present from Rome.

Cleopatra (*proudly*) Beauty from Rome to Egypt indeed! What can Rome give m e that Egypt cannot give me?

Apollodorus. That is true, Cæsar. If the present is to be really beautiful, I shall have to buy it for you in Alexandria.

Cæsar. You are forgetting the treasures for which Rome is most famous, my friend. You cannot buy them in Alexandria.

Apollodorus. What are they, Cæsar?

Cæsar. Her sons. Come, Cleopatra: forgive me and bid me

farewell; and I will send you a man, Roman from head to
heel and Roman of the noblest; not old and ripe for the knife;
not lean in the arms and cold in the heart; not hiding a bald
head under his conqueror's laurels; not stooped with the
weight of the world on his shoulders; but brisk and fresh,
strong and young, hoping in the morning, fighting in the day,
and revelling in the evening. Will you take such an one in
exchange for Cæsar?

Cleopatra (*palpitating*) His name, his name?

Cæsar. Shall it be Mark Antony? (*She throws herself into
his arms*).

Rufio. You are a bad hand at a bargain, mistress, if you
will swop Cæsar for Antony.

Cæsar. So now you are satisfied.

Cleopatra. You will not forget.

Cæsar. I will not forget. Farewell: I do not think we shall
meet again. Farewell. (*He kisses her on the forehead. She
is much affected and begins to sniff. He embarks*).

The Roman Soldiers (*as he sets his foot on the gangway*)
Hail, Cæsar; and farewell!

He reaches the ship and returns Rufio's wave of the hand.

Apollodorus (*to Cleopatra*) No tears, dearest Queen: they
stab your servant to the heart. He will return some day.

Cleopatra. I hope not. But I cant help crying, all the same.
(*She waves her handkerchief to Cæsar; and the ship begins
to move*).

The Roman Soldiers (*drawing their swords and raising them
in the air*) Hail, Cæsar!

NOTES TO CÆSAR AND CLEOPATRA
CLEOPATRA'S CURE FOR BALDNESS

FOR the sake of conciseness in a hurried situation I have made Cleopatra recommend rum. This, I am afraid, is an anachronism: the only real one in the play. To balance it, I give a couple of the remedies she actually believed in. They are quoted by Galen from Cleopatra's book on Cosmetic.

"For bald patches, powder red sulphuret of arsenic and take it up with oak gum, as much as it will bear. Put on a rag and apply, having soaped the place well first. I have mixed the above with a foam of nitre, and it worked well."

Several other receipts follow, ending with: "The following is the best of all, acting for fallen hairs, when applied with oil or pomatum; acts for falling off of eyelashes or for people getting bald all over. It is wonderful. Of domestic mice burnt, one part; of vine rag burnt, one part; of horse's teeth burnt, one part; of bear's grease one; of deer's marrow one; of reed bark one. To be pounded when dry, and mixed with plenty of honey til it gets the consistency of honey; then the bear's grease and marrow to be mixed (when melted), the medicine to be put in a brass flask, and the bald part rubbed til it sprouts."

Concerning these ingredients, my fellow-dramatist Gilbert Murray, who, as a Professor of Greek, has applied to classical antiquity the methods of high scholarship (my own method is pure divination), writes to me as follows: "Some of this I dont understand, and possibly Galen did not, as he quotes your heroine's own language. Foam of nitre is, I think, something like soapsuds. Reed bark is an odd expression. It might mean the outside membrane of a reed: I do not know what it ought to be called. In the burnt mice receipt I take it that you first mixed the solid powders with honey, and then added the grease. I expect Cleopatra preferred it because in most of the others you have to lacerate the skin, prick it, or rub it till it bleeds. I do not know what vine rag is. I translate literally."

APPARENT ANACHRONISMS

The only way to write a play which shall convey to the general public an impression of antiquity is to make the characters speak blank verse and abstain from reference to steam, telegraphy, or any of the material conditions of their existence. The more ignorant men are, the more convinced are they that their little parish and their little chapel is an apex to which civilization and philosophy has painfully struggled up the pyramid of time from a desert of savagery. Savagery, they think, became barbarism; barbarism became ancient civilization; ancient civilization became Pauline Christianity; Pauline Christianity became Roman Catholicism; Roman Catholicism became the Dark Ages; and the Dark Ages were finally enlightened by the Protestant instincts of the English race. The whole process is summed up as Progress with a capital P. And any elderly gentleman of Progressive temperament will testify that the improvement since he was a boy is enormous.

Now if we count the generations of Progressive elderly gentlemen since, say, Plato, and add together the successive enormous improvements to which each of them has testified, it will strike us at once as an unaccountable fact that the world, instead of having been improved in 67 generations out of all recognition, presents, on the whole, a rather less dignified appearance in Ibsen's Enemy of the People than in Plato's Republic. And in truth, the period of time covered by history is far too short to allow of any perceptible progress in the popular sense of Evolution of the Human Species. The notion that there has been any such Progress since Cæsar's time (less than 20 centuries) is too absurd for discussion. All the savagery, barbarism, dark ages and the rest of it which we have any record as existing in the past exists at the present moment. A British carpenter or stonemason may point out that he gets twice as much money for his labor as his father did in the same trade, and that his suburban house, with its bath, its cottage piano, its drawing room suite, and its album of photographs, would have shamed the plainness of his grandmother's. But the descendants of feudal barons, living in squalid lodgings on a salary of fifteen shillings a week instead of in castles on princely revenues, do not congratulate the world on the change. Such changes, in fact, are not to the point. It has been known, as far back as our records go, that man running wild in the woods is different from man kennelled in a city slum; that a dog seems to understand a shepherd better than a hewer of wood and drawer of water can understand an astronomer; and that breeding, gentle nurture, and luxurious food and shelter will produce a kind of man with whom the common laborer is socially incompatible. The same thing is true of horses and dogs. Now there is clearly room for great changes in the world by increasing the percentage of individuals who are carefully bred and gently nurtured, even to finally making the most of every man and woman born. But that possibility existed in the days of the Hittites as much as it does today. It does not give the slightest real support to the common assumption that the civilized contemporaries of the Hittites were unlike their civilized descendants today.

This would appear the tritest commonplace if it were not that the ordinary citizen's ignorance of the past combines with his idealization of the present to mislead and flatter him. Our latest book on the new railway across Asia describes the dulness of the Siberian farmer and the vulgar pursepride of the Siberian man of business without the least consciousness that the string of contemptuous instances given might have been saved by writing simply "Farmers and provincial plutocrats in Siberia are exactly what they are in England." The latest professor descanting on the civilization of the Western Empire in the fifth century feels bound to assume, in the teeth of his own researches, that the Christian was one sort of animal and the Pagan another. It might as well be assumed, as indeed it generally is assumed by implication, that a murder committed with a poisoned arrow is different from a murder committed with a Mauser rifle. All such notions are illusions. Go back to the first syllable of recorded time, and there you will find your Christian and your Pagan, your yokel and your poet, helot and hero, Don Quixote and Sancho, Tamino and Papageno, Newton and bushman unable to count eleven, all alive and contemporaneous, and all convinced that they are the heirs of all the ages and the privileged recipients of THE truth (all others damnable heresies), just as you have them to-day, flourishing in countries each of which is the bravest and best that ever sprang at Heaven's command from out the azure main.

Again, there is the illusion of "increased command over Nature," meaning that cotton is cheap and that ten miles of country road on a bicycle have replaced four on foot. But even if man's increased command over Nature included any increased command over himself (the only sort of command relevant to his evolution into a higher being), the fact remains that it is only by running away from the increased command over Nature to country places where Nature is still in primitive command over Man that he can recover from the effects of the smoke, the stench, the foul air, the overcrowding, the racket, the ugliness, the dirt which the cheap cotton costs us. If manufacturing activity means Progress, the town must be more advanced than the country; and the field laborers and village artisans of today must be much less changed from the servants of Job than the proletariat of modern London from the proletariat of Cæsar's Rome. Yet the cockney proletarian is so inferior to the village laborer that it is only by steady recruiting from the country that London is kept alive. This does not seem as if the change since Job's time were Progress in the popular sense: quite the reverse. The common stock of discoveries in physics has accumulated a little: that is all.

One more illustration. Is the Englishman prepared to admit that the American is his superior as a human being? I ask this question because the scarcity of labor in America relatively to the demand for it has led to a development of machinery there, and a consequent "increase of command over Nature" which makes many of our English methods appear almost medieval to the up-to-date Chicagoan. This means that the American has an advantage over the Englishman of exactly the same nature that the Englishman has over the contemporaries of Cicero. Is the Englishman prepared to draw the same conclusion in both cases? I think not. The American, of course, will draw it cheerfully; but I must then ask him whether, since a modern negro has a greater "command over Nature" than Washington had, we are also to accept the conclusion, involved in his former one, that humanity has progressed from Washington to the *fin de siècle* negro.

Finally, I would point out that if life is crowned by its success and devotion in industrial organization and ingenuity, we had better worship the ant and the bee (as moralists urge us to do in our childhood), and humble ourselves before the arrogance of the birds of Aristophanes.

My reason then for ignoring the popular conception of Progress in Cæsar and Cleopatra is that there is no reason to suppose that any Progress has taken place since their time. But even if I shared the popular delusion, I do not see that I could have made any essential difference in the play. I can only imitate humanity as I know it. Nobody knows whether Shakespear thought that ancient Athenian joiners, weavers, or bellows menders were any different from Elizabethan ones;

but it is quite certain that he could not have made them so, unless, indeed, he had played the literary man and made Quince say, not "Is all our company here?" but "Bottom: was not that Socrates that passed us at the Piræus with Glaucon and Polemarchus on his way to the house of Kephalus?" And so on.

CLEOPATRA

Cleopatra was only sixteen when Cæsar went to Egypt; but in Egypt sixteen is a riper age than it is in England. The childishness I have ascribed to her, as far as it is childishness of character and not lack of experience, is not a matter of years. It may be observed in our own climate at the present day in many women of fifty. It is a mistake to suppose that the difference between wisdom and folly has anything to do with the difference between physical age and physical youth. Some women are younger at seventy than most women at seventeen.

It must be borne in mind, too, that Cleopatra was a queen, and was therefore not the typical Greek-cultured, educated Egyptian lady of her time. To represent her by any such type would be as absurd as to represent George IV by a type founded on the attainments of Sir Isaac Newton. It is true that an ordinarily well educated Alexandrian girl of her time would no more have believed bogey stories about the Romans than the daughter of a modern Oxford professor would believe them about the Germans (though, by the way, it is possible to talk great nonsense at Oxford about foreigners when we are at war with them). But I do not feel bound to believe that Cleopatra was well educated. Her father, the illustrious Flute Blower, was not at all a parent of the Oxford professor type. And Cleopatra was a chip of the old block.

BRITANNUS

I find among those who have read this play in manuscript a strong conviction that an ancient Briton could not possibly

have been like a modern one. I see no reason to adopt this
curious view. It is true that the Roman and Norman conquests
must have for a time disturbed the normal British type produced by the climate. But Britannus, born before these events,
represents the unadulterated Briton who fought Cæsar and
impressed Roman observers much as we should expect the
ancestors of Mr Podsnap to impress the cultivated Italians of
their time.

I am told that it is not scientific to treat national character
as a product of climate. This only shews the wide difference
between common knowledge and the intellectual game called
science. We have men of exactly the same stock, and speaking
the same language, growing in Great Britain, in Ireland, and
in America. The result is three of the most distinctly marked
nationalities under the sun. Racial characteristics are quite
another matter. The difference between a Jew and a Gentile
has nothing to do with the difference between an Englishman
and a German. The characteristics of Britannus are local
characteristics, not race characteristics. In an ancient Briton
they would, I take it, be exaggerated, since modern Britain,
disforested, drained, urbanified and consequently cosmopolized,
is presumably less characteristically British than Cæsar's Britain.

And again I ask does anyone who, in the light of a
competent knowledge of his own age, has studied history
from contemporary documents, believe that 67 generations of
promiscuous marriage have made any appreciable difference
in the human fauna of these isles? Certainly I do not.

JULIUS CÆSAR

As to Cæsar himself, I have purposely avoided the usual
anachronism of going to Cæsar's books, and concluding that
the style is the man. That is only true of authors who have
the specific literary genius, and have practised long enough
to attain complete self-expression in letters. It is not true even
on these conditions in an age when literature is conceived as

a game of style, and not as a vehicle of self-expression by the author. Now Cæsar was an amateur stylist writing books of travel and campaign histories in a style so impersonal that the authenticity of the later volumes is disputed. They reveal some of his qualities just as the Voyage of a Naturalist Round the World reveals some of Darwin's, without expressing his private personality. An Englishman reading them would say that Cæsar was a man of great common sense and good taste, meaning thereby a man without originality or moral courage.

In exhibiting Cæsar as a much more various person than the historian of the Gallic wars, I hope I have not been too much imposed on by the dramatic illusion to which all great men owe part of their reputation and some the whole of it. I admit that reputations gained in war are specially questionable. Able civilians taking up the profession of arms, like Cæsar and Cromwell, in middle age, have snatched all its laurels from opponent commanders bred to it, apparently because capable persons engaged in military pursuits are so scarce that the existence of two of them at the same time in the same hemisphere is extremely rare. The capacity of any conqueror is therefore more likely than not to be an illusion produced by the incapacity of his adversary. At all events, Cæsar might have won his battles without being wiser than Charles XII or Nelson or Joan of Arc, who were, like most modern "self-made" millionaires, half-witted geniuses, enjoying the worship accorded by all races to certain forms of insanity. But Cæsar's victories were only advertisements for an eminence that would never have become popular without them. Cæsar is greater off the battle field than on it. Nelson off his quarterdeck was so quaintly out of the question that when his head was injured at the battle of the Nile, and his conduct became for some years openly scandalous, the difference was not important enough to be noticed. It may, however, be said that peace hath her illusory reputations no less than war. And it is certainly true that in civil life mere capacity for work—the power of killing a dozen secretaries under you, so to speak, as a life-or-death courier kills horses—enables men with common ideas and superstitions to distance all competitors in the strife of political ambition. It was this power of work that astonished Cicero as the most prodigious of Cæsar's gifts, as it astonished later observers in Napoleon before it wore him out. How if Cæsar were nothing but a Nelson and a Gladstone combined! a prodigy of vitality without any special quality of mind! nay, with ideas that were worn out before he was born, as Nelson's and Gladstone's were! I have considered that possibility too, and rejected it. I cannot cite all the stories about Cæsar which seem to me to shew that he was genuinely original; but let me at least point out that I have been careful to attribute nothing but originality to him. Originality gives a man an air of frankness, generosity, and magnanimity by enabling him to estimate the value of truth, money, or success in any particular instance quite independently of convention and moral generalization. He therefore will not, in the ordinary Treasury bench fashion, tell a lie which everybody knows to be a lie (and consequently expects him as a matter of good taste to tell). His lies are not found out: they pass for candors. He understands the paradox of money, and gives it away when he can get most for it: in other words, when its value is least, which is just when a common man tries hardest to get it. He knows that the real moment of success is not the moment apparent to the crowd. Hence, in order to produce an impression of complete disinterestedness and magnanimity, he has only to act with entire selfishness; and this is perhaps the only sense in which a man can be said to be *naturally* great. It is in this sense that I have represented Cæsar as great. Having virtue, he had no need of goodness. He is neither forgiving, frank, nor generous, because a man who is too great to resent has nothing to forgive; a man who says things that other people are afraid to say need be no more frank than Bismarck was; and there is no generosity in giving things you do not want to people of whom you intend to make use. This distinction between virtue and goodness is not understood in England: hence the poverty of our drama in heroes. Our stage attempts at them are mere goody-goodies. Goodness, in its popular British sense of self-denial, implies that man is vicious by nature, and that supreme goodness is supreme martyrdom. Not sharing that pious opinion, I have not given countenance to it in any of my plays. In this I follow the precedent of the ancient myths, which represent the hero as vanquishing his enemies, not in fair fight, but with enchanted sword, superequine horse and magical invulnerability, the possession of which, from the vulgar moralistic point of view, robs his exploits of any merit whatever.

As to Cæsar's sense of humor, there is no more reason to assume that he lacked it than to assume that he was deaf or blind. It is said that on the occasion of his assassination by a conspiracy of moralists (it is always your moralist who makes assassination a duty, on the scaffold or off it), he defended himself until the good Brutus struck him, when he exclaimed "What! you too, Brutus!" and disdained further fight. If this be true, he must have been an incorrigible comedian. But even if we waive this story, or accept the traditional sentimental interpretation of it, there is still abundant evidence of his lightheartedness and adventurousness. Indeed it is clear from his whole history that what has been called his ambition was an instinct for exploration. He had much more of Columbus and Franklin in him than of Henry V.

However, nobody need deny Cæsar a share, at least, of the qualities I have attributed to him. All men, much more Julius Cæsars, possess all qualities in some degree. The really interesting question is whether I am right in assuming that the way to produce an impression of greatness is by exhibiting a man, not as mortifying his nature by doing his duty, in the manner which our system of putting little men into great positions (not having enough great men in our influential families to go round) forces us to inculcate, but as simply doing what he naturally wants to do. For this raises the question whether our world has not been wrong in its moral theory for the last 2,500 years or so. It must be a constant puzzle to many of us that the Christian era, so excellent in its intentions, should have been practically such a very discreditable episode in the history of the race. I doubt if this is altogether due to the vulgar and sanguinary sensationalism of our religious legends, with their substitution of gross physical torments and public executions for the passion of humanity. Islam, substituting voluptuousness for torment (a merely superficial difference, it is true) has done no better. It may have been the failure of Christianity to emancipate itself from expiatory theories of moral responsibility, guilt, innocence, reward, punishment, and the rest of it, that baffled its intention of changing the world. But these are bound up in all philosophies of creation as opposed to cosmism. They may therefore be regarded as the price we pay for popular religion.

Pygmalion

A ROMANCE IN FIVE ACTS

1912

PREFACE TO PYGMALION—
A PROFESSOR OF PHONETICS

AS WILL BE SEEN later on, Pygmalion needs, not a preface, but a sequel, which I have supplied in its due place. The English have no respect for their language, and will not teach their children to speak it. They spell it so abominably that no man can teach himself what it sounds like. It is impossible for an Englishman to open his mouth without making some other Englishman hate or despise him. German and Spanish are accessible to foreigners: English is not accessible even to Englishmen. The reformer England needs today is an energetic phonetic enthusiast: that is why I have made such a one the hero of a popular play. There have been heroes of that kind crying in the wilderness for many years past. When I became interested in the subject towards the end of the eighteen-seventies, the illustrious Alexander Melville Bell, the inventor of Visible Speech, had emigrated to Canada, where his son invented the telephone; but Alexander J. Ellis was still a London patriarch, with an impressive head always covered by a velvet skull cap, for which he would apologize to public meetings in a very courtly manner. He and Tito Pagliardini, another phonetic veteran, were men whom it was impossible to dislike. Henry Sweet, then a young man, lacked their sweetness of character: he was about as conciliatory to conventional mortals as Ibsen or Samuel Butler. His great ability as a phonetician (he was, I think, the best of them all at his job) would have entitled him to high official recognition, and perhaps enabled him to popularize his subject, but for his Satanic contempt for all academic dignitaries and persons in general who thought more of Greek than of phonetics.

Once, in the days when the Imperial Institute rose in South Kensington, and Joseph Chamberlain was booming the Empire, I induced the editor of a leading monthly review to commission an article from Sweet on the imperial importance of his subject. When it arrived, it contained nothing but a savagely derisive attack on a professor of language and literature whose chair Sweet regarded as proper to a phonetic expert only. The article, being libellous, had to be returned as impossible; and I had to renounce my dream of dragging its author into the limelight. When I met him afterwards, for the first time for many years, I found to my astonishment that he, who had been a quite tolerably presentable young man, had actually managed by sheer scorn to alter his personal appearance until he had become a sort of walking repudiation of Oxford and all its traditions. It must have been largely in his own despite that he was squeezed into something called a Readership of phonetics there. The future of phonetics rests probably with his pupils, who all swore by him; but nothing could bring the man himself into any sort of compliance with the university to which he nevertheless clung by divine right in an intensely Oxonian way. I daresay his papers, if he has left any, include some satires that may be published without too destructive results fifty years hence. He was, I believe, not in the least an illnatured man: very much the opposite, I should say; but he would not suffer fools gladly.

Those who knew him will recognize in my third act the allusion to the patent shorthand in which he used to write postcards, and which may be acquired from a four and sixpenny manual published by the Clarendon Press. The postcards which Mrs Higgins describes are such as I have received from Sweet. I would decipher a sound which a cockney would represent by *zerr*, and a Frenchman by *seu*, and then write demanding with some heat what on earth it meant. Sweet, with boundless contempt for my stupidity, would reply that it not only meant but obviously was the word Result, as no other word containing that sound, and capable of making sense with the context, existed in any language spoken on earth. That less expert mortals should require fuller indications was beyond Sweet's patience. Therefore, though the whole point of his Current Shorthand is that it can express every sound in the language perfectly, vowels as well as consonants, and that your hand has to make no stroke except the easy and current ones with which you write m, n, and u, l, p, and q, scribbling them at whatever angle comes easiest to you, his unfortunate determination to make this remarkable and quite legible script serve also as a shorthand reduced it in his own practice to the most inscrutable of cryptograms. His true objective was the provision of a full, accurate, legible script for our noble but ill-dressed language; but he was led past that by his contempt for the popular Pitman system of shorthand, which he called the Pitfall system. The triumph of Pitman was a triumph of business organization: there was a weekly paper to persuade you to learn Pitman: there were cheap textbooks and exercise books and transcripts of speeches for you to copy, and schools where experienced teachers coached you up to the necessary proficiency. Sweet could not organize his market in that fashion. He might as well have been the Sybil who tore up the leaves of prophecy that nobody would attend to. The four and sixpenny manual, mostly in his lithographed handwriting, that was never vulgarly advertized, may perhaps some day be taken up by a syndicate and pushed upon the public as The Times pushed the Encyclopædia Britannica; but until then it will certainly not prevail against Pitman. I have bought three copies of it during my lifetime; and I am informed by the publishers that its cloistered existence is still a steady and healthy one. I actually learned the system two several times; and yet the shorthand in which I am writing these lines is Pitman's. And the reason is, that my secretary cannot transcribe Sweet, having been perforce taught in the schools of Pitman. Therefore, Sweet railed at Pitman as vainly as Thersites railed at Ajax: his raillery, however it may have eased his soul, gave no popular vogue to Current Shorthand.

Pygmalion Higgins is not a portrait of Sweet, to whom the adventure of Eliza Doolittle would have been impossible; still, as will be seen, there are touches of Sweet in the play. With Higgins's physique and temperament Sweet might have set the Thames on fire. As it was, he impressed himself professionally on Europe to an extent that made his comparative personal obscurity, and the failure of Oxford to do justice to his eminence, a puzzle to foreign specialists in his subject. I do not blame Oxford, because I think Oxford is quite right in demanding a certain social amenity from its nurslings (heaven knows it is not exorbitant in its requirements!); for although I well know how hard it is for a man of genius with a seriously underrated subject to maintain serene and kindly relations with the men who underrate it, and who keep all the best places for less important subjects which they profess without originality and sometimes without much capacity for them, still, if he overwhelms them with wrath and disdain, he cannot expect them to heap honors on him.

Of the later generations of phoneticians I know little. Among them towers the Poet Laureate, to whom perhaps Higgins may owe his Miltonic sympathies, though here again I must disclaim all portraiture. But if the play makes the public aware that there are such people as phoneticians, and that they are among the most important people in England at present, it will serve its turn.

I wish to boast that Pygmalion has been an extremely successful play all over Europe and North America as well as at home. It is so intensely and deliberately didactic, and its subject is esteemed so dry, that I delight in throwing it at the heads of the wiseacres who repeat the parrot cry that art should never be didactic. It goes to prove my contention that art should never be anything else.

Finally, and for the encouragement of people troubled with accents that cut them off from all high employment, I may add that the change wrought by Professor Higgins in the flower girl is neither impossible nor uncommon. The modern concierge's daughter who fulfils her ambition by playing the Queen of Spain in Ruy Blas at the Théâtre Français is only one of many thousands of men and women who have sloughed off their native dialects and acquired a new tongue. But the thing has to be done scientifically, or the last state of the aspirant may be worse than the first. An honest and natural slum dialect is more tolerable than the attempt of a phonetically untaught person to imitate the vulgar dialect of the golf club; and I am sorry to say that in spite of the efforts of our Royal Academy of Dramatic Art, there is still too much sham golfing English on our stage, and too little of the noble English of Forbes Robertson.

ACT I

COVENT GARDEN at 11.15 *p.m. Torrents of heavy summer rain. Cab whistles blowing frantically in all directions. Pedestrians running for shelter into the market and under the portico of St Paul's Church, where there are already several people, among them a lady and her daughter in evening dress. They are all peering out gloomily at the rain, except one man with his back turned to the rest, who seems wholly preoccupied with a notebook in which he is writing busily.*

The church clock strikes the first quarter.

The Daughter (in the space between the central pillars, close to the one on her left) I'm getting chilled to the bone. What can Freddy be doing all this time? He's been gone twenty minutes.

The Mother (on her daughter's right) Not so long. But he ought to have got us a cab by this.

A Bystander (on the lady's right) He wont get no cab not until half-past eleven, missus, when they come back after dropping their theatre fares.

The Mother. But we must have a cab. We cant stand here until half-past eleven. It's too bad.

The Bystander. Well, it aint my fault, missus.

The Daughter. If Freddy had a bit of gumption, he would have got one at the theatre door.

The Mother. What could he have done, poor boy?

The Daughter. Other people got cabs. Why couldnt he?

Freddy rushes in out of the rain from the Southampton Street side, and comes between them closing a dripping umbrella. He is a young man of twenty, in evening dress, very wet round the ankles.

The Daughter. Well, havnt you got a cab?

Freddy. Theres not one to be had for love or money.

The Mother. Oh, Freddy, there must be one. You cant have tried.

The Daughter. It's too tiresome. Do you expect us to go and get one ourselves?

Freddy. I tell you theyre all engaged. The rain was so sudden: nobody was prepared; and everybody had to take a cab. Ive been to Charing Cross one way and nearly to Ludgate Circus the other; and they were all engaged.

The Mother. Did you try Trafalgar Square?

Freddy. There wasnt one at Trafalgar Square.

The Daughter. Did you try?

Freddy. I tried as far as Charing Cross Station. Did you expect me to walk to Hammersmith?

The Daughter. You havnt tried at all.

The Mother. You really are very helpless, Freddy. Go again; and dont come back until you have found a cab.

Freddy. I shall simply get soaked for nothing.

The Daughter. And what about us? Are we to stay here all night in this draught, with next to nothing on? You selfish pig—

Freddy. Oh, very well: I'll go, I'll go. (*He opens his umbrella and dashes off Strandwards, but comes into collision with a flower girl, who is hurrying in for shelter, knocking her basket out of her hands. A blinding flash of lightning, followed instantly by a rattling peal of thunder, orchestrates the incident*).

The Flower Girl. Nah then, Freddy: look wh' y' gowin, deah.

Freddy. Sorry (*he rushes off*).

The Flower Girl (*picking up her scattered flowers and replacing them in the basket*) Theres menners f' yer! Te-oo banches o voylets trod into the mad. (*She sits down on the plinth of the column, sorting her flowers, on the lady's right. She is not at all an attractive person. She is perhaps eighteen, perhaps twenty, hardly older. She wears a little sailor hat of black straw that has long been exposed to the dust and soot of London and has seldom if ever been brushed. Her hair needs washing rather badly: its mousy color can hardly be natural. She wears a shoddy black coat that reaches nearly to her knees and is shaped to her waist. She has a brown skirt with a coarse apron. Her boots are much the worse for wear. She is no doubt as clean as she can afford to be; but compared to the ladies she is very dirty. Her features are no worse than theirs; but their condition leaves something to be desired; and she needs the services of a dentist).*

The Mother. How do you know that my son's name is Freddy, pray?

The Flower Girl. Ow, eez ye-ooa san, is e? Wal, fewd dan y' de-ooty bawmz a mather should, eed now bettern to spawl a pore gel's flahrzn than ran awy athaht pyin. Will ye-oo py me f' them? (*Here, with apologies, this desperate attempt to represent her dialect without a phonetic alphabet must be abandoned as unintelligible outside London*).

The Daughter. Do nothing of the sort, mother. The idea!

The Mother. Please allow me, Clara. Have you any pennies?

The Daughter. No. Ive nothing smaller than sixpence.

The Flower Girl (*hopefully*) I can give you change for a tanner, kind lady.

The Mother (*to Clara*) Give it to me. (*Clara parts reluctantly*). Now (*to the girl*) this is for your flowers.

The Flower Girl. Thank you kindly, lady.

The Daughter. Make her give you the change. These things are only a penny a bunch.

The Mother. Do hold your tongue, Clara. (*To the girl*) You can keep the change.

The Flower Girl. Oh, thank you, lady.

The Mother. Now tell me how you know that young gentleman's name.

The Flower Girl. I didnt.

The Mother. I heard you call him by it. Dont try to deceive me.

The Flower Girl (*protesting*) Who's trying to deceive you? I called him Freddy or Charlie same as you might yourself if you was talking to a stranger and wished to be pleasant. (*She sits down beside her basket*).

The Daughter. Sixpence thrown away! Really, mamma, you might have spared Freddy t h a t. (*She retreats in disgust behind the pillar*).

An elderly gentleman of the amiable military type rushes into the shelter, and closes a dripping umbrella. He is in the same plight as Freddy, very wet about the ankles. He is in evening dress, with a light overcoat. He takes the place left vacant by the daughter's retirement.

The Gentleman. Phew!

The Mother (*to the gentleman*) Oh, sir, is there any sign of its stopping?

The Gentleman. I'm afraid not. It started worse than ever about two minutes ago (*He goes to the plinth beside the flower girl; puts up his foot on it; and stoops to turn down his trouser ends*).

The Mother. Oh dear! (*She retires sadly and joins her daughter*).

The Flower Girl (*taking advantage of the military gentleman's proximity to establish friendly relations with him*) If it's worse, it's a sign it's nearly over. So cheer up, Captain; and buy a flower off a poor girl.

The Gentleman. I'm sorry. I havnt any change.

The Flower Girl. I can give you change, Captain.

The Gentleman. For a sovereign? Ive nothing less.

The Flower Girl. Garn! Oh do buy a flower off me, Captain. I can change half-a-crown. Take this for tuppence.

The Gentleman. Now dont be troublesome: theres a good

girl. (*Trying his pockets*) I really havnt any change—Stop: heres three hapence, if thats any use to you (*he retreats to the other pillar*).

The Flower Girl (*disappointed, but thinking three half-pence better than nothing*) Thank you, sir.

The Bystander (*to the girl*) You be careful: give him a flower for it. Theres a bloke here behind taking down every blessed word youre saying. (*All turn to the man who is taking notes*).

The Flower Girl (*springing up terrified*) I aint done nothing wrong by speaking to the gentleman. Ive a right to sell flowers if I keep off the kerb. (*Hysterically*) I'm a respectable girl: so help me, I never spoke to him except to ask him to buy a flower off me. (*General hubbub, mostly sympathetic to the flower girl, but deprecating her excessive sensibility. Cries of* Dont start hollerin. Who's hurting you? Nobody's going to touch you. Whats the good of fussing? Steady on. Easy easy, *etc., come from the elderly staid spectators, who pat her comfortingly. Less patient ones bid her shut her head, or ask her roughly what is wrong with her. A remoter group, not knowing what the matter is, crowd in and increase the noise with question and answer:* Whats the row? Whatshe do? Where is he? A tec taking her down. What! him? Yes: him over there: Took money off the gentleman, etc. *The flower girl, distraught and mobbed, breaks through them to the gentleman, crying wildly*) Oh, sir, dont let him charge me. You dunno what it means to me. Theyll take away my character and drive me on the streets for speaking to gentlemen. They—

The Note Taker (*coming forward on her right, the rest crowding after him*) There, there, there, there! who's hurting you, you silly girl? What do you take me for?

The Bystander. It's all right: he's a gentleman: look at his boots. (*Explaining to the note taker*) She thought you was a copper's nark, sir.

The Note Taker (with quick interest) Whats a copper's nark?

The Bystander (inapt at definition) It's a—well, it's a copper's nark, as you might say. What else would you call it? A sort of informer.

The Flower Girl (still hysterical) I take my Bible oath I never said a word—

The Note Taker (overbearing but good-humored) Oh, shut up, shut up. Do I look like a policeman?

The Flower Girl (far from reassured) Then what did you take down my words for? How do I know whether you took me down right? You just shew me what youve wrote about me. *(The note taker opens his book and holds it steadily under her nose, though the pressure of the mob trying to read it over his shoulders would upset a weaker man)*. Whats that? T h a t aint proper writing. I cant read that.

The Note Taker. I can. *(Reads, reproducing her pronunciation exactly)* "Cheer ap, Keptin; n' baw ya flahr orf a pore gel."

The Flower Girl (much distressed) It's because I called him Captain. I meant no harm. *(To the gentleman)* Oh, sir, dont let him lay a charge agen me for a word like that. You—

The Gentleman. Charge! I make no charge. *(To the note taker)* Really, sir, if you are a detective, you need not begin protecting me against molestation by young women until I ask you. Anybody could see that the girl meant no harm.

The Bystanders Generally (demonstrating against police espionage) Course they could. What business is it of yours? You mind your own affairs. He wants promotion, he does. Taking down people's words! Girl never said a word to him. What harm if she did? Nice thing a girl cant shelter from the rain without being insulted, etc., etc., etc. *(She is conducted by the more sympathetic demonstrators back to her plinth, where she resumes her seat and struggles with her emotion)*.

The Bystander. He aint a tec. He's a blooming busybody: thats what he is. I tell you, look at his boots.

The Note Taker (*turning on him genially*) And how are all your people down at Selsey?

The Bystander (*suspiciously*) Who told you my people come from Selsey?

The Note Taker. Never you mind. They did. (*To the girl*) How do you come to be up so far east? You were born in Lisson Grove.

The Flower Girl (*appalled*) Oh, what harm is there in my leaving Lisson Grove? It wasnt fit for a pig to live in; and I had to pay four-and-six a week. (*In tears*) Oh, boo—hoo—oo—

The Note Taker. Live where you like; but stop that noise.

The Gentleman (*to the girl*) Come, come! he cant touch you: you have a right to live where you please.

A Sarcastic Bystander (*thrusting himself between the note taker and the gentleman*) Park Lane, for instance. I'd like to go into the Housing Question with you, I would.

The Flower Girl (*subsiding into a brooding melancholy over her basket, and talking very low-spiritedly to herself*) I'm a good girl, I am.

The Sarcastic Bystander (*not attending to her*) Do you know where *I* come from?

The Note Taker (*promptly*) Hoxton.

Titterings. Popular interest in the note taker's performance increases.

The Sarcastic One (*amazed*) Well, who said I didnt? Bly me! You know everything, you do.

The Flower Girl (*still nursing her sense of injury*) Aint no call to meddle with me, he aint.

The Bystander (*to her*) Of course he aint. Dont you stand it from him. (*To the note taker*) See here: what call have you to know about people what never offered to meddle with you? Wheres your warrant?

Several Bystanders (*encouraged by this seeming point of law*) Yes: wheres your warrant?

The Flower Girl. Let him say what he likes. I dont want to have no truck with him.

The Bystander. You take us for dirt under your feet, dont you? Catch you taking liberties with a gentleman!

The Sarcastic Bystander. Yes: tell h i m where he come from if you want to go fortune-telling.

The Note Taker. Cheltenham, Harrow, Cambridge, and India.

The Gentleman. Quite right. (*Great laughter. Reaction in the note taker's favor. Exclamations of* He knows all about it. Told him proper. Hear him tell the toff where he come from? etc.). May I ask, sir, do you do this for your living at a music hall?

The Note Taker. Ive thought of that. Perhaps I shall some day.

The rain has stopped; and the persons on the outside of the crowd begin to drop off.

The Flower Girl (*resenting the reaction*) He's no gentleman, he aint, to interfere with a poor girl.

The Daughter (*out of patience, pushing her way rudely to the front and displacing the gentleman, who politely retires to the other side of the pillar*) What on earth is Freddy doing? I shall get pneumonia if I stay in this draught any longer.

The Note Taker (*to himself, hastily making a note of her pronunciation of "monia"*) Earlscourt.

The Daughter (*violently*) Will you please keep your impertinent remarks to yourself.

The Note Taker. Did I say that out loud? I didnt mean to. I beg your pardon. Your mother's Epsom, unmistakeably.

The Mother (*advancing between her daughter and the note taker*) How very curious! I was brought up in Largelady Park, near Epsom.

The Note Taker (*uproariously amused*) Ha! ha! What a devil of a name! Excuse me. (*To the daughter*) You want a cab, do you?

The Daughter. Dont dare speak to me.

The Mother. Oh please, please, Clara. (*Her daughter repudiates her with an angry shrug and retires haughtily*). We should be so grateful to you, sir, if you found us a cab. (*The note taker produces a whistle*). Oh, thank you. (*She joins her daughter*).

The note taker blows a piercing blast.

The Sarcastic Bystander. There! I knowed he was a plainclothes copper.

The Bystander. That aint a police whistle: thats a sporting whistle.

The Flower Girl (*still preoccupied with her wounded feelings*) He's no right to take away my character. My character is the same to me as any lady's.

The Note Taker. I dont know whether youve noticed it; but the rain stopped about two minutes ago.

The Bystander. So it has. Why didnt you say so before? and us losing our time listening to your silliness! (*He walks off towards the Strand*).

The Sarcastic Bystander. I can tell where y o u come from. You come from Anwell. Go back there.

The Note Taker (*helpfully*) Hanwell.

The Sarcastic Bystander (*affecting great distinction of speech*) Thenk you, teacher. Haw haw! So long (*he touches his hat with mock respect and strolls off*).

The Flower Girl. Frightening people like that! How would he like it himself?

The Mother. It's quite fine now, Clara. We can walk to a motor bus. Come. (*She gathers her skirts above her ankles and hurries off towards the Strand*).

The Daughter. But the cab—(*her mother is out of hearing*). Oh, how tiresome! (*She follows angrily*).

All the rest have gone except the note taker, the gentleman, and the flower girl, who sits arranging her basket and still pitying herself in murmurs.

The Flower Girl. Poor girl! Hard enough for her to live without being worrited and chivied.

The Gentleman (*returning to his former place on the note taker's left*) How do you do it, if I may ask?

The Note Taker. Simply phonetics. The science of speech. Thats my profession: also my hobby. Happy is the man who can make a living by his hobby! You can spot an Irishman or a Yorkshireman by his brogue. *I* can place any man within six miles. I can place him within two miles in London. Sometimes within two streets.

The Flower Girl. Ought to be ashamed of himself, unmanly coward!

The Gentleman. But is there a living in that?

The Note Taker. Oh yes. Quite a fat one. This is an age of upstarts. Men begin in Kentish Town with £80 a year, and end in Park Lane with a hundred thousand. They want to drop Kentish Town; but they give themselves away every time they open their mouths. Now I can teach them—

The Flower Girl. Let him mind his own business and leave a poor girl—

The Note Taker (*explosively*) Woman: cease this detestable boohooing instantly; or else seek the shelter of some other place of worship.

The Flower Girl (*with feeble defiance*) Ive a right to be here if I like, same as you.

The Note Taker. A woman who utters such depressing and disgusting sounds has no right to be anywhere—no right to live. Remember that you are a human being with a soul and the divine gift of articulate speech: that your native language is the language of Shakespear and Milton and The Bible: and dont sit there crooning like a bilious pigeon.

The Flower Girl (*quite overwhelmed, looking up at him in mingled wonder and deprecation without daring to raise her head*) Ah-ah-ah-ow-ow-ow-oo!

The Note Taker (*whipping out his book*) Heavens! what a

sound! (*He writes; then holds out the book and reads, reproducing her vowels exactly*) Ah-ah-ah-ow-ow-ow-oo!

The Flower Girl (*tickled by the performance, and laughing in spite of herself*) Garn!

The Note Taker. You see this creature with her kerbstone English: the English that will keep her in the gutter to the end of her days. Well, sir, in three months I could pass that girl off as a duchess at an ambassador's garden party. I could even get her a place as lady's maid or shop assistant, which requires better English. Thats the sort of thing I do for commercial millionaires. And on the profits of it I do genuine scientific work in phonetics, and a little as a poet on Miltonic lines.

The Gentleman. I am myself a student of Indian dialects; and—

The Note Taker (*eagerly*) Are you? Do you know Colonel Pickering, the author of Spoken Sanscrit?

The Gentleman. I a m Colonel Pickering. Who are you?

The Note Taker. Henry Higgins, author of Higgins's Universal Alphabet.

Pickering (*with enthusiasm*) I came from India to meet you.

Higgins. I was going to India to meet you.

Pickering. Where do you live?

Higgins. 27A Wimpole Street. Come and see me to-morrow.

Pickering. I'm at the Carlton. Come with me now and lets have a jaw over some supper.

Higgins. Right you are.

The Flower Girl (*to Pickering, as he passes her*) Buy a flower, kind gentleman. I'm short for my lodging.

Pickering. I really havnt any change. I'm sorry (*he goes away*).

Higgins (*shocked at the girl's mendacity*) Liar. You said you could change half-a-crown.

The Flower Girl (*rising in desperation*) You ought to be

stuffed with nails, you ought. (*Flinging the basket at his feet*)
Take the whole blooming basket for sixpence.

    The church clock strikes the second quarter.

    Higgins (*hearing in it the voice of God, rebuking him for his Pharisaic want of charity to the poor girl*) A reminder. (*He raises his hat solemnly; then throws a handful of money into the basket and follows Pickering*).

    The Flower Girl (*picking up a half-crown*) Ah-ow-ooh! (*Picking up a couple of florins*) Aaah-ow-ooh! (*Picking up several coins*) Aaaaaah-ow-ooh! (*Picking up a half-sovereign*) Aaaaaaaaaaaah-ow-ooh!!!

    Freddy (*springing out of a taxicab*) Got one at last. Hallo! (*To the girl*) Where are the two ladies that were here?

    The Flower Girl. They walked to the bus when the rain stopped.

    Freddy. And left me with a cab on my hands! Damnation!

    The Flower Girl (*with grandeur*) Never mind, young man. I'm going home in a taxi. (*She sails off to the cab. The driver puts his hand behind him and holds the door firmly shut against her. Quite understanding his mistrust, she shews him her handful of money*). Eightpence aint no object to me, Charlie. (*He grins and opens the door*). Angel Court, Drury Lane, round the corner of Micklejohn's oil shop. Lets see how fast you can make her hop it. (*She gets in and pulls the door to with a slam as the taxicab starts*).

    Freddy. Well, I'm dashed!

ACT II

NEXT DAY at 11 a.m. Higgins's laboratory in Wimpole Street. It is a room on the first floor, looking on the street, and was meant for the drawing room. The double doors are in the middle of the back wall; and persons entering find in the corner to their right two tall file cabinets at right angles to one another against the walls. In this corner stands a flat writing-table, on which are a phonograph, a laryngoscope, a row of tiny organ pipes with bellows, a set of lamp chimneys for singing flames with burners attached to a gas plug in the wall by an indiarubber tube, several tuning-forks of different sizes, a life-size image of half a human head, shewing in section the vocal organs, and a box containing a supply of wax cylinders for the phonograph.

Further down the room, on the same side, is a fireplace, with a comfortable leather-covered easy-chair at the side of the hearth nearest the door, and a coal-scuttle. There is a clock on the mantelpiece. Between the fireplace and the phonograph table is a stand for newspapers.

On the other side of the central door, to the left of the visitor, is a cabinet of shallow drawers. On it is a telephone and the telephone directory. The corner beyond, and most of the side wall, is occupied by a grand piano, with the keyboard at the end furthest from the door, and a bench for the player extending the full length of the keyboard. On the piano is a dessert dish heaped with fruit and sweets, mostly chocolates.

The middle of the room is clear. Besides the easy-chair, the piano bench, and two chairs at the phonograph table, there is one stray chair. It stands near the fireplace. On the walls, engravings: mostly Piranesis and mezzotint portraits. No paintings.

Pickering is seated at the table, putting down some cards and a tuning-fork which he has been using. Higgins is standing up near him, closing two or three file drawers which are hanging out. He appears in the morning light as a robust, vital, appetizing sort of man of forty or thereabouts, dressed in a professional-looking black frock-coat with a white linen collar and black silk tie. He is of the energetic, scientific type, heartily, even violently interested in everything that can be studied as a scientific subject, and careless about himself and other people, including their feelings. He is, in fact, but for his years and size, rather like a very impetuous baby "taking notice" eagerly and loudly, and requiring almost as much watching to keep him out of unintended mischief. His manner varies from genial bullying when he is in a good humor to stormy petulance when anything goes wrong; but he is so entirely frank and void of malice that he remains likeable even in his least reasonable moments.

Higgins (*as he shuts the last drawer*) Well, I think thats the whole show.

Pickering. It's really amazing. I havnt taken half of it in, you know.

Higgins. Would you like to go over any of it again?

Pickering (*rising and coming to the fireplace, where he plants himself with his back to the fire*) No, thank you; not now. I'm quite done up for this morning.

Higgins (*following him, and standing beside him on his left*) Tired of listening to sounds?

Pickering. Yes. It's a fearful strain. I rather fancied myself because I can pronounce twenty-four distinct vowel sounds; but your hundred and thirty beat me. I cant hear a bit of difference between most of them.

Higgins (*chuckling, and going over to the piano to eat sweets*) Oh, that comes with practice. You hear no difference at first; but you keep on listening, and presently you find theyre all as different as A from B. (*Mrs Pearce looks in: she is Higgins's housekeeper*). Whats the matter?

Mrs Pearce (*hesitating, evidently perplexed*) A young woman wants to see you sir.

Higgins. A young woman! What does she want?

Mrs Pearce. Well, sir, she says youll be glad to see her when you know what she's come about. She's quite a common girl, sir. Very common indeed. I should have sent her away, only I thought perhaps you wanted her to talk into your machines. I hope Ive not done wrong; but really you see such queer people sometimes—youll excuse me, I'm sure, sir—

Higgins. Oh, thats all right, Mrs Pearce. Has she an interesting accent?

Mrs Pearce. Oh, something dreadful, sir, really. I dont know how you can take an interest in it.

Higgins (*to Pickering*) Lets have her up. Shew her up, Mrs Pearce (*he rushes across to his working table and picks out a cylinder to use on the phonograph*).

Mrs Pearce (*only half resigned to it*) Very well, sir. It's for you to say. (*She goes downstairs*).

Higgins. This is rather a bit of luck. I'll shew you how I make records. We'll set her talking; and I'll take it down first in Bell's Visible Speech; then in broad Romic; and then we'll get her on the phonograph so that you can turn her on as often as you like with the written transcript before you.

Mrs Pearce (*returning*) This is the young woman, sir.

The flower girl enters in state. She has a hat with three ostrich feathers, orange, sky-blue, and red. She has a nearly clean apron, and the shoddy coat has been tidied a little. The pathos of this deplorable figure, with its innocent vanity and consequential air, touches Pickering, who has already straightened himself in the presence of Mrs Pearce. But as to Higgins, the only distinction he makes between men and women is that when he is neither bullying nor exclaiming to the heavens against some feather-weight cross, he coaxes women as a child coaxes its nurse when it wants to get anything out of her.

Higgins (*brusquely, recognizing her with unconcealed disappointment, and at once, babylike, making an intolerable grievance of it*) Why, this is the girl I jotted down last night. She's no use: Ive got all the records I want of the Lisson Grove lingo; and I'm not going to waste another cylinder on it. (*To the girl*) Be off with you: I dont want you.

The Flower Girl. Dont you be so saucy. You aint heard what I come for yet. (*To Mrs Pearce, who is waiting at the door for further instructions*) Did you tell him I come in a taxi?

Mrs Pearce. Nonsense, girl! what do you think a gentleman like Mr Higgins cares what you came in?

The Flower Girl. Oh, we are proud! He aint above giving lessons, not him: I heard him say so. Well, I aint come here to ask for any compliment; and if my money's not good enough I can go elsewhere.

Higgins. Good enough for what?

The Flower Girl. Good enough for ye-oo. Now you know, dont you? I'm come to have lessons, I am. And to pay for em too: make no mistake.

Higgins (*stupent*) Well!!! (*Recovering his breath with a gasp*) What do you expect me to say to you?

The Flower Girl. Well, if you was a gentleman, you might ask me to sit down, I think. Dont I tell you I'm bringing you business?

Higgins. Pickering: shall we ask this baggage to sit down, or shall we throw her out of the window?

The Flower Girl (*running away in terror to the piano, where she turns at bay*) Ah-ah-oh-ow-ow-ow-oo! (*Wounded and whimpering*) I wont be called a baggage when Ive offered to pay like any lady.

Motionless, the two men stare at her from the other side of the room, amazed.

Pickering (*gently*) What is it you want, my girl?

The Flower Girl. I want to be a lady in a flower shop stead of selling at the corner of Tottenham Court Road. But they wont take me unless I can talk more genteel. He said he could teach me. Well, here I am ready to pay him—not asking any favor—and he treats me as if I was dirt.

Mrs Pearce. How can you be such a foolish ignorant girl as to think you could afford to pay Mr Higgins?

The Flower Girl. Why shouldnt I? I know what lessons cost as well as you do; and I'm ready to pay.

Higgins. How much?

The Flower Girl (*coming back to him, triumphant*) Now youre talking! I thought youd come off it when you saw a chance of getting back a bit of what you chucked at me last night. (*Confidentially*) Youd had a drop in, hadnt you?

Higgins (*peremptorily*) Sit down.

The Flower Girl. Oh, if youre going to make a compliment of it—

Higgins (*thundering at her*) Sit down.

Mrs Pearce (*severely*) Sit down, girl. Do as youre told. (*She places the stray chair near the hearthrug between Higgins and Pickering, and stands behind it waiting for the girl to sit down*).

The Flower Girl. Ah-ah-ah-ow-ow-oo! (*She stands, half rebellious, half bewildered*).

Pickering (*very courteous*) Wont you sit down?

The Flower Girl (*coyly*) Dont mind if I do. (*She sits down. Pickering returns to the hearthrug*).

Higgins. Whats your name?

The Flower Girl. Liza Doolittle.

Higgins (*declaiming gravely*)

> Eliza, Elizabeth, Betsy and Bess,
> They went to the woods to get a bird's nes':

Pickering. They found a nest with four eggs in it:

Higgins. They took one apiece, and left three in it.

They laugh heartily at their own wit.

Liza. Oh, dont be silly.

Mrs Pearce. You mustnt speak to the gentleman like that.

Liza. Well, why wont he speak sensible to me?

Higgins. Come back to business. How much do you propose to pay me for the lessons?

Liza. Oh, I know whats right. A lady friend of mine gets French lessons for eighteenpence an hour from a real French gentleman. Well, you wouldnt have the face to ask me the same for teaching me my own language as you would for French; so I wont give more than a shilling. Take it or leave it.

Higgins (walking up and down the room, rattling his keys and his cash in his pockets) You know, Pickering, if you consider a shilling, not as a simple shilling, but as a percentage of this girl's income, it works out as fully equivalent to sixty or seventy guineas from a millionaire.

Pickering. How so?

Higgins. Figure it out. A millionaire has about £150 a day. She earns about half-a-crown.

Liza (haughtily) Who told you I only—

Higgins (continuing) She offers me two-fifths of her day's income for a lesson. Two-fifths of a millionaire's income for a day would be somewhere about £60. It's handsome. By George, it's enormous! it's the biggest offer I ever had.

Liza (rising, terrified) Sixty pounds! What are you talking about? I never offered you sixty pounds. Where would I get—

Higgins. Hold your tongue.

Liza (weeping) But I aint got sixty pounds. Oh—

Mrs Pearce. Dont cry, you silly girl. Sit down. Nobody is going to touch your money.

Higgins. Somebody is going to touch you, with a broomstick, if you dont stop snivelling. Sit down.

Liza (obeying slowly) Ah-ah-ah-ow-oo-o! One would think you was my father.

Higgins. If I decide to teach you, I'll be worse than two fathers to you. Here (*he offers her his silk handkerchief*)!

Liza. Whats this for?

Higgins. To wipe your eyes. To wipe any part of your face that feels moist. Remember: thats your handkerchief; and thats your sleeve. Dont mistake the one for the other if you wish to become a lady in a shop.

Liza, utterly bewildered, stares helplessly at him.

Mrs Pearce. It's no use talking to her like that, Mr Higgins: she doesnt understand you. Besides, youre quite wrong: she doesnt do it that way at all (*she takes the handkerchief*).

Liza (*snatching it*) Here! You give me that handkerchief. He give it to me, not to you.

Pickering (*laughing*) He did. I think it must be regarded as her property, Mrs Pearce.

Mrs Pearce (*resigning herself*) Serve you right, Mr Higgins.

Pickering. Higgins: I'm interested. What about the ambassador's garden party? I'll say youre the greatest teacher alive if you make that good. I'll bet you all the expenses of the experiment you cant do it. And I'll pay for the lessons.

Liza. Oh, you are real good. Thank you, Captain.

Higgins (*tempted, looking at her*) It's almost irresistible. She's so deliciously low—so horribly dirty—

Liza (*protesting extremely*) Ah-ah-ah-ah-ow-ow-oo-oo!!! I aint dirty: I washed my face and hands afore I come, I did.

Pickering. Youre certainly not going to turn her head with flattery, Higgins.

Mrs Pearce (*uneasy*) Oh, dont say that, sir: theres more ways than one of turning a girl's head; and nobody can do it better than Mr Higgins, though he may not always mean it. I do hope, sir, you wont encourage him to do anything foolish.

Higgins (*becoming excited as the idea grows on him*) What is life but a series of inspired follies? The difficulty is to find them to do. Never lose a chance: it doesnt come every day. I shall make a duchess of this draggletailed guttersnipe.

Liza (*strongly deprecating this view of her*) Ah-ah-ah-ow-ow-oo!

Higgins (*carried away*) Yes: in six months—in three if she has a good ear and a quick tongue—I'll take her anywhere and pass her off as anything. We'll start today: now! this moment! Take her away and clean her, Mrs Pearce. Monkey Brand, if it wont come off any other way. Is there a good fire in the kitchen?

Mrs Pearce (*protesting*) Yes; but—

Higgins (*storming on*) Take all her clothes off and burn them. Ring up Whiteley or somebody for new ones. Wrap her up in brown paper til they come.

Liza. Youre no gentleman, youre not, to talk of such things. I'm a good girl, I am; and I know what the like of you are, I do.

Higgins. We want none of your Lisson Grove prudery here, young woman. Youve got to learn to behave like a duchess. Take her away, Mrs Pearce. If she gives you any trouble, wallop her.

Liza (*springing up and running between Pickering and Mrs Pearce for protection*) No! I'll call the police, I will.

Mrs Pearce. But Ive no place to put her.

Higgins. Put her in the dustbin.

Liza. Ah-ah-ah-ow-ow-oo!

Pickering. Oh come, Higgins! be reasonable.

Mrs Pearce (*resolutely*) You m u s t be reasonable, Mr Higgins: really you must. You cant walk over everybody like this.

Higgins, *thus scolded, subsides. The hurricane is succeeded by a zephyr of amiable surprise.*

Higgins (*with professional exquisiteness of modulation*) I walk over everybody! My dear Mrs Pearce, my dear Pickering,

I never had the slightest intention of walking over anyone. All I propose is that we should be kind to this poor girl. We must help her to prepare and fit herself for her new station in life. If I did not express myself clearly it was because I did not wish to hurt her delicacy, or yours.

Liza, reassured, steals back to her chair.

Mrs Pearce (*to Pickering*) Well, did you ever hear anything like that, sir?

Pickering (*laughing heartily*) Never, Mrs Pearce: never.

Higgins (*patiently*) Whats the matter?

Mrs Pearce. Well, the matter is, sir, that you cant take a girl up like that as if you were picking up a pebble on the beach.

Higgins. Why not?

Mrs Pearce. Why not! But you dont know anything about her. What about her parents? She may be married.

Liza. Garn!

Higgins. There! As the girl very properly says, Garn! Married indeed! Dont you know that a woman of that class looks a worn out drudge of fifty a year after she's married?

Liza. Whood marry me?

Higgins (*suddenly resorting to the most thrillingly beautiful low tones in his best elocutionary style*) By George, Eliza, the streets will be strewn with the bodies of men shooting themselves for your sake before Ive done with you.

Mrs Pearce. Nonsense, sir. You mustnt talk like that to her.

Liza (*rising and squaring herself determinedly*) I'm going away. He's off his chump, he is. I dont want no balmies teaching me.

Higgins (*wounded in his tenderest point by her insensibility to his elocution*) Oh, indeed! I'm mad, am I? Very well, Mrs Pearce: you neednt order the new clothes for her. Throw her out.

Liza (*whimpering*) Nah-ow. You got no right to touch me.

Mrs Pearce. You see now what comes of being saucy. (*Indicating the door*) This way, please.

Liza (*almost in tears*) I didnt want no clothes. I wouldnt have taken them (*she throws away the handkerchief*). I can buy my own clothes.

Higgins (*deftly retrieving the handkerchief and intercepting her on her reluctant way to the door*) Youre an ungrateful wicked girl. This is my return for offering to take you out of the gutter and dress you beautifully and make a lady of you.

Mrs Pearce. Stop, Mr Higgins. I wont allow it. It's you that are wicked. Go home to your parents, girl; and tell them to take better care of you.

Liza. I aint got no parents. They told me I was big enough to earn my own living and turned me out.

Mrs Pearce. Wheres your mother?

Liza. I aint got no mother. Her that turned me out was my sixth stepmother. But I done without them. And I'm a good girl, I am.

Higgins. Very well, then, what on earth is all this fuss about? The girl doesnt belong to anybody—is no use to anybody but me. (*He goes to Mrs Pearce and begins coaxing*). You can adopt her, Mrs Pearce: I'm sure a daughter would be a great amusement to you. Now dont make any more fuss. Take her downstairs; and—

Mrs Pearce. But whats to become of her? Is she to be paid anything? Do be sensible, sir.

Higgins. Oh, pay her whatever is necessary: put it down in the housekeeping book. (*Impatiently*) What on earth will she want with money? She'll have her food and her clothes. She'll only drink if you give her money.

Liza (*turning on him*) Oh you a r e a brute. It's a lie: nobody ever saw the sign of liquor on me. (*She goes back to her chair and plants herself there defiantly*).

Pickering (*in good-humored remonstrance*) Does it occur to you, Higgins, that the girl has some feelings?

Higgins (*looking critically at her*) Oh no, I dont think so. Not any feelings that we need bother about. (*Cheerily*) Have you, Eliza?

Liza. I got my feelings same as anyone else.

Higgins (*to Pickering, reflectively*) You see the difficulty?

Pickering. Eh? What difficulty?

Higgins. To get her to talk grammar. The mere pronunciation is easy enough.

Liza. I dont want to talk grammar. I want to talk like a lady.

Mrs Pearce. Will you please keep to the point, Mr Higgins? I want to know on what terms the girl is to be here. Is she to have any wages? And what is to become of her when youve finished your teaching? You must look ahead a little.

Higgins (*impatiently*) Whats to become of her if I leave her in the gutter? Tell me that, Mrs Pearce.

Mrs Pearce. Thats her own business, not yours, Mr Higgins.

Higgins. Well, when Ive done with her, we can throw her back into the gutter; and then it will be her own business again; so thats all right.

Liza. Oh, youve no feeling heart in you: you dont care for nothing but yourself (*she rises and takes the floor resolutely*). Here! Ive had enough of this. I'm going (*making for the door*). You ought to be ashamed of yourself, you ought.

Higgins (*snatching a chocolate cream from the piano, his eyes suddenly beginning to twinkle with mischief*) Have some chocolates, Eliza.

Liza (*halting, tempted*) How do I know what might be in them? Ive heard of girls being drugged by the like of you.

Higgins whips out his penknife; cuts a chocolate in two; puts one half into his mouth and bolts it; and offers her the other half.

Higgins. Pledge of good faith, Eliza. I eat one half: you eat the other. (*Liza opens her mouth to retort: he pops the half chocolate into it*). You shall have boxes of them, barrels of them, every day. You shall live on them. Eh?

Liza (*who has disposed of the chocolate after being nearly choked by it*) I wouldnt have ate it, only I'm too ladylike to take it out of my mouth.

Higgins. Listen, Eliza. I think you said you came in a taxi.

Liza. Well, what if I did? Ive as good a right to take a taxi as anyone else.

Higgins. You have, Eliza; and in future you shall have as many taxis as you want. You shall go up and down and round the town in a taxi every day. Think of that, Eliza.

Mrs Pearce. Mr Higgins: youre tempting the girl. It's not right. She should think of the future.

Higgins. At her age! Nonsense! Time enough to think of the future when you havnt any future to think of. No, Eliza: do as this lady does: think of other people's futures; but never think of your own. Think of chocolates, and taxis, and gold, and diamonds.

Liza. No: I dont want no gold and no diamonds. I'm a good girl, I am. (*She sits down again, with an attempt at dignity*).

Higgins. You shall remain so, Eliza, under the care of Mrs Pearce. And you shall marry an officer in the Guards, with a beautiful moustache: the son of a marquis, who will disinherit him for marrying you, but will relent when he sees your beauty and goodness—

Pickering. Excuse me, Higgins; but I really must interfere. Mrs Pearce is quite right. If this girl is to put herself in your hands for six months for an experiment in teaching, she must understand thoroughly what she's doing.

Higgins. How can she? She's incapable of understanding anything. Besides, do any of us understand what we are doing? If we did, would we ever do it?

Pickering. Very clever, Higgins; but not sound sense. (*To Eliza*) Miss Doolittle—

Liza (*overwhelmed*) Ah-ah-ow-oo!

Higgins. There! Thats all youll get out of Eliza. Ah-ah-ow-oo! No use explaining. As a military man you ought to know that. Give her her orders: thats what she wants. Eliza: you are to live here for the next six months, learning how to speak beautifully, like a lady in a florist's shop. If youre good and do whatever youre told, you shall sleep in a proper bedroom, and have lots to eat, and money to buy chocolates and take rides in taxis. If youre naughty and idle you will sleep in the back kitchen among the black beetles, and be walloped by Mrs Pearce with a broomstick. At the end of six months you shall go to Buckingham Palace in a carriage, beautifully dressed. If the King finds out youre not a lady, you will be taken by the police to the Tower of London, where your head will be cut off as a warning to other presumptuous flower girls. If you are not found out, you shall have a present of seven-and-sixpence to start life with as a lady in a shop. If you refuse this offer you will be a most ungrateful and wicked girl; and the angels will weep for you. (*To Pickering*) Now are you satisfied, Pickering? (*To Mrs Pearce*) Can I put it more plainly and fairly, Mrs Pearce?

Mrs Pearce (*patiently*) I think youd better let me speak to the girl properly in private. I dont know that I can take charge of her or consent to the arrangement at all. Of course I know you dont mean her any harm; but when you get what you call interested in people's accents, you never think or care what may happen to them or you. Come with me, Eliza.

Higgins. Thats all right. Thank you, Mrs Pearce. Bundle her off to the bathroom.

Liza (*rising reluctantly and suspiciously*) Youre a great bully, you are. I wont stay here if I dont like. I wont let nobody wallop me. I never asked to go to Bucknam Palace, I didnt. I was never in trouble with the police, not me. I'm a good girl—

Mrs Pearce. Dont answer back, girl. You dont understand the gentleman. Come with me. (*She leads the way to the door, and holds it open for Eliza*).

Liza (*as she goes out*) Well, what I say is right. I wont go near the King, not if I'm going to have my head cut off. If I'd known what I was letting myself in for, I wouldnt have come here. I always been a good girl; and I never offered to say a word to him; and I dont owe him nothing; and I dont care; and I wont be put upon; and I have my feelings the same as anyone else—

Mrs Pearce shuts the door; and Eliza's plaints are no longer audible. Pickering comes from the hearth to the chair and sits astride it with his arms on the back.

Pickering. Excuse the straight question, Higgins. Are you a man of good character where women are concerned?

Higgins (moodily) Have you ever met a man of good character where women are concerned?

Pickering. Yes: very frequently.

Higgins (dogmatically, lifting himself on his hands to the level of the piano, and sitting on it with a bounce) Well, I havnt. I find that the moment I let a woman make friends with me, she becomes jealous, exacting, suspicious, and a damned nuisance. I find that the moment I let myself make friends with a woman, I become selfish and tyrannical. Women upset everything. When you let them into your life, you find that the woman is driving at one thing and youre driving at another.

Pickering. At what, for example?

Higgins (coming off the piano restlessly) Oh, Lord knows! I suppose the woman wants to live her own life; and the man wants to live his; and each tries to drag the other on to the wrong track. One wants to go north and the other south; and the result is that both have to go east, though they both hate the east wind. *(He sits down on the bench at the keyboard).* So here I am, a confirmed old bachelor, and likely to remain so.

Pickering (rising and standing over him gravely) Come, Higgins! You know what I mean. If I'm to be in this business I shall feel responsible for that girl. I hope it's understood that no advantage is to be taken of her position.

Higgins. What! That thing! Sacred, I assure you. (*Rising to explain*) You see, she'll be a pupil; and teaching would be impossible unless pupils were sacred. Ive taught scores of American millionairesses how to speak English: the best looking women in the world. I'm seasoned. They might as well be blocks of wood. *I* might as well be a block of wood. It's—

Mrs Pearce opens the door. She has Eliza's hat in her hand. Pickering retires to the easy-chair at the hearth and sits down.

Higgins (*eagerly*) Well, Mrs Pearce: is it all right?

Mrs Pearce (*at the door*) I just wish to trouble you with a word, if I may, Mr Higgins.

Higgins. Yes, certainly. Come in. (*She comes forward*). Dont burn that, Mrs Pearce. I'll keep it as a curiosity. (*He takes the hat*).

Mrs Pearce. Handle it carefully, sir, p l e a s e. I had to promise her not to burn it; but I had better put it in the oven for a while.

Higgins (*putting it down hastily on the piano*) Oh! thank you. Well, what have you to say to me?

Pickering. Am I in the way?

Mrs Pearce. Not at all, sir. Mr Higgins: will you please be very particular what you say before the girl?

Higgins (*sternly*) Of course. I'm always particular about what I say. Why do you say this to me?

Mrs Pearce (*unmoved*) No, sir: youre not at all particular when youve mislaid anything or when you get a little impatient. Now it doesnt matter before me: I'm used to it. But you really must not swear before the girl.

Higgins (*indignantly*) I swear! (*Most emphatically*) I never swear. I detest the habit. What the devil do you mean?

Mrs Pearce (*stolidly*) Thats what I mean, sir. You swear a great deal too much. I dont mind your damning and blasting, and w h a t the devil and w h e r e the devil and w h o the devil—

Higgins. Mrs Pearce: this language from your lips! Really!

Mrs Pearce (*not to be put off*)—but there is a certain word I must ask you not to use. The girl has just used it herself because the bath was too hot. It begins with the same letter as bath. She knows no better: she learnt it at her mother's knee. But she must not hear it from y o u r lips.

Higgins (*loftily*) I cannot charge myself with having ever uttered it, Mrs Pearce. (*She looks at him steadfastly. He adds, hiding an uneasy conscience with a judicial air*) Except perhaps in a moment of extreme and justifiable excitement.

Mrs Pearce. Only this morning, sir, you applied it to your boots, to the butter, and to the brown bread.

Higgins. Oh, that! Mere alliteration, Mrs Pearce, natural to a poet.

Mrs Pearce. Well, sir, whatever you choose to call it, I beg you not to let the girl hear you repeat it.

Higgins. Oh, very well, very well. Is that all?

Mrs Pearce. No, sir. We shall have to be very particular with this girl as to personal cleanliness.

Higgins. Certainly. Quite right. Most important.

Mrs Pearce. I mean not to be slovenly about her dress or untidy in leaving things about.

Higgins (*going to her solemnly*) Just so. I intended to call your attention to that. (*He passes on to Pickering, who is enjoying the conversation immensely*). It is these little things that matter, Pickering. Take care of the pence and the pounds will take care of themselves is as true of personal habits as of money. (*He comes to anchor on the hearthrug, with the air of a man in an unassailable position*).

Mrs Pearce. Yes, sir. Then might I ask you not to come down to breakfast in your dressing-gown, or at any rate not to use it as a napkin to the extent you do, sir. And if you would be so good as not to eat everything off the same plate, and to remember not to put the porridge saucepan out of your hand on the clean tablecloth, it would be a better example to the girl. You know you nearly choked yourself with a fishbone in the jam only last week.

Higgins (*routed from the hearthrug and drifting back to the piano*) I may do these things sometimes in absence of mind; but surely I dont do them habitually. (*Angrily*) By the way: my dressing-gown smells most damnably of benzine.

Mrs Pearce. No doubt it does, Mr Higgins. But if you will wipe your fingers—

Higgins (*yelling*) Oh very well, very well: I'll wipe them in my hair in future.

Mrs Pearce. I hope youre not offended, Mr Higgins.

Higgins (*shocked at finding himself thought capable of an unamiable sentiment*) Not at all, not at all. Youre quite right, Mrs Pearce: I shall be particularly careful before the girl. Is that all?

Mrs Pearce. No, sir. Might she use some of those Japanese dresses you brought from abroad? I really cant put her back into her old things.

Higgins. Certainly. Anything you like. Is t h a t all?

Mrs Pearce. Thank you, sir. Thats all. (*She goes out*).

Higgins. You know, Pickering, that woman has the most extraordinary ideas about me. Here I am, a shy, diffident sort of man. Ive never been able to feel really grown-up and tremendous, like other chaps. And yet she's firmly persuaded that I'm an arbitrary overbearing bossing kind of person. I cant account for it.

Mrs Pearce returns.

Mrs Pearce. If you please, sir, the trouble's beginning already. Theres a dustman downstairs, Alfred Doolittle, wants to see you. He says you have his daughter here.

Pickering (*rising*) Phew! I say! (*He retreats to the hearthrug*).

Higgins (*promptly*) Send the blackguard up.

Mrs Pearce. Oh, very well, sir. (*She goes out*).

Pickering. He may not be a blackguard, Higgins.

Higgins. Nonsense. Of course he's a blackguard.

Pickering. Whether he is or not, I'm afraid we shall have some trouble with him.

Higgins (*confidently*) Oh no: I think not. If theres any trouble he shall have it with me, not I with him. And we are sure to get something interesting out of him.

Pickering. About the girl?

Higgins. No. I mean his dialect.

Pickering. Oh!

Mrs Pearce (*at the door*) Doolittle, sir. (*She admits Doolittle and retires*).

Alfred Doolittle is an elderly but vigorous dustman, clad in the costume of his profession, including a hat with a black brim covering his neck and shoulders. He has well marked and rather interesting features, and seems equally free from fear and conscience. He has a remarkably expressive voice, the result of a habit of giving vent to his feelings without reserve. His present pose is that of wounded honor and stern resolution.

Doolittle (*at the door, uncertain which of the two gentlemen is his man*) Professor Higgins?

Higgins. Here. Good morning. Sit down.

Doolittle. Morning, Governor. (*He sits down magisterially*) I come about a very serious matter, Governor.

Higgins (*to Pickering*) Brought up in Hounslow. Mother Welsh, I should think. (*Doolittle opens his mouth, amazed. Higgins continues*) What do you want, Doolittle?

Doolittle (*menacingly*) I want my daughter: thats what I want. See?

Higgins. Of course you do. Youre her father, arnt you? You dont suppose anyone else wants her, do you? I'm glad to see you have some spark of family feeling left. She's upstairs. Take her away at once.

Doolittle (*rising, fearfully taken aback*) What!

Higgins. Take her away. Do you suppose I'm going to keep your daughter for you?

Doolittle (*remonstrating*) Now, now, look here, Governor. Is this reasonable? Is it fairity to take advantage of a man like this? The girl belongs to me. You got her. Where do I come in? (*He sits down again*).

Higgins. Your daughter had the audacity to come to my house and ask me to teach her how to speak properly so that she could get a place in a flower-shop. This gentleman and my housekeeper have been here all the time. (*Bullying him*) How dare you come here and attempt to blackmail me? You sent her here on purpose.

Doolittle (*protesting*) No, Governor.

Higgins. You must have. How else could you possibly know that she is here?

Doolittle. Dont take a man up like that, Governor.

Higgins. The police shall take you up. This is a plant— a plot to extort money by threats. I shall telephone for the police. (*He goes resolutely to the telephone and opens the directory*).

Doolittle. Have I asked you for a brass farthing? I leave it to the gentleman here: have I said a word about money?

Higgins (*throwing the book aside and marching down on Doolittle with a poser*) What else did you come for?

Doolittle (*sweetly*) Well, what w o u l d a man come for? Be human, Governor.

Higgins (*disarmed*) Alfred: did you put her up to it?

Doolittle. So help me, Governor, I never did. I take my Bible oath I aint seen the girl these two months past.

Higgins. Then how did you know she was here?

Doolittle ("*most musical, most melancholy*") I'll tell you, Governor, if youll only let me get a word in. I'm willing to tell you. I'm wanting to tell you. I'm waiting to tell you.

Higgins. Pickering: this chap has a certain natural gift of rhetoric. Observe the rhythm of his native woodnotes wild. "I'm willing to tell you: I'm wanting to tell you: I'm waiting to tell you." Sentimental rhetoric! thats the Welsh strain in him. It also accounts for his mendacity and dishonesty.

Pickering. Oh, p l e a s e , Higgins: I'm west country myself. (*To Doolittle*) How did you know the girl was here if you didnt send her?

Doolittle. It was like this, Governor. The girl took a boy in the taxi to give him a jaunt. Son of her landlady, he is. He hung about on the chance of her giving him another ride home. Well, she sent him back for her luggage when she heard you was willing for her to stop here. I met the boy at the corner of Long Acre and Endell Street.

Higgins. Public house. Yes?

Doolittle. The poor man's club, Governor: why shouldnt I?

Pickering. Do let him tell his story, Higgins.

Doolittle. He told me what was up. And I ask you, what was my feelings and my duty as a father? I says to the boy, "You bring me the luggage," I says—

Pickering. Why didnt you go for it yourself?

Doolittle. Landlady wouldnt have trusted me with it, Governor. She's that kind of woman: you know. I had to give the boy a penny afore he trusted me with it, the little swine. I brought it to her just to oblige you like, and make myself agreeable. Thats all.

Higgins. How much luggage?

Doolittle. Musical instrument, Governor. A few pictures, a trifle of jewlery, and a bird-cage. She said she didnt want no clothes. What was I to think from that, Governor? I ask you as a parent what was I to think?

Higgins. So you came to rescue her from worse than death, eh?

Doolittle (*appreciatively: relieved at being so well under-stood*) Just so, Governor. Thats right.

Pickering. But why did you bring her luggage if you intended to take her away?

Doolittle. Have I said a word about taking her away? Have I now?

Higgins (*determinedly*) Youre going to take her away, double quick. (*He crosses to the hearth and rings the bell*).

Doolittle (*rising*) No, Governor. Dont say that. I'm not the man to stand in my girl's light. Heres a career opening for her, as you might say; and—

Mrs Pearce opens the door and awaits orders.

Higgins. Mrs Pearce: this is Eliza's father. He has come to her away. Give her to him. (*He goes back to the piano, with an air of washing his hands of the whole affair*).

Doolittle. No. This is a misunderstanding. Listen here—

Mrs Pearce. He cant take her away, Mr Higgins: how can he? You told me to burn her clothes.

Doolittle. Thats right. I cant carry the girl through the streets like a blooming monkey, can I? I put it to you.

Higgins. You have put it to me that you want your daughter. Take your daughter. If she has no clothes go out and buy her some.

Doolittle (*desperate*) Wheres the clothes she come in? Did I burn them or did your missus here?

Mrs Pearce. I am the housekeeper, if you please. I have sent for some clothes for your girl. When they come you can take her away. You can wait in the kitchen. This way, please.

Doolittle, much troubled, accompanies her to the door; then hesitates; finally turns confidently to Higgins.

Doolittle. Listen here, Governor. You and me is men of the world, aint we?

Higgins. Oh! Men of the world, are we? Youd better go, Mrs Pearce.

Mrs Pearce. I think so, indeed, sir. (*She goes, with dignity*).

Pickering. The floor is yours, Mr Doolittle.

Doolittle (*to Pickering*) I thank you, Governor. (*To Hig-*

gins, who takes refuge on the piano bench, a little overwhelmed
by the proximity of his visitor; for Doolittle has a professional
flavor of dust about him). Well, the truth is, Ive taken a sort
of fancy to you, Governor; and if you want the girl, I'm not
so set on having her back home again but what I might be
open to an arrangement. Regarded in the light of a young
woman, she's a fine handsome girl. As a daughter she's not
worth her keep; and so I tell you straight. All I ask is my rights
as a father; and youre the last man alive to expect me to let
her go for nothing; for I can see youre one of the straight
sort, Governor. Well, whats a five-pound note to you? And
whats Eliza to me? (He returns to his chair and sits down
judicially).

Pickering. I think you ought to know, Doolittle, that Mr
Higgins's intentions are entirely honorable.

Doolittle. Course they are, Governor. If I thought they wasnt,
I'd ask fifty.

Higgins (revolted) Do you mean to say, you callous rascal,
that you would sell your daughter for £50?

Doolittle. Not in a general way I wouldnt; but to oblige
a gentleman like you I'd do a good deal, I do assure you.

Pickering. Have you no morals, man?

Doolittle (unabashed) Cant afford them, Governor. Neither
could you if you was as poor as me. Not that I mean any
harm, you know. But if Liza is going to have a bit out of this,
why not me too?

Higgins (troubled) I dont know what to do, Pickering.
There can be no question that as a matter of morals it's a
positive crime to give this chap a farthing. And yet I feel a
sort of rough justice in his claim.

Doolittle. Thats it, Governor. Thats all I say. A father's
heart, as it were.

Pickering. Well, I know the feeling; but really it seems
hardly right—

Doolittle. Dont say that, Governor. Dont look at it that

way. What am I, Governors both? I ask you, what am I? I'm
one of the undeserving poor: thats what I am. Think of what
that means to a man. It means that he's up agen middle class
morality all the time. If theres anything going, and I put in
for a bit of it, it's always the same story: "Youre undeserving;
so you cant have it." But my needs is as great as the most
deserving widow's that ever got money out of six different
charities in one week for the death of the same husband. I
dont need less than a deserving man: I need more. I dont
eat less hearty than him; and I drink a lot more. I want
a bit of amusement, cause I'm a thinking man. I want cheerfulness and a song and a band when I feel low. Well, they
charge me just the same for everything as they charge the
deserving. What is middle class morality? Just an excuse for
never giving me anything. Therefore, I ask you, as two gentlemen, not to play that game on me. I'm playing straight with
you. I aint pretending to be deserving. I'm undeserving; and
I mean to go on being undeserving. I like it; and thats the
truth. Will you take advantage of a man's nature to do him
out of the price of his own daughter what he's brought up
and fed and clothed by the sweat of his brow until she's
growed big enough to be interesting to you two gentlemen?
Is five pounds unreasonable? I put it to you; and I leave it to
you.

   Higgins (rising, and going over to Pickering) Pickering:
if we were to take this man in hand for three months, he
could choose between a seat in the Cabinet and a popular
pulpit in Wales.

   Pickering. What do you say to that, Doolittle?

   Doolittle. Not me, Governor, thank you kindly. Ive heard
all the preachers and all the prime ministers—for I'm a thinking man and game for politics or religion or social reform same
as all the other amusements—and I tell you it's a dog's life
any way you look at it. Undeserving poverty is my line.

Taking one station in society with another, it's—it's—well, it's the only one that has any ginger in it, to my taste.

Higgins. I suppose we must give him a fiver.

Pickering. He'll make a bad use of it, I'm afraid.

Doolittle. Not me, Governor, so help me I wont. Dont you be afraid that I'll save it and spare it and live idle on it. There wont be a penny of it left by Monday: I'll have to go to work same as if I'd never had it. It wont pauperize me, you bet. Just one good spree for myself and the missus, giving pleasure to ourselves and employment to others, and satisfaction to you to think it's not been throwed away. You couldnt spend it better.

Higgins (taking out his pocket book and coming between Doolittle and the piano) This is irresistible. Lets give him ten. *(He offers two notes to the dustman).*

Doolittle. No, Governor. She wouldnt have the heart to spend ten; and perhaps I shouldnt neither. Ten pounds is a lot of money: it makes a man feel prudent like; and then goodbye to happiness. You give me what I ask you, Governor: not a penny more, and not a penny less.

Pickering. Why dont you marry that missus of yours? I rather draw the line at encouraging that sort of immorality.

Doolittle. Tell her so, Governor: tell her so. I'm willing. It's me that suffers by it. Ive no hold on her. I got to be agreeable to her. I got to give her presents. I got to buy her clothes something sinful. I'm a slave to that woman, Governor, just because I'm not her lawful husband. And she knows it too. Catch her marrying me! Take my advice, Governor: marry Eliza while she's young and dont know no better. If you dont youll be sorry for it after. If you do, s h e'l l be sorry for it after; but better her than you, because youre a man, and she's only a woman and dont know how to be happy anyhow.

Higgins. Pickering: if we listen to this man another minute, we shall have no convictions left. *(To Doolittle)* Five pounds I think you said.

Doolittle. Thank you kindly, Governor.

Higgins. Youre sure you wont take ten?

Doolittle. Not now. Another time, Governor.

Higgins (*handing him a five-pound note*) Here you are.

Doolittle. Thank you, Governor. Good morning. (*He hurries to the door, anxious to get away with his booty. When he opens it he is confronted with a dainty and exquisitely clean young Japanese lady in a simple blue cotton kimono printed cunningly with small white jasmine blossoms. Mrs Pearce is with her. He gets out of her way deferentially and apologizes*). Beg pardon, miss.

The Japanese Lady. Garn! Dont you know your own daughter?

Doolittle	exclaiming	Bly me! it's Eliza!
Higgins	simul-	Whats that! This!
Pickering	taneously	By Jove!

Liza. Dont I look silly?

Higgins. Silly?

Mrs Pearce (*at the door*) Now, Mr Higgins, please dont say anything to make the girl conceited about herself.

Higgins (*conscientiously*) Oh! Quite right, Mrs Pearce. (*To Eliza*) Yes: damned silly.

Mrs Pearce. Please, sir.

Higgins (*correcting himself*) I mean extremely silly.

Liza. I should look all right with my hat on. (*She takes up her hat; puts it on; and walks across the room to the fireplace with a fashionable air*).

Higgins. A new fashion, by George! And it ought to look horrible!

Doolittle (*with fatherly pride*) Well, I never thought she'd clean up as good looking as that, Governor. She's a credit to me, aint she?

Liza. I tell you, it's easy to clean up here. Hot and cold water on tap, just as much as you like, there is. Woolly towels, there is; and a towel horse so hot, it burns your fingers. Soft

brushes to scrub yourself, and a wooden bowl of soap smelling
like primroses. Now I know why ladies is so clean. Washing's
a treat for them. Wish they saw what it is for the like of me.

Higgins. I'm glad the bathroom met with your approval.

Liza. It didnt: not all of it; and I dont care who hears me
say it. Mrs Pearce knows.

Higgins. What was wrong, Mrs Pearce?

Mrs Pearce (blandly) Oh, nothing, sir. It doesnt matter.

Liza. I had a good mind to break it. I didnt know which
way to look. But I hung a towel over it, I did.

Higgins. Over what?

Mrs Pearce. Over the looking glass, sir.

Higgins. Doolittle: you have brought your daughter up too
strictly.

Doolittle. Me! I never brought her up at all, except to give
her a lick of a strap now and again. Dont put it on me, Governor. She aint accustomed to it, you see: thats all. But she'll soon
pick up your free-and-easy ways.

Liza. I'm a good girl, I am; and I wont pick up no free-and-
easy ways.

Higgins. Eliza: if you say again that youre a good girl, your
father shall take you home.

Liza. Not him. You dont know my father. All he come here
for was to touch you for some money to get drunk on.

Doolittle. Well, what else would I want money for? To put
into the plate in church, I suppose. (*She puts out her tongue
at him. He is so incensed by this that Pickering presently
finds it necessary to step between them*). Dont you give me
none of your lip; and dont let me hear you giving this gentleman any of it neither, or youll hear from me about it. See?

Higgins. Have you any further advice to give her before
you go, Doolittle? Your blessing, for instance.

Doolittle. No, Governor: I aint such a mug as to put up my
children to all I know myself. Hard enough to hold them in
without that. If you want Eliza's mind improved, Governor,

you do it yourself with a strap. So long, gentlemen. (*He turns to go*).

Higgins (*impressively*) Stop. Youll come regularly to see your daughter. It's your duty, you know. My brother is a clergyman; and he could help you in your talks with her.

Doolittle (*evasively*) Certainly. I'll come, Governor. Not just this week, because I have a job at a distance. But later on you may depend on me. Afternoon, gentlemen. Afternoon, maam. (*He takes off his hat to Mrs Pearce, who disdains the salutation and goes out. He winks at Higgins, thinking him probably a fellow-sufferer from Mrs Pearce's difficult disposition, and follows her*).

Liza. Dont you believe the old liar. He'd as soon you set a bull-dog on him as a clergyman. You wont see him again in a hurry.

Higgins. I dont want to, Eliza. Do you?

Liza. Not me. I dont want never to see him again, I dont. He's a disgrace to me, he is, collecting dust, instead of working at his trade.

Pickering. What is his trade, Eliza?

Liza. Taking money out of other people's pockets into his own. His proper trade's a navvy; and he works at it sometimes too—for exercise—and earns good money at it. Aint you going to call me Miss Doolittle any more?

Pickering. I beg your pardon, Miss Doolittle. It was a slip of the tongue.

Liza. Oh, I dont mind; only it sounded so genteel. I s h o u l d just like to take a taxi to the corner of Tottenham Court Road and get out there and tell it to wait for me, just to put the girls in their place a bit. I wouldnt speak to them, you know.

Pickering. Better wait til we get you something really fashionable.

Higgins. Besides, you shouldnt cut your old friends now that you have risen in the world. Thats what we call snobbery.

Liza. You dont call the like of them my friends now, I should hope. Theyve took it out of me often enough with their ridicule when they had the chance; and now I mean to get a bit of my own back. But if I'm to have fashionable clothes, I'll wait. I should like to have some. Mrs Pearce says youre going to give me some to wear in bed at night different to what I wear in the daytime; but it do seem a waste of money when you could get something to shew. Besides, I never could fancy changing into cold things on a winter night.

Mrs Pearce (coming back) Now, Eliza. The new things have come for you to try on.

Liza. Ah-ow-oo-ooh! *(She rushes out)*.

Mrs Pearce (following her) Oh, dont rush about like that, girl. *(She shuts the door behind her)*.

Higgins. Pickering: we have taken on a stiff job.

Pickering (with conviction) Higgins: we have.

ACT III

IT IS Mrs Higgins's at-home day. Nobody has yet arrived. Her drawing room, in a flat on Chelsea Embankment, has three windows looking on the river; and the ceiling is not so lofty as it would be in an older house of the same pretension. The windows are open, giving access to a balcony with flowers in pots. If you stand with your face to the windows, you have the fireplace on your left and the door in the right-hand wall close to the corner nearest the windows.

Mrs Higgins was brought up on Morris and Burne Jones; and her room, which is very unlike her son's room in Wimpole Street, is not crowded with furniture and little tables and nick-nacks. In the middle of the room there is a big ottoman; and this, with the carpet, the Morris wall-papers, and the Morris chintz window curtains and brocade covers of the ottoman and its cushions, supply all the ornament, and are much too handsome to be hidden by odds and ends of useless things. A few good oil-paintings from the exhibitions in the Grosvenor Gallery thirty years ago (the Burne Jones, not the Whistler side of them) are on the walls. The only landscape is a Cecil Lawson on the scale of a Rubens. There is a portrait of Mrs Higgins as she was when she defied fashion in her youth in one of the beautiful Rosettian costumes which, when caricatured by people who did not understand, led to the absurdities of popular estheticism in the eighteen-seventies.

In the corner diagonally opposite the door Mrs Higgins, now over sixty and long past taking the trouble to dress out of the fashion, sits writing at an elegantly simple writing-table with a bell button within reach of her hand. There is a Chippendale chair further back in the room between her and the window nearest her side. At the other side of the room, further forward, is an Elizabethan chair roughly carved in the taste of Inigo

Jones. On the same side a piano in a decorated case. The corner between the fireplace and the window is occupied by a divan cushioned in Morris chintz.

It is between four and five in the afternoon.

The door is opened violently; and Higgins enters with his hat on.

Mrs Higgins (*dismayed*) Henry (*scolding him*)! What are you doing here to-day? It is my at-home day: you promised not to come. (*As he bends to kiss her, she takes his hat off, and presents it to him*).

Higgins. Oh bother! (*He throws the hat down on the table*).

Mrs Higgins. Go home at once.

Higgins (*kissing her*) I know, mother. I came on purpose.

Mrs Higgins. But you mustnt. I'm serious, Henry. You offend all my friends: they stop coming whenever they meet you.

Higgins. Nonsense! I know I have no small talk; but people dont mind. (*He sits on the settee*).

Mrs Higgins. Oh! dont they? Small talk indeed! What about your large talk? Really, dear, you mustnt stay.

Higgins. I must. Ive a job for you. A phonetic job.

Mrs Higgins. No use, dear. I'm sorry; but I cant get round your vowels; and though I like to get pretty postcards in your patent shorthand, I always have to read the copies in ordinary writing you so thoughtfully send me.

Higgins. Well, this isnt a phonetic job.

Mrs Higgins. You said it was.

Higgins. Not your part of it. Ive picked up a girl.

Mrs Higgins. Does that mean that some girl has picked you up?

Higgins. Not at all. I dont mean a love affair.

Mrs Higgins. What a pity!

Higgins. Why?

Mrs Higgins. Well, you never fall in love with anyone

under forty-five. When will you discover that there are some rather nice-looking young women about?

Higgins. Oh, I cant be bothered with young women. My idea of a lovable woman is something as like you as possible. I shall never get into the way of seriously liking young women: some habits lie too deep to be changed. (*Rising abruptly and walking about, jingling his money and his keys in his trouser pockets*) Besides, theyre all idiots.

Mrs Higgins. Do you know what you would do if you really loved me, Henry?

Higgins. Oh bother! What? Marry, I suppose?

Mrs Higgins. No. Stop fidgeting and take your hands out of your pockets. (*With a gesture of despair, he obeys and sits down again*). Thats a good boy. Now tell me about the girl.

Higgins. She's coming to see you.

Mrs Higgins. I dont remember asking her.

Higgins. You didnt. *I* asked her. If youd known her you wouldnt have asked her.

Mrs Higgins. Indeed! Why?

Higgins. Well, it's like this. She's a common flower girl. I picked her off the kerbstone.

Mrs Higgins. And invited her to my at-home!

Higgins (*rising and coming to her to coax her*) Oh, thatll be all right. Ive taught her to speak properly; and she has strict orders as to her behavior. She's to keep to two subjects: the weather and everybody's health—Fine day and How do you do, you know—and not to let herself go on things in general. That will be safe.

Mrs Higgins. Safe! To talk about our health! about our in-sides! perhaps about our outsides! How could you be so silly, Henry?

Higgins (*impatiently*) Well, she must talk about something. (*He controls himself and sits down again*). Oh, she'll be all right: dont you fuss. Pickering is in it with me. Ive a sort of bet on that I'll pass her off as a duchess in six months. I

started on her some months ago; and she's getting on like a
house on fire. I shall win my bet. She has a quick ear; and
she's been easier to teach than my middle class pupils because
she's had to learn a complete new language. She talks English
almost as you talk French.

Mrs Higgins. Thats satisfactory, at all events.

Higgins. Well, it is and it isnt.

Mrs Higgins. What does that mean?

Higgins. You see, Ive got her pronunciation all right; but
you have to consider not only h o w a girl pronounces, but
w h a t she pronounces; and thats where—

They are interrupted by the parlor-maid, announcing guests.

The Parlor-Maid. Mrs and Miss Eynsford Hill. (*She withdraws*).

Higgins. Oh Lord! (*He rises; snatches his hat from the table;
and makes for the door; but before he reaches it his mother
introduces him*).

*Mrs and Miss Eynsford Hill are the mother and daughter
who sheltered from the rain in Covent Garden. The mother is
well bred, quiet, and has the habitual anxiety of straitened
means. The daughter has acquired a gay air of being very much
at home in society: the bravado of genteel poverty.*

Mrs Eynsford Hill (*to Mrs Higgins*) How do you do? (*They
shake hands*).

Miss Eynsford Hill. How d'you do? (*She shakes*).

Mrs Higgins (*introducing*) My son Henry.

Mrs Eynsford Hill. Your celebrated son! I have so longed
to meet you, Professor Higgins.

Higgins (*glumly, making no movement in her direction*)
Delighted. (*He backs against the piano and bows brusquely*).

Miss Eynsford Hill (*going to him with confident familiarity*) How do you do?

Higgins (*staring at her*) Ive seen you before somewhere.
I havnt the ghost of a notion where; but Ive heard your voice.
(*Drearily*) It doesnt matter. Youd better sit down.

Mrs Higgins. I'm sorry to say that my celebrated son has no manners. You mustnt mind him.

Miss Eynsford Hill (*gaily*) I dont. (*She sits in the Elizabethan chair*).

Mrs Eynsford Hill (*a little bewildered*) Not at all. (*She sits on the ottoman between her daughter and Mrs Higgins, who has turned her chair away from the writing-table*).

Higgins. Oh, have I been rude? I didnt mean to be.

He goes to the central window, through which, with his back to the company, he contemplates the river and the flowers in Battersea Park on the opposite bank as if they were a frozen desert.

The parlor-maid returns, ushering in Pickering.

The Parlor-Maid. Colonel Pickering. (*She withdraws*).

Pickering. How do you do, Mrs Higgins?

Mrs Higgins. So glad youve come. Do you know Mrs Eynsford Hill—Miss Eynsford Hill? (*Exchange of bows. The Colonel brings the Chippendale chair a little forward between Mrs Hill and Mrs Higgins, and sits down*).

Pickering. Has Henry told you what weve come for?

Higgins (*over his shoulder*) We were interrupted: damn it!

Mrs Higgins. Oh Henry, Henry, really!

Mrs Eynsford Hill (*half rising*) Are we in the way?

Mrs Higgins (*rising and making her sit down again*) No, no. You couldnt have come more fortunately: we want you to meet a friend of ours.

Higgins (*turning hopefully*) Yes, by George! We want two or three people. Youll do as well as anybody else.

The parlor-maid returns, ushering Freddy.

The Parlor-Maid. Mr Eynsford Hill.

Higgins (*almost audibly, past endurance*) God of Heaven! another of them.

Freddy (*shaking hands with Mrs Higgins*) Ahdedo?

Mrs Higgins. Very good of you to come. (*Introducing*) Colonel Pickering.

Freddy (*bowing*) Ahdedo?

Mrs Higgins. I dont think you know my son, Professor Higgins.

Freddy (*going to Higgins*) Ahdedo?

Higgins (*looking at him much as if he were a pickpocket*) I'll take my oath Ive met y o u before somewhere. Where was it?

Freddy. I dont think so.

Higgins (*resignedly*) It dont matter, anyhow. Sit down.

He shakes Freddy's hand, and almost slings him on to the ottoman with his face to the windows; then comes round to the other side of it.

Higgins. Well, here we are, anyhow! (*He sits down on the ottoman next Mrs Eynsford Hill, on her left*). And now, what the devil are we going to talk about until Eliza comes?

Mrs Higgins. Henry: you are the life and soul of the Royal Society's soirées; but really youre rather trying on more commonplace occasions.

Higgins. Am I? Very sorry. (*Beaming suddenly*) I suppose I am, you know. (*Uproariously*) Ha, ha!

Miss Eynsford Hill (*who considers Higgins quite eligible matrimonially*) I sympathize. I havnt any small talk. If people would only be frank and say what they really think!

Higgins (*relapsing into gloom*) Lord forbid!

Mrs Eynsford Hill (*taking up her daughter's cue*) But why?

Higgins. What they think they ought to think is bad enough, Lord knows; but what they really think would break up the whole show. Do you suppose it would be really agreeable if I were to come out now with what I really think?

Miss Eynsford Hill (*gaily*) Is it so very cynical?

Higgins. Cynical! Who the dickens said it was cynical? I mean it wouldnt be decent.

Mrs Eynsford Hill (*seriously*) Oh! I'm sure you dont mean that, Mr Higgins.

Higgins. You see, we're all savages, more or less. We're supposed to be civilized and cultured—to know all about poetry and philosophy and art and science, and so on; but how many of us know even the meanings of these names? (*To Miss Hill*) What do y o u know of poetry? (*To Mrs Hill*) What do y o u know of science? (*Indicating Freddy*) What does h e know of art or science or anything else? What the devil do you imagine I know of philosophy?

Mrs Higgins (*warningly*) Or of manners, Henry?

The Parlor-Maid (*opening the door*) Miss Doolittle. (*She withdraws*).

Higgins (*rising hastily and running to Mrs Higgins*) Here she is, mother. (*He stands on tiptoe and makes signs over his mother's head to Eliza to indicate to her which lady is her hostess*).

Eliza, who is exquisitely dressed, produces an impression of such remarkable distinction and beauty as she enters that they all rise, quite fluttered. Guided by Higgins's signals, she comes to Mrs Higgins with studied grace.

Liza (*speaking with pedantic correctness of pronunciation and great beauty of tone*) How do you do, Mrs Higgins? (*She gasps slightly in making sure of the H in Higgins, but is quite successful*). Mr Higgins told me I might come.

Mrs Higgins (*cordially*) Quite right: I'm very glad indeed to see you.

Pickering. How do you do, Miss Doolittle?

Liza (*shaking hands with him*) Colonel Pickering, is it not?

Mrs Eynsford Hill. I feel sure we have met before, Miss Doolittle. I remember your eyes.

Liza. How do you do? (*She sits down on the ottoman gracefully in the place just left vacant by Higgins*).

Mrs Eynsford Hill (*introducing*) My daughter Clara.

Liza. How do you do?

Clara (*impulsively*) How do you do? (*She sits down on the ottoman beside Eliza, devouring her with her eyes*).

Freddy (*coming to their side of the ottoman*) Ive certainly had the pleasure.

Mrs Eynsford Hill (*introducing*) My son Freddy.

Liza. How do you do?

Freddy bows and sits down in the Elizabethan chair, in-fatuated.

Higgins (*suddenly*) By George, yes: it all comes back to me! (*They stare at him*). Covent Garden! (*Lamentably*) What a damned thing!

Mrs Higgins. Henry, please! (*He is about to sit on the edge of the table*) Dont sit on my writing-table: youll break it.

Higgins (*sulkily*) Sorry.

He goes to the divan, stumbling into the fender and over the fire-irons on his way; extricating himself with muttered imprecations; and finishing his disastrous journey by throwing himself so impatiently on the divan that he almost breaks it. Mrs Higgins looks at him, but controls herself and says nothing.

A long and painful pause ensues.

Mrs Higgins (*at last, conversationally*) Will it rain, do you think?

Liza. The shallow depression in the west of these islands is likely to move slowly in an easterly direction. There are no indications of any great change in the barometrical situation.

Freddy. Ha! ha! how awfully funny!

Liza. What is wrong with that, young man? I bet I got it right.

Freddy. Killing!

Mrs Eynsford Hill. I'm sure I hope it wont turn cold. Theres so much influenza about. It runs right through our whole family regularly every spring.

Liza (*darkly*) My aunt died of influenza: so they said.

Mrs Eynsford Hill (*clicks her tongue sympathetically*)!!!

Liza (*in the same tragic tone*) But it's my belief they done the old woman in.

Mrs Higgins (*puzzled*) Done her in?

Liza. Y-e-e-e-es, Lord love you! Why should s h e die of in fluenza? She come through diphtheria right enough the year before. I saw her with my own eyes. Fairly blue with it, she was. They all thought she was dead; but my father he kept ladling gin down her throat til she came to so sudden that she bit the bowl off the spoon.

Mrs Eynsford Hill (*startled*) Dear me!

Liza (*piling up the indictment*) What call would a woman with that strength in her have to die of influenza? What become of her new straw hat that should have come to me? Somebody pinched it; and what I say is, them as pinched it done her in.

Mrs Eynsford Hill. What does doing her in mean?

Higgins (*hastily*) Oh, thats the new small talk. To do a person in means to kill them.

Mrs Eynsford Hill (*to Eliza, horrified*) You surely dont believe that your aunt was killed?

Liza. Do I not! Them she lived with would have killed her for a hat-pin, let alone a hat.

Mrs Eynsford Hill. But it cant have been right for your father to pour spirits down her throat like that. It might have killed her.

Liza. Not her. Gin was mother's milk to her. Besides, he'd poured so much down his own throat that he knew the good of it.

Mrs Eynsford Hill. Do you mean that he drank?

Liza. Drank! My word! Something chronic.

Mrs Eynsford Hill. How dreadful for you!

Liza. Not a bit. It never did him no harm what I could see. But then he did not keep it up regular. (*Cheerfully*) On the burst, as you might say, from time to time. And always more agreeable when he had a drop in. When he was out of work, my mother used to give him fourpence and tell him to go out and not come back until he'd drunk himself cheerful and loving-like. Theres lots of women has to make their husbands drunk to make them fit to live with. (*Now quite at her ease*) You see, it's like this. If a man has a bit of a conscience, it always takes him when he's sober; and then it makes him low-spirited. A drop of booze just takes that off and makes him happy. (*To Freddy, who is in convulsions of suppressed laughter*) Here! what are you sniggering at?

Freddy. The new small talk. You do it so awfully well.

Liza. If I was doing it proper, what was you laughing at? (*To Higgins*) Have I said anything I oughtnt?

Mrs Higgins (*interposing*) Not at all, Miss Doolittle.

Liza. Well, thats a mercy, anyhow. (*Expansively*) What I always say is—

Higgins (*rising and looking at his watch*) Ahem!

Liza (*looking round at him; taking the hint; and rising*) Well: I must go. (*They all rise. Freddy goes to the door*). So pleased to have met you. Goodbye. (*She shakes hands with Mrs Higgins*).

Mrs Higgins. Goodbye.

Liza. Goodbye, Colonel Pickering.

Pickering. Goodbye, Miss Doolittle. (*They shake hands*).

Liza (*nodding to the others*) Goodbye, all.

Freddy (*opening the door for her*) Are you walking across the Park, Miss Doolittle? If so—

Liza. Walk! Not bloody likely. (*Sensation*). I am going in a taxi. (*She goes out*).

Pickering gasps and sits down. Freddy goes out on the balcony to catch another glimpse of Eliza.

Mrs Eynsford Hill (*suffering from shock*) Well, I really cant get used to the new ways.

Clara (*throwing herself discontentedly into the Elizabethan chair*) Oh, it's all right, mamma, quite right. People will think we never go anywhere or see anybody if you are so old-fashioned.

Mrs Eynsford Hill. I daresay I am very old-fashioned; but I do hope you wont begin using that expression, Clara. I have got accustomed to hear you talking about men as rotters, and calling everything filthy and beastly; though I do think it horrible and unladylike. But this last is really too much. Dont you think so, Colonel Pickering?

Pickering. Dont ask me. Ive been away in India for several years; and manners have changed so much that I sometimes dont know whether I'm at a respectable dinner-table or in a ship's forecastle.

Clara. It's all a matter of habit. Theres no right or wrong in it. Nobody means anything by it. And it's so quaint, and gives such a smart emphasis to things that are not in themselves very witty. I find the new small talk delightful and quite innocent.

Mrs Eynsford Hill (rising) Well, after that, I think it's time for us to go.

Pickering and Higgins rise.

Clara (rising) Oh yes: we have three at-homes to go to still. Goodbye, Mrs Higgins. Goodbye, Colonel Pickering. Goodbye, Professor Higgins.

Higgins (coming grimly at her from the divan, and accompanying her to the door) Goodbye. Be sure you try on that small talk at the three at-homes. Dont be nervous about it. Pitch it in strong.

Clara (all smiles) I will. Goodbye. Such nonsense, all this early Victorian prudery!

Higgins (tempting her) Such damned nonsense!

Clara. Such bloody nonsense!

Mrs Eynsford Hill (convulsively) Clara!

Clara. Ha! ha! (*She goes out radiant, conscious of being thoroughly up to date, and is heard descending the stairs in a stream of silvery laughter*).

Freddy (to the heavens at large) Well, I ask you— (*He gives it up, and comes to Mrs Higgins*). Goodbye.

Mrs Higgins (shaking hands) Goodbye. Would you like to meet Miss Doolittle again?

Freddy (eagerly) Yes, I should, most awfully.

Mrs Higgins. Well, you know my days.

Freddy. Yes. Thanks awfully. Goodbye. (*He goes out*).

Mrs Eynsford Hill. Goodbye, Mr Higgins.

Higgins. Goodbye. Goodbye.

Mrs Eynsford Hill (*to Pickering*) It's no use. I shall never be able to bring myself to use that word.

Pickering. Dont. It's not compulsory, you know. Youll get on quite well without it.

Mrs Eynsford Hill. Only, Clara is so down on me if I am not positively reeking with the latest slang. Goodbye.

Pickering. Goodbye (*They shake hands*).

Mrs Eynsford Hill (*to Mrs Higgins*) You mustnt mind Clara. (*Pickering, catching from her lowered tone that this is not meant for him to hear, discreetly joins Higgins at the window*). We're so poor! and she gets so few parties, poor child! She doesnt quite know. (*Mrs Higgins, seeing that her eyes are moist, takes her hand sympathetically and goes with her to the door*). But the boy is nice. Dont you think so?

Mrs Higgins. Oh, quite nice. I shall always be delighted to see him.

Mrs Eynsford Hill. Thank you, dear. Goodbye. (*She goes out*).

Higgins (*eagerly*) Well? Is Eliza presentable? (*He swoops on his mother and drags her to the ottoman, where she sits down in Eliza's place with her son on her left*).

Pickering returns to his chair on her right.

Mrs Higgins. You silly boy, of course she's not presentable. She's a triumph of your art and of her dressmaker's; but if you suppose for a moment that she doesnt give herself away in every sentence she utters, you must be perfectly cracked about her.

Pickering. But dont you think something might be done? I mean something to eliminate the sanguinary element from her conversation.

Mrs Higgins. Not as long as she is in Henry's hands.

Higgins (*aggrieved*) Do you mean that m y language is im-proper?

Mrs Higgins. No, dearest: it would be quite proper—say on a canal barge; but it would not be proper for her at a garden party.

Higgins (*deeply injured*) Well I must say—

Pickering (*interrupting him*) Come, Higgins: you must learn to know yourself. I havnt heard such language as yours since we used to review the volunteers in Hyde Park twenty years ago.

Higgins (*sulkily*) Oh, well, if y o u say so, I suppose I dont always talk like a bishop.

Mrs Higgins (*quieting Henry with a touch*) Colonel Pickering: will you tell me what is the exact state of things in Wimpole Street?

Pickering (*cheerfully: as if this completely changed the subject*) Well, I have come to live there with Henry. We work together at my Indian Dialects; and we think it more con-venient—

Mrs Higgins. Quite so. I know all about that: it's an excel-lent arrangement. But where does this girl live?

Higgins. With us, of course. Where s h o u l d she live?

Mrs Higgins. But on what terms? Is she a servant? If not, what is she?

Pickering (*slowly*) I think I know what you mean, Mrs Higgins.

Higgins. Well, dash me if I do! Ive had to work at the girl every day for months to get her to her present pitch. Besides, she's useful. She knows where my things are, and remembers my appointments and so forth.

Mrs Higgins. How does your housekeeper get on with her?

Higgins. Mrs Pearce? Oh, she's jolly glad to get so much taken off her hands; for before Eliza came, s h e used to have to find things and remind me of my appointments. But she's got some silly bee in her bonnet about Eliza. She keeps saying "You dont t h i n k, sir": doesnt she, Pick?

Pickering. Yes: thats the formula. "You dont t h i n k, sir." Thats the end of every conversation about Eliza.

Higgins. As if I ever stop thinking about the girl and her confounded vowels and consonants. I'm worn out, thinking about her, and watching her lips and her teeth and her tongue, not to mention her soul, which is the quaintest of the lot.

Mrs Higgins. You certainly are a pretty pair of babies, playing with your live doll.

Higgins. Playing! The hardest job I ever tackled: make no mistake about that, mother. But you have no idea how frightfully interesting it is to take a human being and change her into a quite different human being by creating a new speech for her. It's filling up the deepest gulf that separates class from class and soul from soul.

Pickering (*drawing his chair closer to Mrs Higgins and bending over to her eagerly*) Yes: it's enormously interesting. I assure you, Mrs Higgins, we take Eliza very seriously. Every week—every day almost—there is some new change. (*Closer again*) We keep records of every stage—dozens of gramophone disks and photographs—

Higgins (*assailing her at the other ear*) Yes, by George: it's the most absorbing experiment I ever tackled. She regularly fills our lives up: doesnt she, Pick?

Pickering. We're always talking Eliza.

Higgins. Teaching Eliza.

Pickering. Dressing Eliza.

Mrs Higgins. What!

Higgins. Inventing new Elizas.

Higgins.		You know, she has the most extraordinary quickness of ear:
Pickering.	(*speaking together*)	I assure you, my dear Mrs Higgins, that girl

Higgins.	just like a parrot. Ive tried her with every
Pickering.	is a genius. She can play the piano quite beautifully.
Higgins.	possible sort of sound that a human being can make—
Pickering.	We have taken her to classical concerts and to music
Higgins.	Continental dialects, African dialects, Hottentot
Pickering.	halls; and it's all the same to her: she plays everything
Higgins.	clicks, things it took me years to get hold of; and
Pickering.	she hears right off when she comes home, whether it's
Higgins.	she picks them up like a shot, right away, as if she had
Pickering.	Beethoven and Brahms or Lehar and Lionel Monckton;
Higgins.	been at it all her life.
Pickering.	though six months ago, she'd never as much as touched a piano—

Mrs Higgins (putting her fingers in her ears, as they are by this time shouting one another down with an intolerable noise) Sh-sh-sh—sh! (They stop).

Pickering. I beg your pardon. (He draws his chair back apologetically).

Higgins. Sorry. When Pickering starts shouting nobody can get a word in edgeways.

Mrs Higgins. Be quiet, Henry. Colonel Pickering: dont you realize that when Eliza walked into Wimpole Street, something walked in with her?

Pickering. Her father did. But Henry soon got rid of him.

Mrs Higgins. It would have been more to the point if her mother had. But as her mother didnt something else did.

Pickering. But what?

Mrs Higgins (unconsciously dating herself by the word) A problem.

Pickering. Oh, I see. The problem of how to pass her off as a lady.

Higgins. I'll solve that problem. Ive half solved it already.

Mrs Higgins. No, you two infinitely stupid male creatures: the problem of what is to be done with her afterwards.

Higgins. I dont see anything in that. She can go her own way, with all the advantages I have given her.

Mrs Higgins. The advantages of that poor woman who was here just now! The manners and habits that disqualify a fine lady from earning her own living without giving her a fine lady's income! Is that what you mean?

Pickering (indulgently, being rather bored) Oh, that will be all right, Mrs Higgins. *(He rises to go).*

Higgins (rising also) We'll find her some light employment.

Pickering. She's happy enough. Dont you worry about her. Goodbye. *(He shakes hands as if he were consoling a frightened child, and makes for the door).*

Higgins. Anyhow, theres no good bothering now. The thing's done. Goodbye, mother. *(He kisses her, and follows Pickering).*

Pickering (turning for a final consolation) There are plenty of openings. We'll do whats right. Goodbye.

Higgins (to Pickering as they go out together) Let's take her to the Shakespear exhibition at Earls Court.

Pickering. Yes: lets. Her remarks will be delicious.

Higgins. She'll mimic all the people for us when we get home.

Pickering. Ripping. *(Both are heard laughing as they go downstairs).*

Mrs Higgins (rises with an impatient bounce, and returns to her work at the writing-table. She sweeps a litter of disarranged papers out of her way; snatches a sheet of paper from her stationery case; and tries resolutely to write. At the third line she gives it up; flings down her pen; grips the table angrily and exclaims) Oh, men! men!! men!!!

ACT IV

THE Wimpole Street laboratory. Midnight. Nobody in the room. The clock on the mantelpiece strikes twelve. The fire is not alight: it is a summer night.

Presently Higgins and Pickering are heard on the stairs.

Higgins (calling down to Pickering) I say, Pick: lock up, will you? I shant be going out again.

Pickering. Right. Can Mrs Pearce go to bed? We dont want anything more, do we?

Higgins. Lord, no!

Eliza opens the door and is seen on the lighted landing in opera cloak, brilliant evening dress, and diamonds, with fan, flowers, and all accessories. She comes to the hearth, and switches on the electric lights there. She is tired: her pallor contrasts strongly with her dark eyes and hair; and her expression is almost tragic. She takes off her cloak; puts her fan and flowers on the piano; and sits down on the bench, brooding and silent. Higgins, in evening dress, with overcoat and hat, comes in, carrying a smoking jacket which he has picked up downstairs. He takes off the hat and overcoat; throws them carelessly on the newspaper stand; disposes of his coat in the same way; puts on the smoking jacket; and throws himself wearily into the easy-chair at the hearth. Pickering, similarly attired, comes in. He also takes off his hat and overcoat, and is about to throw them on Higgins's when he hesitates.

Pickering. I say: Mrs Pearce will row if we leave these things lying about in the drawing room.

Higgins. Oh, chuck them over the bannisters into the hall. She'll find them there in the morning and put them away all right. She'll think we were drunk.

Pickering. We are, slightly. Are there any letters?

Higgins. I didnt look. (*Pickering takes the overcoats and hats and goes downstairs. Higgins begins half singing half yawning an air from La Fanciulla del Golden West. Suddenly he stops and exclaims*) I wonder where the devil my slippers are!

Eliza looks at him darkly; then rises suddenly and leaves the room.

Higgins yawns again, and resumes his song.

Pickering returns, with the contents of the letter-box in his hand.

Pickering. Only circulars, and this coroneted billet-doux for you. (*He throws the circulars into the fender, and posts himself on the hearthrug, with his back to the grate*).

Higgins (*glancing at the billet-doux*) Money-lender. (*He throws the letter after the circulars*).

Eliza returns with a pair of large down-at-heel slippers. She places them on the carpet before Higgins, and sits as before without a word.

Higgins (*yawning again*) Oh Lord! What an evening! What a crew! What a silly tomfoolery! (*He raises his shoe to unlace it, and catches sight of the slippers. He stops unlacing and looks at them as if they had appeared there of their own accord*). Oh! theyre there, are they?

Pickering (*stretching himself*) Well, I feel a bit tired. It's been a long day. The garden party, a dinner party, and the opera! Rather too much of a good thing. But youve won your bet, Higgins. Eliza did the trick, and something to spare, eh?

Higgins (*fervently*) Thank God it's over!

Eliza flinches violently; but they take no notice of her; and she recovers herself and sits stonily as before.

Pickering. Were you nervous at the garden party? I was. Eliza didnt seem a bit nervous.

Higgins. Oh, s h e wasnt nervous. I knew she'd be all right. No: it's the strain of putting the job through all these months that has told on me. It was interesting enough at first, while we were at the phonetics; but after that I got deadly sick of it. If I hadnt backed myself to do it I should have chucked the whole thing up two months ago. It was a silly notion: the whole thing has been a bore.

Pickering. Oh come! the garden party was frightfully exciting. My heart began beating like anything.

Higgins. Yes, for the first three minutes. But when I saw we were going to win hands down, I felt like a bear in a cage, hanging about doing nothing. The dinner was worse: sitting gorging there for over an hour, with nobody but a damned fool of a fashionable woman to talk to! I tell you, Pickering, never again for me. No more artificial duchesses. The whole thing has been simple purgatory.

Pickering. Youve never been broken in properly to the social routine. (*Strolling over to the piano*) I rather enjoy dipping into it occasionally myself: it makes me feel young again. Anyhow, it was a great success: an immense success. I was quite frightened once or twice because Eliza was doing it so well. You see, lots of the real people cant do it at all: theyre such fools that they think style comes by nature to people in their position; and so they never learn. Theres always something professional about doing a thing superlatively well.

Higgins. Yes: thats what drives me mad: the silly people dont know their own silly business. (*Rising*) However, it's over and done with; and now I can go to bed at last without dreading tomorrow.

Eliza's beauty becomes murderous.

Pickering. I think I shall turn in too. Still, it's been a great occasion: a triumph for you. Goodnight. (*He goes*).

Higgins (*following him*) Goodnight. (*Over his shoulder, at the door*) Put out the lights, Eliza; and tell Mrs Pearce not to make coffee for me in the morning: I'll take tea. (*He goes out*).

Eliza tries to control herself and feel indifferent as she rises and walks across to the hearth to switch off the lights. By the time she gets there she is on the point of screaming. She sits down in Higgins's chair and holds on hard to the arms. Finally she gives way and flings herself furiously on the floor, raging.

Higgins (*in despairing wrath outside*) What the devil have I done with my slippers? (*He appears at the door*).

Liza (*snatching up the slippers, and hurling them at him one after the other with all her force*) There are your slippers. And there. Take your slippers; and may you never have a day's luck with them!

Higgins (*astounded*) What on earth—! (*He comes to her*). Whats the matter? Get up. (*He pulls her up*). Anything wrong?

Liza (*breathless*) Nothing wrong—with you. Ive won your bet for you, havnt I? Thats enough for you. *I* dont matter, I suppose.

Higgins. Y o u won my bet! You! Presumptuous insect! *I* won it. What did you throw those slippers at me for?

Liza. Because I wanted to smash your face. I'd like to kill you, you selfish brute. Why didnt you leave me where you picked me out of—in the gutter? You thank God it's all over, and that now you can throw me back again there, do you? (*She crisps her fingers frantically*).

Higgins (*looking at her in cool wonder*) The creature is nervous, after all.

Liza (*gives a suffocated scream of fury, and instinctively darts her nails at his face*)!!

Higgins (*catching her wrists*) Ah! would you? Claws in, you cat. How dare you shew your temper to me? Sit down and be quiet. (*He throws her roughly into the easy-chair*).

Liza (*crushed by superior strength and weight*) Whats to become of me? Whats to become of me?

Higgins. How the devil do I know whats to become of you? What does it matter what becomes of you?

Liza. You dont care. I know you dont care. You wouldnt

care if I was dead. I'm nothing to you—not so much as them slippers.

Higgins (thundering) T h o s e slippers.

Liza (with bitter submission) Those slippers. I didnt think it made any difference now.

A pause. Eliza hopeless and crushed. Higgins a little uneasy.

Higgins (in his loftiest manner) Why have you begun going on like this? May I ask whether you complain of your treatment here?

Liza. No.

Higgins. Has anybody behaved badly to you? Colonel Pickering? Mrs Pearce? Any of the servants?

Liza. No.

Higgins. I presume you dont pretend that *I* have treated you badly?

Liza. No.

Higgins. I am glad to hear it. (*He moderates his tone*). Perhaps youre tired after the strain of the day. Will you have a glass of champagne? (*He moves towards the door*).

Liza. No. (*Recollecting her manners*) Thank you.

Higgins (good-humored again) This has been coming on you for some days. I suppose it was natural for you to be anxious about the garden party. But thats all over now. (*He pats her kindly on the shoulder. She writhes*). Theres nothing more to worry about.

Liza. No. Nothing more for y o u to worry about. (*She suddenly rises and gets away from him by going to the piano bench, where she sits and hides her face*). Oh God! I wish I was dead.

Higgins (staring after her in sincere surprise) Why? In heaven's name, why? (*Reasonably, going to her*) Listen to me, Eliza. All this irritation is purely subjective.

Liza. I dont understand. I'm too ignorant.

Higgins. It's only imagination. Low spirits and nothing else

Nobody's hurting you. Nothing's wrong. You go to bed like a good girl and sleep it off. Have a little cry and say your prayers: that will make you comfortable.

Liza. I heard your prayers. "Thank God it's all over!"

Higgins (impatiently) Well, d o n t you thank God it's all over? Now you are free and can do what you like.

Liza (pulling herself together in desperation) What am I fit for? What have you left me fit for? Where am I to go? What am I to do? Whats to become of me?

Higgins (enlightened, but not at all impressed) Oh thats whats worrying you, is it? (*He thrusts his hands into his pockets, and walks about in his usual manner, rattling the contents of his pockets, as if condescending to a trivial subject out of pure kindness*). I shouldnt bother about it if I were you. I should imagine you wont have much difficulty in settling yourself somewhere or other, though I hadnt quite realized that you were going away. (*She looks quickly at him: he does not look at her, but examines the dessert stand on the piano and decides that he will eat an apple*). You might marry, you know. (*He bites a large piece out of the apple and munches it noisily*). You see, Eliza, all men are not confirmed old bachelors like me and the Colonel. Most men are the marrying sort (poor devils!); and youre not bad-looking: it's quite a pleasure to look at you sometimes—not now, of course, because youre crying and looking as ugly as the very devil; but when youre all right and quite yourself, youre what I should call attractive. That is, to the people in the marrying line, you understand. You go to bed and have a good nice rest; and then get up and look at yourself in the glass; and you wont feel so cheap.

Eliza again looks at him, speechless, and does not stir.

The look is quite lost on him: he eats his apple with a dreamy expression of happiness, as it is quite a good one.

Higgins (a genial afterthought occurring to him) I daresay my mother could find some chap or other who would do very well.

Liza. We were above that at the corner of Tottenham Court Road.

Higgins (waking up) What do you mean?

Liza. I sold flowers. I didnt sell myself. Now youve made a lady of me I'm not fit to sell anything else. I wish youd left me where you found me.

Higgins (slinging the core of the apple decisively into the grate) Tosh, Eliza. Dont you insult human relations by dragging all this cant about buying and selling into it. You neednt marry the fellow if you dont like him.

Liza. What else am I to do?

Higgins. Oh, lots of things. What about your old idea of a florist's shop? Pickering could set you up in one: he's lots of money. *(Chuckling)* He'll have to pay for all those togs you have been wearing to-day; and that, with the hire of the jewellery, will make a big hole in two hundred pounds. Why, six months ago you would have thought it the millennium to have a flower shop of your own. Come! youll be all right. I must clear off to bed: I'm devilish sleepy. By the way, I came down for something: I forget what it was.

Liza. Your slippers.

Higgins. Oh yes, of course. You shied them at me. *(He picks them up, and is going out when she rises and speaks to him).*

Liza. Before you go, sir—

Higgins (dropping the slippers in his surprise at her calling him Sir) Eh?

Liza. Do my clothes belong to me or to Colonel Pickering?

Higgins (coming back into the room as if her question were the very climax of unreason) What the devil use would they be to Pickering?

Liza. He might want them for the next girl you pick up to experiment on.

Higgins (shocked and hurt) Is t h a t the way you feel towards us?

Liza. I dont want to hear anything more about that. All I

want to know is whether anything belongs to me. My own clothes were burnt.

Higgins. But what does it matter? Why need you start bothering about that in the middle of the night?

Liza. I want to know what I may take away with me. I dont want to be accused of stealing.

Higgins (now deeply wounded) Stealing! You shouldnt have said that, Eliza. That shews a want of feeling.

Liza. I'm sorry. I'm only a common ignorant girl; and in my station I have to be careful. There cant be any feelings between the like of you and the like of me. Please will you tell me what belongs to me and what doesnt?

Higgins (very sulky) You may take the whole damned houseful if you like. Except the jewels. Theyre hired. Will that satisfy you? (He turns on his heel and is about to go in extreme dudgeon).

Liza (drinking in his emotion like nectar, and nagging him to provoke a further supply) Stop, please. (She takes off her jewels). Will you take these to your room and keep them safe? I dont want to run the risk of their being missing.

Higgins (furious) Hand them over. (She puts them into his hands). If these belonged to me instead of to the jeweller, I'd ram them down your ungrateful throat. (He perfunctorily thrusts them into his pockets, unconsciously decorating himself with the protruding ends of the chains).

Liza (taking a ring off) This ring isnt the jeweller's: it's the one you bought me in Brighton. I dont want it now. (Higgins dashes the ring violently into the fireplace, and turns on her so threateningly that she crouches over the piano with her hands over her face, and exclaims) Dont you hit me.

Higgins. Hit you! You infamous creature, how dare you accuse me of such a thing? It is you who have hit me. You have wounded me to the heart.

Liza (thrilling with hidden joy) I'm glad. Ive got a little of my own back, anyhow.

Higgins (*with dignity, in his finest professional style*) You have caused me to lose my temper: a thing that has hardly ever happened to me before. I prefer to say nothing more to-night. I am going to bed.

Liza (*pertly*) You'd better leave a note for Mrs Pearce about the coffee; for she wont be told by me.

Higgins (*formally*) Damn Mrs Pearce; and damn the coffee; and damn you; and damn my own folly in having lavished hard-earned knowledge and the treasure of my regard and intimacy on a heartless guttersnipe. (*He goes out with impressive decorum, and spoils it by slamming the door savagely*).

Eliza smiles for the first time; expresses her feelings by a wild pantomime in which an imitation of Higgins's exit is confused with her own triumph; and finally goes down on her knees on the hearthrug to look for the ring.

ACT V

MRS HIGGINS'S *drawing room. She is at her writing-table as before. The parlor-maid comes in.*

The Parlor-Maid (*at the door*) Mr Henry, maam, is downstairs with Colonel Pickering.

Mrs Higgins. Well, shew them up.

The Parlor-Maid. Theyre using the telephone, maam. Telephoning to the police, I think.

Mrs Higgins. What!

The Parlor-Maid (*coming further in and lowering her voice*) Mr Henry is in a state, maam. I thought I'd better tell you.

Mrs Higgins. If you had told me that Mr Henry was not in a state it would have been more surprising. Tell them to come up when theyve finished with the police. I suppose he's lost something.

The Parlor-Maid. Yes, maam (*going*).

Mrs Higgins. Go upstairs and tell Miss Doolittle that Mr Henry and the Colonel are here. Ask her not to come down til I send for her.

The Parlor-Maid. Yes, maam.

Higgins bursts in. He is, as the parlor-maid has said, in a state.

Higgins. Look here, mother: heres a confounded thing!

Mrs Higgins. Yes, dear. Good morning. (*He checks his impatience and kisses her, whilst the parlor-maid goes out*). What is it?

Higgins. Eliza's bolted.

Mrs Higgins (*calmly continuing her writing*) You must have frightened her.

Higgins. Frightened her! nonsense! She was left last night, as usual, to turn out the lights and all that; and instead of

going to bed she changed her clothes and went right off: her
bed wasnt slept in. She came in a cab for her things before
seven this morning; and that fool Mrs Pearce let her have them
without telling me a word about it. What am I to do?

Mrs Higgins. Do without, I'm afraid, Henry. The girl has
a perfect right to leave if she chooses.

Higgins (wandering distractedly across the room) But I
cant find anything. I dont know what appointments Ive got.
I'm—(*Pickering comes in. Mrs Higgins puts down her pen
and turns away from the writing-table*).

Pickering (shaking hands) Good morning, Mrs Higgins.
Has Henry told you? (*He sits down on the ottoman*).

Higgins. What does that ass of an inspector say? Have you
offered a reward?

Mrs Higgins (rising in indignant amazement) You dont
mean to say you have set the police after Eliza.

Higgins. Of course. What are the police for? What else
could we do? (*He sits in the Elizabethan chair*).

Pickering. The inspector made a lot of difficulties. I really
think he suspected us of some improper purpose.

Mrs Higgins. Well, of course he did. What right have you
to go to the police and give the girl's name as if she were a
thief, or a lost umbrella, or something? Really! (*She sits down
again, deeply vexed*).

Higgins. But we want to find her.

Pickering. We cant let her go like this, you know, Mrs
Higgins. What were we to do?

Mrs Higgins. You have no more sense, either of you, than
two children. Why—

The parlor-maid comes in and breaks off the conversation.

The Parlor-Maid. Mr Henry: a gentleman wants to see you
very particular. He's been sent on from Wimpole Street.

Higgins. Oh, bother! I cant see anyone now. Who is it?

The Parlor-Maid. A Mr Doolittle, sir.

Pickering. Doolittle! Do you mean the dustman?

The Parlor-Maid. Dustman! Oh no, sir: a gentleman.

Higgins (springing up excitedly) By George, Pick, it's some relative of hers that she's gone to. Somebody we know nothing about. (*To the parlor-maid*) Send him up, quick.

The Parlor-Maid. Yes, sir. (*She goes*).

Higgins (eagerly, going to his mother) Genteel relatives! now we shall hear something. (*He sits down in the Chippendale chair*).

Mrs Higgins. Do you know any of her people?

Pickering. Only her father: the fellow we told you about.

The Parlor-Maid (announcing) Mr Doolittle. (*She withdraws*).

Doolittle enters. He is brilliantly dressed in a new fashionable frock-coat, with white waistcoat and grey trousers. A flower in his buttonhole, a dazzling silk hat, and patent leather shoes complete the effect. He is too concerned with the business he has come on to notice Mrs Higgins. He walks straight to Higgins, and accosts him with vehement reproach.

Doolittle (indicating his own person) See here! Do you see this? You done this.

Higgins. Done what, man?

Doolittle. This, I tell you. Look at it. Look at this hat. Look at this coat.

Pickering. Has Eliza been buying you clothes?

Doolittle. Eliza! not she. Not half. Why would she buy me clothes?

Mrs Higgins. Good morning, Mr Doolittle. Wont you sit down?

Doolittle (taken aback as he becomes conscious that he has forgotten his hostess) Asking your pardon, maam. (*He approaches her and shakes her proffered hand*). Thank you. (*He sits down on the ottoman, on Pickering's right*). I am that full of what has happened to me that I cant think of anything else.

Higgins. What the dickens h a s happened to you?

Doolittle. I shouldnt mind if it had only happened to me:

anything might happen to anybody and nobody to blame but Providence, as you might say. But this is something that you done to me: yes, you, Henry Higgins.

Higgins. Have you found Eliza? Thats the point.

Doolittle. Have you lost her?

Higgins. Yes.

Doolittle. You have all the luck, you have. I aint found her; but she'll find me quick enough now after what you done to me.

Mrs Higgins. But what has my son done to you, Mr Doolittle?

Doolittle. Done to me! Ruined me. Destroyed my happiness. Tied me up and delivered me into the hands of middle class morality.

Higgins (rising intolerantly and standing over Doolittle) Youre raving. Youre drunk. Youre mad. I gave you five pounds. After that I had two conversations with you, at half-a-crown an hour. Ive never seen you since.

Doolittle. Oh! Drunk! am I? Mad? am I? Tell me this. Did you or did you not write a letter to an old blighter in America that was giving five millions to found Moral Reform Societies all over the world, and that wanted you to invent a universal language for him?

Higgins. What! Ezra D. Wannafeller! He's dead. (*He sits down again carelessly*).

Doolittle. Yes: he's dead; and I'm done for. Now did you or did you not write a letter to him to say that the most original moralist at present in England, to the best of your knowledge, was Alfred Doolittle, a common dustman.

Higgins. Oh, after your last visit I remember making some silly joke of the kind.

Doolittle. Ah! you may well call it a silly joke. It put the lid on me right enough. Just give him the chance he wanted to shew that Americans is not like us: that they recognize and respect merit in every class of life, however humble. Them

words is in his blooming will, in which, Henry Higgins, thanks
to your silly joking, he leaves me a share in his Pre-digested
Cheese Trust worth three thousand a year on condition that
I lecture for his Wannafeller Moral Reform World League
as often as they ask me up to six times a year.

Higgins. The devil he does! Whew! (*Brightening suddenly*)
What a lark!

Pickering. A safe thing for you, Doolittle. They wont ask
you twice.

Doolittle. It aint the lecturing I mind. I'll lecture them
blue in the face, I will, and not turn a hair. It's making a
gentleman of me that I object to. Who asked him to make
a gentleman of me? I was happy. I was free. I touched pretty
nigh everybody for money when I wanted it, same as I touched
you, Henry Higgins. Now I am worrited; tied neck and heels;
and everybody touches me for money. It's a fine thing for you,
says my solicitor. Is it? says I. You mean it's a good thing for
you, I says. When I was a poor man and had a solicitor once
when they found a pram in the dust cart, he got me off, and
got shut of me and got me shut of him as quick as he could.
Same with the doctors: used to shove me out of the hospital
before I could hardly stand on my legs, and nothing to pay.
Now they finds out that I'm not a healthy man and cant live
unless they looks after me twice a day. In the house I'm not
let do a hand's turn for myself: somebody else must do it and
touch me for it. A year ago I hadnt a relative in the world
except two or three that wouldnt speak to me. Now Ive fifty,
and not a decent week's wages among the lot of them. I have to
live for others and not for myself: thats middle class morality.
You talk of losing Eliza. Dont you be anxious: I bet she's on
my doorstep by this: she that could support herself easy by
selling flowers if I wasnt respectable. And the next one to
touch me will be you, Henry Higgins. I'll have to learn to
speak middle class language from you, instead of speaking

proper English. Thats where youll come in; and I daresay thats what you done it for.

Mrs Higgins. But, my dear Mr Doolittle, you need not suffer all this if you are really in earnest. Nobody can force you to accept this bequest. You can repudiate it. Isnt that so, Colonel Pickering?

Pickering. I believe so.

Doolittle (softening his manner in deference to her sex) Thats the tragedy of it, maam. It's easy to say chuck it; but I havnt the nerve. Which of us has? We're all intimidated. Intimidated, maam: thats what we are. What is there for me if I chuck it but the workhouse in my old age? I have to dye my hair already to keep my job as a dustman. If I was one of the deserving poor, and had put by a bit, I could chuck it; but then why should I, acause the deserving poor might as well be millionaires for all the happiness they ever has. They dont know what happiness is. But I, as one of the undeserving poor, have nothing between me and the pauper's uniform but this here blasted three thousand a year that shoves me into the middle class. (Excuse the expression, maam: youd use it yourself if you had my provocation.) Theyve got you every way you turn: it's a choice between the Skilly of the workhouse and the Char Bydis of the middle class; and I havnt the nerve for the workhouse. Intimidated: thats what I am. Broke. Brought up. Happier men than me will call for my dust, and touch me for their tip; and I'll look on helpless, and envy them. And thats what your son has brought me to. (*He is overcome by emotion*).

Mrs Higgins. Well, I'm very glad youre not going to do anything foolish, Mr Doolittle. For this solves the problem of Eliza's future. You can provide for her now.

Doolittle (with melancholy resignation) Yes, maam: I'm expected to provide for everyone now, out of three thousand a year.

Higgins (*jumping up*) Nonsense! he cant provide for her. He shant provide for her. She doesnt belong to him. I paid him five pounds for her. Doolittle: either youre an honest man or a rogue.

Doolittle (*tolerantly*) A little of both, Henry, like the rest of us: a little of both.

Higgins. Well, you took that money for the girl; and you have no right to take her as well.

Mrs Higgins. Henry: dont be absurd. If you want to know where Eliza is, she is upstairs.

Higgins (*amazed*) Upstairs!!! Then I shall jolly soon fetch her downstairs. (*He makes resolutely for the door*).

Mrs Higgins (*rising and following him*) Be quiet, Henry. Sit down.

Higgins. I—

Mrs Higgins. Sit down, dear; and listen to me.

Higgins. Oh very well, very well, very well. (*He throws himself ungraciously on the ottoman, with his face towards the windows*). But I think you might have told us this half an hour ago.

Mrs Higgins. Eliza came to me this morning. She passed the night partly walking about in a rage, partly trying to throw herself into the river and being afraid to, and partly in the Carlton Hotel. She told me of the brutal way you two treated her.

Higgins (*bounding up again*) What!

Pickering (*rising also*) My dear Mrs Higgins, she's been telling you stories. We didnt treat her brutally. We hardly said a word to her; and we parted on particularly good terms. (*Turning on Higgins*). Higgins: did you bully her after I went to bed?

Higgins. Just the other way about. She threw my slippers in my face. She behaved in the most outrageous way. I never gave her the slightest provocation. The slippers came bang into my face the moment I entered the room—before I had uttered a word. And used perfectly awful language.

Pickering (*astonished*) But why? What did we do to her?

Mrs Higgins. I think I know pretty well what you did. The girl is naturally rather affectionate, I think. Isnt she, Mr Doolittle?

Doolittle. Very tender-hearted, maam. Takes after me.

Mrs Higgins. Just so. She had become attached to you both. She worked very hard for you, Henry! I dont think you quite realize what anything in the nature of brain work means to a girl like that. Well, it seems that when the great day of trial came, and she did this wonderful thing for you without making a single mistake, you two sat there and never said a word to her, but talked together of how glad you were that it was all over and how you had been bored with the whole thing. And then you were surprised because she threw your slippers at you! *I* should have thrown the fire-irons at you.

Higgins. We said nothing except that we were tired and wanted to go to bed. Did we, Pick?

Pickering (*shrugging his shoulders*) That was all.

Mrs Higgins (*ironically*) Quite sure?

Pickering. Absolutely. Really, that was all.

Mrs Higgins. You didnt thank her, or pet her, or admire her, or tell her how splendid she'd been.

Higgins (*impatiently*) But she knew all about that. We didnt make speeches to her, if thats what you mean.

Pickering (*conscience stricken*) Perhaps we were a little inconsiderate. Is she very angry?

Mrs Higgins (*returning to her place at the writing-table*) Well, I'm afraid she wont go back to Wimpole Street, especially now that Mr Doolittle is able to keep up the position you have thrust on her; but she says she is quite willing to meet you on friendly terms and to let bygones be bygones.

Higgins (*furious*) Is she, by George? Ho!

Mrs Higgins. If you promise to behave yourself, Henry, I'll ask her to come down. If not, go home; for you have taken up quite enough of my time.

Higgins. Oh, all right. Very well. Pick: you behave yourself. Let us put on our best Sunday manners for this creature that we picked out of the mud. (*He flings himself sulkily into the Elizabethan chair*).

Doolittle (*remonstrating*) Now, now, Henry Higgins! have some consideration for my feelings as a middle class man.

Mrs Higgins. Remember your promise, Henry. (*She presses the bell-button on the writing-table*). Mr Doolittle: will you be so good as to step out on the balcony for a moment. I dont want Eliza to have the shock of your news until she has made it up with these two gentlemen. Would you mind?

Doolittle. As you wish, lady. Anything to help Henry to keep her off my hands. (*He disappears through the window*).

The parlor-maid answers the bell. Pickering sits down in Doolittle's place.

Mrs Higgins. Ask Miss Doolittle to come down, please.

The Parlor-Maid. Yes, maam. (*She goes out*).

Mrs Higgins. Now, Henry: be good.

Higgins. I am behaving myself perfectly.

Pickering. He is doing his best, Mrs Higgins.

A pause. Higgins throws back his head; stretches out his legs; and begins to whistle.

Mrs Higgins. Henry, dearest, you dont look at all nice in that attitude.

Higgins (*pulling himself together*) I was not trying to look nice, mother.

Mrs Higgins. It doesnt matter, dear. I only wanted to make you speak.

Higgins. Why?

Mrs Higgins. Because you cant speak and whistle at the same time.

Higgins groans. Another very trying pause.

Higgins (springing up, out of patience) Where the devil is that girl? Are we to wait here all day?

Eliza enters, sunny, self-possessed, and giving a staggeringly convincing exhibition of ease of manner. She carries a little work-basket, and is very much at home. Pickering is too much taken aback to rise.

LIZA. How do you do, Professor Higgins? Are you quite well?

Higgins (choking) Am I—(*He can say no more*).

LIZA. But of course you are: you are never ill. So glad to see you again, Colonel Pickering. (*He rises hastily; and they shake hands*). Quite chilly this morning, isnt it? (*She sits down on his left. He sits beside her*).

HIGGINS. Dont you dare try this game on me. I taught it to you; and it doesnt take me in. Get up and come home; and dont be a fool.

Eliza takes a piece of needlework from her basket, and begins to stitch at it, without taking the least notice of this outburst.

MRS HIGGINS. Very nicely put, indeed, Henry. No woman could resist such an invitation.

HIGGINS. You let her alone, mother. Let her speak for herself. You will jolly soon see whether she has an idea that I havnt put into her head or a word that I havnt put into her mouth. I tell you I have created this thing out of the squashed cabbage leaves of Covent Garden; and now she pretends to play the fine lady with me.

Mrs Higgins (placidly) Yes, dear; but youll sit down, wont you?

Higgins sits down again, savagely.

LIZA (*to Pickering, taking no apparent notice of Higgins, and working away deftly*) Will y o u drop me altogether now that the experiment is over, Colonel Pickering?

PICKERING. Oh dont. You mustnt think of it as an experiment. It shocks me, somehow.

LIZA. Oh, I'm only a squashed cabbage leaf—

Pickering (*impulsively*) No.

Liza (*continuing quietly*)—but I owe so much to you that I should be very unhappy if you forgot me.

Pickering. It's very kind of you to say so, Miss Doolittle.

Liza. It's not because you paid for my dresses. I know you are generous to everybody with money. But it was from you that I learnt really nice manners; and that is what makes one a lady, isnt it? You see it was so very difficult for me with the example of Professor Higgins always before me. I was brought up to be just like him, unable to control myself, and using bad language on the slightest provocation. And I should never have known that ladies and gentlemen didnt behave like that if you hadnt been there.

Higgins. Well!!

Pickering. Oh, thats only his way, you know. He doesnt mean it.

Liza. Oh, *I* didnt mean it either, when I was a flower girl. It was only my way. But you see I did it; and thats what makes the difference after all.

Pickering. No doubt. Still, he taught you to speak; and I couldnt have done that, you know.

Liza (*trivially*) Of course: that is his profession.

Higgins. Damnation!

Liza (*continuing*) It was just like learning to dance in the fashionable way: there was nothing more than that in it. But do you know what began my real education?

Pickering. What?

Liza (*stopping her work for a moment*) Your calling me Miss Doolittle that day when I first came to Wimpole Street. That was the beginning of self-respect for me. (*She resumes her stitching*). And there were a hundred little things you never noticed, because they came naturally to you. Things about standing up and taking off your hat and opening doors—

Pickering. Oh, that was nothing.

Liza. Yes: things that shewed you thought and felt about

me as if I were something better than a scullery-maid; though
of course I know you would have been just the same to a
scullery-maid if she had been let into the drawing room. You
never took off your boots in the dining room when I was there.

Pickering. You mustnt mind that. Higgins takes off his
boots all over the place.

Liza. I know. I am not blaming him. It is his way, isnt it?
But it made s u c h a difference to me that you didnt do it. You
see, really and truly, apart from the things anyone can pick
up (the dressing and the proper way of speaking, and so on),
the difference between a lady and a flower girl is not how she
behaves, but how she's treated. I shall always be a flower girl
to Professor Higgins, because he always treats me as a flower
girl, and always will; but I know I can be a lady to you, because you always treat me as a lady, and always will.

Mrs Higgins. Please dont grind your teeth, Henry.

Pickering. Well, this is really very nice of you, Miss Doolittle.

Liza. I should like you to call me Eliza, now, if you would.

Pickering. Thank you. Eliza, of course.

Liza. And I should like Professor Higgins to call me Miss
Doolittle.

Higgins. I'll see you damned first.

Mrs Higgins. Henry! Henry!

Pickering (*laughing*) Why dont you slang back at him?
Dont stand it. It would do him a lot of good.

Liza. I cant. I could have done it once; but now I cant go
back to it. Last night, when I was wandering about, a girl spoke
to me; and I tried to get back into the old way with her; but
it was no use. You told me, you know, that when a child is
brought to a foreign country, it picks up the language in a few
weeks, and forgets its own. Well, I am a child in your country.
I have forgotten my own language, and can speak nothing but
yours. Thats the real break-off with the corner of Tottenham
Court Road. Leaving Wimpole Street finishes it.

Pickering (*much alarmed*) Oh! but youre coming back to Wimpole Street, arnt you? Youll forgive Higgins?

Higgins (*rising*) Forgive! Will she, by George! Let her go. Let her find out how she can get on without us. She will relapse into the gutter in three weeks without me at her elbow.

Doolittle appears at the centre window. With a look of dignified reproach at Higgins, he comes slowly and silently to his daughter, who, with her back to the window, is unconscious of his approach.

Pickering. He's incorrigible, Eliza. You wont relapse, will you?

Liza. No: not now. Never again. I have learnt my lesson. I dont believe I could utter one of the old sounds if I tried. (*Doolittle touches her on her left shoulder. She drops her work, losing her self-possession utterly at the spectacle of her father's splendor*) A-a-a-a-a-ah-ow-ooh!

Higgins (*with a crow of triumph*) Aha! Just so. A-a-a-a-ahowooh! A-a-a-a-ahowooh! A-a-a-a-ahowooh! Victory! Victory! (*He throws himself on the divan, folding his arms, and spraddling arrogantly*).

Doolittle. Can you blame the girl? Dont look at me like that, Eliza. It aint my fault. Ive come into some money.

Liza. You must have touched a millionaire this time, dad.

Doolittle. I have. But I'm dressed something special today. I'm going to St George's, Hanover Square. Your stepmother is going to marry me.

Liza (*angrily*) Youre going to let yourself down to marry that low common woman!

Pickering (*quietly*) He ought to, Eliza. (*To Doolittle*) Why has she changed her mind?

Doolittle (*sadly*) Intimidated, Governor. Intimidated. Middle class morality claims its victim. Wont you put on your hat, Liza, and come and see me turned off?

Liza. If the Colonel says I must, I—I'll (*almost sobbing*) I'll demean myself. And get insulted for my pains, like enough.

Doolittle. Dont be afraid: she never comes to words with anyone now, poor woman! respectability has broke all the spirit out of her.

Pickering (squeezing Eliza's elbow gently) Be kind to them, Eliza. Make the best of it.

Liza (forcing a little smile for him through her vexation) Oh well, just to shew theres no ill feeling. I'll be back in a moment. *(She goes out)*.

Doolittle (sitting down beside Pickering) I feel uncommon nervous about the ceremony, Colonel. I wish youd come and see me through it.

Pickering. But youve been through it before, man. You were married to Eliza's mother.

Doolittle. Who told you that, Colonel?

Pickering. Well, nobody told me. But I concluded—naturally—

Doolittle. No: that aint the natural way, Colonel: it's only the middle class way. My way was always the undeserving way. But dont say nothing to Eliza. She dont know: I always had a delicacy about telling her.

Pickering. Quite right. We'll leave it so, if you dont mind.

Doolittle. And youll come to the church, Colonel, and put me through straight?

Pickering. With pleasure. As far as a bachelor can.

Mrs Higgins. May I come, Mr Doolittle? I should be very sorry to miss your wedding.

Doolittle. I should indeed be honored by your condescension, maam; and my poor old woman would take it as a tremenjous compliment. She's been very low, thinking of the happy days that are no more.

Mrs Higgins (rising) I'll order the carriage and get ready. *(The men rise, except Higgins)*. I shant be more than fifteen minutes. *(As she goes to the door Eliza comes in, hatted and buttoning her gloves)*. I'm going to the church to see your father married, Eliza. You had better come in the brougham with me. Colonel Pickering can go on with the bridegroom.

Mrs Higgins goes out. Eliza comes to the middle of the room between the centre window and the ottoman. Pickering joins her.

Doolittle. Bridegroom! What a word! It makes a man realize his position, somehow. (*He takes up his hat and goes towards the door*).

Pickering. Before I go, Eliza, do forgive him and come back to us.

Liza. I dont think papa would allow me. Would you, dad?

Doolittle (*sad but magnanimous*) They played you off very cunning, Eliza, them two sportsmen. If it had been only one of them, you could have nailed him. But you see, there was two; and one of them chaperoned the other, as you might say. (*To Pickering*) It was artful of you, Colonel; but I bear no malice: I should have done the same myself. I been the victim of one woman after another all my life; and I dont grudge you two getting the better of Eliza. I shant interfere. It's time for us to go, Colonel. So long, Henry. See you in St George's, Eliza. (*He goes out*).

Pickering (*coaxing*) Do stay with us, Eliza. (*He follows Doolittle*).

Eliza goes out on the balcony to avoid being alone with Higgins. He rises and joins her there. She immediately comes back into the room and makes for the door; but he goes along the balcony quickly and gets his back to the door before she reaches it.

Higgins. Well, Eliza, youve had a bit of your own back, as you call it. Have you had enough? and are you going to be reasonable? Or do you want any more?

Liza. You want me back only to pick up your slippers and put up with your tempers and fetch and carry for you.

Higgins. I havnt said I wanted you back at all.

Liza. Oh, indeed. Then what are we talking about?

Higgins. About you, not about me. If you come back I shall treat you just as I have always treated you. I cant change my nature; and I dont intend to change my manners. My manners are exactly the same as Colonel Pickering's.

Liza. Thats not true. He treats a flower girl as if she was a duchess.

Higgins. And I treat a duchess as if she was a flower girl.

Liza. I see. (*She turns away composedly, and sits on the ottoman, facing the window*). The same to everybody.

Higgins. Just so.

Liza. Like father.

Higgins (*grinning, a little taken down*) Without accepting the comparison at all points, Eliza, it's quite true that your father is not a snob, and that he will be quite at home in any station of life to which his eccentric destiny may call him. (*Seriously*) The great secret, Eliza, is not having bad manners or good manners or any other particular sort of manners, but having the same manner for all human souls: in short, behaving as if you were in Heaven, where there are no third-class carriages, and one soul is as good as another.

Liza. Amen. You are a born preacher.

Higgins (*irritated*) The question is not whether I treat you rudely, but whether you ever heard me treat anyone else better.

Liza (*with sudden sincerity*) I dont care how you treat me. I dont mind your swearing at me. I dont mind a black eye: Ive had one before this. But (*standing up and facing him*) I wont be passed over.

Higgins. Then get out of my way; for I wont stop for you. You talk about me as if I were a motor bus.

Liza. So you are a motor bus: all bounce and go, and no consideration for anyone. But I can do without you: dont think I cant.

Higgins. I know you can. I told you you could.

Liza (*wounded, getting away from him to the other side of the ottoman with her face to the hearth*) I know you did, you brute. You wanted to get rid of me.

Higgins. Liar.

Liza. Thank you. (*She sits down with dignity*).

Higgins. You never asked yourself, I suppose, whether *I* could do without you.

Liza (*earnestly*) Dont you try to get round me. Youll h a v e to do without me.

Higgins (*arrogant*) I can do without anybody. I have my own soul: my own spark of divine fire. But (*with sudden humility*) I shall miss you, Eliza. (*He sits down near her on the ottoman*). I have learnt something from your idiotic notions: I confess that humbly and gratefully. And I have grown accustomed to your voice and appearance. I like them, rather.

Liza. Well, you have both of them on your gramophone and in your book of photographs. When you feel lonely without me, you can turn the machine on. It's got no feelings to hurt.

Higgins. I cant turn your soul on. Leave me those feelings; and you can take away the voice and the face. They are not you.

Liza. Oh, you a r e a devil. You can twist the heart in a girl as easy as some could twist her arms to hurt her. Mrs Pearce warned me. Time and again she has wanted to leave you; and you always got round her at the last minute. And you dont care a bit for her. And you dont care a bit for me.

Higgins. I care for life, for humanity; and you are a part of it that has come my way and been built into my house. What more can you or anyone ask?

Liza. I wont care for anybody that doesnt care for me.

Higgins. Commercial principles, Eliza. Like (*reproducing her Covent Garden pronunciation with professional exactness*) s'yollin voylets (*selling violets*), isnt it?

Liza. Dont sneer at me. It's mean to sneer at me.

Higgins. I have never sneered in my life. Sneering doesnt become either the human face or the human soul. I am expressing my righteous contempt for Commercialism. I dont and wont trade in affection. You call me a brute because you couldnt buy a claim on me by fetching my slippers and finding my spectacles. You were a fool: I think a woman fetching a man's slippers is a disgusting sight: did I ever fetch y o u r slippers? I think a good deal more of you for throwing them in my face. No use slaving for me and then saying you want to be cared for: who cares for a slave? If you come back, come back for the sake of good fellowship; for youll get nothing else. Youve had a thousand times as much out of me as I have out of you; and if you dare to set up your little dog's tricks of fetching and carrying slippers against my creation of a Duchess Eliza, I'll slam the door in your silly face.

Liza. What did you do it for if you didnt care for me?

Higgins (heartily) Why, because it was my job.

Liza. You never thought of the trouble it would make for me.

Higgins. Would the world ever have been made if its maker had been afraid of making trouble? Making life means making trouble. Theres only one way of escaping trouble; and thats killing things. Cowards, you notice, are always shrieking to have troublesome people killed.

Liza. I'm no preacher: I dont notice things like that. I notice that you dont notice me.

Higgins (jumping up and walking about intolerantly) Eliza: youre an idiot. I waste the treasures of my Miltonic mind by spreading them before you. Once for all, understand that I go my way and do my work without caring twopence what happens to either of us. I am not intimidated, like your father and your stepmother. So you can come back or go to the devil: which you please.

Liza. What am I to come back for?

Higgins (bouncing up on his knees on the ottoman and leaning over it to her) For the fun of it. Thats why I took you on.

Liza (*with averted face*) And you may throw me out to-morrow if I dont do everything you want me to?

Higgins. Yes; and you may walk out to-morrow if I dont do everything y o u want me to.

Liza. And live with my stepmother?

Higgins. Yes, or sell flowers.

Liza. Oh! if I only c o u l d go back to my flower basket! I should be independent of both you and father and all the world! Why did you take my independence from me? Why did I give it up? I'm a slave now, for all my fine clothes.

Higgins. Not a bit. I'll adopt you as my daughter and settle money on you if you like. Or would you rather marry Pickering?

Liza (*looking fiercely round at him*) I wouldnt marry y o u if you asked me; and youre nearer my age than what he is.

Higgins (*gently*) Than he is: not "than what he is."

Liza (*losing her temper and rising*) I'll talk as I like. Youre not my teacher now.

Higgins (*reflectively*) I dont suppose Pickering would, though. He's as confirmed an old bachelor as I am.

Liza. Thats not what I want; and dont you think it. Ive always had chaps enough wanting me that way. Freddy Hill writes to me twice and three times a day, sheets and sheets.

Higgins (*disagreeably surprised*) Damn his impudence! (*He recoils and finds himself sitting on his heels*).

Liza. He has a right to if he likes, poor lad. And he does love me.

Higgins (*getting off the ottoman*) You have no right to encourage him.

Liza. Every girl has a right to be loved.

Higgins. What! By fools like that?

Liza. Freddy's not a fool. And if he's weak and poor and wants me, may be he'd make me happier than my betters that bully me and dont want me.

Higgins. Can he m a k e anything of you? Thats the point.

Liza. Perhaps I could make something of him. But I never thought of us making anything of one another; and you never think of anything else. I only want to be natural.

Higgins. In short, you want me to be as infatuated about you as Freddy? Is that it?

Liza. No I dont. Thats not the sort of feeling I want from you. And dont you be too sure of yourself or of me. I could have been a bad girl if I'd liked. Ive seen more of some things than you, for all your learning. Girls like me can drag gentlemen down to make love to them easy enough. And they wish each other dead the next minute.

Higgins. Of course they do. Then what in thunder are we quarrelling about?

Liza (much troubled) I want a little kindness. I know I'm a common ignorant girl, and you a book-learned gentleman; but I'm not dirt under your feet. What I done (*correcting herself*) what I did was not for the dresses and the taxis: I did it because we were pleasant together and I come—came—to care for you; not to want you to make love to me, and not forgetting the difference between us, but more friendly like.

Higgins. Well, of course. Thats just how I feel. And how Pickering feels. Eliza: youre a fool.

Liza. Thats not a proper answer to give me (*she sinks on the chair at the writing-table in tears*).

Higgins. It's all youll get until you stop being a common idiot. If youre going to be a lady, youll have to give up feeling neglected if the men you know dont spend half their time snivelling over you and the other half giving you black eyes. If you cant stand the coldness of my sort of life, and the strain of it, go back to the gutter. Work til you are more a brute than a human being; and then cuddle and squabble and drink til you fall asleep. Oh, it's a fine life, the life of the gutter. It's real: it's warm: it's violent: you can feel it through the thickest skin: you can taste it and smell it without any training or any work. Not like Science and Literature and Classical Music and

Philosophy and Art. You find me cold, unfeeling, selfish, dont you? Very well: be off with you to the sort of people you like. Marry some sentimental hog or other with lots of money, and a thick pair of lips to kiss you with and a thick pair of boots to kick you with. If you cant appreciate what youve got, youd better get what you can appreciate.

Liza (desperate) Oh, you a r e a cruel tyrant. I cant talk to you: you turn everything against me: I'm always in the wrong. But you know very well all the time that youre nothing but a bully. You know I cant go back to the gutter, as you call it, and that I have no real friends in the world but you and the Colonel. You know well I couldnt bear to live with a low common man after you two; and it's wicked and cruel of you to insult me by pretending I could. You think I must go back to Wimpole Street because I have nowhere else to go but father's. But dont you be too sure that you have me under your feet to be trampled on and talked down. I'll marry Freddy, I will, as soon as he's able to support me.

Higgins (sitting down beside her) Rubbish! you shall marry an ambassador. You shall marry the Governor-General of India or the Lord-Lieutenant of Ireland, or somebody who wants a deputy-queen. I'm not going to have my masterpiece thrown away on Freddy.

Liza. You think I like you to say that. But I havnt forgot what you said a minute ago; and I wont be coaxed round as if I was a baby or a puppy. If I cant have kindness, I'll have independence.

Higgins. Independence? Thats middle class blasphemy. We are all dependent on one another, every soul of us on earth.

Liza (rising determinedly) I'll let you see whether I'm dependent on you. If you can preach, I can teach. I'll go and be a teacher.

Higgins. Whatll you teach, in heaven's name?

Liza. What you taught me. I'll teach phonetics.

Higgins. Ha! ha! ha!

Liza. I'll offer myself as an assistant to Professor Nepean.

Higgins (*rising in a fury*) What! That impostor! that humbug! that toadying ignoramus! Teach him m y methods! m y discoveries! You take one step in his direction and I'll wring your neck. (*He lays hands on her*). Do you hear?

Liza (*defiantly non-resistant*) Wring away. What do I care? I knew youd strike me some day. (*He lets her go, stamping with rage at having forgotten himself, and recoils so hastily that he stumbles back into his seat on the ottoman*). Aha! Now I know how to deal with you. What a fool I was not to think of it before! You cant take away the knowledge you gave me. You said I had a finer ear than you. And I can be civil and kind to people, which is more than you can. Aha! Thats done you, Henry Higgins, it has. Now I dont care t h a t (*snapping her fingers*) for your bullying and your big talk. I'll advertize it in the papers that your duchess is only a flower girl that you taught, and that she'll teach anybody to be a duchess just the same in six months for a thousand guineas. Oh, when I think of myself crawling under your feet and being trampled on and called names, when all the time I had only to lift up my finger to be as good as you, I could just kick myself.

Higgins (*wondering at her*) You damned impudent slut, you! But it's better than snivelling; better than fetching slippers and finding spectacles, isnt it? (*Rising*) By George, Eliza, I said I'd make a woman of you; and I have. I like you like this.

Liza. Yes: you turn round and make up to me now that I'm not afraid of you, and can do without you.

Higgins. Of course I do, you little fool. Five minutes ago you were like a millstone round my neck. Now youre a tower of strength: a consort battleship. You and I and Pickering will be three old bachelors together instead of only two men and a silly girl.

Mrs Higgins returns, dressed for the wedding. Eliza instantly becomes cool and elegant.

Mrs Higgins. The carriage is waiting, Eliza. Are you ready?

Liza. Quite. Is the Professor coming?

Mrs Higgins. Certainly not. He cant behave himself in church. He makes remarks out loud all the time on the clergyman's pronunciation.

Liza. Then I shall not see you again, Professor. Goodbye. (*She goes to the door*).

Mrs Higgins (*coming to Higgins*) Goodbye, dear.

Higgins. Goodbye, mother. (*He is about to kiss her, when he recollects something*). Oh, by the way, Eliza, order a ham and a Stilton cheese, will you? And buy me a pair of reindeer gloves, number eights, and a tie to match that new suit of mine, at Eale & Binman's. You can choose the color. (*His cheerful, careless, vigorous voice shows that he is incorrigible*).

Liza (*disdainfully*) Buy them yourself. (*She sweeps out*).

Mrs Higgins. I'm afraid youve spoiled that girl, Henry. But never mind, dear: I'll buy you the tie and gloves.

Higgins (*sunnily*) Oh, dont bother. She'll buy em all right enough. Goodbye.

They kiss. Mrs Higgins runs out. Higgins, left alone, rattles his cash in his pocket; chuckles; and disports himself in a highly self-satisfied manner.

*   *   *   *   *   *

The rest of the story need not be shewn in action, and indeed, would hardly need telling if our imaginations were not so enfeebled by their lazy dependence on the ready-mades and reach-me-downs of the ragshop in which Romance keeps its stock of "happy endings" to misfit all stories. Now, the history of Eliza Doolittle, though called a romance because the transfiguration it records seems exceedingly improbable, is common enough. Such transfigurations have been achieved by hundreds of resolutely ambitious young women since Nell Gwynne set them the example by playing queens and fascinating kings in the theatre in which she began by selling oranges. Nevertheless, people in all directions have assumed, for no other reason than that she became the heroine of a romance, that she must have married the hero of it. This is unbearable, not only because her little drama, if acted on such a thoughtless assumption, must be spoiled, but because the true sequel is patent to anyone with a sense of human nature in general, and of feminine instinct in particular.

Eliza, in telling Higgins she would not marry him if he asked her, was not coquetting: she was announcing a well-considered decision. When a bachelor interests, and dominates, and teaches, and becomes important to a spinster, as Higgins with Eliza, she always, if she has character enough to be capable of it, considers very seriously indeed whether she will play for becoming that bachelor's wife, especially if he is so little interested in marriage that a determined and devoted woman might capture him if she set herself resolutely to do it. Her decision will depend a good deal on whether she is really free to choose; and that, again, will depend on her age and income. If she is at the end of her youth, and has no security for her livelihood, she will marry him because she must marry anybody who will provide for her. But at Eliza's age a good-looking girl does not feel that pressure: she feels free to pick and choose. She is therefore guided by her instinct in the matter. Eliza's instinct tells her not to marry Higgins. It does not tell her to give him up. It is not in the slightest doubt as to his remaining one of the strongest personal interests in her life. It would be very sorely strained if there was another woman likely to supplant her with him. But as she feels sure of him on that last point, she has no doubt at all as to her course, and would not have any, even if the difference of twenty years in age, which seems so great to youth, did not exist between them.

As our own instincts are not appealed to by her conclusion, let us see whether we cannot discover some reason in it. When Higgins excused his indifference to young women on the ground that they had an irresistible rival in his mother, he gave the clue to his inveterate old-bachelordom. The case is

uncommon only to the extent that remarkable mothers are uncommon. If an imaginative boy has a sufficiently rich mother
who has intelligence, personal grace, dignity of character without harshness, and a cultivated sense of the best art of her
time to enable her to make her house beautiful, she sets a
standard for him against which very few women can struggle,
besides effecting for him a disengagement of his affections, his
sense of beauty, and his idealism from his specifically sexual
impulses. This makes him a standing puzzle to the huge number of uncultivated people who have been brought up in taste-
less homes by commonplace or disagreeable parents, and to
whom, consequently, literature, painting, sculpture, music, and
affectionate personal relations come as modes of sex if they
come at all. The word passion means nothing else to them; and
that Higgins could have a passion for phonetics and idealize
his mother instead of Eliza, would seem to them absurd and
unnatural. Nevertheless, when we look round and see that
hardly anyone is too ugly or disagreeable to find a wife or a
husband if he or she wants one, whilst many old maids and
bachelors are above the average in quality and culture, we cannot help suspecting that the disentanglement of sex from the
associations with which it is so commonly confused, a disentanglement which persons of genius achieve by sheer intellectual analysis, is sometimes produced or aided by parental fascination.

Now, though Eliza was incapable of thus explaining to
herself Higgins's formidable powers of resistance to the charm
that prostrated Freddy at the first glance, she was instinctively
aware that she could never obtain a complete grip of him, or
come between him and his mother (the first necessity of the
married woman). To put it shortly, she knew that for some
mysterious reason he had not the makings of a married man
in him, according to her conception of a husband as one to
whom she would be his nearest and fondest and warmest interest. Even had there been no mother-rival, she would still

have refused to accept an interest in herself that was secondary
to philosophic interests. Had Mrs Higgins died, there would
still have been Milton and the Universal Alphabet. Landor's
remark that to those who have the greatest power of loving,
love is a secondary affair, would not have recommended Landor to Eliza. Put that along with her resentment of Higgins's
domineering superiority, and her mistrust of his coaxing cleverness in getting round her and evading her wrath when he had
gone too far with his impetuous bullying, and you will see
that Eliza's instinct had good grounds for warning her not to
marry her Pygmalion.

And now, whom did Eliza marry? For if Higgins was a predestinate old bachelor, she was most certainly not a predestinate
old maid. Well, that can be told very shortly to those who have
not guessed it from the indications she has herself given them.

Almost immediately after Eliza is stung into proclaiming
her considered determination not to marry Higgins, she men-
tions the fact that young Mr Frederick Eynsford Hill is pouring out his love for her daily through the post. Now Freddy
is young, practically twenty years younger than Higgins: he
is a gentleman (or, as Eliza would qualify him, a toff), and
speaks like one; he is nicely dressed, is treated by the Colonel
as an equal, loves her unaffectedly, and is not her master, nor
ever likely to dominate her in spite of his advantage of social
standing. Eliza has no use for the foolish romantic tradition
that all women love to be mastered, if not actually bullied and
beaten. "When you go to women," says Nietzsche, "take your
whip with you." Sensible despots have never confined that
precaution to women: they have taken their whips with them
when they have dealt with men, and been slavishly idealized
by the men over whom they have flourished the whip much
more than by women. No doubt there are slavish women as
well as slavish men: and women, like men, admire those that
are stronger than themselves. But to admire a strong person
and to live under that strong person's thumb are two different

things. The weak may not be admired and hero-worshipped; but they are by no means disliked or shunned; and they never seem to have the least difficulty in marrying people who are too good for them. They may fail in emergencies; but life is not one long emergency: it is mostly a string of situations for which no exceptional strength is needed, and with which even rather weak people can cope if they have a stronger partner to help them out. Accordingly, it is a truth everywhere in evidence that strong people, masculine or feminine, not only do not marry stronger people, but do not shew any preference for them in selecting their friends. When a lion meets another with a louder roar "the first lion thinks the last a bore." The man or woman who feels strong enough for two, seeks for every other quality in a partner than strength.

The converse is also true. Weak people want to marry strong people who do not frighten them too much; and this often leads them to make the mistake we describe metaphorically as "biting off more than they can chew." They want too much for too little; and when the bargain is unreasonable beyond all bearing, the union becomes impossible: it ends in the weaker party being either discarded or borne as a cross, which is worse. People who are not only weak, but silly or obtuse as well, are often in these difficulties.

This being the state of human affairs, what is Eliza fairly sure to do when she is placed between Freddy and Higgins? Will she look forward to a lifetime of fetching Higgins's slippers or to a lifetime of Freddy fetching hers? There can be no doubt about the answer. Unless Freddy is biologically repulsive to her, and Higgins biologically attractive to a degree that overwhelms all her other instincts, she will, if she marries either of them, marry Freddy.

And that is just what Eliza did.

Complications ensued; but they were economic, not romantic. Freddy had no money and no occupation. His mother's jointure, a last relic of the opulence of Largelady Park, had enabled her to struggle along in Earlscourt with an air of gentility, but not to procure any serious secondary education for her children, much less give the boy a profession. A clerkship at thirty shillings a week was beneath Freddy's dignity, and extremely distasteful to him besides. His prospects consisted of a hope that if he kept up appearances somebody would do something for him. The something appeared vaguely to his imagination as a private secretaryship or a sinecure of some sort. To his mother it perhaps appeared as a marriage to some lady of means who could not resist her boy's niceness. Fancy her feelings when he married a flower girl who had become déclassée under extraordinary circumstances which were now notorious!

It is true that Eliza's situation did not seem wholly inelegible. Her father, though formerly a dustman, and now fantastically disclassed, had become extremely popular in the smartest society by a social talent which triumphed over every prejudice and every disadvantage. Rejected by the middle class, which he loathed, he had shot up at once into the highest circles by his wit, his dustmanship (which he carried like a banner), and his Nietzschean transcendence of good and evil. At intimate ducal dinners he sat on the right hand of the Duchess; and in country houses he smoked in the pantry and was made much of by the butler when he was not feeding in the dining room and being consulted by cabinet ministers. But he found it almost as hard to do all this on four thousand a year as Mrs Eynsford Hill to live in Earlscourt on an income so pitiably smaller that I have not the heart to disclose its exact figure. He absolutely refused to add the last straw to his burden by contributing to Eliza's support.

Thus Freddy and Eliza, now Mr and Mrs Eynsford Hill, would have spent a penniless honeymoon but for a wedding present of £500 from the Colonel to Eliza. It lasted a long time because Freddy did not know how to spend money, never having had any to spend, and Eliza, socially trained by a pair of old bachelors, wore her clothes as long as they held together and looked pretty, without the least regard to their being many months out of fashion. Still, £500 will not last two young people for ever; and they both knew, and Eliza felt as well, that they must shift for themselves in the end. She could quarter herself on Wimpole Street because it had come to be her home; but she was quite aware that she ought not to quarter Freddy there, and that it would not be good for his character if she did.

Not that the Wimpole Street bachelors objected. When she consulted them, Higgins declined to be bothered about her housing problem when that solution was so simple. Eliza's desire to have Freddy in the house with her seemed of no more importance than if she had wanted an extra piece of bedroom furniture. Pleas as to Freddy's character, and the moral obligation on him to earn his own living, were lost on Higgins. He denied that Freddy had any character, and declared that if he tried to do any useful work some competent person would have the trouble of undoing it: a procedure involving a net loss to the community, and great unhappiness to Freddy himself, who was obviously intended by Nature for such light work as amusing Eliza, which, Higgins declared, was a much more useful and honorable occupation than working in the city. When Eliza referred again to her project of teaching phonetics, Higgins abated not a jot of his violent opposition to it. He said she was not within ten years of being qualified to meddle with his pet subject; and as it was evident that the Colonel agreed with him, she felt she could not go against them in this grave matter, and that she had no right, without Higgins's consent, to exploit the knowledge he had given her; for his knowledge seemed to her as much his private property as his watch: Eliza was no communist. Besides, she was superstitiously devoted to them both, more entirely and frankly after her marriage than before it.

It was the Colonel who finally solved the problem, which

had cost him much perplexed cogitation. He one day asked Eliza, rather shyly, whether she had quite given up her notion of keeping a flower shop. She replied that she had thought of it, but had put it out of her head, because the Colonel had said, that day at Mrs Higgins's, that it would never do. The Colonel confessed that when he said that, he had not quite recovered from the dazzling impression of the day before. They broke the matter to Higgins that evening. The sole comment vouchsafed by him very nearly led to a serious quarrel with Eliza. It was to the effect that she would have in Freddy an ideal errand boy.

Freddy himself was next sounded on the subject. He said he had been thinking of a shop himself; though it had presented itself to his pennilessness as a small place in which Eliza should sell tobacco at one counter whilst he sold newspapers at the opposite one. But he agreed that it would be extraordinarily jolly to go early every morning with Eliza to Covent Garden and buy flowers on the scene of their first meeting: a sentiment which earned him many kisses from his wife. He added that he had always been afraid to propose anything of the sort, because Clara would make an awful row about a step that must damage her matrimonial chances, and his mother could not be expected to like it after clinging for so many years to that step of the social ladder on which retail trade is impossible.

This difficulty was removed by an event highly unexpected by Freddy's mother. Clara, in the course of her incursions into those artistic circles which were the highest within her reach, discovered that her conversational qualifications were expected to include a grounding in the novels of Mr H. G. Wells. She borrowed them in various directions so energetically that she swallowed them all within two months. The result was a conversion of a kind quite common today. A modern Acts of the Apostles would fill fifty whole Bibles if anyone were capable of writing it.

Poor Clara, who appeared to Higgins and his mother as a disagreeable and ridiculous person, and to her own mother as in some inexplicable way a social failure, had never seen herself in either light; for, though to some extent ridiculed and mimicked in West Kensington like everybody else there, she was accepted as a rational and normal—or shall we say inevitable?—sort of human being. At worst they called her The Pusher; but to them no more than to herself had it ever occurred that she was pushing the air, and pushing it in a wrong direction. Still, she was not happy. She was growing desperate. Her one asset, the fact that her mother was what the Epsom greengrocer called a carriage lady, had no exchange value, apparently. It had prevented her from getting educated, because the only education she could have afforded was education with the Earlscourt greengrocer's daughter. It had led her to seek the society of her mother's class; and that class simply would not have her, because she was much poorer than the greengrocer, and, far from being able to afford a maid, could not afford even a housemaid, and had to scrape along at home with an illiberally treated general servant. Under such circumstances nothing could give her an air of being a genuine product of Largelady Park. And yet its tradition made her regard a marriage with anyone within her reach as an unbearable humiliation. Commercial people and professional people in a small way were odious to her. She ran after painters and novelists; but she did not charm them; and her bold attempts to pick up and practice artistic and literary talk irritated them. She was, in short, an utter failure, an ignorant, incompetent, pretentious, unwelcome, penniless, useless little snob; and though she did not admit these disqualifications (for nobody ever faces unpleasant truths of this kind until the possibility of a way out dawns on them) she felt their effects too keenly to be satisfied with her position.

Clara had a startling eyeopener when, on being suddenly wakened to enthusiasm by a girl of her own age who dazzled her and produced in her a gushing desire to take her for a model, and gain her friendship, she discovered that this exquisite apparition had graduated from the gutter in a few months time. It shook her so violently, that when Mr H. G. Wells lifted her on the point of his puissant pen, and placed her at the angle of view from which the life she was leading and the society to which she clung appeared in its true relation to real human needs and worthy social structure, he effected a conversion and a conviction of sin comparable to the most sensational feats of General Booth or Gypsy Smith. Clara's snobbery went bang. Life suddenly began to move with her. Without knowing how or why, she began to make friends and enemies. Some of the acquaintances to whom she had been a tedious or indifferent or ridiculous affliction, dropped her: others became cordial. To her amazement she found that some "quite nice" people were saturated with Wells, and that this accessibility to ideas was the secret of their niceness. People she had thought deeply religious, and had tried to conciliate on that tack with disastrous results, suddenly took an interest in her, and revealed a hostility to conventional religion which she had never conceived possible except among the most desperate characters. They made her read Galsworthy; and Galsworthy exposed the vanity of Largelady Park and finished her. It exasperated her to think that the dungeon in which she had languished for so many unhappy years had been unlocked all the time, and that the impulses she had so carefully struggled with and stifled for the sake of keeping well with society, were precisely those by which alone she could have come into any sort of sincere human contact. In the radiance of these discoveries, and the tumult of their reaction, she made a fool of herself as freely and conspicuously as when she so rashly adopted Eliza's expletive in Mrs Higgins's drawing room; for the new-born Wellsian had to find her bearings almost as ridiculously as a baby; but nobody hates a baby for its ineptitudes, or thinks the worse of it for trying to eat the matches; and Clara lost no friends by her follies. They laughed at her to her face this time; and she had to defend herself and fight it out as best she could.

When Freddy paid a visit to Earlscourt (which he never did when he could possibly help it) to make the desolating announcement that he and his Eliza were thinking of blackening the Largelady scutcheon by opening a shop, he found the little household already convulsed by a prior announcement from Clara that she also was going to work in an old furniture shop in Dover Street, which had been started by a fellow Wellsian. This appointment Clara owed, after all, to her old social accomplishment of Push. She had made up her mind that, cost what it might, she would see Mr Wells in the flesh; and she had achieved her end at a garden party. She had better luck than so rash an enterprise deserved. Mr Wells came up to her expectations. Age had not withered him, nor could custom stale his infinite variety in half an hour. His pleasant neatness and compactness, his small hands and feet, his teeming ready brain, his unaffected accessibility, and a certain fine apprehensiveness which stamped him as susceptible from his topmost hair to his tipmost toe, proved irresistible. Clara talked of nothing else for weeks and weeks afterwards. And as she happened to talk to the lady of the furniture shop, and that lady also desired above all things to know Mr Wells and sell pretty things to him, she offered Clara a job on the chance of achieving that end through her.

And so it came about that Eliza's luck held, and the expected opposition to the flower shop melted away. The shop is in the arcade of a railway station not very far from the Victoria and Albert Museum; and if you live in that neighborhood you may go there any day and buy a buttonhole from Eliza.

Now here is a last opportunity for romance. Would you not like to be assured that the shop was an immense success, thanks to Eliza's charms and her early business experience in Covent Garden? Alas! the truth is the truth: the shop did not pay for a long time, simply because Eliza and her Freddy did not know how to keep it. True, Eliza had not to begin at the very beginning: she knew the names and prices of the cheaper flowers; and her elation was unbounded when she found that Freddy, like all youths educated at cheap, pretentious, and thoroughly inefficient schools, knew a little Latin. It was very little, but enough to make him appear to her a Porson or Bentley, and to put him at his ease with botanical nomenclature. Unfortunately he knew nothing else; and Eliza, though she could count money up to eighteen shillings or so, and had acquired a certain familiarity with the language of Milton from her struggles to qualify herself for winning Higgins's bet, could not write out a bill without utterly disgracing the establishment. Freddy's power of stating in Latin that Balbus built a wall and that Gaul was divided into three parts did not carry with it the slightest knowledge of accounts or business: Colonel Pickering had to explain to him what a cheque book and a bank account meant. And the pair were by no means easily teachable. Freddy backed up Eliza in her obstinate refusal to believe that they could save money by engaging a bookkeeper with some knowledge of the business. How, they argued, could you possibly save money by going to extra expense when you already could not make both ends meet? But the Colonel, after making the ends meet over and over again, at last gently insisted; and Eliza, humbled to the dust by having to beg from him so often, and stung by the uproarious derision of Higgins, to whom the notion of Freddy succeeding at anything was a joke that never palled, grasped the fact that business, like phonetics, has to be learned.

On the piteous spectacle of the pair spending their evenings in shorthand schools and polytechnic classes, learning bookkeeping and typewriting with incipient junior clerks, male and female, from the elementary schools, let me not dwell. There were even classes at the London School of Economics, and a humble personal appeal to the director of that institution to recommend a course bearing on the flower business. He, being a humorist, explained to them the method of the celebrated Dickensian essay on Chinese Metaphysics by the gentleman who read an article on China and an article on Metaphysics and combined the information. He suggested that they should combine the London School with Kew Gardens. Eliza, to whom the procedure of the Dickensian gentleman seemed perfectly correct (as in fact it was) and not in the least funny (which was only her ignorance), took his advice with entire gravity. But the effort that cost her the deepest humiliation was a request to Higgins, whose pet artistic fancy, next to Milton's verse, was calligraphy, and who himself wrote a most beautiful Italian hand, that he would teach her to write. He declared that she was congenitally incapable of forming a single letter worthy of the least of Milton's words; but she persisted; and again he suddenly threw himself into the task of teaching her with a combination of stormy intensity, concentrated patience, and occasional bursts of interesting disquisition on the beauty and nobility, the august mission and destiny, of human hand-writing. Eliza ended by acquiring an extremely uncommercial script which was a positive extension of her personal beauty, and spending three times as much on stationery as anyone else because certain qualities and shapes of paper became indispensable to her. She could not even address an envelope in the usual way because it made the margins all wrong.

Their commercial schooldays were a period of disgrace and despair for the young couple. They seemed to be learning nothing about flower shops. At last they gave it up as hopeless, and shook the dust of the shorthand schools, and the polytechnics, and the London School of Economics from their feet for ever. Besides, the business was in some mysterious way beginning to take care of itself. They had somehow forgotten their objections to employing other people. They came to the conclusion that their own way was the best, and that they had really a remarkable talent for business. The Colonel, who had been compelled for some years to keep a sufficient sum on current account at his bankers to make up their deficits, found that the provision was unnecessary: the young people were prospering. It is true that there was not quite fair play between them and their competitors in trade. Their week-ends in the country cost them nothing, and saved them the price of their Sunday dinners; for the motor car was the Colonel's; and he and Higgins paid the hotel bills. Mr F. Hill, florist and greengrocer (they soon discovered that there was money in asparagus; and asparagus led to other vegetables), had an air which stamped the business as classy; and in private life he was still Frederick Eynsford Hill, Esquire. Not that there was any swank about him: nobody but Eliza knew that he had been christened Frederick Challoner. Eliza herself swanked like anything.

That is all. That is how it has turned out. It is astonishing how much Eliza still manages to meddle in the housekeeping at Wimpole Street in spite of the shop and her own family. And it is notable that though she never nags her husband, and frankly loves the Colonel as if she were his favorite daughter, she has never got out of the habit of nagging Higgins that was established on the fatal night when she won his bet for him. She snaps his head off on the faintest provocation, or on none. He no longer dares to tease her by assuming an abysmal inferiority of Freddy's mind to his own. He storms and bullies and derides: but she stands up to him so ruthlessly that the Colonel has to ask her from time to time to be kinder to Higgins; and it is the only request of his that brings a mulish expression into her face. Nothing but some emergency or calamity great enough to break down all likes and dislikes, and throw them both back on their common humanity—and may they be spared any such trial!—will ever alter this. She knows that Higgins does not need her, just as her father did not need her. The very scrupulousness with which he told her that day that he had become used to having her there, and dependent on

her for all sorts of little services, and that he should miss her
if she went away (it would never have occurred to Freddy or
the Colonel to say anything of the sort) deepens her inner certainty that she is "no more to him than them slippers"; yet she
has a sense, too, that his indifference is deeper than the infat-
uation of commoner souls. She is immensely interested in him.
She has even secret mischievous moments in which she wishes
she could get him alone, on a desert island, away from all ties
and with nobody else in the world to consider, and just drag
him off his pedestal and see him making love like any common
man. We all have private imaginations of that sort. But when
it comes to business, to the life that she really leads as distinguished from the life of dreams and fancies, she likes Freddy
and she likes the Colonel; and she does not like Higgins and
Mr Doolittle. Galatea never does quite like Pygmalion: his
relation to her is too godlike to be altogether agreeable.

Heartbreak House

A FANTASIA IN THE RUSSIAN MANNER ON ENGLISH THEMES

1917

HEARTBREAK HOUSE AND HORSEBACK HALL
WHERE HEARTBREAK HOUSE STANDS

HEARTBREAK HOUSE is not merely the name of the play which follows this preface. It is cultured, leisured Europe before the war. When the play was begun not a shot had been fired; and only the professional diplomatists and the very few amateurs whose hobby is foreign policy even knew that the guns were loaded. A Russian playwright, Tchekov, had produced four fascinating dramatic studies of Heartbreak House, of which three, The Cherry Orchard, Uncle Vanya, and The Seagull, had been performed in England. Tolstoy, in his Fruits of Enlightenment, had shewn us through it in his most ferociously contemptuous manner. Tolstoy did not waste any sympathy on it: it was to him the house in which Europe was stifling its soul; and he knew that our utter enervation and futilization in that overheated drawing-room atmosphere was delivering the world over to the control of ignorant and soulless cunning and energy, with the frightful consequences which have now overtaken it. Tolstoy was no pessimist: he was not disposed to leave the house standing if he could bring it down about the ears of its pretty and amiable voluptuaries; and he wielded the pickaxe with a will. He treated the case of the inmates as one of opium poisoning, to be dealt with by seizing the patients roughly and exercising them violently until they were broad awake. Tchekov, more of a fatalist, had no faith in these charming people extricating themselves. They would, he thought, be sold up and sent adrift by the bailiffs; therefore he had no scruple in exploiting and even flattering their charm.

THE INHABITANTS

Tchekov's plays, being less lucrative than swings and round-abouts, got no further in England, where theatres are only ordinary commercial affairs, than a couple of performances by the Stage Society. We stared and said, "How Russian!" They did not strike me in that way. Just as Ibsen's intensely Norwegian plays exactly fitted every middle and professional class suburb in Europe, these intensely Russian plays fitted all the country houses in Europe in which the pleasures of music, art, literature, and the theatre had supplanted hunting, shooting, fishing, flirting, eating, and drinking. The same nice people, the same utter futility. The nice people could read; some of them could write; and they were the only repositories of culture who had social opportunities of contact with our politicians, administrators, and newspaper proprietors, or any chance of sharing or influencing their activities. But they shrank from that contact. They hated politics. They did not wish to realize Utopia for the common people: they wished to realize their favorite fictions and poems in their own lives; and, when they could, they lived without scruple on incomes which they did nothing to earn. The women in their girlhood made themselves look like variety theatre stars, and settled down later into the types of beauty imagined by the previous generation of painters. They took the only part of our society in which there was leisure for high culture, and made it an economic, political, and, as far as practicable, a moral vacuum; and as Nature, abhorring the vacuum, immediately filled it up with sex and with all sorts of refined pleasures, it was a very delightful place at its best for moments of relaxation. In other moments it was disastrous. For prime ministers and their like, it was a veritable Capua.

HORSEBACK HALL

But where were our front benchers to nest if not here? The alternative to Heartbreak House was Horseback Hall, consisting of a prison for horses with an annex for the ladies and gentlemen who rode them, hunted them, talked about them, bought them and sold them, and gave nine-tenths of their lives to them, dividing the other tenth between charity, churchgoing (as a substitute for religion), and conservative electioneering (as a substitute for politics). It is true that the two establishments got mixed at the edges. Exiles from the library, the music room, and the picture gallery would be found languishing among the stables, miserably discontented; and hardy horsewomen who slept at the first chord of Schumann were born, horribly misplaced, into the garden of Klingsor; but sometimes one came upon horsebreakers and heartbreakers who could make the best of both worlds. As a rule, however, the two were apart and knew little of one another; so the prime minister folk had to choose between barbarism and Capua. And of the two atmospheres it is hard to say which was the more fatal to statesmanship.

REVOLUTION ON THE SHELF

Heartbreak House was quite familiar with revolutionary ideas on paper. It aimed at being advanced and free-thinking, and hardly ever went to church or kept the Sabbath except by a little extra fun at week-ends. When you spent a Friday to Tuesday in it you found on the shelf in your bedroom not only the books of poets and novelists, but of revolutionary biologists and even economists. Without at least a few plays by myself and Mr Granville Barker, and a few stories by Mr H. G. Wells, Mr Arnold Bennett, and Mr John Galsworthy, the house would have been out of the movement. You would find Blake among the poets, and beside him Bergson, Butler, Scott Haldane, the poems of Meredith and Thomas Hardy, and, generally speaking, all the literary implements for forming the mind of the perfect modern Socialist and Creative Evolutionist. It was a curious experience to spend Sunday in dipping into these books, and on Monday morning to read in the daily paper that the country had just been brought to the verge of anarchy be-

cause a new Home Secretary or chief of police, without an idea
in his head that his great-grandmother might not have had to
apologize for, had refused to "recognize" some powerful Trade
Union, just as a gondola might refuse to recognize a 20,000-
ton liner.

In short, power and culture were in separate compartments.
The barbarians were not only literally in the saddle, but on the
front bench in the House of Commons, with nobody to correct
their incredible ignorance of modern thought and political science but upstarts from the counting-house, who had spent their
lives furnishing their pockets instead of their minds. Both, however, were practised in dealing with money and with men, as
far as acquiring the one and exploiting the other went; and
although this is as undesirable an expertness as that of the
medieval robber baron, it qualifies men to keep an estate or a
business going in its old routine without necessarily understanding it, just as Bond Street tradesmen and domestic servants keep fashionable society going without any instruction in
sociology.

THE CHERRY ORCHARD

The Heartbreak people neither could nor would do anything
of the sort. With their heads as full of the Anticipations of
Mr H. G. Wells as the heads of our actual rulers were empty
even of the anticipations of Erasmus or Sir Thomas More, they
refused the drudgery of politics, and would have made a very
poor job of it if they had changed their minds. Not that they
would have been allowed to meddle anyhow, as only through
the accident of being a hereditary peer can anyone in these
days of Votes for Everybody get into parliament if handicapped
by a serious modern cultural equipment; but if they had, their
habit of living in a vacuum would have left them helpless and
ineffective in public affairs. Even in private life they were
often helpless wasters of their inheritance, like the people in
Tchekov's Cherry Orchard. Even those who lived within their

incomes were really kept going by their solicitors and agents, being unable to manage an estate or run a business without continual prompting from those who have to learn how to do such things or starve.

From what is called Democracy no corrective to this state of things could be hoped. It is said that every people has the Government it deserves. It is more to the point that every Government has the electorate it deserves; for the orators of the front bench can edify or debauch an ignorant electorate at will. Thus our democracy moves in a vicious circle of reciprocal worthiness and unworthiness.

NATURE'S LONG CREDITS

Nature's way of dealing with unhealthy conditions is unfortunately not one that compels us to conduct a solvent hygiene on a cash basis. She demoralizes us with long credits and reckless overdrafts, and then pulls us up cruelly with catastrophic bankruptcies. Take, for example, common domestic sanitation. A whole city generation may neglect it utterly and scandalously, if not with absolute impunity, yet without any evil consequences that anyone thinks of tracing to it. In a hospital two generations of medical students may tolerate dirt and carelessness, and then go out into general practice to spread the doctrine that fresh air is a fad, and sanitation an imposture set up to make profits for plumbers. Then suddenly Nature takes her revenge. She strikes at the city with a pestilence and at the hospital with an epidemic of hospital gangrene, slaughtering right and left until the innocent young have paid for the guilty old, and the account is balanced. And then she goes to sleep again and gives another period of credit, with the same result.

This is what has just happened in our political hygiene. Political science has been as recklessly neglected by Governments and electorates during my lifetime as sanitary science was in the days of Charles the Second. In international rela-

tions diplomacy has been a boyishly lawless affair of family
intrigues, commercial and territorial brigandage, torpors of
pseudo-goodnature produced by laziness, and spasms of fero-
cious activity produced by terror. But in these islands we mud-
dled through. Nature gave us a longer credit than she gave to
France or Germany or Russia. To British centenarians who
died in their beds in 1914, any dread of having to hide underground in London from the shells of an enemy seemed more
remote and fantastic than a dread of the appearance of a colony
of cobras and rattlesnakes in Kensington Gardens. In the
prophetic works of Charles Dickens we were warned against
many evils which have since come to pass; but of the evil of
being slaughtered by a foreign foe on our own door-steps there
was no shadow. Nature gave us a very long credit; and we
abused it to the utmost. But when she struck at last she struck
with a vengeance. For four years she smote our firstborn and
heaped on us plagues of which Egypt never dreamed. They
were all as preventible as the great Plague of London, and
came solely because they had not been prevented. They were
not undone by winning the war. The earth is still bursting
with the dead bodies of the victors.

THE WICKED HALF CENTURY

It is difficult to say whether indifference and neglect are
worse than false doctrine; but Heartbreak House and Horseback Hall unfortunately suffered from both. For half a century
before the war civilization had been going to the devil very
precipitately under the influence of a pseudo-science as disastrous as the blackest Calvinism. Calvinism taught that as we
are predestinately saved or damned, nothing that we do can
alter our destiny. Still, as Calvinism gave the individual no
clue as to whether he had drawn a lucky number or an unlucky one, it left him a fairly strong interest in encouraging his
hopes of salvation and allaying his fear of damnation by behaving as one of the elect might be expected to behave rather than

as one of the reprobate. But in the middle of the XIX century naturalists and physicists assured the world, in the name of Science, that salvation and damnation are all nonsense, and that pre-destination is the central truth of religion, inasmuch as human beings are produced by their environment, their sins and good deeds being only a series of chemical and mechanical reactions over which they have no control. Such figments as mind, choice, purpose, conscience, will, and so forth, are, they taught, mere illusions, produced because they are useful in the continual struggle of the human machine to maintain its environment in a favorable condition, a process incidentally involving the ruthless destruction or subjection of its competitors for the supply (assumed to be limited) of subsistence available. We taught Prussia this religion; and Prussia bettered our instruction so effectively that we presently found ourselves confronted with the necessity of destroying Prussia to prevent Prussia destroying us. And that has just ended in each destroying the other to an extent doubtfully reparable in our time.

It may be asked how so imbecile and dangerous a creed ever came to be accepted by intelligent beings. I will answer that question more fully in my next volume of plays, which will be entirely devoted to the subject. For the present I will only say that there were better reasons than the obvious one that such sham science as this opened a scientific career to very stupid men, and all the other careers to shameless rascals, provided they were industrious enough. It is true that this motive operated very powerfully; but when the new departure in scientific doctrine which is associated with the name of the great naturalist Charles Darwin began, it was not only a reaction against a barbarous pseudo-evangelical teleology intolerably obstructive to all scientific progress, but was accompanied, as it happened, by discoveries of extraordinary interest in physics, chemistry, and that lifeless method of evolution which its investigators called Natural Selection. Howbeit, there was only one result possible in the ethical sphere, and that was the banishment of conscience from human affairs, or, as Samuel Butler vehemently put it, "of mind from the universe."

HYPOCHONDRIA

Now Heartbreak House, with Butler and Bergson and Scott Haldane alongside Blake and the other major poets on its shelves (to say nothing of Wagner and the tone poets), was not so completely blinded by the doltish materialism of the laboratories as the uncultured world outside. But being an idle house it was a hypochondriacal house, always running after cures. It would stop eating meat, not on valid Shelleyan grounds, but in order to get rid of a bogey called Uric Acid; and it would actually let you pull all its teeth out to exorcise another demon named Pyorrhea. It was superstitious, and addicted to table-rapping, materialization séances, clairvoyance, palmistry, crystal-gazing and the like to such an extent that it may be doubted whether ever before in the history of the world did soothsayers, astrologers, and unregistered therapeutic specialists of all sorts flourish as they did during this half century of the drift to the abyss. The registered doctors and surgeons were hard put to it to compete with the unregistered. They were not clever enough to appeal to the imagination and sociability of the Heartbreakers by the arts of the actor, the orator, the poet, the winning conversationalist. They had to fall back coarsely on the terror of infection and death. They prescribed inoculations and operations. Whatever part of a human being could be cut out without necessarily killing him they cut out; and he often died (unnecessarily of course) in consequence. From such trifles as uvulas and tonsils they went on to ovaries and appendices until at last no one's inside was safe. They explained that the human intestine was too long, and that nothing could make a child of Adam healthy except short circuiting the pylorus by cutting a length out of the lower intestine and fastening it directly to the stomach. As their mechanist theory taught them that medicine was the business of the chemist's laboratory, and surgery of the carpenter's shop, and also that Science (by which they meant their practices) was so important that no consideration for the interests of any individual creature, whether frog or philosopher, much less the vulgar commonplaces of sentimental ethics, could weigh for a moment against the remotest off-chance of an addition to the body of scientific knowledge, they operated and vivisected and inoculated and lied on a stupendous scale, clamoring for and actually acquiring such legal powers over the bodies of their fellow-citizens as neither king, pope, nor parliament dare ever have claimed. The Inquisition itself was a Liberal institution compared to the General Medical Council.

THOSE WHO DO NOT KNOW HOW TO LIVE MUST MAKE A MERIT OF DYING

Heartbreak House was far too lazy and shallow to extricate itself from this palace of evil enchantment. It rhapsodized about love; but it believed in cruelty. It was afraid of the cruel people; and it saw that cruelty was at least effective. Cruelty did things that made money, whereas Love did nothing but prove the soundness of Larochefoucauld's saying that very few people would fall in love if they had never read about it. Heartbreak House, in short, did not know how to live, at which point all that was left to it was the boast that at least it knew how to die: a melancholy accomplishment which the outbreak of war presently gave it practically unlimited opportunities of displaying. Thus were the firstborn of Heartbreak House smitten; and the young, the innocent, the hopeful expiated the folly and worthlessness of their elders.

WAR DELIRIUM

Only those who have lived through a first-rate war, not in the field, but at home, and kept their heads, can possibly understand the bitterness of Shakespear and Swift, who both went through this experience. The horror of Peer Gynt in the madhouse, when the lunatics, exalted by illusions of splendid talent and visions of a dawning millennium, crowned him as their emperor, was tame in comparison. I do not know whether anyone really kept his head completely except those who had to keep it because they had to conduct the war at first hand. I should not have kept my own (as far as I did keep it) if I had not at once understood that as a scribe and speaker I too was under the most serious public obligation to keep my grip on realities; but this did not save me from a considerable degree of hyperaesthesia. There were of course some happy people to whom the war meant nothing: all political and general matters lying outside their little circle of interest. But the ordinary war-conscious civilian went mad, the main symptom being a conviction that the whole order of nature had been reversed. All foods, he felt, must now be adulterated. All schools must be closed. No advertisements must be sent to the newspapers, of which new editions must appear and be bought up every ten minutes. Travelling must be stopped, or, that being impossible, greatly hindered. All pretences about fine art and culture and the like must be flung off as an intolerable affectation; and the picture galleries and museums and schools at once occupied by war workers. The British Museum itself was saved only by a hairsbreadth. The sincerity of all this, and of much more which would not be believed if I chronicled it, may be established by one con- clusive instance of the general craziness. Men were seized with the illusion that they could win the war by giving away money. And they not only subscribed millions to Funds of all sorts with no discoverable object, and to ridiculous voluntary organizations for doing what was plainly the business of the civil and military authorities, but actually handed out money to any thief in the street who had the presence of mind to pretend that he (or she) was "collecting" it for the annihilation of the enemy. Swindlers were emboldened to take offices; label themselves Anti-Enemy Leagues; and simply pocket the money that was heaped on them. Attractively dressed young women found that they had nothing to do but parade the streets, collecting box in hand, and live gloriously on the profits. Many months elapsed before, as a first sign of returning sanity, the police swept an Anti-Enemy secretary into prison *pour encourager les autres,* and the passionate penny collecting of the Flag Days was brought under some sort of regulation.

MADNESS IN COURT

The demoralization did not spare the Law Courts. Soldiers were acquitted, even on fully proved indictments for wilful murder, until at last the judges and magistrates had to announce that what was called the Unwritten Law, which meant simply that a soldier could do what he liked with impunity in civil life, was not the law of the land, and that a Victoria Cross did not carry with it a perpetual plenary indulgence. Unfortunately the insanity of the juries and magistrates did not always manifest itself in indulgence. No person unlucky enough to be charged with any sort of conduct, however reasonable and salutary, that did not smack of war delirium had the slightest chance of acquittal. There were in the country, too, a certain number of people who had conscientious objections to war as criminal or unchristian. The Act of Parliament introducing Compulsory Military Service thoughtlessly exempted these persons, merely requiring them to prove the genuineness of their convictions. Those who did so were very ill-advised from the point of view of their own personal interest; for they were persecuted with savage logicality in spite of the law; whilst those who made no pretence of having any objection to war at all, and had not only had military training in Officers' Training Corps, but had proclaimed on public occasions that they were perfectly ready to engage in civil war on behalf of their political opinions, were allowed the benefit of the Act on the ground that they did not approve of this particular war. For the Christians there was no mercy.

In cases where the evidence as to their being killed by ill treatment was so unequivocal that the verdict would certainly have been one of wilful murder had the prejudice of the coroner's jury been on the other side, their tormentors were gratuitously declared to be blameless. There was only one virtue, pugnacity: only one vice, pacifism. That is an essential condition of war; but the Government had not the courage to legislate accordingly; and its law was set aside for Lynch law.

The climax of legal lawlessness was reached in France. The greatest Socialist statesman in Europe, Jaurès, was shot and killed by a gentleman who resented his efforts to avert the war. M. Clemenceau was shot by another gentleman of less popular opinions, and happily came off no worse than having to spend a precautionary couple of days in bed. The slayer of Jaurès was recklessly acquitted: the would-be slayer of M. Clemenceau was carefully found guilty. There is no reason to doubt that the same thing would have happened in England if the war had begun with a successful attempt to assassinate Keir Hardie, and ended with an unsuccessful one to assassinate Mr Lloyd George.

THE LONG ARM OF WAR

The pestilence which is the usual accompaniment of war was called influenza. Whether it was really a war pestilence or not was made doubtful by the fact that it did its worst in places remote from the battle-fields, notably on the west coast of North America and in India. But the moral pestilence, which was unquestionably a war pestilence, reproduced this phenomenon. One would have supposed that the war fever would have raged most furiously in the countries actually under fire, and that the others would be more reasonable. Belgium and Flanders, where over large districts literally not one stone was left upon another as the opposed armies drove each other back and forward over it after terrific preliminary bombardments, might have been pardoned for relieving their feelings more emphatically than by shrugging their shoulders and saying "C'est la guerre." England, inviolate for so many centuries that the swoop of war on her homesteads had long ceased to be more credible than a return of the Flood, could hardly be expected to keep her temper sweet when she knew at last what it was to hide in cellars and underground railway stations, or lie quaking in bed, whilst bombs crashed, houses crumbled, and aircraft guns distributed shrapnel on friend and foe alike until certain shop windows in London, formerly full of fashionable hats, were filled with steel helmets. Slain and mutilated women and children, and burnt and wrecked dwellings, excuse a good deal of violent language, and produce a wrath on which many suns go down before it is appeased. Yet it was in the United States of America, where nobody slept the worse for the war, that the war fever went beyond all sense and reason. In European Courts there was vindictive illegality: in American Courts there was raving lunacy. It is not for me to chronicle the extravagances of an Ally: let some candid American do that. I can only say that to us sitting in our gardens in England, with the guns in France making themselves felt by a throb in the air as unmistakeable as an audible sound, or with tightening hearts studying the phases of the moon in London in their bearing on the chances whether our houses would be standing or ourselves alive next morning, the newspaper accounts of the sentences American Courts were passing on young girls and old men alike for the expression of opinions which were being uttered amid thundering applause before huge audiences in England, and the more private records of the methods by which the American War Loans were raised, were so amazing that they put the guns and the possibilities of a raid clean out of our heads for the moment.

THE RABID WATCHDOGS OF LIBERTY

Not content with these rancorous abuses of the existing law, the war maniacs made a frantic rush to abolish all constitutional guarantees of liberty and well-being. The ordinary law was superseded by Acts under which newspapers were seized and their printing machinery destroyed by simple police raids *à la Russe,* and persons arrested and shot without any pretence of trial by jury or publicity of procedure or evidence. Though it was urgently necessary that production should be increased by the most scientific organization and economy of labor, and though no fact was better established than that excessive duration and intensity of toil reduces production heavily instead of increasing it, the factory laws were suspended, and men and women recklessly overworked until the loss of their efficiency became too glaring to be ignored. Remonstrances and warnings were met either with an accusation of pro-Germanism or the formula, "Remember that we are at war now." I have said that men assumed that war had reversed the order of nature, and that all was lost unless we did the exact opposite of everything we had found necessary and beneficial in peace. But the truth was worse than that. The war did not change men's minds in any such impossible way. What really happened was that the impact of physical death and destruction, the one reality that every fool can understand, tore off the masks of education, art, science, and religion from our ignorance and barbarism, and left us glorying grotesquely in the licence suddenly accorded to our vilest passions and most abject terrors. Ever since Thucydides wrote his history, it has been on record that when the angel of death sounds his trumpet the pretences of civilization are blown from men's heads into the mud like hats in a gust of wind. But when this scripture was fulfilled among us, the shock was not the less appalling because a few students of Greek history were not surprised by it. Indeed these students threw themselves into the orgy as shamelessly as the illiterate. The Christian priest joining in the war dance without even throwing off his cassock first, and the respectable school governor expelling the German professor with insult and bodily violence, and declaring that no English child

should ever again be taught the language of Luther and
Goethe, were kept in countenance by the most impudent
repudiations of every decency of civilization and every lesson
of political experience on the part of the very persons who, as
university professors, historians, philosophers, and men of science, were the accredited custodians of culture. It was crudely
natural, and perhaps necessary for recruiting purposes, that
German militarism and German dynastic ambition should be
painted by journalists and recruiters in black and red as European dangers (as in fact they are), leaving it to be inferred
that our own militarism and our own political constitution are
millennially democratic (which they certainly are not); but
when it came to frantic denunciations of German chemistry,
German biology, German poetry, German music, German literature, German philosophy, and even German engineering, as
malignant abominations standing towards British and French
chemistry and so forth in the relation of heaven to hell, it
was clear that the utterers of such barbarous ravings had never
really understood or cared for the arts and sciences they
professed and were profaning, and were only the appallingly
degenerate descendants of the men of the seventeenth and
eighteenth centuries who, recognizing no national frontiers in
the great realm of the human mind, kept the European comity
of that realm loftily and even ostentatiously above the rancors
of the battle-field. Tearing the Garter from the Kaiser's leg,
striking the German dukes from the roll of our peerage, changing the King's illustrious and historically appropriate surname
for that of a traditionless locality, was not a very dignified
business; but the erasure of German names from the British
rolls of science and learning was a confession that in England
the little respect paid to science and learning is only an affectation which hides a savage contempt for both. One felt that
the figure of St George and the Dragon on our coinage should
be replaced by that of the soldier driving his spear through
Archimedes. But by that time there was no coinage: only

paper money in which ten shillings called itself a pound as confidently as the people who were disgracing their country called themselves patriots.

THE SUFFERINGS OF THE SANE

The mental distress of living amid the obscene din of all these carmagnoles and corobberies was not the only burden that lay on sane people during the war. There was also the emotional strain, complicated by the offended economic sense, produced by the casualty lists. The stupid, the selfish, the narrow-minded, the callous and unimaginative were spared a great deal. "Blood and destruction shall be so in use that mothers shall but smile when they behold their infants quartered by the hands of war," was a Shakespearean prophecy that very nearly came true; for when nearly every house had a slaughtered son to mourn, we should all have gone quite out of our senses if we had taken our own and our friends' bereavements at their peace value. It became necessary to give them a false value; to proclaim the young life worthily and gloriously sacrificed to redeem the liberty of mankind, instead of to expiate the heedlessness and folly of their fathers, and expiate it in vain. We had even to assume that the parents and not the children had made the sacrifice, until at last the comic papers were driven to satirize fat old men, sitting comfortably in club chairs, and boasting of the sons they had "given" to their country.

No one grudged these anodynes to acute personal grief; but they only embittered those who knew that the young men were having their teeth set on edge because their parents had eaten sour political grapes. Then think of the young men themselves! Many of them had no illusions about the policy that led to the war: they went clear-sighted to a horribly repugnant duty. Men essentially gentle and essentially wise, with really valuable work in hand, laid it down voluntarily and spent months forming fours in the barrack yard, and stabbing sacks of straw in the public eye, so that they might go out to kill and maim men as gentle as themselves. These men, who were perhaps, as a class, our most efficient soldiers (Frederick Keeling, for example), were not duped for a moment by the hypocritical melodrama that consoled and stimulated the others. They left their creative work to drudge at destruction, exactly as they would have left it to take their turn at the pumps in a sinking ship. They did not, like some of the conscientious objectors, hold back because the ship had been neglected by its officers and scuttled by its wreckers. The ship had to be saved, even if Newton had to leave his fluxions and Michael Angelo his marbles to save it; so they threw away the tools of their beneficent and ennobling trades, and took up the bloodstained bayonet and the murderous bomb, forcing themselves to pervert their divine instinct for perfect artistic execution to the effective handling of these diabolical things, and their economic faculty for organization to the contriving of ruin and slaughter. For it gave an ironic edge to their tragedy that the very talents they were forced to prostitute made the prostitution not only effective, but even interesting; so that some of them were rapidly promoted, and found themselves actually becoming artists in war, with a growing relish for it, like Napoleon and all the other scourges of mankind, in spite of themselves. For many of them there was not even this consolation. They "stuck it," and hated it, to the end.

EVIL IN THE THRONE OF GOOD

This distress of the gentle was so acute that those who shared it in civil life, without having to shed blood with their own hands, or witness destruction with their own eyes, hardly care to obtrude their own woes. Nevertheless, even when sitting at home in safety, it was not easy for those who had to write and speak about the war to throw away their highest conscience, and deliberately work to a standard of inevitable evil instead of to the ideal of life more abundant. I can answer for

at least one person who found the change from the wisdom of
Jesus and St Francis to the morals of Richard III and the
madness of Don Quixote extremely irksome. But that change
had to be made; and we are all the worse for it, except those
for whom it was not really a change at all, but only a relief
from hypocrisy.

Think, too, of those who, though they had neither to write
nor to fight, and had no children of their own to lose, yet
knew the inestimable loss to the world of four years of the
life of a generation wasted on destruction. Hardly one of the
epoch-making works of the human mind might not have
been aborted or destroyed by taking their authors away from
their natural work for four critical years. Not only were
Shakespears and Platos being killed outright; but many of the
best harvests of the survivors had to be sown in the barren
soil of the trenches. And this was no mere British consideration.
To the truly civilized man, to the good European, the slaughter
of the German youth was as disastrous as the slaughter of the
English. Fools exulted in "German losses." They were our
losses as well. Imagine exulting in the death of Beethoven
because Bill Sikes dealt him his death blow!

STRAINING AT THE GNAT AND SWALLOWING THE CAMEL

But most people could not comprehend these sorrows. There
was a frivolous exultation in death for its own sake, which
was at bottom an inability to realize that the deaths were real
deaths and not stage ones. Again and again, when an air
raider dropped a bomb which tore a child and its mother limb
from limb, the people who saw it, though they had been reading with great cheerfulness of thousands of such happenings
day after day in their newspapers, suddenly burst into furious
imprecations on "the Huns" as murderers, and shrieked for
savage and satisfying vengeance. At such moments it became
clear that the deaths they had not seen meant no more to them

than the mimic deaths of the cinema screen. Sometimes it was not necessary that death should be actually witnessed: it had only to take place under circumstances of sufficient novelty and proximity to bring it home almost as sensationally and effectively as if it had been actually visible.

For example, in the spring of 1915 there was an appalling slaughter of our young soldiers at Neuve Chapelle and at the Gallipoli landing. I will not go so far as to say that our civilians were delighted to have such exciting news to read at breakfast. But I cannot pretend that I noticed either in the papers, or in general intercourse, any feeling beyond the usual one that the cinema show at the front was going splendidly, and that our boys were the bravest of the brave. Suddenly there came the news that an Atlantic liner, the Lusitania, had been torpedoed, and that several well-known first class passengers, including a famous theatrical manager and the author of a popular farce, had been drowned, among others. The others included Sir Hugh Lane; but as he had only laid the country under great obligations in the sphere of the fine arts, no great stress was laid on that loss.

Immediately an amazing frenzy swept through the country. Men who up to that time had kept their heads now lost them utterly. "Killing saloon passengers! What next?" was the essence of the whole agitation; but it is far too trivial a phrase to convey the faintest notion of the rage which possessed us. To me, with my mind full of the hideous cost of Neuve Chapelle, Ypres, and the Gallipoli landing, the fuss about the Lusitania seemed almost a heartless impertinence, though I was well acquainted personally with the three best-known victims, and understood, better perhaps than most people, the misfortune of the death of Lane. I even found a grim satisfaction, very intelligible to all soldiers, in the fact that the civilians who found the war such splendid British sport should get a sharp taste of what it was to the actual combatants. I expressed my impatience very freely, and found that my very straightforward and natural feeling in the matter was received as a monstrous and heartless paradox. When I asked those who gaped at me whether they had anything to say about the holocaust of Festubert, they gaped wider than before, having totally forgotten it, or rather, having never realized it. They were not heartless any more than I was; but the big catastrophe was too big for them to grasp, and the little one had been just the right size for them. I was not surprised. Have I not seen a public body for just the same reason pass a vote for £30,000 without a word, and then spend three special meetings, prolonged into the night, over an item of seven shillings for refreshments?

LITTLE MINDS AND BIG BATTLES

Nobody will be able to understand the vagaries of public feeling during the war unless they bear constantly in mind that the war in its entire magnitude did not exist for the average civilian. He could not conceive even a battle, much less a campaign. To the suburbs the war was nothing but a suburban squabble. To the miner and navvy it was only a series of bayonet fights between German champions and English ones. The enormity of it was quite beyond most of us. Its episodes had to be reduced to the dimensions of a railway accident or a shipwreck before it could produce any effect on our minds at all. To us the ridiculous bombard- ments of Scarborough and Ramsgate were colossal tragedies, and the battle of Jutland a mere ballad. The words "after thorough artillery preparation" in the news from the front meant nothing to us; but when our seaside trippers learned that an elderly gentleman at breakfast in a week-end marine hotel had been interrupted by a bomb dropping into his egg- cup, their wrath and horror knew no bounds. They declared that this would put a new spirit into the army, and had no suspicion that the soldiers in the trenches roared with laughter

over it for days, and told each other that it would do the
blighters at home good to have a taste of what the army was
up against. Sometimes the smallness of view was pathetic. A
man would work at home regardless of the call "to make the
world safe for democracy." His brother would be killed at the
front. Immediately he would throw up his work and take up
the war as a family blood feud against the Germans. Sometimes
it was comic. A wounded man, entitled to his discharge, would
return to the trenches with a grim determination to find the
Hun who had wounded him and pay him out for it.

It is impossible to estimate what proportion of us, in khaki
or out of it, grasped the war and its political antecedents as
a whole in the light of any philosophy of history or knowledge
of what war is. I doubt whether it was as high as our proportion of higher mathematicians. But there can be no doubt
that it was prodigiously outnumbered by the comparatively
ignorant and childish. Remember that these people had to be
stimulated to make the sacrifices demanded by the war, and
that this could not be done by appeals to a knowledge which
they did not possess, and a comprehension of which they were
incapable. When the armistice at last set me free to tell the
truth about the war at the following general election, a soldier
said to a candidate whom I was supporting "If I had known
all that in 1914, they would never have got me into khaki."
And that, of course, was precisely why it had been necessary
to stuff him with a romance that any diplomatist would have
laughed at. Thus the natural confusion of ignorance was increased by a deliberately propagated confusion of nursery bogey
stories and melodramatic nonsense, which at last overreached
itself and made it impossible to stop the war before we had
not only achieved the triumph of vanquishing the German
army and thereby overthrowing its militarist monarchy, but
made the very serious mistake of ruining the centre of Europe,
a thing that no sane European State could afford to do.

THE DUMB CAPABLES AND THE NOISY INCAPABLES

Confronted with this picture of insensate delusion and folly, the critical reader will immediately counterplead that England all this time was conducting a war which involved the organization of several millions of fighting men and of the workers who were supplying them with provisions, munitions, and transport, and that this could not have been done by a mob of hysterical ranters. This is fortunately true. To pass from the newspaper offices and political platforms and club fenders and suburban drawing-rooms to the Army and the munition factories was to pass from Bedlam to the busiest and sanest of workaday worlds. It was to rediscover England, and find solid ground for the faith of those who still believed in her. But a necessary condition of this efficiency was that those who were efficient should give all their time to their business and leave the rabble raving to its hearts' content. Indeed the raving was useful to the efficient, because, as it was always wide of the mark, it often distracted attention very conveniently from operations that would have been defeated or hindered by publicity. A precept which I endeavored vainly to popularize early in the war, "If you have anything to do go and do it: if not, for heaven's sake get out of the way," was only half carried out. Certainly the capable people went and did it; but the incapables would by no means get out of the way: they fussed and bawled and were only prevented from getting very seriously into the way by the blessed fact that they never knew where the way was. Thus whilst all the efficiency of England was silent and invisible, all its imbecility was deafening the heavens with its clamor and blotting out the sun with its dust. It was also unfortunately intimidating the Government by its blusterings into using the irresistible powers of the State to intimidate the sensible people, thus enabling a despicable minority of would-be lynchers to set up a reign of terror which could at any time have been broken by a single stern word from a responsible minister. But our ministers had not that sort of courage: neither Heartbreak House nor Horseback Hall had bred it, much less the suburbs. When matters at last came to the looting of shops by criminals under patriotic pretexts, it was the police force and not the Government that put its foot down. There was even one deplorable moment, during the submarine scare, in which the Government yielded to a childish cry for the maltreatment of naval prisoners of war, and, to our great disgrace, was forced by the enemy to behave itself. And yet behind all this public blundering and misconduct and futile mischief, the effective England was carrying on with the most formidable capacity and activity. The ostensible England was making the empire sick with its incontinences, its ignorances, its ferocities, its panics, and its endless and intolerable blarings of Allied national anthems in season and out. The esoteric England was proceeding irresistibly to the conquest of Europe.

THE PRACTICAL BUSINESS MEN

From the beginning the useless people set up a shriek for "practical business men." By this they meant men who had become rich by placing their personal interests before those of the country, and measuring the success of every activity by the pecuniary profit it brought to them and to those on whom they depended for their supplies of capital. The pitiable failure of some conspicuous samples from the first batch we tried of these poor devils helped to give the whole public side of the war an air of monstrous and hopeless farce. They proved not only that they were useless for public work, but that in a well-ordered nation they would never have been allowed to control private enterprise.

HOW THE FOOLS SHOUTED THE WISE
MEN DOWN

Thus, like a fertile country flooded with mud, England shewed no sign of her greatness in the days when she was putting forth all her strength to save herself from the worst consequences of her littleness. Most of the men of action, occupied to the last hour of their time with urgent practical work, had to leave to idler people, or to professional rhetoricians, the presentation of the war to the reason and imagination of the country and the world in speeches, poems, manifestoes, picture posters, and newspaper articles. I have had the privilege of hearing some of our ablest commanders talking about their work; and I have shared the common lot of reading the accounts of that work given to the world by the newspapers. No two experiences could be more different. But in the end the talkers obtained a dangerous ascendancy over the rank and file of the men of action; for though the great men of action are always inveterate talkers and often very clever writers, and therefore cannot have their minds formed for them by others, the average man of action, like the average fighter with the bayonet, can give no account of himself in words even to himself, and is apt to pick up and accept what he reads about himself and other people in the papers, except when the writer is rash enough to commit himself on technical points. It was not uncommon during the war to hear a soldier, or a civilian engaged on war work, describing events within his own experience that reduced to utter absurdity the ravings and maunderings of his daily paper, and yet echo the opinions of that paper like a parrot. Thus, to escape from the prevailing confusion and folly, it was not enough to seek the company of the ordinary man of action: one had to get into contact with the master spirits. This was a privilege which only a handful of people could enjoy. For the unprivileged citizen there was no escape. To him the whole country seemed mad, futile, silly, incompetent, with no hope of victory except the hope that the enemy might be just as mad. Only by very resolute reflection and reasoning could he reassure himself that if there was nothing more solid beneath these appalling appearances the war could not possibly have gone on for a single day without a total breakdown of its organization.

THE MAD ELECTION

Happy were the fools and the thoughtless men of action in those days. The worst of it was that the fools were very strongly represented in parliament, as fools not only elect fools, but can persuade men of action to elect them too. The election that immediately followed the armistice was perhaps the maddest that has ever taken place. Soldiers who had done voluntary and heroic service in the field were defeated by persons who had apparently never run a risk or spent a farthing that they could avoid, and who even had in the course of the election to apologize publicly for bawling Pacifist or Pro-German at their opponent. Party leaders seek such followers, who can always be depended on to walk tamely into the lobby at the party whip's orders, provided the leader will make their seats safe for them by the process which was called, in derisive reference to the war rationing system, "giving them the coupon." Other incidents were so grotesque that I cannot mention them without enabling the reader to identify the parties, which would not be fair, as they were no more to blame than thousands of others who must necessarily be nameless. The general result was patently absurd; and the electorate, disgusted at its own work, instantly recoiled to the opposite extreme, and cast out all the coupon candidates at the earliest bye-elections by equally silly majorities. But the mischief of the general election could not be undone; and the Government had not only to pretend to abuse its European victory as it had promised, but actually to do it by starving the enemies who had thrown down their arms. It had, in short, won the election by pledg-

ing itself to be thriftlessly wicked, cruel, and vindictive; and
it did not find it as easy to escape from this pledge as it had
from nobler ones. The end, as I write, is not yet; but it is clear
that this thoughtless savagery will recoil on the heads of the
Allies so severely that we shall be forced by the sternest necessity to take up our share of healing the Europe we have
wounded almost to death instead of attempting to complete
her destruction.

YAHOO AND THE ANGRY APE

Contemplating this picture of a state of mankind so recent
that no denial of its truth is possible, one understands
Shakespear comparing Man to an angry ape, Swift describing
him as a Yahoo rebuked by the superior virtue of the horse,
and Wellington declaring that the British can behave themselves neither in victory nor defeat. Yet none of the three
had seen war as we have seen it. Shakespear blamed great
men, saying that "Could great men thunder as Jove himself
does Jove would ne'er be quiet; for every pelting petty officer
would use his heaven for thunder: nothing but thunder." What
would Shakespear have said if he had seen something far
more destructive than thunder in the hand of every village
laborer, and found on the Messines Ridge the craters of the
nineteen volcanoes that were let loose there at the touch of a
finger that might have been a child's finger without the result
being a whit less ruinous? Shakespear may have seen a Stratford cottage struck by one of Jove's thunderbolts, and have
helped to extinguish the lighted thatch and clear away the
bits of the broken chimney. What would he have said if he
had seen Ypres as it is now, or returned to Stratford, as French
peasants are returning to their homes today, to find the old
familiar signpost inscribed "To Stratford, 1 mile," and at the
end of the mile nothing but some holes in the ground and a
fragment of a broken churn here and there? Would not the
spectacle of the angry ape endowed with powers of destruc-

tion that Jove never pretended to, have beggared even his command of words?

And yet, what is there to say except that war puts a strain on human nature that breaks down the better half of it, and makes the worse half a diabolical virtue? Better for us if it broke it down altogether; for then the warlike way out of our difficulties would be barred to us, and we should take greater care not to get into them. In truth, it is, as Byron said, "not difficult to die," and enormously difficult to live: that explains why, at bottom, peace is not only better than war, but infinitely more arduous. Did any hero of the war face the glorious risk of death more bravely than the traitor Bolo faced the ignominious certainty of it? Bolo taught us all how to die: can we say that he taught us all how to live? Hardly a week passes now without some soldier who braved death in the field so recklessly that he was decorated or specially commended for it, being haled before our magistrates for having failed to resist the paltriest temptations of peace, with no better excuse than the old one that "a man must live." Strange that one who, sooner than do honest work, will sell his honor for a bottle of wine, a visit to the theatre, and an hour with a strange woman, all obtained by passing a worthless cheque, could yet stake his life on the most desperate chances of the battle-field! Does it not seem as if, after all, the glory of death were cheaper than the glory of life? If it is not easier to attain, why do so many more men attain it? At all events it is clear that the kingdom of the Prince of Peace has not yet become the kingdom of this world. His attempts at invasion have been resisted far more fiercely than the Kaiser's. Successful as that resistance has been, it has piled up a sort of National Debt that is not the less oppressive because we have no figures for it and do not intend to pay it. A blockade that cuts off "the grace of our Lord" is in the long run less bearable than the blockades which merely cut off raw materials; and against that blockade our Armada is impotent. In the blockader's house, he has assured us, there are many mansions; but I am afraid they do not include either Heartbreak House or Horseback Hall.

PLAGUE ON BOTH YOUR HOUSES!

Meanwhile the Bolshevist picks and petards are at work on the foundations of both buildings; and though the Bolshevists may be buried in the ruins, their deaths will not save the edifices. Unfortunately they can be built again. Like Doubting Castle, they have been demolished many times by successive Greathearts, and rebuilt by Simple, Sloth, and Presumption, by Feeble Mind and Much Afraid, and by all the jurymen of Vanity Fair. Another generation of "secondary education" at our ancient public schools and the cheaper institutions that ape them will be quite sufficient to keep the two going until the next war.

For the instruction of that generation I leave these pages as a record of what civilian life was during the war: a matter on which history is usually silent. Fortunately it was a very short war. It is true that the people who thought it could not last more than six months were very signally refuted by the event. As Sir Douglas Haig has pointed out, its Waterloos lasted months instead of hours. But there would have been nothing surprising in its lasting thirty years. If it had not been for the fact that the blockade achieved the amazing feat of starving out Europe, which it could not possibly have done had Europe been properly organized for war, or even for peace, the war would have lasted until the belligerents were so tired of it that they could no longer be compelled to compel themselves to go on with it. Considering its magnitude, the war of 1914–18 will certainly be classed as the shortest in history. The end came so suddenly that the combatants literally stumbled over it; and yet it came a full year later than it should have come if the belligerents had not been far too afraid of one another to face the situation sensibly. Germany, having failed to provide for the war she began, failed again to surrender before she was dangerously exhausted. Her opponents, equally improvident, went as much too close to bankruptcy as Germany to starvation. It was a bluff at which both were bluffed. And, with the usual irony of war, it remains doubtful whether Germany and Russia, the defeated, will not be the gainers; for the victors are already busy fastening on themselves the chains they have struck from the limbs of the vanquished.

HOW THE THEATRE FARED

Let us now contract our view rather violently from the European theatre of war to the theatre in which the fights are sham fights, and the slain, rising the moment the curtain has fallen, go comfortably home to supper after washing off their rosepink wounds. It is nearly twenty years since I was last obliged to introduce a play in the form of a book for lack of an opportunity of presenting it in its proper mode by a performance in a theatre. The war has thrown me back on this expedient. Heartbreak House has not yet reached the stage. I have withheld it because the war has completely upset the economic conditions which formerly enabled serious drama to pay its way in London. The change is not in the theatres nor in the management of them, nor in the authors and actors, but in the audiences. For four years the London theatres were crowded every night with thousands of soldiers on leave from the front. These soldiers were not seasoned London playgoers. A childish experience of my own gave me a clue to their condition. When I was a small boy I was taken to the opera. I did not then know what an opera was, though I could whistle a good deal of opera music. I had seen in my mother's album photographs of all the great opera singers, mostly in evening dress. In the theatre I found myself before a gilded balcony filled with persons in evening dress whom I took to be the opera singers. I picked out one massive dark lady as Alboni, and wondered how soon she would stand up and sing. I was puzzled by the fact that I was made to sit with my back to the singers instead of facing them. When the curtain went up, my astonishment and delight were unbounded.

THE SOLDIER AT THE THEATRE FRONT

In 1915 I saw in the theatres men in khaki in just the same predicament. To everyone who had my clue to their state of mind it was evident that they had never been in a theatre before and did not know what it was. At one of our great variety theatres I sat beside a young officer, not at all a rough specimen, who, even when the curtain rose and enlightened him as to the place where he had to look for his entertainment, found the dramatic part of it utterly incomprehensible. He did not know how to play his part of the game. He could understand the people on the stage singing and dancing and performing gymnastic feats. He not only understood but intensely enjoyed an artist who imitated cocks crowing and pigs squeaking. But the people who pretended that they were somebody else, and that the painted picture behind them was real, bewildered him. In his presence I realized how very sophisticated the natural man has to become before the conventions of the theatre can be easily acceptable, or the purpose of the drama obvious to him.

Well, from the moment when the routine of leave for our soldiers was established, such novices, accompanied by damsels (called flappers) often as innocent as themselves, crowded the theatres to the doors. It was hardly possible at first to find stuff crude enough to nurse them on. The best music-hall comedians ransacked their memories for the oldest quips and the most childish antics to avoid carrying the military spectators out of their depth. I believe that this was a mistake as far as the novices were concerned. Shakespear, or the dramatized histories of George Barnwell, Maria Martin, or the Demon Barber of Fleet Street, would probably have been quite popular with them. But the novices were only a minority after all. The cultivated soldier, who in time of peace would look at nothing theatrical except the most advanced post-Ibsen plays in the most artistic settings, found himself, to his own astonishment, thirsting for silly jokes, dances, and brainlessly sensuous exhibitions of pretty girls. The author of some of the most grimly serious plays of our time told me that after enduring the trenches for months without a glimpse of the female of his species, it gave him an entirely innocent but delightful pleasure merely to see a flapper. The reaction from the battlefield produced a condition of hyperaesthesia in which all the theatrical values were altered. Trivial things gained intensity and stale things novelty. The actor, instead of having to coax his audiences out of the boredom which had driven them to the theatre in an ill humor to seek some sort of distraction, had only to exploit the bliss of smiling men who were no longer under fire and under military discipline, but actually clean and comfortable and in a mood to be pleased with anything and everything that a bevy of pretty girls and a funny man, or even a bevy of girls pretending to be pretty and a man pretending to be funny, could do for them.

Then could be seen every night in the theatres old-fashioned farcical comedies, in which a bedroom, with four doors on each side and a practicable window in the middle, was understood to resemble exactly the bedroom in the flats beneath and above, all three inhabited by couples consumed with jealousy. When these people came home drunk at night; mistook their neighbors' flats for their own; and in due course got into the wrong beds, it was not only the novices who found the resulting complications and scandals exquisitely ingenious and amusing, nor their equally verdant flappers who could not help squealing in a manner that astonished the oldest performers when the gentleman who had just come in drunk through the window pretended to undress, and allowed glimpses of his naked person to be descried from time to time. Men who had just read the news that Charles Wyndham was dying, and were thereby sadly reminded of Pink Dominos and the torrent of farcical comedies that followed it in his heyday until every trick of that trade had become so stale that the laughter they provoked turned to loathing: these veterans also, when they returned from the field, were as much pleased by what they knew to be stale and foolish as the novices by what they thought fresh and clever.

COMMERCE IN THE THEATRE

Wellington said that an army moves on its belly. So does a London theatre. Before a man acts he must eat. Before he performs plays he must pay rent. In London we have no theatres for the welfare of the people: they are all for the sole purpose of producing the utmost obtainable rent for the proprietor. If the twin flats and twin beds produce a guinea more than Shakespear, out goes Shakespear and in come the twin flats and the twin beds. If the brainless bevy of pretty girls and the funny man outbid Mozart, out goes Mozart.

UNSER SHAKESPEAR

Before the war an effort was made to remedy this by establishing a national theatre in celebration of the tercentenary of the death of Shakespear. A committee was formed; and all sorts of illustrious and influential persons lent their names to a grand appeal to our national culture. My play, The Dark Lady of The Sonnets, was one of the incidents of that appeal. After some years of effort the result was a single handsome subscription from a German gentleman. Like the celebrated swearer in the anecdote when the cart containing all his household goods lost its tailboard at the top of the hill and let its contents roll in ruin to the bottom, I can only say, "I cannot do justice to this situation," and let it pass without another word.

THE HIGHER DRAMA PUT OUT OF ACTION

The effect of the war on the London theatres may now be imagined. The beds and the bevies drove every higher form of art out of it. Rents went up to an unprecedented figure. At the same time prices doubled everywhere except at the theatre pay boxes, and raised the expenses of management to such a degree that unless the houses were quite full every night, profit was impossible. Even bare solvency could not be attained without a very wide popularity. Now what had made serious drama possible to a limited extent before the war was that a play could pay its way even if the theatre were only half full until Saturday and three-quarters full then. A manager who was an enthusiast and a desperately hard worker, with an occasional grant-in-aid from an artistically disposed millionaire, and a due proportion of those rare and happy accidents by which plays of the higher sort turn out to be potboilers as well, could hold out for some years, by which time a relay might arrive in the person of another enthusiast. Thus and not otherwise occurred that remarkable revival of the British drama at the beginning of the century which made my own career as a playwright possible in England. In America I had already established myself, not as part of the ordinary theatre system, but in association with the exceptional genius of Richard Mansfield. In Germany and Austria I had no difficulty: the system of publicly aided theatres there, Court and Municipal, kept drama of the kind I dealt in alive; so that I was indebted to the Emperor of Austria for magnificent productions of my works at a time when the sole official attention paid me by the British Court was the announcement to the English-speaking world that certain plays of mine were unfit for public performance, a substantial set-off against this being that the British Court, in the course of its private playgoing, paid no regard to the bad character given me by the chief officer of its household.

Howbeit, the fact that my plays effected a lodgment on the London stage, and were presently followed by the plays of Granville Barker, Gilbert Murray, John Masefield, St John Hankin, Laurence Housman, Arnold Bennett, John Galsworthy, John Drinkwater, and others which would in the XIX century have stood rather less chance of production at a London theatre than the Dialogues of Plato, not to mention revivals of the ancient Athenian drama, and a restoration to the stage of Shakespear's plays as he wrote them, was made economically possible solely by a supply of theatres which could hold nearly twice as much money as it cost to rent and maintain them. In such theatres work appealing to a relatively small class of cultivated persons, and therefore attracting only from half to three-quarters as many spectators as the more popular pastimes, could nevertheless keep going in the hands of young adventurers who were doing it for its own sake, and had not yet been forced by advancing age and responsibilities to consider the commercial value of their time and energy too closely. The war struck this foundation away in the manner I have just described. The expenses of running the cheapest west-end theatres rose to a sum which exceeded by twenty-five per cent the utmost that the higher drama can, as an ascertained matter of fact, be depended on to draw. Thus the higher drama, which has never really been a commercially sound speculation, now became an impossible one. Accordingly, attempts are being made to provide a refuge for it in suburban theatres in London and repertory theatres in the provinces. But at the moment when the army has at last disgorged the survivors of the gallant band of dramatic pioneers whom it swallowed, they find that the economic conditions which formerly made their work no worse than precarious now put it out of the question altogether, as far as the west end of London is concerned.

CHURCH AND THEATRE

I do not suppose many people care particularly. We are not brought up to care; and a sense of the national importance of the theatre is not born in mankind: the natural man, like so many of the soldiers at the beginning of the war, does not know what a theatre is. But please note that all these soldiers who did not know what a theatre was, knew what a church was. And they had been taught to respect churches. Nobody had ever warned them against a church as a place where frivolous women paraded in their best clothes; where stories of improper females like Potiphar's wife, and erotic poetry like the Song of Songs, were read aloud; where the sensuous and sentimental music of Schubert, Mendelssohn, Gounod, and Brahms was more popular than severe music by greater composers; where the prettiest sort of pretty pictures of pretty saints assailed the imagination and senses through stained-glass windows; and where sculpture and architecture came to the help of painting. Nobody ever reminded them that these things had sometimes produced such developments of erotic idolatry that men who were not only enthusiastic amateurs of literature, painting, and music, but famous practitioners of them, had actually exulted when mobs and even regular troops under express command had mutilated church statues, smashed church windows, wrecked church organs, and torn up the sheets from which the church music was read and sung. When they saw broken statues in churches, they were told that this was the work of wicked godless rioters, instead of, as it was, the work partly of zealots bent on driving the world, the flesh, and the devil out of the temple, and partly of insurgent men who had become intolerably poor because the temple had become a den of thieves. But all the sins and perversions that were so carefully hidden from them in the history of the Church were laid on the shoulders of the Theatre: that stuffy, uncomfortable place of penance in which we suffer so much

inconvenience on the slenderest chance of gaining a scrap of
food for our starving souls. When the Germans bombed the
Cathedral of Rheims the world rang with the horror of the
sacrilege. When they bombed the Little Theatre in the Adel-
phi, and narrowly missed bombing two writers of plays who
lived within a few yards of it, the fact was not even mentioned
in the papers. In point of appeal to the senses no theatre ever
built could touch the fane at Rheims: no actress could rival
its Virgin in beauty, nor any operatic tenor look otherwise
than a fool beside its David. Its picture glass was glorious even
to those who had seen the glass of Chartres. It was wonderful
in its very grotesques: who would look at the Blondin Donkey
after seeing its leviathans? In spite of the Adam-Adelphian
decoration on which Miss Kingston had lavished so much taste
and care, the Little Theatre was in comparison with Rheims
the gloomiest of little conventicles: indeed the cathedral must,
from the Puritan point of view, have debauched a million
voluptuaries for every one whom the Little Theatre had sent
home thoughtful to a chaste bed after Mr Chesterton's Magic
or Brieux's *Les Avariés*. Perhaps that is the real reason why
the Church is lauded and the Theatre reviled. Whether or no,
the fact remains that the lady to whose public spirit and sense
of the national value of the theatre I owed the first regular
public performance of a play of mine had to conceal her action as if it had been a crime, whereas if she had given
the money to the Church she would have worn a halo for it.
And I admit, as I have always done, that this state of things
may have been a very sensible one. I have asked Londoners
again and again why they pay half a guinea to go to a theatre
when they can go to St Paul's or Westminster Abbey for
nothing. Their only possible reply is that they want to see
something new and possibly something wicked; but the
theatres mostly disappoint both hopes. If ever a revolution
makes me Dictator, I shall establish a heavy charge for admission to our churches. But everyone who pays at the church

door shall receive a ticket entitling him or her to free admission
to one performance at any theatre he or she prefers. Thus shall
the sensuous charms of the church service be made to subsidize
the sterner virtue of the drama.

THE NEXT PHASE

The present situation will not last. Although the newspaper I read at breakfast this morning before writing these
words contains a calculation that no less than twenty-three
wars are at present being waged to confirm the peace, England is no longer in khaki; and a violent reaction is setting
in against the crude theatrical fare of the four terrible years.
Soon the rents of theatres will once more be fixed on the
assumption that they cannot always be full, nor even on the
average half full week in and week out. Prices will change.
The higher drama will be at no greater disadvantage than
it was before the war; and it may benefit, first, by the fact
that many of us have been torn from the fools' paradise in
which the theatre formerly traded, and thrust upon the
sternest realities and necessities until we have lost both faith
in and patience with the theatrical pretences that had no
root either in reality or necessity; second, by the startling change
made by the war in the distribution of income. It seems only
the other day that a millionaire was a man with £50,000 a
year. Today, when he has paid his income tax and super tax,
and insured his life for the amount of his death duties, he is
lucky if his net income is £10,000, though his nominal property
remains the same. And this is the result of a Budget which is
called "a respite for the rich." At the other end of the scale
millions of persons have had regular incomes for the first time
in their lives; and their men have been regularly clothed, fed,
lodged, and taught to make up their minds that certain things
have to be done, also for the first time in their lives. Hundreds
of thousands of women have been taken out of their domestic
cages and tasted both discipline and independence. The

thoughtless and snobbish middle classes have been pulled up
short by the very unpleasant experience of being ruined to
an unprecedented extent. We have all had a tremendous jolt;
and although the widespread notion that the shock of the war
would automatically make a new heaven and a new earth, and
that the dog would never go back to his vomit nor the sow
to her wallowing in the mire, is already seen to be a delusion,
yet we are far more conscious of our condition than we were,
and far less disposed to submit to it. Revolution, lately only a
sensational chapter in history or a demagogic claptrap, is now
a possibility so imminent that hardly by trying to suppress it
in other countries by arms and defamation, and calling the
process anti-Bolshevism, can our Government stave it off at
home.

Perhaps the most tragic figure of the day is the American
President who was once a historian. In those days it became
his task to tell us how, after that great war in America which
was more clearly than any other war of our time a war for
an idea, the conquerors, confronted with a heroic task of
reconstruction, turned recreant, and spent fifteen years in
abusing their victory under cover of pretending to accomplish
the task they were doing what they could to make impossible.
Alas! Hegel was right when he said that we learn from history
that men never learn anything from history. With what
anguish of mind the President sees that we, the new conquerors, forgetting everything we professed to fight for, are
sitting down with watering mouths to a good square meal of
ten years' revenge upon and humiliation of our prostrate foe,
can only be guessed by those who know, as he does, how
hopeless is remonstrance, and how happy Lincoln was in
perishing from the earth before his inspired messages became
scraps of paper. He knows well that from the Peace Conference
will come, in spite of his utmost, no edict on which he will
be able, like Lincoln, to invoke "the considerate judgment

of mankind, and the gracious favor of Almighty God." He led his people to destroy the militarism of Zabern; and the army they rescued is busy in Cologne imprisoning every German who does not salute a British officer; whilst the Government at home, asked whether it approves, replies that it does not propose even to discontinue this Zabernism when the Peace is concluded, but in effect looks forward to making Germans salute British officers until the end of the world. That is what war makes of men and women. It will wear off; and the worst it threatens is already proving impracticable; but before the humble and contrite heart ceases to be despised, the President and I, being of the same age, will be dotards. In the meantime there is, for him, another history to write; for me, another comedy to stage. Perhaps, after all, that is what wars are for, and what historians and playwrights are for. If men will not learn until their lessons are written in blood, why, blood they must have, their own for preference.

THE EPHEMERAL THRONES AND THE ETERNAL THEATRE

To the theatre it will not matter. Whatever Bastilles fall, the theatre will stand. Apostolic Hapsburg has collapsed; All Highest Hohenzollern languishes in Holland, threatened with trial on a capital charge of fighting for his country against England; Imperial Romanoff, said to have perished miserably by a more summary method of murder, is perhaps alive or perhaps dead: nobody cares more than if he had been a peasant; the lord of Hellas is level with his lackeys in republican Switzerland; Prime Ministers and Commanders-in-Chief have passed from a brief glory as Solons and Caesars into failure and obscurity as closely on one another's heels as the descendants of Banquo; but Euripides and Aristophanes, Shakespear and Molière, Goethe and Ibsen remain fixed in their everlasting seats.

HOW WAR MUZZLES THE DRAMATIC POET

As for myself, why, it may be asked, did I not write two plays about the war instead of two pamphlets on it? The answer is significant. You cannot make war on war and on your neighbor at the same time. War cannot bear the terrible castigation of comedy, the ruthless light of laughter that glares on the stage. When men are heroically dying for their country, it is not the time to shew their lovers and wives and fathers and mothers how they are being sacrificed to the blunders of boobies, the cupidity of capitalists, the ambition of conquerors, the electioneering of demagogues, the Pharisaism of patriots, the lusts and lies and rancors and bloodthirsts that love war because it opens their prison doors, and sets them in the thrones of power and popularity. For unless these things are mercilessly exposed they will hide under the mantle of the ideals on the stage just as they do in real life.

And though there may be better things to reveal, it may not, and indeed cannot, be militarily expedient to reveal them whilst the issue is still in the balance. Truth telling is not compatible with the defence of the realm. We are just now reading the revelations of our generals and admirals, un-muzzled at last by the armistice. During the war, General A, in his moving despatches from the field, told how General B had covered himself with deathless glory in such and such a battle. He now tells us that General B came within an ace of losing us the war by disobeying his orders on that occasion, and fighting instead of running away as he ought to have done. An excellent subject for comedy now that the war is over, no doubt; but if General A had let this out at the time, what would have been the effect on General B's soldiers? And had the stage made known what the Prime Minister and the Secretary of State for War who overruled General A thought of him, and what he thought of them, as now revealed in raging controversy, what would have been the effect on the nation?

That is why comedy, though sorely tempted, had to be loyally silent; for the art of the dramatic poet knows no patriotism; recognizes no obligation but truth to natural history; cares not whether Germany or England perish; is ready to cry with Brynhild, "Lass' uns verderben, lachend zu grunde geh'n" sooner than deceive or be deceived; and thus becomes in time of war a greater military danger than poison, steel, or trinitrotoluene. That is why I had to withhold Heartbreak House from the footlights during the war; for the Germans might on any night have turned the last act from play into earnest, and even then might not have waited for their cues.

june 1919.

ACT I

THE HILLY country in the middle of the north edge of Sussex, looking very pleasant on a fine evening at the end of September, is seen through the windows of a room which has been built so as to resemble the after part of an old-fashioned high-pooped ship with a stern gallery; for the windows are ship built with heavy timbering, and run right across the room as continuously as the stability of the wall allows. A row of lockers under the windows provides an unupholstered window-seat interrupted by twin glass doors, respectively halfway between the stern post and the sides. Another door strains the illusion a little by being apparently in the ship's port side, and yet leading, not to the open sea, but to the entrance hall of the house. Between this door and the stern gallery are bookshelves. There are electric light switches beside the door leading to the hall and the glass doors in the stern gallery. Against the starboard wall is a carpenter's bench. The vice has a board in its jaws; and the floor is littered with shavings, overflowing from a waste-paper basket. A couple of planes and a centrebit are on the bench. In the same wall, between the bench and the windows, is a narrow doorway with a half door, above which a glimpse of the room beyond shews that it is a shelved pantry with bottles and kitchen crockery.

On the starboard side, but close to the middle, is a plain oak drawing-table with drawing-board, T-square, straightedges, set squares, mathematical instruments, saucers of water color, a tumbler of discolored water, Indian ink, pencils, and brushes on it. The drawing-board is set so that the draughtsman's chair has the window on its left hand. On the floor at the end of the table, on his right, is a ship's fire bucket. On the port side of the room, near the bookshelves, is a sofa with its back to the windows. It is a sturdy mahogany article, oddly upholstered in

364

sailcloth, including the bolster, with a couple of blankets hanging over the back. Between the sofa and the drawing-table is a big wicker chair, with broad arms and a low sloping back, with its back to the light. A small but stout table of teak, with a round top and gate legs, stands against the port wall between the door and the bookcase. It is the only article in the room that suggests (not at all convincingly) a woman's hand in the furnishing. The uncarpeted floor of narrow boards is caulked and holystoned like a deck.

The garden to which the glass doors lead dips to the south before the landscape rises again to the hills. Emerging from the hollow is the cupola of an observatory. Between the observatory and the house is a flagstaff on a little esplanade, with a hammock on the east side and a long garden seat on the west.

A young lady, gloved and hatted, with a dust coat on, is sitting in the window-seat with her body twisted to enable her to look out at the view. One hand props her chin: the other hangs down with a volume of the Temple Shakespear in it, and her finger stuck in the page she has been reading.

A clock strikes six.

The young lady turns and looks at her watch. She rises with an air of one who waits and is almost at the end of her patience. She is a pretty girl, slender, fair, and intelligent looking, nicely but not expensively dressed, evidently not a smart idler.

With a sigh of weary resignation she comes to the draughtsman's chair; sits down; and begins to read Shakespear. Presently the book sinks to her lap; her eyes close; and she dozes into a slumber.

An elderly womanservant comes in from the hall with three unopened bottles of rum on a tray. She passes through and disappears in the pantry without noticing the young lady. She places the bottles on the shelf and fills her tray with empty bottles. As she returns with these, the young lady lets her

*book drop, awakening herself, and startling the womanservant
so that she all but lets the tray fall.*

The Womanservant. God bless us! (*The young lady picks
up the book and places it on the table*). Sorry to wake you,
miss, I'm sure; but you are a stranger to me. What might you
be waiting here for now?

The Young Lady. Waiting for somebody to shew some
signs of knowing that I have been invited here.

The Womanservant. Oh, youre invited, are you? And has
nobody come? Dear! dear!

The Young Lady. A wild-looking old gentleman came and
looked in at the window; and I heard him calling out "Nurse:
there is a young and attractive female waiting in the poop.
Go and see what she wants." Are you the nurse?

The Womanservant. Yes, miss: I'm Nurse Guinness. That
was old Captain Shotover, Mrs Hushabye's father. I heard
him roaring; but I thought it was for something else. I suppose
it was Mrs Hushabye that invited you, ducky?

The Young Lady. I understood her to do so. But really I
think I'd better go.

Nurse Guinness. Oh, dont think of such a thing, miss. If
Mrs Hushabye has forgotten all about it, it will be a pleasant
surprise for her to see you, wont it?

The Young Lady. It has been a very unpleasant surprise to
me to find that nobody expects me.

Nurse Guinness. Youll get used to it, miss: this house is full
of surprises for them that dont know our ways.

Captain Shotover (*looking in from the hall suddenly: an
ancient but still hardy man with an immense white beard, in
a reefer jacket with a whistle hanging from his neck*) Nurse:
there is a hold-all and a handbag on the front steps for everybody to fall over. Also a tennis racquet. Who the devil left
them there?

The Young Lady. They are mine, I'm afraid.

The Captain (*advancing to the drawing-table*) Nurse: who is this misguided and unfortunate young lady?

Nurse Guinness. She says Miss Hessy invited her, sir.

The Captain. And had she no friend, no parents, to warn her against my daughter's invitations? This is a pretty sort of house, by heavens! A young and attractive lady is invited here. Her luggage is left on the steps for hours; and she herself is deposited in the poop and abandoned, tired and starving. This is our hospitality. These are our manners. No room ready. No hot water. No welcoming hostess. Our visitor is to sleep in the toolshed, and to wash in the duckpond.

Nurse Guinness. Now it's all right, Captain: I'll get the lady some tea; and her room shall be ready before she has finished it. (*To the young lady*) Take off your hat, ducky; and make yourself at home. (*She goes to the door leading to the hall*).

The Captain (*as she passes him*) Ducky! Do you suppose, woman, that because this young lady has been insulted and neglected, you have the right to address her as you address my wretched children, whom you have brought up in ignorance of the commonest decencies of social intercourse?

Nurse Guinness. Never mind him, doty. (*Quite unconcerned, she goes out into the hall on her way to the kitchen*).

The Captain. Madam: will you favor me with your name? (*He sits down in the big wicker chair*).

The Young Lady. My name is Ellie Dunn.

The Captain. Dunn! I had a boatswain whose name was Dunn. He was originally a pirate in China. He set up as a ship's chandler with stores which I have every reason to believe he stole from me. No doubt he became rich. Are you his daughter?

Ellie (*indignant*) No: certainly not. I am proud to be able to say that though my father has not been a successful man, nobody has ever had one word to say against him. I think my father is the best man I have ever known.

The Captain. He must be greatly changed. Has he attained the seventh degree of concentration?

Ellie. I dont understand.

The Captain. But how could he, with a daughter? I, madam, have two daughters. One of them is Hesione Hushabye, who invited you here. I keep this house: she upsets it. I desire to attain the seventh degree of concentration: she invites visitors and leaves me to entertain them. (*Nurse Guinness returns with the tea-tray, which she places on the teak table*). I have a second daughter who is, thank God, in a remote part of the Empire with her numskull of a husband. As a child she thought the figure-head of my ship, the Dauntless, the most beautiful thing on earth. He resembled it. He had the same expression: wooden yet enterprising. She married him, and will never set foot in this house again.

Nurse Guinness (*carrying the table, with the tea-things on it, to Ellie's side*) Indeed you never were more mistaken. She is in England this very moment. You have been told three times this week that she is coming home for a year for her health. And very glad you should be to see your own daughter again after all these years.

The Captain. I am not glad. The natural term of the affection of the human animal for its offspring is six years. My daughter Ariadne was born when I was forty-six. I am now eighty-eight. If she comes, I am not at home. If she wants anything, let her take it. If she asks for me, let her be informed that I am extremely old, and have totally forgotten her.

Nurse Guinness. Thats no talk to offer to a young lady. Here, ducky, have some tea; and dont listen to him. (*She pours out a cup of tea*).

The Captain (*rising wrathfully*) Now before high heaven they have given this innocent child Indian tea: the stuff they tan their own leather insides with. (*He seizes the cup and the tea-pot and empties both into the leathern bucket*).

Ellie (almost in tears) Oh, please! I am so tired. I should have been glad of anything.

Nurse Guinness. Oh, what a thing to do! The poor lamb is ready to drop.

The Captain. You shall have some of my tea. Do not touch that fly-blown cake: nobody eats it here except the dogs. (*He disappears into the pantry*).

Nurse Guinness. Theres a man for you! They say he sold himself to the devil in Zanzibar before he was a captain; and the older he grows the more I believe them.

A Woman's Voice (in the hall) Is anyone at home? Hesione! Nurse! Papa! Do come, somebody; and take in my luggage.

Thumping heard, as of an umbrella, on the wainscot.

Nurse Guinness. My gracious! It's Miss Addy, Lady Utterword, Mrs Hushabye's sister: the one I told the Captain about. (*Calling*) Coming, miss, coming.

She carries the table back to its place by the door, and is hurrying out when she is intercepted by Lady Utterword, who bursts in much flustered. Lady Utterword, a blonde, is very handsome, very well dressed, and so precipitate in speech and action that the first impression (erroneous) is one of comic silliness.

Lady Utterword. Oh, is that you, Nurse? How are you? You dont look a day older. Is nobody at home? Where is Hesione? Doesnt she expect me? Where are the servants? Whose luggage is that on the steps? Where's papa? Is everybody asleep? (*Seeing Ellie*) Oh! I beg your pardon. I suppose you are one of my nieces. (*Approaching her with outstretched arms*) Come and kiss your aunt, darling.

Ellie. I'm only a visitor. It is my luggage on the steps.

Nurse Guinness. I'll go get you some fresh tea, ducky. (*She takes up the tray*).

Ellie. But the old gentleman said he would make some himself.

Nurse Guinness. Bless you! he's forgotten what he went for already. His mind wanders from one thing to another.

Lady Utterword. Papa, I suppose?

Nurse Guinness. Yes, miss.

Lady Utterword (vehemently) Dont be silly, Nurse. Dont call me miss.

Nurse Guinness (placidly) No, lovey. *(She goes out with the tea-tray)*.

Lady Utterword (sitting down with a flounce on the sofa) I know what you must feel. Oh, this house, this house! I come back to it after twenty-three years; and it is just the same: the luggage lying on the steps, the servants spoilt and impossible, nobody at home to receive anybody, no regular meals, nobody ever hungry because they are always gnawing bread and butter or munching apples, and, what is worse, the same disorder in ideas, in talk, in feeling. When I was a child I was used to it: I had never known anything better, though I was unhappy, and longed all the time—oh, how I longed!—to be respectable, to be a lady, to live as others did, not to have to think of everything for myself. I married at nineteen to escape from it. My husband is Sir Hastings Utterword, who has been governor of all the crown colonies in succession. I have always been the mistress of Government House. I have been so happy: I had forgotten that people could live like this. I wanted to see my father, my sister, my nephews and nieces (one ought to, you know), and I was looking forward to it. And now the state of the house! the way I'm received! the casual impudence of that woman Guinness, our old nurse! really Hesione might at least have been here: s o m e preparation might have been made for me. You must excuse my going on in this way; but I am really very much hurt and annoyed and disillusioned: and if I had realized it was to be like this, I wouldnt have come. I have a great mind to go away without another word. *(She is on the point of weeping)*.

Ellie (also very miserable) Nobody has been here to receive me either. I thought I ought to go away too. But how can I, Lady Utterword? My luggage is on the steps; and the station fly has gone.

The Captain emerges from the pantry with a tray of Chinese lacquer and a very fine tea-set on it. He rests it provisionally on the end of the table; snatches away the drawing-board, which he stands on the floor against the table legs; and puts the tray in the space thus cleared. Ellie pours out a cup greedily.

The Captain. Your tea, young lady. What! another lady! I must fetch another cup. (*He makes for the pantry*).

Lady Utterword (*rising from the sofa, suffused with emotion*) Papa! Don't you know me? I'm your daughter.

The Captain. Nonsense! my daughter's upstairs asleep. (*He vanishes through the half door*).

Lady Utterword retires to the window to conceal her tears.

Ellie (*going to her with the cup*) Dont be so distressed. Have this cup of tea. He is very old and very strange: he has been just like that to me. I know how dreadful it must be: my own father is all the world to me. Oh, I'm sure he didnt mean it.

The Captain returns with another cup.

The Captain. Now we are complete. (*He places it on the tray*).

Lady Utterword (*hysterically*) Papa: you cant have forgotten me. I am Ariadne. I'm little Paddy Patkins. Wont you kiss me? (*She goes to him and throws her arms round his neck*).

The Captain (*woodenly enduring her embrace*) How can you be Ariadne? You are a middle-aged woman: well-preserved, madam, but no longer young.

Lady Utterword. But think of all the years and years I have been away, papa. I have had to grow old, like other people.

The Captain (*disengaging himself*) You should grow out of

kissing strange men: they may be striving to attain the seventh degree of concentration.

Lady Utterword. But I'm your daughter. You havnt seen me for years.

The Captain. So much the worse! When our relatives are at home, we have to think of all their good points or it would be impossible to endure them. But when they are away, we console ourselves for their absence by dwelling on their vices. That is how I have come to think my absent daughter Ariadne a perfect fiend; so do not try to ingratiate yourself here by impersonating her. (*He walks firmly away to the other side of the room*).

Lady Utterword. Ingratiating myself indeed! (*With dignity*) Very well, papa. (*She sits down at the drawing-table and pours out tea for herself*).

The Captain. I am neglecting my social duties. You remember Dunn? Billy Dunn?

Lady Utterword. Do you mean that villainous sailor who robbed you?

The Captain (*introducing Ellie*) His daughter. (*He sits down on the sofa*).

Ellie (*protesting*) No—

Nurse Guinness returns with fresh tea.

The Captain. Take that hogwash away. Do you hear?

Nurse. Youve actually remembered about the tea! (*To Ellie*) O, miss, he didnt forget you after all! You h a v e made an impression.

The Captain (*gloomily*) Youth! beauty! novelty! They are badly wanted in this house. I am excessively old. Hesione is only moderately young. Her children are not youthful.

Lady Utterword. How can children be expected to be youthful in this house? Almost before we could speak we were filled with notions that might have been all very well for pagan philosophers of fifty, but were certainly quite unfit for respectable people of any age.

Nurse. You were always for respectability, Miss Addy.

Lady Utterword. Nurse: will you please remember that I am Lady Utterword, and not Miss Addy, nor lovey, nor darling, nor doty? Do you hear?

Nurse. Yes, ducky: all right. I'll tell them all they must call you my lady. (*She takes her tray out with undisturbed placidity*).

Lady Utterword. What comfort? what sense is there in having servants with no manners?

Ellie (*rising and coming to the table to put down her empty cup*) Lady Utterword: do you think Mrs Hushabye really expects me?

Lady Utterword. Oh, dont ask me. You can see for yourself that Ive just arrived; her only sister, after twenty-three years absence! and it seems that I am not expected.

The Captain. What does it matter whether the young lady is expected or not? She is welcome. There are beds: there is food. I'll find a room for her myself. (*He makes for the door*).

Ellie (*following him to stop him*) Oh please— (*He goes out*). Lady Utterword: I dont know what to do. Your father persists in believing that my father is some sailor who robbed him.

Lady Utterword. You had better pretend not to notice it. My father is a very clever man; but he always forgot things; and now that he is old, of course he is worse. And I must warn you that it is sometimes very hard to feel quite sure that he really forgets.

Mrs Hushabye bursts into the room tempestuously, and embraces Ellie. She is a couple of years older than Lady Utterword, and even better looking. She has magnificent black hair, eyes like the fishpools of Heshbon, and a nobly modelled neck, short at the back and low between her shoulders in front. Unlike her sister she is uncorseted and dressed anyhow in a rich robe of black pile that shews off her white skin and statuesque contour.

Mrs Hushabye. Ellie, my darling, my pettikins (*kissing her*): how long have you been here? Ive been at home all the time: I was putting flowers and things in your room; and when I just sat down for a moment to try how comfortable the arm-chair was I went off to sleep. Papa woke me and told me you were here. Fancy your finding no one, and being neglected and abandoned. (*Kissing her again*) My poor love! (*She deposits Ellie on the sofa. Meanwhile Ariadne has left the table and come over to claim her share of attention*). Oh! youve brought someone with you. Introduce me.

Lady Utterword. Hesione: is it possible that y o u dont know me?

Mrs Hushabye (*conventionally*) Of course I remember your face quite well. Where have we met?

Lady Utterword. Didnt papa tell you I was here? Oh! this is really too much. (*She throws herself sulkily into the big chair*).

Mrs Hushabye. Papa!

Lady Utterword. Yes: Papa. O u r papa, you unfeeling wretch. (*Rising angrily*) I'll go straight to a hotel.

Mrs Hushabye (*seizing her by the shoulders*) My goodness gracious goodness, you dont mean to say that youre Addy!

Lady Utterword. I certainly am Addy; and I dont think I can be so changed that you would not have recognized me if you had any real affection for me. And papa didnt think me even worth mentioning!

Mrs Hushabye. What a lark! Sit down. (*She pushes her back into the chair instead of kissing her, and posts herself behind it*). You d o look a swell. Youre much handsomer than you used to be. Youve made the acquaintance of Ellie, of course. She is going to marry a perfect hog of a millionaire for the sake of her father, who is as poor as a church mouse; and you must help me to stop her.

Ellie. Oh p l e a s e, Hesione.

Mrs Hushabye. My pettikins, the man's coming here today

with your father to begin persecuting you; and everybody will see the state of the case in ten minutes; so whats the use of making a secret of it?

Ellie. He is not a hog, Hesione. You dont know how wonderfully good he was to my father, and how deeply grateful I am to him.

Mrs Hushabye (to Lady Utterword) Her father is a very remarkable man, Addy. His name is Mazzini Dunn. Mazzini was a celebrity of some kind who knew Ellie's grandparents. They were both poets, like the Brownings; and when her father came into the world Mazzini said "Another soldier born for freedom!" So they christened him Mazzini; and he has been fighting for freedom in his quiet way ever since. Thats why he is so poor.

Ellie. I am proud of his poverty.

Mrs Hushabye. Of course you are, pettikins. Why not leave him in it, and marry someone you love?

Lady Utterword (rising suddenly and explosively) Hesione: are you going to kiss me or are you not?

Mrs Hushabye. What do you want to be kissed for?

Lady Utterword. I d o n t want to be kissed; but I do want you to behave properly and decently. We are sisters. We have been separated for twenty-three years. You o u g h t to kiss me.

Mrs Hushabye. To-morrow morning, dear, before you make up. I hate the smell of powder.

Lady Utterword. Oh! you unfeeling— *(She is interrupted by the return of the Captain).*

The Captain (to Ellie) Your room is ready. *(Ellie rises).* The sheets were damp; but I have changed them. *(He makes for the garden door on the port side).*

Lady Utterword. Oh! What about m y sheets?

The Captain (halting at the door) Take my advice: air them; or take them off and sleep in blankets. You shall sleep in Ariadne's old room.

Lady Utterword. Indeed I shall do nothing of the sort. That little hole! I am entitled to the best spare room.

The Captain (*continuing unmoved*) She married a numskull. She told me she would marry anyone to get away from home.

Lady Utterword. You are pretending not to know me on purpose. I will leave the house.

Mazzini Dunn enters from the hall. He is a little elderly man with bulging credulous eyes and earnest manners. He is dressed in a blue serge jacket suit with an unbuttoned mackintosh over it, and carries a soft black hat of clerical cut.

Ellie. At last! Captain Shotover: here is my father.

The Captain. This! Nonsense! not a bit like him. (*He goes away through the garden, shutting the door sharply behind him*).

Lady Utterword. I will not be ignored and pretended to be somebody else. I will have it out with papa now, this instant. (*To Mazzini*) Excuse me. (*She follows the Captain out, making a hasty bow to Mazzini, who returns it*).

Mrs Hushabye (*hospitably, shaking hands*) How good of you to come, Mr Dunn! You dont mind papa, do you? He is as mad as a hatter, you know, but quite harmless, and extremely clever. You will have some delightful talks with him.

Mazzini. I hope so. (*To Ellie*) So here you are, Ellie, dear. (*He draws her arm affectionately through his*). I must thank you, Mrs Hushabye, for your kindness to my daughter. I'm afraid she would have had no holiday if you had not invited her.

Mrs Hushabye. Not at all. Very nice of her to come and attract young people to the house for us.

Mazzini (*smiling*) I'm afraid Ellie is not interested in young men, Mrs Hushabye. Her taste is on the graver, solider side.

Mrs Hushabye (*with a sudden rather hard brightness in her manner*) Wont you take off your overcoat, Mr Dunn? You will find a cupboard for coats and hats and things in the corner of the hall.

Mazzini (hastily releasing Ellie) Yes—thank you—I had better— *(He goes out)*.

Mrs Hushabye (emphatically) The old brute!

Ellie. Who?

Mrs. Hushabye. Who! Him. He. It. *(Pointing after Mazzini)*. "Graver, solider tastes," indeed!

Ellie (aghast) You dont mean that you were speaking like that of my father!

Mrs Hushabye. I was. You know I was.

Ellie (with dignity) I will leave your house at once. *(She turns to the door)*.

Mrs Hushabye. If you attempt it, I'll tell your father why.

Ellie (turning again) Oh! How can you treat a visitor like this, Mrs Hushabye?

Mrs Hushabye. I thought you were going to call me Hesione.

Ellie. Certainly not now?

Mrs Hushabye. Very well: I'll tell your father.

Ellie (distressed) Oh!

Mrs Hushabye. If you turn a hair—if you take his part against me and against your own heart for a moment, I'll give that born soldier of freedom a piece of my mind that will stand him on his selfish old head for a week.

Ellie. Hesione! My father selfish! How little you know—

She is interrupted by Mazzini, who returns, excited and perspiring.

Mazzini. Ellie: Mangan has come: I thought youd like to know. Excuse me, Mrs Hushabye: the strange old gentleman——

Mrs Hushabye. Papa. Quite so.

Mazzini. Oh, I beg your pardon: of course: I was a little confused by his manner. He is making Mangan help him with something in the garden; and he wants me to—

A powerful whistle is heard.

The Captain's Voice. Bosun ahoy! (*The whistle is repeated*).

Mazzini (*flustered*) Oh dear! I believe he is whistling for me. (*He hurries out*).

Mrs Hushabye. Now m y father is a wonderful man if you like.

Ellie. Hesione: listen to me. You dont understand. My father and Mr Mangan were boys together. Mr Ma—

Mrs Hushabye. I dont care what they were: we must sit down if you are going to begin as far back as that. (*She snatches at Ellie's waist, and makes her sit down on the sofa beside her*). Now, pettikins: tell me all about Mr Mangan. They call him Boss Mangan, dont they? He is a Napoleon of industry and disgustingly rich, isnt he? Why isnt your father rich?

Ellie. My poor father should never have been in business. His parents were poets; and they gave him the noblest ideas; but they could not afford to give him a profession.

Mrs Hushabye. Fancy your grandparents, with their eyes in fine frenzy rolling! And so your poor father had to go into business. Hasnt he succeeded in it?

Ellie. He always used to say he could succeed if he only had some capital. He fought his way along, to keep a roof over our heads and bring us up well; but it was always a struggle: always the same difficulty of not having capital enough. I dont know how to describe it to you.

Mrs Hushabye. Poor Ellie! I know. Pulling the devil by the tail.

Ellie (*hurt*) Oh no. Not like that. It was at least dignified.

Mrs Hushabye. That made it all the harder, didnt it? I shouldn't have pulled the devil by the tail with dignity. I should have pulled hard—(*between her teeth*) h a r d. Well? Go on.

Ellie. At last it seemed that all our troubles were at an end. Mr Mangan did an extraordinarily noble thing out of pure friendship for my father and respect for his character. He asked him how much capital he wanted, and gave it to him. I dont mean that he lent it to him, or that he invested it in his business. He just simply made him a present of it. Wasnt that splendid of him?

Mrs Hushabye. On condition that you married him?

Ellie. Oh no, no, no. This was when I was a child. He had never even seen me: he never came to our house. It was absolutely disinterested. Pure generosity.

Mrs Hushabye. Oh! I beg the gentleman's pardon. Well, what became of the money?

Ellie. We all got new clothes and moved into another house. And I went to another school for two years.

Mrs Hushabye. Only two years?

Ellie. That was all; for at the end of two years my father was utterly ruined.

Mrs Hushabye. How?

Ellie. I dont know. I never could understand. But it was dreadful. When we were poor my father had never been in debt. But when he launched out into business on a large scale, he had to incur liabilities. When the business went into liquidation he owed more money than Mr Mangan had given him.

Mrs Hushabye. Bit off more than he could chew, I suppose.

Ellie. I think you are a little unfeeling about it.

Mrs Hushabye. My pettikins: you mustnt mind my way of talking. I was quite as sensitive and particular as you once; but I have picked up so much slang from the children that I am really hardly presentable. I suppose your father had no head for business, and made a mess of it.

Ellie. Oh, that just shews how entirely you are mistaken about him. The business turned out a great success. It now pays forty-four per cent after deducting the excess profits tax.

Mrs Hushabye. Then why arnt you rolling in money?

Ellie. I dont know. It seems very unfair to me. You see, my father was made bankrupt. It nearly broke his heart, because he had persuaded several of his friends to put money into the business. He was sure it would succeed; and events proved that he was quite right. But they all lost their money. It was dreadful. I dont know what we should have done but for Mr Mangan.

Mrs Hushabye. What! Did the Boss come to the rescue again, after all his money being thrown away?

Ellie. He did indeed, and never uttered a reproach to my father. He bought what was left of the business—the buildings and the machinery and things—from the official trustee for enough money to enable my father to pay six and eightpence in the pound and get his discharge. Everyone pitied papa so much, and saw so plainly that he was an honorable man, that they let him off at six and eightpence instead of ten shillings. Then Mr Mangan started a company to take up the business, and made my father a manager in it to save us from starvation; for I wasnt earning anything then.

Mrs Hushabye. Quite a romance. And when did the Boss develop the tender passion?

Ellie. Oh, that was years after, quite lately. He took the chair one night at a sort of people's concert. I was singing there. As an amateur, you know: half a guinea for expenses and three songs with three encores. He was so pleased with my singing that he asked might he walk home with me. I never saw anyone so taken aback as he was when I took him home and introduced him to my father: his own manager. It was then that my father told me how nobly he had behaved. Of course it was considered a great chance for me, as he is so rich. And—and—we drifted into a sort of understanding—I suppose I should call it an engagement— (*She is distressed and cannot go on*).

Mrs Hushabye (*rising and marching about*) You may have drifted into it; but you will bounce out of it, my pettikins, if I am to have anything to do with it.

Ellie (hopelessly) No: it's no use. I am bound in honor and gratitude. I will go through with it.

Mrs Hushabye (behind the sofa, scolding down at her) You know, of course, that it's not honorable or grateful to marry a man you dont love. Do you love this Mangan man?

Ellie. Yes. At least—

Mrs Hushabye. I dont want to know about "the least": I want to know the worst. Girls of your age fall in love with all sorts of impossible people, especially old people.

Ellie. I like Mr Mangan very much; and I shall always be—

Mrs Hushabye (impatiently completing the sentence and prancing away intolerantly to starboard) —grateful to him for his kindness to dear father. I know. Anybody else?

Ellie. What do you mean?

Mrs Hushabye. Anybody else? Are you in love with anybody else?

Ellie. Of course not.

Mrs Hushabye. Humph! (*The book on the drawing-table catches her eye. She picks it up, and evidently finds the title very unexpected. She looks at Ellie, and asks, quaintly*). Quite sure youre not in love with an actor?

Ellie. No, no. Why? What put such a thing into your head?

Mrs Hushabye. This is yours, isnt it? Why else should you be reading Othello?

Ellie. My father taught me to love Shakespear.

Mrs Hushabye (flinging the book down on the table) Really! your father does seem to be about the limit.

Ellie (naïvely) Do you never read Shakespear, Hesione? That seems to me so extraordinary. I like Othello.

Mrs Hushabye. Do you indeed? He was jealous, wasnt he?

Ellie. Oh, not that. I think all the part about jealousy is horrible. But dont you think it must have been a wonderful experience for Desdemona, brought up so quietly at home, to meet a man who had been out in the world doing all sorts of brave things and having terrible adventures, and yet finding something in her that made him love to sit and talk with her and tell her about them?

Mrs Hushabye. Thats your idea of romance, is it?

Ellie. Not romance, exactly. It might really happen.

Ellie's eyes shew that she is not arguing, but in a daydream. Mrs Hushabye, watching her inquisitively, goes deliberately back to the sofa and resumes her seat beside her.

Mrs Hushabye. Ellie darling: have you noticed that some of those stories that Othello told Desdemona couldnt have happened?

Ellie. Oh no. Shakespear thought they could have happened.

Mrs Hushabye. Hm! Desdemona thought they could have happened. But they didnt.

Ellie. Why do you look so enigmatic about it? You are such a sphinx: I never know what you mean.

Mrs Hushabye. Desdemona would have found him out if she had lived, you know. I wonder was that why he strangled her!

Ellie. Othello was not telling lies.

Mrs Hushabye. How do you know?

Ellie. Shakespear would have said if he was. Hesione: there are men who have done wonderful things: men like Othello, only, of course, white, and very handsome, and—

Mrs Hushabye. Ah! Now we're coming to it. Tell me all about him. I knew there must be somebody, or youd never have been so miserable about Mangan: youd have thought it quite a lark to marry him.

Ellie (blushing vividly) Hesione: you are dreadful. But I dont want to make a secret of it, though of course I dont tell everybody. Besides, I dont know him.

Mrs Hushabye. Dont know him! What does that mean?

Ellie. Well, of course I know him to speak to.

Mrs Hushabye. But you want to know him ever so much more intimately, eh?

Ellie. No no: I know him quite—almost intimately.

Mrs Hushabye. You dont know him; and you know him almost intimately. How lucid!

Ellie. I mean that he does not call on us. I—I got into conversation with him by chance at a concert.

Mrs Hushabye. You seem to have rather a gay time at your concerts, Ellie.

Ellie. Not at all: we talk to everyone in the greenroom waiting for our turns. I thought he was one of the artists: he looked so splendid. But he was only one of the committee. I happened to tell him that I was copying a picture at the National Gallery. I make a little money that way. I cant paint much; but as it's always the same picture I can do it pretty quickly and get two or three pounds for it. It happened that he came to the National Gallery one day.

Mrs Hushabye. One student's day. Paid sixpence to stumble about through a crowd of easels, when he might have come in next day for nothing and found the floor clear! Quite by accident?

Ellie (*triumphantly*) No. On purpose. He liked talking to me. He knows lots of the most splendid people. Fashionable women who are all in love with him. But he ran away from them to see me at the National Gallery and persuade me to come with him for a drive round Richmond Park in a taxi.

Mrs Hushabye. My pettikins, you have been going it. It's wonderful what you good girls can do without anyone saying a word.

Ellie. I am not in society, Hesione. If I didnt make acquaintances in that way I shouldnt have any at all.

Mrs Hushabye. Well, no harm if you know how to take care of yourself. May I ask his name?

Ellie (*slowly and musically*) Marcus Darnley.

Mrs Hushabye (*echoing the music*) Marcus Darnley! What a splendid name!

Ellie. Oh, I'm so glad you think so. I think so too; but I was afraid it was only a silly fancy of my own.

Mrs Hushabye. Hm! Is he one of the Aberdeen Darnleys?

Ellie. Nobody knows. Just fancy! He was found in an antique chest—

Mrs Hushabye. A what?

Ellie. An antique chest, one summer morning in a rose garden, after a night of the most terrible thunderstorm.

Mrs Hushabye. What on earth was he doing in the chest? Did he get into it because he was afraid of the lightning?

Ellie. Oh no, no: he was a baby. The name Marcus Darnley was embroidered on his babyclothes. And five hundred pounds in gold.

Mrs Hushabye (looking hard at her) Ellie!

Ellie. The garden of the Viscount—

Mrs Hushabye. —de Rougemont?

Ellie (innocently) No: de Larochejaquelin. A French family. A vicomte. His life has been one long romance. A tiger—

Mrs Hushabye. Slain by his own hand?

Ellie. Oh no: nothing vulgar like that. He saved the life of the tiger from a hunting party: one of King Edward's hunting parties in India. The King was furious: that was why he never had his military services properly recognized. But he doesnt care. He is a Socialist and despises rank, and has been in three revolutions fighting on the barricades.

Mrs Hushabye. How can you sit there telling me such lies? You, Ellie, of all people! And I thought you were a perfectly simple, straightforward, good girl.

Ellie (rising, dignified but very angry) Do you mean to say you dont believe me?

Mrs Hushabye. Of course I dont believe you. Youre inventing every word of it. Do you take me for a fool?

Ellie stares at her. Her candor is so obvious that Mrs Hushabye is puzzled.

Ellie. Goodbye, Hesione. I'm very sorry. I see now that it sounds very improbable as I tell it. But I cant stay if you think that way about me.

Mrs Hushabye (*catching her dress*) You shant go. I couldnt be so mistaken: I know too well what liars are like. Somebody has really told you all this.

Ellie (*flushing*) Hesione: dont say that you dont believe h i m. I couldn't bear that.

Mrs Hushabye (*soothing her*) Of course I believe him, dearest. But you should have broken it to me by degrees. (*Drawing her back to her seat*) Now tell me all about him. Are you in love with him?

Ellie. Oh no. I'm not so foolish. I dont fall in love with people. I'm not so silly as you think.

Mrs Hushabye. I see. Only something to think about—to give some interest and pleasure to life.

Ellie. Just so. Thats all, really.

Mrs Hushabye. It makes the hours go fast, doesnt it? No tedious waiting to go to sleep at nights and wondering whether you will have a bad night. How delightful it makes waking up in the morning! How much better than the happiest dream! All life transfigured! No more wishing one had an interesting book to read, because life is so much happier than any book! No desire but to be alone and not to have to talk to anyone: to be alone and just think about it.

Ellie (*embracing her*) Hesione: you are a witch. How do you know? Oh, you are the most sympathetic woman in the world.

Mrs Hushabye (*caressing her*) Pettikins, my pettikins: how I envy you! and how I pity you!

Ellie. Pity me! Oh, why?

A very handsome man of fifty, with mousquetaire moustaches, wearing a rather dandified curly brimmed hat, and carrying an elaborate walking-stick, comes into the room from the hall, and stops short at sight of the women on the sofa.

Ellie (*seeing him and rising in glad surprise*) Oh! Hesione: this is Mr Marcus Darnley.

Mrs Hushabye (*rising*) What a lark! He is my husband.

Ellie. But how— (*She stops suddenly; then turns pale and sways*).

Mrs Hushabye (*catching her and sitting down with her on the sofa*) Steady, my pettikins.

The Man (*with a mixture of confusion and effrontery, depositing his hat and stick on the teak table*) My real name, Miss Dunn, is Hector Hushabye. I leave you to judge whether that is a name any sensitive man would care to confess to. I never use it when I can possibly help it. I have been away for nearly a month; and I had no idea you knew my wife, or that you were coming here. I am none the less delighted to find you in our little house.

Ellie (*in great distress*) I dont know what to do. Please, may I speak to papa? Do leave me. I cant bear it.

Mrs Hushabye. Be off, Hector.

Hector. I—

Mrs Hushabye. Quick, quick. Get out.

Hector. If you think it better— (*He goes out, taking his hat with him but leaving the stick on the table*).

Mrs Hushabye (*laying Ellie down at the end of the sofa*) Now, pettikins, he is gone. Theres nobody but me. You can let yourself go. Dont try to control yourself. Have a good cry.

Ellie (*raising her head*) Damn!

Mrs Hushabye. Splendid! Oh, what a relief! I thought you were going to be broken-hearted. Never mind me. Damn him again.

Ellie. I am not damning him: I am damning myself for being such a fool. (*Rising*) How could I let myself be taken in so? (*She begins prowling to and fro, her bloom gone, looking curiously older and harder*).

Mrs Hushabye (*cheerfully*) Why not, pettikins? Very few

young women can resist Hector. I couldnt when I was your age. He is really rather splendid, you know.

Ellie (turning on her) Splendid! Yes: splendid l o o k i n g, of course. But how can you love a liar?

Mrs Hushabye. I dont know. But you can, fortunately. Otherwise there wouldnt be much love in the world.

Ellie. But to lie like that! To be a boaster! a coward!

Mrs Hushabye (rising in alarm) Pettikins: none of that, if you please. If you hint the slightest doubt of Hector's courage, he will go straight off and do the most horribly dangerous things to convince himself that he isnt a coward. He has a dreadful trick of getting out of one third-floor window and coming in at another, just to test his nerve. He has a whole drawerful of Albert Medals for saving people's lives.

Ellie. He never told me that.

Mrs Hushabye. He never boasts of anything he really did: he cant bear it; and it makes him shy if anyone else does. All his stories are made-up stories.

Ellie (coming to her) Do you mean that he is really brave, and really has adventures, and yet tells lies about things that he never did and that never happened?

Mrs Hushabye. Yes, pettikins, I do. People dont have their virtues and vices in sets: they have them anyhow: all mixed.

Ellie (staring at her thoughtfully) Theres something odd about this house, Hesione, and even about you. I dont know why I'm talking to you so calmly. I have a horrible fear that my heart is broken, but that heartbreak is not like what I thought it must be.

Mrs Hushabye (fondling her) It's only life educating you, pettikins. How do you feel about Boss Mangan now?

Ellie (disengaging herself with an expression of distaste) Oh, how can you remind me of him, Hesione?

Mrs Hushabye. Sorry, dear. I think I hear Hector coming back. You dont mind now, do you, dear?

Ellie. Not in the least. I'm quite cured.

Mazzini Dunn and Hector come in from the hall.

Hector (*as he opens the door and allows Mazzini to pass in*) One second more, and she would have been a dead woman!

Mazzini. Dear! dear! what an escape! Ellie, my love: Mr Hushabye has just been telling me the most extraordinary—

Ellie. Yes: Ive heard it. (*She crosses to the other side of the room*).

Hector (*following her*) Not this one· I'll tell it to you after dinner. I think youll like it. The truth is, I made it up for you, and was looking forward to the pleasure of telling it to you. But in a moment of impatience at being turned out of the room, I threw it away on your father.

Ellie (*turning at bay with her back to the carpenter's bench, scornfully self-possessed*) It was not thrown away. He believes it. I should not have believed it.

Mazzini (*benevolently*) Ellie is very naughty, Mr Hushabye. Of course she does not really think that. (*He goes to the bookshelves, and inspects the titles of the volumes*).

Boss Mangan comes in from the hall, followed by the Captain. Mangan, carefully frock-coated as for church or for a directors' meeting, is about fifty-five, with a careworn, mistrustful expression, standing a little on an entirely imaginary dignity, with a dull complexion, straight, lustreless hair, and features so entirely commonplace that it is impossible to describe them.

Captain Shotover (*to Mrs Hushabye, introducing the newcomer*) Says his name is Mangan. Not ablebodied.

Mrs Hushabye (*graciously*) How do you do, Mr Mangan?

Mangan (*shaking hands*) Very pleased.

Captain Shotover. Dunn's lost his muscle, but recovered his nerve. Men seldom do after three attacks of delirium tremens. (*He goes into the pantry*).

Mrs Hushabye. I congratulate you, Mr Dunn.

Mazzini (*dazed*) I am a lifelong teetotaler.

Mrs Hushabye. You will find it far less trouble to let papa have his own way than try to explain.

Mazzini. But three attacks of delirium tremens, really!

Mrs Hushabye (to Mangan) Do you know my husband, Mr Mangan? *(She indicates Hector).*

Mangan (going to Hector, who meets him with outstretched hand) Very pleased. *(Turning to Ellie)* I hope, Miss Ellie, you have not found the journey down too fatiguing. *(They shake hands).*

Mrs Hushabye. Hector: shew Mr Dunn his room.

Hector. Certainly. Come along, Mr Dunn. *(He takes Mazzini out).*

Ellie. You havnt shewn me my room yet, Hesione.

Mrs Hushabye. How stupid of me! Come along. Make yourself quite at home, Mr Mangan. Papa will entertain you. *(She calls to the Captain in the pantry)* Papa: come and explain the house to Mr Mangan.

She goes out with Ellie. The Captain comes from the pantry.

Captain Shotover. Youre going to marry Dunn's daughter. Dont. Youre too old.

Mangan (staggered) Well! Thats fairly blunt, Captain.

Captain Shotover. It's true.

Mangan. She doesnt think so.

Captain Shotover. She does.

Mangan. Older men than I have—

Captain Shotover (finishing the sentence for him)—made fools of themselves. That, also, is true.

Mangan (asserting himself) I dont see that this is any business of yours.

Captain Shotover. It is everybody's business. The stars in their courses are shaken when such things happen.

Mangan. I'm going to marry her all the same.

Captain Shotover. How do you know?

Mangan (playing the strong man) I intend to. I mean to. See? I never made up my mind to do a thing yet that I didnt bring it off. Thats the sort of man I am; and there will be a better understanding between us when you make up your mind to that, Captain.

Captain Shotover. You frequent picture palaces.

Mangan. Perhaps I do. Who told you?

Captain Shotover. Talk like a man, not like a movy. You mean that you make a hundred thousand a year.

Mangan. I dont boast. But when I meet a man that makes a hundred thousand a year, I take off my hat to that man, and stretch out my hand to him and call him brother.

Captain Shotover. Then you also make a hundred thousand a year, hey?

Mangan. No. I cant say that. Fifty thousand, perhaps.

Captain Shotover. His half brother only. (*He turns away from Mangan with his usual abruptness, and collects the empty tea-cups on the Chinese tray*).

Mangan (*irritated*) See here, Captain Shotover. I dont quite understand my position here. I came here on your daughter's invitation. Am I in her house or in yours?

Captain Shotover. You are beneath the dome of heaven, in the house of God. What is true within these walls is true outside them. Go out on the seas; climb the mountains; wander through the valleys. She is still too young.

Mangan (*weakening*) But I'm very little over fifty.

Captain Shotover. You are still less under sixty. Boss Mangan: you will not marry the pirate's child. (*He carries the tray away into the pantry*).

Mangan (*following him to the half door*) What pirate's child? What are you talking about?

Captain Shotover (*in the pantry*) Ellie Dunn. You will not marry her.

Mangan. Who will stop me?

Captain Shotover (*emerging*) My daughter. (*He makes for the door leading to the hall*).

Mangan (following him) Mrs Hushabye! Do you mean to say she brought me down here to break it off?

Captain Shotover (stopping and turning on him) I know nothing more than I have seen in her eye. She will break it off. Take my advice: marry a West Indian negress: they make excellent wives. I was married to one myself for two years.

Mangan. Well, I a m damned!

Captain Shotover. I thought so. I was, too, for many years. The negress redeemed me.

Mangan (feebly) This is queer. I ought to walk out of this house.

Captain Shotover. Why?

Mangan. Well, many men would be offended by your style of talking.

Captain Shotover. Nonsense! It's the other sort of talking that makes quarrels. Nobody ever quarrels with me.

A gentleman, whose firstrate tailoring and frictionless manners proclaim the wellbred West Ender, comes in from the hall. He has an engaging air of being young and unmarried, but on close inspection is found to be at least over forty.

The Gentleman. Excuse my intruding in this fashion; but there is no knocker on the door; and the bell does not seem to ring.

Captain Shotover. Why should there be a knocker? Why should the bell ring? The door is open.

The Gentleman. Precisely. So I ventured to come in.

Captain Shotover. Quite right. I will see about a room for you. (*He makes for the door*).

The Gentleman (stopping him) But I'm afraid you dont know who I am.

Captain Shotover. Do you suppose that at my age I make distinctions between one fellowcreature and another? (*He goes out. Mangan and the newcomer stare at one another*).

Mangan. Strange character, Captain Shotover, sir.

The Gentleman. Very.

Captain Shotover (*shouting outside*) Hesione: another person has arrived and wants a room. Man about town, well dressed, fifty.

The Gentleman. Fancy Hesione's feelings! May I ask are you a member of the family?

Mangan. No.

The Gentleman. I am. At least a connexion.

Mrs Hushabye comes back.

Mrs Hushabye. How do you do? How good of you to come!

The Gentleman. I am very glad indeed to make your acquaintance, Hesione. (*Instead of taking her hand he kisses her. At the same moment the Captain appears in the doorway*). You will excuse my kissing your daughter, Captain, when I tell you that—

Captain Shotover. Stuff! Everyone kisses my daughter. Kiss her as much as you like. (*He makes for the pantry*).

The Gentleman. Thank you. One moment, Captain. (*The Captain halts and turns. The gentleman goes to him affably*). Do you happen to remember—but probably you dont, as it occurred many years ago—that your younger daughter married a numskull?

Captain Shotover. Yes. She said she'd marry anybody to get away from this house. I should not have recognized you: your head is no longer like a walnut. Your aspect is softened. You have been boiled in bread and milk for years and years, like other married men. Poor devil! (*He disappears into the pantry*).

Mrs Hushabye (*going past Mangan to the gentleman and scrutinizing him*). I dont believe you are Hastings Utterword.

The Gentleman. I am not.

Mrs Hushabye. Then what business had you to kiss me?

The Gentleman. I thought I would like to. The fact is, I am Randall Utterword, the unworthy younger brother of Hastings. I was abroad diplomatizing when he was married.

Lady Utterword (dashing in) Hesione: where is the key of the wardrobe in my room? My diamonds are in my dressing-bag: I must lock it up— *(Recognizing the stranger with a shock)* Randall: how dare you? *(She marches at him past Mrs Hushabye, who retreats and joins Mangan near the sofa).*

Randall. How dare I what? I am not doing anything.

Lady Utterword. Who told you I was here?

Randall. Hastings. You had just left when I called on you at Claridge's; so I followed you down here. You are looking extremely well.

Lady Utterword. Dont presume to tell me so.

Mrs Hushabye. What is wrong with Mr Randall, Addy?

Lady Utterword (recollecting herself) Oh, nothing. But he has no right to come bothering you and papa without being invited. *(She goes to the window-seat and sits down, turning away from them ill-humoredly and looking into the garden where Hector and Ellie are now seen strolling together).*

Mrs Hushabye. I think you have not met Mr Mangan, Addy.

Lady Utterword (turning her head and nodding coldly to Mangan) I beg your pardon. Randall: you have flustered me so: I made a perfect fool of myself.

Mrs. Hushabye. Lady Utterword. My sister. My y o u n g e r sister.

Mangan (bowing) Pleased to meet you, Lady Utterword.

Lady Utterword (with marked interest) Who is that gentleman walking in the garden with Miss Dunn?

Mrs Hushabye. I dont know. She quarrelled mortally with my husband only ten minutes ago; and I didnt know anyone else had come. It must be a visitor. *(She goes to the window to look).* Oh, it i s Hector. Theyve made it up.

Lady Utterword. Your husband! That handsome man?

Mrs Hushabye. Well, why shouldnt my husband be a handsome man?

Randall (joining them at the window) One's husband never is, Ariadne. *(He sits by Lady Utterword, on her right).*

Mrs Hushabye. One's sister's husband always is, Mr Randall.

Lady Utterword. Dont be vulgar, Randall. And you, Hesione, are just as bad.

Ellie and Hector come in from the garden by the starboard door. Randall rises. Ellie retires into the corner near the pantry. Hector comes forward; and Lady Utterword rises looking her very best.

Mrs Hushabye. Hector: this is Addy.

Hector (apparently surprised) Not this lady.

Lady Utterword (smiling) Why not?

Hector (looking at her with a piercing glance of deep but respectful admiration, his moustache bristling) I thought— *(Pulling himself together)* I beg your pardon, Lady Utterword. I am extremely glad to welcome you at last under our roof. *(He offers his hand with grave courtesy).*

Mrs Hushabye. She wants to be kissed, Hector.

Lady Utterword. Hesione! *(But she still smiles).*

Mrs Hushabye. Call her Addy; and kiss her like a good brother-in-law; and have done with it. *(She leaves them to themselves).*

Hector. Behave yourself, Hesione. Lady Utterword is entitled not only to hospitality but to civilization.

Lady Utterword (gratefully) Thank you, Hector. *(They shake hands cordially).*

Mazzini Dunn is seen crossing the garden from starboard to port.

Captain Shotover (coming from the pantry and addressing Ellie) Your father has washed himself.

Ellie (quite self-possessed) He often does, Captain Shotover.

Captain Shotover. A strange conversion! I saw him through the pantry window.

Mazzini Dunn enters through the port window door, newly

washed and brushed, and stops, smiling benevolently, between Mangan and Mrs Hushabye.

Mrs Hushabye (introducing) Mr Mazzini Dunn, Lady Ut—oh, I forgot: youve met. *(Indicating Ellie)* Miss Dunn.

Mazzini (walking across the room to take Ellie's hand, and beaming at his own naughty irony) I have met Miss Dunn also. She is my daughter. *(He draws her arm through his caressingly).*

Mrs Hushabye. Of course: how stupid! Mr Utterword, my sister's—er—

Randall (shaking hands agreeably) Her brother-in-law, Mr Dunn. How do you do?

Mrs Hushabye. This is my husband.

Hector. We have met, dear. Dont introduce us any more. *(He moves away to the big chair, and adds)* Wont you sit down, Lady Utterword? *(She does so very graciously).*

Mrs Hushabye. Sorry. I hate it: it's like making people shew their tickets.

Mazzini (sententiously) How little it tells us, after all! The great question is, not who we are, but what we are.

Captain Shotover. Ha! What are you?

Mazzini (taken aback) What am I?

Captain Shotover. A thief, a pirate, and a murderer.

Mazzini. I assure you you are mistaken.

Captain Shotover. An adventurous life; but what does it end in? Respectability. A ladylike daughter. The language and appearance of a city missionary. Let it be a warning to all of you. *(He goes out through the garden).*

Dunn. I hope nobody here believes that I am a thief, a pirate, or a murderer. Mrs Hushabye: will you excuse me a moment? I must really go and explain. *(He follows the Captain).*

Mrs Hushabye (as he goes) It's no use. Youd really better— *(But Dunn has vanished).* We had better all go out and look for some tea. We never have regular tea; but you can always get some when you want: the servants keep it stewing all day. The kitchen veranda is the best place to ask. May I shew you? (*She goes to the starboard door*).

Randall (*going with her*) Thank you, I dont think I'll take any tea this afternoon. But if you will shew me the garden—?

Mrs Hushabye. Theres nothing to see in the garden except papa's observatory, and a gravel pit with a cave where he keeps dynamite and things of that sort. However, it's pleasanter out of doors; so come along.

Randall. Dynamite! Isnt that rather risky?

Mrs Hushabye. Well, we dont sit in the gravel pit when theres a thunderstorm.

Lady Utterword. Thats something new. What is the dynamite for?

Hector. To blow up the human race if it goes too far. He is trying to discover a psychic ray that will explode all the explosives at the will of a Mahatma.

Ellie. The Captain's tea is delicious, Mr Utterword.

Mrs Hushabye (*stopping in the doorway*) Do you mean to say that youve had some of my father's tea? that you got round him before you were ten minutes in the house?

Ellie. I did.

Mrs Hushabye. You little devil! (*She goes out with Randall*).

Mangan. Wont you come, Miss Ellie?

Ellie. I'm too tired. I'll take a book up to my room and rest a little. (*She goes to the bookshelf*).

Mangan. Right. You cant do better. But I'm disappointed. (*He follows Randall and Mrs Hushabye*).

Ellie, Hector, and Lady Utterword are left. Hector is close to Lady Utterword. They look at Ellie, waiting for her to go.

Ellie (*looking at the title of a book*) Do you like stories of adventure, Lady Utterword?

Lady Utterword (*patronizingly*) Of course, dear.

Ellie. Then I'll leave you to Mr Hushabye. (*She goes out through the hall*).

Hector. That girl is mad about tales of adventure. The lies I have to tell her!

Lady Utterword (*not interested in Ellie*) When you saw me what did you mean by saying that you thought, and then stopping short? What did you think?

Hector (*folding his arms and looking down at her magnetically*) May I tell you?

Lady Utterword. Of course.

Hector. It will not sound very civil. I was on the point of saying "I thought you were a plain woman."

Lady Utterword. Oh for shame, Hector! What right had you to notice whether I am plain or not?

Hector. Listen to me, Ariadne. Until today I have seen only photographs of you; and no photograph can give the strange fascination of the daughters of that supernatural old man. There is some damnable quality in them that destroys men's moral sense, and carries them beyond honor and dishonor. You know that, dont you?

Lady Utterword. Perhaps I do, Hector. But let me warn you once for all that I am a rigidly conventional woman. You may think because I'm a Shotover that I'm a Bohemian, because we are all so horribly Bohemian. But I'm not. I hate and loathe Bohemianism. No child brought up in a strict Puritan household ever suffered from Puritanism as I suffered from our Bohemianism.

Hector. Our children are like that. They spend their holidays in the houses of their respectable schoolfellows.

Lady Utterword. I shall invite them for Christmas.

Hector. Their absence leaves us both without our natural chaperons.

Lady Utterword. Children are certainly very inconvenient sometimes. But intelligent people can always manage, unless they are Bohemians.

Hector. You are no Bohemian; but you are no Puritan either: your attraction is alive and powerful. What sort of woman do you count yourself?

Lady Utterword. I am a woman of the world, Hector; and I can assure you that if you will only take the trouble always to do the perfectly correct thing, and to say the perfectly correct thing, you can do just what you like. An ill-conducted, careless woman gets simply no chance. An ill-conducted, careless man is never allowed within arms length of any woman worth knowing.

Hector. I see. You are neither a Bohemian woman nor a Puritan woman. You are a dangerous woman.

Lady Utterword. On the contrary, I am a safe woman.

Hector. You are a most accursedly attractive woman. Mind: I am not making love to you. I do not like being attracted. But you had better know how I feel if you are going to stay here.

Lady Utterword. You are an exceedingly clever ladykiller, Hector. And terribly handsome. I am quite a good player, myself, at that game. Is it quite understood that we are only playing?

Hector. Quite. I am deliberately playing the fool, out of sheer worthlessness.

Lady Utterword (rising brightly) Well, you are my brother-in-law. Hesione asked you to kiss me. (*He seizes her in his arms, and kisses her strenuously*). Oh! that was a little more than play, brother-in-law. (*She pushes him suddenly away*). You shall not do that again.

Hector. In effect, you got your claws deeper into me than I intended.

Mrs Hushabye (coming in from the garden) Dont let me disturb you: I only want a cap to put on daddiest. The sun is setting; and he'll catch cold. (*She makes for the door leading to the hall*).

Lady Utterword. Your husband is quite charming, darling.

He has actually condescended to kiss me at last. I shall go into the garden: it's cooler now. (*She goes out by the port door*).

Mrs Hushabye. Take care, dear child. I dont believe any man can kiss Addy without falling in love with her. (*She goes into the hall*).

Hector (*striking himself on the chest*) Fool! Goat!

Mrs Hushabye comes back with the Captain's cap.

Hector. Your sister is an extremely enterprising old girl. Wheres Miss Dunn!

Mrs Hushabye. Mangan says she has gone up to her room for a nap. Addy wont let you talk to Ellie: she has marked you for her own.

Hector. She has the diabolical family fascination. I began making love to her automatically. What am I to do? I cant fall in love; and I cant hurt a woman's feelings by telling her so when she falls in love with me. And as women are always falling in love with my moustache I get landed in all sorts of tedious and terrifying flirtations in which I'm not a bit in earnest.

Mrs Hushabye. Oh, neither is Addy. She has never been in love in her life, though she has always been trying to fall in head over ears. She is worse than you, because you had one real go at least, with me.

Hector. That was a confounded madness. I cant believe that such an amazing experience is common. It has left its mark on me. I believe that is why I have never been able to repeat it.

Mrs Hushabye (*laughing and caressing his arm*) We were frightfully in love with one another, Hector. It was such an enchanting dream that I have never been able to grudge it to you or anyone else since. I have invited all sorts of pretty women to the house on the chance of giving you another turn. But it has never come off.

Hector. I dont know that I want it to come off. It was damned dangerous. You fascinated me; but I loved you; so it was heaven. This sister of yours fascinates me; but I hate her; so it is hell. I shall kill her if she persists.

Mrs Hushabye. Nothing will kill Addy: she is as strong as a horse. (*Releasing him*) Now I am going off to fascinate somebody.

Hector. The Foreign Office toff? Randall?

Mrs Hushabye. Goodness gracious, no! Why should I fascinate him?

Hector. I presume you dont mean the bloated capitalist, Mangan?

Mrs Hushabye. Hm! I think he had better be fascinated by me than by Ellie. (*She is going into the garden when the Captain comes in from it with some sticks in his hand*). What have you got there, daddiest?

Captain Shotover. Dynamite.

Mrs Hushabye. Youve been to the gravel pit. Dont drop it about the house: theres a dear. (*She goes into the garden, where the evening light is now very red*).

Hector. Listen, O sage. How long dare you concentrate on a feeling without risking having it fixed in your consciousness all the rest of your life?

Captain Shotover. Ninety minutes. An hour and a half. (*He goes into the pantry*).

Hector, left alone, contracts his brows, and falls into a day-dream. He does not move for some time. Then he folds his arms. Then, throwing his hands behind him, and gripping one with the other, he strides tragically once to and fro. Suddenly he snatches his walking-stick from the teak table, and draws it; for it is a sword-stick. He fights a desperate duel with an imaginary antagonist, and after many vicissitudes runs him through the body up to the hilt. He sheathes his sword and throws it on the sofa, falling into another reverie as he does so. He looks straight into the eyes of an imaginary woman; seizes her by the arms; and says in a deep and thrilling tone "Do you love me!" *The Captain comes out of the pantry at this moment; and Hector, caught with his arms stretched out and his fists clenched, has to account for his attitude by going through a series of gymnastic exercises.*

Captain Shotover. That sort of strength is no good. You will never be as strong as a gorilla.

Hector. What is the dynamite for?

Captain Shotover. To kill fellows like Mangan.

Hector. No use. They will always be able to buy more dynamite than you.

Captain Shotover. I will make a dynamite that he cannot explode.

Hector. And that you can, eh?

Captain Shotover. Yes: when I have attained the seventh degree of concentration.

Hector. Whats the use of that? You never do attain it.

Captain Shotover. What then is to be done? Are we to be kept for ever in the mud by these hogs to whom the universe is nothing but a machine for greasing their bristles and filling their snouts?

Hector. Are Mangan's bristles worse than Randall's love-locks?

Captain Shotover. We must win powers of life and death over them both. I refuse to die until I have invented the means.

Hector. Who are we that we should judge them?

Captain Shotover. What are they that they should judge us? Yet they do, unhesitatingly. There is enmity between our seed and their seed. They know it and act on it, strangling our souls. They believe in themselves. When we believe in ourselves, we shall kill them.

Hector. It is the same seed. You forget that your pirate has a very nice daughter. Mangan's son may be a Plato: Randall's a Shelley. What was my father?

Captain Shotover. The damndest scoundrel I ever met. (*He replaces the drawing-board; sits down at the table; and begins to mix a wash of color*).

Hector. Precisely. Well, dare you kill his innocent grand-children?

Captain Shotover. They are mine also.

Hector. Just so. We are members one of another. (*He throws himself carelessly on the sofa*). I tell you I have often thought of this killing of human vermin. Many men have thought of it. Decent men are like Daniel in the lion's den: their survival is a miracle; and they do not always survive. We live among the Mangans and Randalls and Billy Dunns as they, poor devils, live among the disease germs and the doctors and the lawyers and the parsons and the restaurant chefs and the tradesmen and the servants and all the rest of the parasites and blackmailers. What are our terrors to theirs? Give me the power to kill them; and I'll spare them in sheer—

Captain Shotover (*cutting in sharply*) Fellow feeling?

Hector. No. I should kill myself if I believed that. I must believe that my spark, small as it is, is divine, and that the red light over their door is hell fire. I should spare them in simple magnanimous pity.

Captain Shotover. You cant spare them until you have the power to kill them. At present they have the power to kill you. There are millions of blacks over the water for them to train and let loose on us. Theyre going to do it. Theyre doing it already.

Hector. They are too stupid to use their power.

Captain Shotover (*throwing down his brush and coming to the end of the sofa*) Do not deceive yourself: they do use it. We kill the better half of ourselves every day to propitiate them. The knowledge that these people are there to render all our aspirations barren prevents us having the aspirations. And when we are tempted to seek their destruction they bring forth demons to delude us, disguised as pretty daughters, and singers and poets and the like, for whose sake we spare them.

Hector (*sitting up and leaning towards him*) May not Hesione be such a demon, brought forth by you lest I should slay you?

Captain Shotover. That is possible. She has used you up, and left you nothing but dreams, as some women do.

Hector. Vampire women, demon women.

Captain Shotover. Men think the world well lost for them, and lose it accordingly. Who are the men that do things? The husbands of the shrew and of the drunkard, the men with the thorn in the flesh. (*Walking distractedly away towards the pantry*) I must think these things out. (*Turning suddenly*) But I go on with the dynamite none the less. I will discover a ray mightier than any X-ray: a mind ray that will explode the ammunition in the belt of my adversary before he can point his gun at me. And I must hurry. I am old: I have no time to waste in talk. (*He is about to go into the pantry, and Hector is making for the hall, when Hesione comes back*).

Mrs Hushabye. Daddiest: you and Hector must come and help me to entertain all these people. What on earth were you shouting about?

Hector (*stopping in the act of turning the door handle*) He is madder than usual.

Mrs Hushabye. We all are.

Hector. I must change. (*He resumes his door opening*).

Mrs Hushabye. Stop, stop. Come back, both of you. Come back. (*They return, reluctantly*). Money is running short.

Hector. Money! Where are my April dividends?

Mrs Hushabye. Where is the snow that fell last year?

Captain Shotover. Where is all the money you had for that patent lifeboat I invented?

Mrs Hushabye. Five hundred pounds; and I have made it last since Easter!

Captain Shotover. Since Easter! Barely four months! Monstrous extravagance! I could live for seven years on £500.

Mrs Hushabye. Not keeping open house as we do here, daddiest.

Captain Shotover. Only £500 for that lifeboat! I got twelve thousand for the invention before that.

Mrs Hushabye. Yes, dear; but that was for the ship with the magnetic keel that sucked up submarines. Living at the rate we do, you cannot afford life-saving inventions. Cant you think of something that will murder half Europe at one bang?

Captain Shotover. No. I am ageing fast. My mind does not dwell on slaughter as it did when I was a boy. Why doesnt your husband invent something? He does nothing but tell lies to women.

Hector. Well, that is a form of invention, is it not? However, you are right: I ought to support my wife.

Mrs Hushabye. Indeed you shall do nothing of the sort: I should never see you from breakfast to dinner. I want my husband.

Hector (*bitterly*) I might as well be your lapdog.

Mrs Hushabye. Do you want to be my breadwinner, like the other poor husbands?

Hector. No, by thunder! What a damned creature a husband is anyhow!

Mrs Hushabye (*to the Captain*) What about that harpoon cannon?

Captain Shotover. No use. It kills whales, not men.

Mrs Hushabye. Why not? You fire the harpoon out of a cannon. It sticks in the enemy's general; you wind him in; and there you are.

Hector. You are your father's daughter, Hesione.

Captain Shotover. There is something in it. Not to wind in generals: they are not dangerous. But one could fire a grapnel and wind in a machine gun or even a tank. I will think it out.

Mrs Hushabye (squeezing the Captain's arm affectionately) Saved! You a r e a darling, daddiest. Now we must go back to these dreadful people and entertain them.

Captain Shotover. They have had no dinner. Dont forget that.

Hector. Neither have I. And it is dark: it must be all hours.

Mrs Hushabye. Oh, Guinness will produce some sort of dinner for them. The servants always take jolly good care that there is food in the house.

Captain Shotover (raising a strange wail in the darkness) What a house! What a daughter!

Mrs Hushabye (raving) What a father!

Hector (following suit) What a husband!

Captain Shotover. Is there no thunder in heaven?

Hector. Is there no beauty, no bravery, on earth?

Mrs Hushabye. What do men want? They have their food, their firesides, their clothes mended, and our love at the end of the day. Why are they not satisfied? Why do they envy us the pain with which we bring them into the world, and make strange dangers and torments for themselves to be even with us?

Captain Shotover (weirdly chanting)

> I built a house for my daughters, and opened the
>   doors thereof,
> That men might come for their choosing, and their betters
>   spring from their love;
> But one of them married a numskull;

Hector (taking up the rhythm)

>   The other a liar wed;

Mrs Hushabye (completing the stanza)

> And now must she lie beside him, even as she made her
>   bed.

Lady Utterword (*calling from the garden*) Hesione! Hesione! Where are you?

Hector. The cat is on the tiles.

Mrs Hushabye. Coming, darling, coming. (*She goes quickly into the garden*).

The Captain goes back to his place at the table.

Hector (*going into the hall*) Shall I turn up the lights for you?

Captain Shotover. No. Give me deeper darkness. Money is not made in the light.

ACT II

THE SAME ROOM, with the lights turned up and the curtains drawn. Ellie comes in, followed by Mangan. Both are dressed for dinner. She strolls to the drawing-table. He comes between the table and the wicker chair.

Mangan. What a dinner! I dont call it a dinner: I call it a meal.

Ellie. I am accustomed to meals, Mr Mangan, and very lucky to get them. Besides, the Captain cooked some macaroni for me.

Mangan (shuddering liverishly) Too rich: I cant eat such things. I suppose it's because I have to work so much with my brain. Thats the worst of being a man of business: you are always thinking, thinking, thinking. By the way, now that we are alone, may I take the opportunity to come to a little understanding with you?

Ellie (settling into the draughtsman's seat) Certainly. I should like to.

Mangan (taken aback) Should you? That surprises me; for I thought I noticed this afternoon that you avoided me all you could. Not for the first time either.

Ellie. I was very tired and upset. I wasn't used to the ways of this extraordinary house. Please forgive me.

Mangan. Oh, thats all right: I dont mind. But Captain Shotover has been talking to me about you. You and me, you know.

Ellie (interested) The Captain! What did he say?

Mangan. Well, he noticed the difference between our ages.

Ellie. He notices everything.

Mangan. You dont mind, then?

Ellie. Of course I know quite well that our engagement—

Mangan. Oh! you call it an engagement.

Ellie. Well, isnt it?

Mangan. Oh, yes, yes: no doubt it is if you hold to it. This is the first time youve used the word; and I didnt quite know where we stood: thats all. (*He sits down in the wicker chair; and resigns himself to allow her to lead the conversation*). You were saying—?

Ellie. Was I? I forget. Tell me. Do you like this part of the country? I heard you ask Mr Hushabye at dinner whether there are any nice houses to let down here.

Mangan. I like the place. The air suits me. I shouldnt be surprised if I settled down here.

Ellie. Nothing would please me better. The air suits me too. And I want to be near Hesione.

Mangan (*with growing uneasiness*) The air may suit us; but the question is, should we suit one another? Have you thought about that?

Ellie. Mr Mangan: we must be sensible, mustnt we? It's no use pretending that we are Romeo and Juliet. But we can get on very well together if we choose to make the best of it. Your kindness of heart will make it easy for me.

Mangan (*leaning forward, with the beginning of something like deliberate unpleasantness in his voice*) Kindness of heart, eh? I ruined your father, didnt I?

Ellie. Oh, not intentionally.

Mangan. Yes I did. Ruined him on purpose.

Ellie. On purpose!

Mangan. Not out of ill-nature, you know. And youll admit that I kept a job for him when I had finished with him. But business is business; and I ruined him as a matter of business.

Ellie. I dont understand how that can be. Are you trying to make me feel that I need not be grateful to you, so that I may choose freely?

Mangan (*rising aggressively*) No. I mean what I say.

Ellie. But how could it possibly do you any good to ruin my father? The money he lost was yours.

Mangan (with a sour laugh) W a s mine! It i s mine, Miss Ellie, and all the money the other fellows lost too. (*He shoves his hands into his pockets and shews his teeth*). I just smoked them out like a hive of bees. What do you say to that? A bit of a shock, eh?

Ellie. It would have been, this morning. N o w! you cant think how little it matters. But it's quite interesting. Only, you must explain it to me. I dont understand it. (*Propping her elbows on the drawing-board and her chin on her hands, she composes herself to listen with a combination of conscious curiosity with unconscious contempt which provokes him to more and more unpleasantness, and an attempt at patronage of her ignorance*).

Mangan. Of course you dont understand: what do you know about business? You just listen and learn. Your father's business was a new business; and I dont start new businesses: I let other fellows start them. They put all their money and their friends' money into starting them. They wear out their souls and bodies trying to make a success of them. Theyre what you call enthusiasts. But the first dead lift of the thing is too much for them; and they havnt enough financial experience. In a year or so they have either to let the whole show go bust, or sell out to a new lot of fellows for a few deferred ordinary shares: that is, if theyre lucky enough to get anything at all. As likely as not the very same thing happens to the new lot. They put in more money and a couple of years more work; and then perhaps t h e y have to sell out to a third lot. If it's really a big thing the third lot will have to sell out too, and leave t h e i r work and t h e i r money behind them. And thats where the real business man comes in: where I come in. But I'm cleverer than some: I dont mind dropping a little money to start the process. I took your father's measure. I saw that he had a sound idea, and that he would work himself silly for it if he got the chance. I saw that he was a child in business, and was dead certain to outrun his expenses and be in too great a hurry to wait for his market. I knew that the surest way to ruin a man who doesnt know how to handle money is to give him some. I explained my idea to some friends in the city, and they found the money; for I take no risks in ideas, even when theyre my own. Your father and the friends that ventured their money with him were no more to me than a heap of squeezed lemons. Youve been wasting your gratitude: my kind heart is all rot. I'm sick of it. When I see your father beaming at me with his moist, grateful eyes, regularly wallowing in gratitude, I sometimes feel I must tell him the truth or burst. What stops me is that I know he wouldnt believe me. He'd think it was my modesty, as you did just now. He'd think anything rather than the truth, which is that he's a blamed fool, and I am a man that knows how to take care of himself. (*He throws himself back into the big chair with large self-approval*). Now what do you think of me, Miss Ellie?

Ellie (*dropping her hands*) How strange! that my mother, who knew nothing at all about business, should have been quite right about you! She always said—not before papa, of course, but to us children—that you were just that sort of man.

Mangan (*sitting up, much hurt*) Oh! did she? And yet she'd have let you marry me.

Ellie. Well, you see, Mr Mangan, my mother married a very good man—for whatever you may think of my father as a man of business, he is the soul of goodness—and she is not at all keen on my doing the same.

Mangan. Anyhow, you dont want to marry me now, do you?

Ellie (*very calmly*) Oh, I think so. Why not?

Mangan (*rising aghast*) Why not!

Ellie. I dont see why we shouldnt get on very well together.

Mangan. Well, but look here, you know— (*He stops, quite at a loss*).

Ellie (*patiently*) Well?

Mangan. Well, I thought you were rather particular about people's characters.

Ellie. If we women were particular about men's characters, we should never get married at all, Mr Mangan.

Mangan. A child like you talking of "we women"! What next! Youre not in earnest?

Ellie. Yes I am. Arnt you?

Mangan. You mean to hold me to it?

Ellie. Do you wish to back out of it?

Mangan. Oh no. Not exactly back out of it.

Ellie. Well?

He has nothing to say. With a long whispered whistle, he drops into the wicker chair and stares before him like a beggared gambler. But a cunning look soon comes into his face. He leans over towards her on his right elbow, and speaks in a low steady voice.

Mangan. Suppose I told you I was in love with another woman!

Ellie (*echoing him*) Suppose I told you I was in love with another man!

Mangan (*bouncing angrily out of his chair*) I'm not joking.

Ellie. Who told you I was?

Mangan. I tell you I'm serious. Youre too young to be serious; but youll have to believe me. I want to be near your friend Mrs Hushabye. I'm in love with her. Now the murder's out.

Ellie. I want to be near your friend Mr Hushabye. I'm in love with him. (*She rises and adds with a frank air*) Now we are in one another's confidence, we shall be real friends. Thank you for telling me.

Mangan (*almost beside himself*) Do you think I'll be made a convenience of like this?

Ellie. Come, Mr Mangan! you made a business convenience of my father. Well, a woman's business is marriage. Why shouldnt I make a domestic convenience of you?

Mangan. Because I dont choose, see? Because I'm not a silly gull like your father. Thats why.

Ellie (*with serene contempt*) You are not good enough to clean my father's boots, Mr Mangan; and I am paying you a great compliment in condescending to make a convenience of you, as you call it. Of course you are free to throw over our engagement if you like; but, if you do, youll never enter Hesione's house again: I will take care of that.

Mangan (*gasping*) You little devil, youve done me. (*On the point of collapsing into the big chair again he recovers himself*) Wait a bit, though: youre not so cute as you think. You cant beat Boss Mangan as easy as that. Suppose I go straight to Mrs Hushabye and tell her that youre in love with her husband.

Ellie. She knows it.

Mangan. You told her!!!

Ellie. She told me.

Mangan (*clutching at his bursting temples*) Oh, this is a crazy house. Or else I'm going clean off my chump. Is she making a swop with you—she to have your husband and you to have hers?

Ellie. Well, you dont want us both, do you?

Mangan (*throwing himself into the chair distractedly*) My brain wont stand it. My head's going to split. Help! Help me to hold it. Quick: hold it: squeeze it. Save me. (*Ellie comes behind his chair; clasps his head hard for a moment; then begins to draw her hands from his forehead back to his ears*). Thank you. (*Drowsily*) Thats very refreshing. (*Waking a little*) Don't you hypnotize me, though. Ive seen men made fools of by hypnotism.

Ellie (*steadily*) Be quiet. Ive seen men made fools of without hypnotism.

Mangan (*humbly*) You dont dislike touching me, I hope. You never touched me before, I noticed.

Ellie. Not since you fell in love naturally with a grown-up nice woman, who will never expect you to make love to her. And I will never expect him to make love to me.

Mangan. He may, though.

Ellie (*making her passes rhythmically*) Hush. Go to sleep. Do you hear? You are to go to sleep, go to sleep, go to sleep; be quiet, deeply deeply quiet; sleep, sleep, sleep, sleep, sleep.

He falls asleep. Ellie steals away; turns the light out; and goes into the garden.

Nurse Guinness opens the door and is seen in the light which comes in from the hall.

Guinness (*speaking to someone outside*) Mr Mangan's not here, ducky: theres no one here. It's all dark.

Mrs Hushabye (*without*) Try the garden. Mr Dunn and I will be in my boudoir. Shew him the way.

Guinness. Yes, ducky. (*She makes for the garden door in the dark; stumbles over the sleeping Mangan; and screams*). Ahoo! Oh Lord, sir! I beg your pardon, I'm sure: I didnt see you in the dark. Who is it? (*She goes back to the door and turns on the light*). Oh, Mr Mangan, sir, I hope I havnt hurt you plumping into your lap like that. (*Coming to him*) I was looking for you, sir. Mrs Hushabye says will you please— (*Noticing that he remains quite insensible*) Oh, my good Lord, I hope I havnt killed him. Sir! Mr Mangan! Sir! (*She shakes him; and he is rolling inertly off the chair on the floor when she holds him up and props him against the cushion*). Miss Hessy! Miss Hessy! Quick, doty darling. Miss Hessy! (*Mrs Hushabye comes in from the hall, followed by Mazzini Dunn*). Oh, Miss Hessy, Ive been and killed him.

Mazzini runs round the back of the chair to Mangan's right hand, and sees that the nurse's words are apparently only too true.

Mazzini. What tempted you to commit such a crime, woman?

Mrs Hushabye (trying not to laugh) Do you mean you did it on purpose?

Guinness. Now is it likely I'd kill any man on purpose? I fell over him in the dark; and I'm a pretty tidy weight. He never spoke nor moved until I shook him; and then he would have dropped dead on the floor. Isnt it tiresome?

Mrs Hushabye (going past the nurse to Mangan's side, and inspecting him less credulously than Mazzini) Nonsense! he is not dead: he is only asleep. I can see him breathing.

Guinness. But why wont he wake?

Mazzini (speaking very politely into Mangan's ear) Mangan! My dear Mangan! *(He blows into Mangan's ear).*

Mrs Hushabye. Thats no good. *(She shakes him vigorously).* Mr Mangan: wake up. Do you hear? *(He begins to roll over).* Oh! Nurse, nurse: he's falling: help me.

Nurse Guinness rushes to the rescue. With Mazzini's assistance, Mangan is propped safely up again.

Guinness (behind the chair; bending over to test the case with her nose) Would he be drunk, do you think, pet?

Mrs Hushabye. Had he any of papa's rum?

Mazzini. It cant be that: he is most abstemious. I am afraid he drank too much formerly, and has to drink too little now. You know, Mrs Hushabye, I really think he has been hypnotized.

Guinness. Hip no what, sir?

Mazzini. One evening at home, after we had seen a hypnotizing performance, the children began playing at it; and Ellie stroked my head. I assure you I went off dead asleep; and they had to send for a professional to wake me up after I had slept eighteen hours. They had to carry me upstairs; and as the poor children were not very strong, they let me slip; and I rolled right down the whole flight and never woke up.

(*Mrs Hushabye splutters*). Oh, you may laugh, Mrs Hushabye; but I might have been killed.

Mrs Hushabye. I couldnt have helped laughing even if you had been, Mr Dunn. So Ellie has hypnotized him. What fun!

Mazzini. Oh no, no, no. It was such a terrible lesson to her: nothing would induce her to try such a thing again.

Mrs Hushabye. Then who did it? *I* didnt.

Mazzini. I thought perhaps the Captain might have done it unintentionally. He is so fearfully magnetic: I feel vibrations whenever he comes close to me.

Guinness. The Captain will get him out of it anyhow, sir: I'll back him for that. I'll go fetch him. (*She makes for the pantry*).

Mrs Hushabye. Wait a bit. (*To Mazzini*) You say he is all right for eighteen hours?

Mazzini. Well, *I* was asleep for eighteen hours.

Mrs Hushabye. Were you any the worse for it?

Mazzini. I dont quite remember. They had poured brandy down my throat, you see; and—

Mrs Hushabye. Quite. Anyhow, you survived. Nurse, darling: go and ask Miss Dunn to come to us here. Say I want to speak to her particularly. You will find her with Mr Hushabye probably.

Guinness. I think not, ducky: Miss Addy is with him. But I'll find her and send her to you. (*She goes out into the garden*).

Mrs Hushabye (*calling Mazzini's attention to the figure on the chair*) Now, Mr Dunn, look. Just look. Look hard. Do you still intend to sacrifice your daughter to that thing?

Mazzini (*troubled*) You have completely upset me, Mrs Hushabye, by all you have said to me. That anyone could imagine that I—I, a consecrated soldier of freedom, if I may say so—could sacrifice Ellie to anybody or anyone, or that I should ever have dreamed of forcing her inclinations in any way, is a most painful blow to my—well, I suppose you would say to my good opinion of myself.

Mrs Hushabye (*rather stolidly*) Sorry.

Mazzini (*looking forlornly at the body*) What is your objection to poor Mangan, Mrs Hushabye? He looks all right to me. But then I am so accustomed to him.

Mrs Hushabye. Have you no heart? Have you no sense? Look at the brute! Think of poor weak innocent Ellie in the clutches of this slavedriver, who spends his life making thousands of rough violent workmen bend to his will and sweat for him: a man accustomed to have great masses of iron beaten into shape for him by steam-hammers! to fight with women and girls over a halfpenny an hour ruthlessly! a captain of industry, I think you call him, dont you? Are you going to fling your delicate, sweet, helpless child into such a beast's claws just because he will keep her in an expensive house and make her wear diamonds to shew how rich he is?

Mazzini (*staring at her in wide-eyed amazement*) Bless you, dear Mrs Hushabye, what romantic ideas of business you have! Poor dear Mangan isnt a bit like that.

Mrs Hushabye (*scornfully*) Poor dear Mangan indeed!

Mazzini. But he doesnt know anything about machinery. He never goes near the men: he couldnt manage them: he is afraid of them. I never can get him to take the least interest in the works: he hardly knows more about them than you do. People are cruelly unjust to Mangan: they think he is all rugged strength just because his manners are bad.

Mrs Hushabye. Do you mean to tell me he isnt strong enough to crush poor little Ellie?

Mazzini. Of course it's very hard to say how any marriage will turn out; but speaking for myself, I should say that he wont have a dog's chance against Ellie. You know, Ellie has remarkable strength of character. I think it is because I taught her to like Shakespear when she was very young.

Mrs Hushabye (*contemptuously*) Shakespear! The next

thing you will tell me is that you could have made a great deal more money than Mangan. (*She retires to the sofa, and sits down at the port end of it in the worst of humors*).

Mazzini (*following her and taking the other end*) No: I'm no good at making money. I dont care enough for it, somehow. I'm not ambitious! that must be it. Mangan is wonderful about money: he thinks of nothing else. He is so dreadfully afraid of being poor. I am always thinking of other things: even at the works I think of the things we are doing and not of what they cost. And the worst of it is, poor Mangan doesnt know what to do with his money when he gets it. He is such a baby that he doesnt know even what to eat and drink: he has ruined his liver eating and drinking the wrong things; and now he can hardly eat at all. Ellie will diet him splendidly. You will be surprised when you come to know him better: he is really the most helpless of mortals. You get quite a protective feeling towards him.

Mrs Hushabye. Then who manages his business, pray?

Mazzini. I do. And of course other people like me.

Mrs Hushabye. Footling people, you mean.

Mazzini. I suppose youd think us so.

Mrs Hushabye. And pray why dont you do without him if youre all so much cleverer?

Mazzini. Oh, we couldnt: we should ruin the business in a year. I've tried; and I know. We should spend too much on everything. We should improve the quality of the goods and make them too dear. We should be sentimental about the hard cases among the workpeople. But Mangan keeps us in order. He is down on us about every extra halfpenny. We could never do without him. You see, he will sit up all night thinking of how to save sixpence. Wont Ellie make him jump, though, when she takes his house in hand!

Mrs Hushabye. Then the creature is a fraud even as a captain of industry!

Mazzini. I am afraid all the captains of industry are what y o u call frauds, Mrs Hushabye. Of course there are some manufacturers who really do understand their own works; but they dont make as high a rate of profit as Mangan does. I assure you Mangan is quite a good fellow in his way. He means well.

Mrs Hushabye. He doesnt look well. He is not in his first youth, is he?

Mazzini. After all, no husband is in his first youth for very long, Mrs Hushabye. And men cant afford to marry in their first youth nowadays.

Mrs Hushabye. Now if I said that, it would sound witty. Why cant y o u say it wittily? What on earth is the matter with you? Why dont you inspire everybody with confidence? with respect?

Mazzini (humbly) I think that what is the matter with me is that I am poor. You dont know what that means at home. Mind: I dont say they have ever complained. Theyve all been wonderful: theyve been proud of my poverty. Theyve even joked about it quite often. But my wife has had a very poor time of it. She has been quite resigned—

Mrs Hushabye (shuddering involuntarily)!!

Mazzini. There! You see, Mrs Hushabye. I dont want Ellie to live on resignation.

Mrs Hushabye. Do you want her to have to resign herself to living with a man she doesnt love?

Mazzini (wistfully) Are you sure that would be worse than living with a man she did love, if he was a footling person?

Mrs Hushabye (relaxing her contemptuous attitude, quite interested in Mazzini now) You know, I really think you must love Ellie very much; for you become quite clever when you talk about her.

Mazzini. I didnt know I was so very stupid on other subjects.

Mrs Hushabye. You are, sometimes.

Mazzini (turning his head away; for his eyes are wet) I

have learnt a good deal about myself from you, Mrs Hushabye; and I'm afraid I shall not be the happier for your plain speaking. But if you thought I needed it to make me think of Ellie's happiness you were very much mistaken.

Mrs Hushabye (leaning towards him kindly) Have I been a beast?

Mazzini (pulling himself together) It doesnt matter about me, Mrs Hushabye. I think you like Ellie; and that is enough for me.

Mrs Hushabye. I'm beginning to like you a little. I perfectly loathed you at first. I thought you the most odious, self-satisfied, boresome elderly prig I ever met.

Mazzini (resigned, and now quite cheerful) I daresay I am all that. I never have been a favorite with gorgeous women like you. They always frighten me.

Mrs Hushabye (pleased) Am I a gorgeous woman, Mazzini? I shall fall in love with you presently.

Mazzini (with placid gallantry) No you wont, Hesione. But you would be quite safe. Would you believe it that quite a lot of women have flirted with me because I am quite safe? But they get tired of me for the same reason.

Mrs Hushabye (mischievously). Take care. You may not be so safe as you think.

Mazzini. Oh yes, quite safe. You see, I have been in love really: the sort of love that only happens once. *(Softly)* Thats why Ellie is such a lovely girl.

Mrs Hushabye. Well, really, you a r e coming out. Are you quite sure you wont let me tempt you into a second grand passion?

Mazzini. Quite. It wouldnt be natural. The fact is, you dont strike on my box, Mrs Hushabye; and I certainly dont strike on yours.

Mrs Hushabye. I see. Your marriage was a safety match.

Mazzini. What a very witty application of the expression I used. I should never have thought of it.

Ellie comes in from the garden, looking anything but happy.

Mrs Hushabye (rising) Oh! here is Ellie at last. (*She goes behind the sofa*).

Ellie (on the threshold of the starboard door) Guinness said you wanted me: you and papa.

Mrs Hushabye. You have kept us waiting so long that it almost came to—well, never mind. Your father is a very wonderful man (*she ruffles his hair affectionately*): the only one I ever met who could resist me when I made myself really agreeable. (*She comes to the big chair, on Mangan's left*). Come here. I have something to shew you. (*Ellie strolls listlessly to the other side of the chair*). Look.

Ellie (contemplating Mangan without interest) I know. He is only asleep. We had a talk after dinner; and he fell asleep in the middle of it.

Mrs Hushabye. You did it, Ellie. You put him asleep.

Mazzini (rising quickly and coming to the back of the chair) Oh, I hope not. Did you, Ellie?

Ellie (wearily) He asked me to.

Mazzini. But it's dangerous. You know what happened to me.

Ellie (utterly indifferent) Oh, I daresay I can wake him. If not, somebody else can.

Mrs Hushabye. It doesnt matter, anyhow, because I have at last persuaded your father that you dont want to marry him.

Ellie (suddenly coming out of her listlessness, much vexed) But why did you do that, Hesione? I do want to marry him. I fully intend to marry him.

Mazzini. Are you quite sure, Ellie? Mrs Hushabye has made me feel that I may have been thoughtless and selfish about it.

Ellie (very clearly and steadily) Papa. When Mrs Hushabye takes it on herself to explain to you what I think or dont think, shut your ears tight; and shut your eyes too. Hesione knows nothing about me: she hasnt the least notion of the sort of person I am, and never will. I promise you I wont do anything I dont want to do and mean to do for my own sake.

Mazzini. You are quite, quite sure?

Ellie. Quite, quite sure. Now you must go away and leave me to talk to Mrs Hushabye.

Mazzini. But I should like to hear. Shall I be in the way?

Ellie (*inexorable*) I had rather talk to her alone.

Mazzini (*affectionately*) Oh, well, I know what a nuisance parents are, dear. I will be good and go. (*He goes to the garden door*). By the way, do you remember the address of that professional who woke me up? Dont you think I had better telegraph to him?

Mrs Hushabye (*moving towards the sofa*) It's too late to telegraph tonight.

Mazzini. I suppose so. I do hope he'll wake up in the course of the night. (*He goes out into the garden*).

Ellie (*turning vigorously on Hesione the moment her father is out of the room*) Hesione: what the devil do you mean by making mischief with my father about Mangan?

Mrs Hushabye (*promptly losing her temper*) Dont you dare speak to me like that, you little minx. Remember that you are in my house.

Ellie. Stuff! Why dont you mind your own business? What is it to you whether I choose to marry Mangan or not?

Mrs Hushabye. Do you suppose you can bully me, you miserable little matrimonial adventurer?

Ellie. Every woman who hasnt any money is a matrimonial adventurer. It's easy for you to talk: you have never known what it is to want money; and you can pick up men as if they were daisies. I am poor and respectable—

Mrs Hushabye (*interrupting*) Ho! respectable! How did you pick up Mangan? How did you pick up my husband? You have the audacity to tell me that I am a—a—a—

Ellie. A siren. So you are. You were born to lead men by
the nose: if you werent, Marcus would have waited for me,
perhaps.

Mrs Hushabye (suddenly melting and half laughing) Oh,
my poor Ellie, my pettikins, my unhappy darling! I am so sorry
about Hector. But what can I do? It's not my fault: I'd give
him to you if I could.

Ellie. I dont blame you for that.

Mrs Hushabye. What a brute I was to quarrel with you and
call you names! Do kiss me and say youre not angry with me.

Ellie (fiercely) Oh, dont slop and gush and be sentimental.
Dont you see that unless I can be hard—as hard as nails—I
shall go mad? I dont care a damn about your calling me names:
do you think a woman in my situation can feel a few hard
words?

Mrs Hushabye. Poor little woman! Poor little situation!

Ellie. I suppose you think youre being sympathetic. You are
just foolish and stupid and selfish. You see me getting a smasher
right in the face that kills a whole part of my life: the best part
that can never come again; and you think you can help me
over it by a little coaxing and kissing. When I want all the
strength I can get to lean on: something iron, something stony,
I dont care how cruel it is, you go all mushy and want to slob-
ber over me. I'm not angry; I'm not unfriendly; but for God's
sake do pull yourself together; and dont think that because
youre on velvet and always have been, women who are in hell
can take it as easily as you.

Mrs Hushabye (shrugging her shoulders) Very well. *(She
sits down on the sofa in her old place).* But I warn you that
when I am neither coaxing and kissing nor laughing, I am just
wondering how much longer I can stand living in this cruel,
damnable world. You object to the siren: well, I drop the siren.
You want to rest your wounded bosom against a grindstone.
Well *(folding her arms)*, here is the grindstone.

Ellie (*sitting down beside her, appeased*) Thats better: you really have the trick of falling in with everyone's mood; but you dont understand, because you are not the sort of woman for whom there is only one man and only one chance.

Mrs Hushabye. I certainly dont understand how your marrying that object (*indicating Mangan*) will console you for not being able to marry Hector.

Ellie. Perhaps you dont understand why I was quite a nice girl this morning, and am now neither a girl nor particularly nice.

Mrs Hushabye. Oh yes, I do. It's because you have made up your mind to do something despicable and wicked.

Ellie. I dont think so, Hesione. I must make the best of my ruined house.

Mrs Hushabye. Pooh! Youll get over it. Your house isnt ruined.

Ellie. Of course I shall get over it. You dont suppose I'm going to sit down and die of a broken heart, I hope, or be an old maid living on a pittance from the Sick and Indigent Roomkeepers' Association. But my heart i s broken, all the same. What I mean by that is that I know that what has happened to me with Marcus will not happen to me ever again. In the world for me there is Marcus and a lot of other men of whom one is just the same as another. Well, if I cant have love, thats no reason why I should have poverty. If Mangan has nothing else, he has money.

Mrs Hushabye. And are there no y o u n g men with money?

Ellie. Not within my reach. Besides, a young man would have the right to expect love from me, and would perhaps leave me when he found I could not give it to him. Rich young men can get rid of their wives, you know, pretty cheaply. But this object, as you call him, can expect nothing more from me than I am prepared to give him.

Mrs Hushabye. He will be your owner, remember. If he buys you, he will make the bargain pay him and not you. Ask your father.

Ellie (rising and strolling to the chair to contemplate their subject) You need not trouble on that score, Hesione. I have more to give Boss Mangan than he has to give me: it is I who am buying him, and at a pretty good price too, I think. Women are better at that sort of bargain than men. I have taken the Boss's measure; and ten Boss Mangans shall not prevent me doing far more as I please as his wife than I have ever been able to do as a poor girl. *(Stooping to the recumbent figure)* Shall they, Boss? I think not. *(She passes on to the drawing-table, and leans against the end of it, facing the windows).* I shall not have to spend most of my time wondering how long my gloves will last, anyhow.

Mrs Hushabye (rising superbly) Ellie: you are a wicked sordid little beast. And to think that I actually condescended to fascinate that creature there to save you from him! Well, let me tell you this: if you make this disgusting match, you will never see Hector again if I can help it.

Ellie (unmoved) I nailed Mangan by telling him that if he did not marry me he should never see you again. *(She lifts herself on her wrists and seats herself on the end of the table).*

Mrs Hushabye (recoiling) Oh!

Ellie. So you see I am not unprepared for your playing that trump against me. Well, you just try it: thats all. I should have made a man of Marcus, not a household pet.

Mrs Hushabye (flaming) You dare!

Ellie (looking almost dangerous) Set him thinking about me if y o u dare.

Mrs Hushabye. Well, of all the impudent little fiends I ever met! Hector says there is a certain point at which the only answer you can give to a man who breaks all the rules is to knock him down. What would you say if I were to box your ears?

Ellie (calmly) I should pull your hair.

Mrs Hushabye (mischievously) That wouldnt hurt me. Perhaps it comes off at night.

Ellie (so taken aback that she drops off the table and runs to her) Oh, you dont mean to say, Hesione, that your beautiful black hair is false?

Mrs Hushabye (patting it) Dont tell Hector. He believes in it.

Ellie (groaning) Oh! Even the hair that ensnared him false! Everything false!

Mrs Hushabye. Pull it and try. Other women can snare men in their hair; but I can swing a baby on mine. Aha! You cant do that, Goldylocks.

Ellie (heartbroken) No. You have stolen m y babies.

Mrs Hushabye. Pettikins: dont make me cry. You know, what you said about my making a household pet of him is a little true. Perhaps he ought to have waited for you. Would any other woman on earth forgive you?

Ellie. Oh, what right had you to take him all for yourself! *(Pulling herself together)* There! You couldnt help it: neither of us could help it. He couldnt help it. No: dont say anything more: I cant bear it. Let us wake the object. *(She begins stroking Mangan's head, reversing the movement with which she put him to sleep).* Wake up, do you hear? You are to wake up at once. Wake up, wake up, wake—

Mangan (bouncing out of the chair in a fury and turning on them) Wake up! So you think Ive been asleep, do you? *(He kicks the chair violently back out of his way, and gets between them).* You throw me into a trance so that I cant move hand or foot—I might have been buried alive! it's a mercy I wasnt—and then you think I was only asleep. If youd let me drop the two times you rolled me about, my nose would have been flattened for life against the floor. But Ive found you all out, anyhow. I know the sort of people I'm among now. Ive heard every word youve said, you and your precious father, and *(to Mrs Hushabye)* you too. So I'm an object, am I? I'm a thing, am I? I'm a fool that hasnt sense enough to feed myself properly, am I? I'm afraid of the men that would starve if it werent for the wages I give them, am I? I'm nothing but a disgusting old skinflint to be made a convenience of by designing women and fool managers of my works, am I? I'm—

Mrs Hushabye (*with the most elegant aplomb*) Sh-sh-sh-sh-sh! Mr Mangan: you are bound in honor to obliterate from your mind all you heard while you were pretending to be asleep. It was not meant for you to hear.

Mangan. Pretending to be asleep! Do you think if I was only pretending that I'd have sprawled there helpless, and listened to such unfairness, such lies, such injustice and plotting and backbiting and slandering of me, if I could have up and told you what I thought of you! I wonder I didnt burst.

Mrs Hushabye (*sweetly*) You dreamt it all, Mr Mangan. We were only saying how beautifully peaceful you looked in your sleep. That was all, wasnt it, Ellie? Believe me, Mr Mangan, all those unpleasant things came into your mind in the last half second before you woke. Ellie rubbed your hair the wrong way; and the disagreeable sensation suggested a disagreeable dream.

Mangan (*doggedly*) I believe in dreams.

Mrs Hushabye. So do I. But they go by contraries, dont they?

Mangan (*depths of emotion suddenly welling up in him*) I shant forget, to my dying day, that when you gave me the glad eye that time in the garden, you were making a fool of me. That was a dirty low mean thing to do. You had no right to let me come near you if I disgusted you. It isnt my fault if I'm old and havnt a moustache like a bronze candlestick as your husband has. There are things no decent woman would do to a man—like a man hitting a woman in the breast.

Hesione, utterly shamed, sits down on the sofa and covers her face with her hands. Mangan sits down also on his chair and begins to cry like a child. Ellie stares at them. Mrs Hushabye, at the distressing sound he makes, takes down her hands and looks at him. She rises and runs to him.

Mrs Hushabye. Dont cry: I cant bear it. Have I broken your heart? I didnt know you had one. How could I?

Mangan. I'm a man aint I?

Mrs Hushabye (half coaxing, half rallying, altogether tenderly) Oh no: not what I call a man. Only a Boss: just that and nothing else. What business has a Boss with a heart?

Mangan. Then youre not a bit sorry for what you did, nor ashamed?

Mrs Hushabye. I was ashamed for the first time in my life when you said that about hitting a woman in the breast, and I found out what I'd done. My very bones blushed red. Youve had your revenge, Boss. Arnt you satisfied?

Mangan. Serve you right! Do you hear? Serve you right! Youre just cruel. Cruel.

Mrs Hushabye. Yes: cruelty would be delicious if one could only find some sort of cruelty that didnt really hurt. By the way *(sitting down beside him on the arm of the chair)*, whats your name? It's not really Boss, is it?

Mangan (shortly) if you want to know, my name's Alfred.

Mrs Hushabye (springing up) Alfred! Ellie: he was christened after Tennyson!!!

Mangan (rising) I was christened after my uncle, and never had a penny from him, damn him! What of it?

Mrs Hushabye. It comes to me suddenly that you are a real person: that you had a mother, like anyone else. *(Putting her hands on his shoulders and surveying him)* Little Alf!

Mangan. Well, you have a nerve.

Mrs Hushabye. And you have a heart, Alfy, a whimpering little heart, but a real one. *(Releasing him suddenly)* Now run and make it up with Ellie. She has had time to think what to say to you, which is more than I had. *(She goes out quickly into the garden by the port door)*.

Mangan. That woman has a pair of hands that go right through you.

Ellie. Still in love with her, in spite of all we said about you?

Mangan. Are all women like you two? Do they never think of anything about a man except what they can get out of him? Y o u werent even thinking that about me. You were only thinking whether your gloves would last.

Ellie. I shall not have to think about that when we are married.

Mangan. And you think I am going to marry you after what I heard there!

Ellie. You heard nothing from me that I did not tell you before.

Mangan. Perhaps you think I cant do without you.

Ellie. I think you would feel lonely without us all now, after coming to know us so well.

Mangan (*with something like a yell of despair*) Am I never to have the last word?

Captain Shotover (*appearing at the starboard garden door*) There is a soul in torment here. What is the matter?

Mangan. This girl doesnt want to spend her life wondering how long her gloves will last.

Captain Shotover (*passing through*) Dont wear any. I never do. (*He goes into the pantry*).

Lady Utterword (*appearing at the port garden door, in a handsome dinner dress*) Is anything the matter?

Ellie. This gentleman wants to know is he never to have the last word?

Lady Utterword (*coming forward to the sofa*) I should let him have it, my dear. The important thing is not to have the last word, but to have your own way.

Mangan. She wants both.

Lady Utterword. She wont get them, Mr Mangan. Providence always has the last word.

Mangan (*desperately*) Now y o u are going to come religion over me. In his house a man's mind might as well be a football. I'm going. (*He makes for the hall, but is stopped by a hail from the Captain, who has just emerged from his pantry*).

Captain Shotover. Whither away, Boss Mangan?

Mangan. To hell out of this house: let that be enough for you and all here.

Captain Shotover. You were welcome to come: you are free to go. The wide earth, the high seas, the spacious skies are waiting for you outside.

Lady Utterword. But your things, Mr Mangan. Your bags, your comb and brushes, your pyjamas—

Hector (who has just appeared in the port doorway in a handsome Arab costume) Why should the escaping slave take his chains with him?

Mangan. Thats right, Hushabye. Keep the pyjamas, my lady; and much good may they do you.

Hector (advancing to Lady Utterword's left hand) Let us all go out into the night and leave everything behind us.

Mangan. You stay where you are, the lot of you. I want no company, especially female company.

Ellie. Let him go. He is unhappy here. He is angry with us.

Captain Shotover. Go, Boss Mangan; and when you have found the land where there is happiness and where there are no women, send me its latitude and longitude; and I will join you there.

Lady Utterword. You will certainly not be comfortable without your luggage, Mr Mangan.

Ellie (impatient) Go, go: why dont you go? It is a heavenly night: you can sleep on the heath. Take my waterproof to lie on: it is hanging up in the hall.

Hector. Breakfast at nine, unless you prefer to breakfast with the Captain at six.

Ellie. Good night, Alfred.

Hector. Alfred! (*He runs back to the door and calls into the garden*) Randall: Mangan's Christian name is Alfred.

Randall (appearing in the starboard doorway in evening dress) Then Hesione wins her bet.

Mrs Hushabye appears in the port doorway. She throws her

*left arm round Hector's neck; draws him with her to the back
of the sofa; and throws her right arm round Lady Utterword's
neck.*

Mrs Hushabye. They wouldnt believe me, Alf.

They contemplate him.

Mangan. Is there any more of you coming in to look at me, as
if I was the latest thing in a menagerie?

Mrs Hushabye. You a r e the latest thing in this menagerie.

*Before Mangan can retort, a fall of furniture is heard from
upstairs; then a pistol shot, and a yell of pain. The staring
group breaks up in consternation.*

Mazzini's Voice (from above) Help! A burglar! Help!

Hector (his eyes blazing) A burglar!!!

Mrs Hushabye. No, Hector: youll be shot. (*But it is too
late: he has dashed out past Mangan, who hastily moves towards the bookshelves out of his way*).

Captain Shotover (blowing his whistle) All hands aloft! (*He
strides out after Hector*).

Lady Utterword. My diamonds! (*She follows the Captain*).

Randall (rushing after her) No, Ariadne. Let me.

Ellie. Oh, is papa shot? (*She runs out*).

Mrs Hushabye. Are you frightened, Alf?

Mangan. No. It aint my house, thank God.

Mrs Hushabye. If they catch a burglar, shall we have to go
into court as witnesses, and be asked all sorts of questions about
our private lives?

Mangan. You wont be believed if you tell the truth.

*Mazzini, terribly upset, with a duelling pistol in his hand,
comes from the hall, and makes his way to the drawing-table.*

Mazzini. Oh, my dear Mrs Hushabye, I might have killed
him. (*He throws the pistol on the table and staggers round to
the chair*). I hope you wont believe I really intended to.

*Hector comes in, marching an old and villainous looking
man before him by the collar. He plants him in the middle of
the room and releases him.*

Ellie follows, and immediately runs across to the back of her father's chair and pats his shoulders.

Randall (entering with a poker) Keep your eye on this door, Mangan. I'll look after the other. *(He goes to the starboard door and stands on guard there).*

Lady Utterword comes in after Randall, and goes between Mrs Hushabye and Mangan.

Nurse Guinness brings up the rear, and waits near the door, on Mangan's left.

Mrs Hushabye. What has happened?

Mazzini. Your housekeeper told me there was somebody upstairs, and gave me a pistol that Mr Hushabye had been practising with. I thought it would frighten him; but it went off at a touch.

The Burglar. Yes, and took the skin off my ear. Precious near took the top off my head. Why dont you have a proper revolver instead of a thing like that, that goes off if you as much as blow on it?

Hector. One of my duelling pistols. Sorry.

Mazzini. He put his hands up and said it was a fair cop.

The Burglar. So it was. Send for the police.

Hector. No, by thunder! It was not a fair cop. We were four to one.

Mrs Hushabye. What will they do to him?

The Burglar. Ten years. Beginning with solitary. Ten years off my life. I shant serve it all: I'm too old. It will see me out.

Lady Utterword. You should have thought of that before you stole my diamonds.

The Burglar. Well, youve got them back, lady: havnt you? Can you give me back the years of my life you are going to take from me?

Mrs Hushabye. Oh, we cant bury a man alive for ten years for a few diamonds.

The Burglar. Ten little shining diamonds! Ten long black years!

Lady Utterword. Think of what it is for us to be dragged through the horrors of a criminal court, and have all our family affairs in the papers! If you were a native, and Hastings could order you a good beating and send you away, I shouldnt mind; but here in England there is no real protection for any respectable person.

The Burglar. I'm too old to be giv a hiding, lady. Send for the police and have done with it. It's only just and right you should.

Randall (*who has relaxed his vigilance on seeing the burglar so pacifically disposed, and comes forward swinging the poker between his fingers like a well-folded umbrella*) It is neither just nor right that we should be put to a lot of inconvenience to gratify your moral enthusiasm, my friend. You had better get out, while you have the chance.

The Burglar (*inexorably*) No. I must work my sin off my conscience. This has come as a sort of call to me. Let me spend the rest of my life repenting in a cell. I shall have my reward above.

Mangan (*exasperated*) The very burglars cant behave naturally in this house.

Hector. My good sir: you must work out your salvation at somebody else's expense. Nobody here is going to charge you.

The Burglar. Oh, you wont charge me, wont you?

Hector. No. I'm sorry to be inhospitable; but will you kindly leave the house?

The Burglar. Right. I'll go to the police station and give myself up. (*He turns resolutely to the door; but Hector stops him*).

Hector.	Oh no. You mustnt do that.
Randall.	No, no. Clear out, man, cant you; and dont be a fool.
Mrs Hushabye.	Dont be so silly. Cant you repent at home?

Lady Utterword. You will have to do as you are told.

The Burglar. It's compounding a felony, you know.

Mrs Hushabye. This is utterly ridiculous. Are we to be forced to prosecute this man when we dont want to?

The Burglar. Am I to be robbed of my salvation to save you the trouble of spending a day at the sessions? Is that justice? Is it right? Is it fair to me?

Mazzini (*rising and leaning across the table persuasively as if it were a pulpit desk or a shop counter*) Come, come! let me shew you how you can turn your very crimes to account. Why not set up as a locksmith? You must know more about locks than most honest men?

The Burglar. Thats true, sir. But I couldnt set up as a lock-smith under twenty pounds.

Randall. Well, you can easily steal twenty pounds. You will find it in the nearest bank.

The Burglar (*horrified*) Oh what a thing for a gentleman to put into the head of a poor criminal scrambling out of the bottomless pit as it were! Oh, shame on you, sir! Oh, God forgive you! (*He throws himself into the big chair and covers his face as if in prayer*).

Lady Utterword. Really, Randall!

Hector. It seems to me that we shall have to take up a collection for this inopportunely contrite sinner.

Lady Utterword. But twenty pounds is ridiculous.

The Burglar (*looking up quickly*) I shall have to buy a lot of tools, lady.

Lady Utterword. Nonsense: you have your burgling kit.

The Burglar. Whats a jimmy and a centrebit and an acetylene welding plant and a bunch of skeleton keys? I shall want a forge, and a smithy, and a shop, and fittings. I cant hardly do it for twenty.

Hector. My worthy friend, we havnt got twenty pounds.

The Burglar (*now master of the situation*) You can raise it among you, cant you?

Mrs Hushabye. Give him a sovereign, Hector, and get rid of him.

Hector (*giving him a pound*) There! Off with you.

The Burglar (*rising and taking the money very ungratefully*) I wont promise nothing. You have more on you than a quid: all the lot of you, I mean.

Lady Utterword (*vigorously*) Oh, let us prosecute him and have done with it. I have a conscience too, I hope; and I do not feel at all sure that we have any right to let him go, especially if he is going to be greedy and impertinent.

The Burglar (*quickly*) All right, lady, all right. Ive no wish to be anything but agreeable. Good evening, ladies and gentlemen; and thank you kindly.

He is hurrying out when he is confronted in the doorway by Captain Shotover.

Captain Shotover (*fixing the burglar with a piercing regard*) Whats this? Are there two of you?

The Burglar (*falling on his knees before the Captain in abject terror*) Oh my good Lord, what have I done? Dont tell me its y o u r house Ive broken into, Captain Shotover.

The Captain seizes him by the collar; drags him to his feet; and leads him to the middle of the group, Hector falling back beside his wife to make way for them.

Captain Shotover (*turning him towards Ellie*) Is that your daughter? (*He releases him*).

The Burglar. Well, how do I know, Captain? You know the sort of life you and me has led. Any young lady of that age might be my daughter anywhere in the wide world, as you might say.

Captain Shotover (*to Mazzini*) You are not Billy Dunn. This is Billy Dunn. Why have you imposed on me?

The Burglar (*indignantly to Mazzini*) Have you been giving yourself out to be me? You, that nigh blew my head off! Shooting y o u r s e l f , in a manner of speaking!

Mazzini. My dear Captain Shotover, ever since I came into

this house I have done hardly anything else but assure you that I am not Mr William Dunn, but Mazzini Dunn, a very different person.

The Burglar. He dont belong to my branch, Captain. Theres two sets in the family: the thinking Dunns and the drinking Dunns, each going their own ways. I'm a drinking Dunn: he's a thinking Dunn. But that didnt give him any right to shoot me.

Captain Shotover. So youve turned burglar, have you?

The Burglar. No, Captain: I wouldnt disgrace our old sea calling by such a thing. I am no burglar.

Lady Utterword. What were you doing with my diamonds?

Guinness. What did you break into the house for if youre no burglar?

Randall. Mistook the house for your own and came in by the wrong window, eh?

The Burglar. Well, it's no use my telling you a lie: I can take in most captains, but not Captain Shotover, because he sold himself to the devil in Zanzibar, and can divine water, spot gold, explode a cartridge in your pocket with a glance of his eye, and see the truth hidden in the heart of man. But I'm no burglar.

Captain Shotover. Are you an honest man?

The Burglar. I dont set up to be better than my fellow-creatures, and never did, as you well know, Captain. But what I do is innocent and pious. I enquire about for houses where the right sort of people live. I work it on them same as I worked it here. I break into the house; put a few spoons or diamonds in my pocket; make a noise; get caught; and take up a collection. And you wouldnt believe how hard it is to get caught when youre actually trying to. I have knocked over all the chairs in a room without a soul paying any attention to me. In the end I have had to walk out and leave the job.

Randall. When that happens, do you put back the spoons and diamonds?

The Burglar. Well, I dont fly in the face of Providence, if thats what you want to know.

Captain Shotover. Guinness: you remember this man?

Guinness. I should think I do, seeing I was married to him, the blackguard!

Hesione	(*exclaiming*	Married to him!
Lady Utterword	*together*)	Guinness!!

The Burglar. It wasnt legal. Ive been married to no end of women. No use coming that over me.

Captain Shotover. Take him to the forecastle. (*He flings him to the door with a strength beyond his years*).

Guinness. I suppose you mean the kitchen. They wont have him there. Do you expect servants to keep company with thieves and all sorts?

Captain Shotover. Land-thieves and water-thieves are the same flesh and blood. I'll have no boatswain on my quarter-deck. Off with you both.

The Burglar. Yes, Captain. (*He goes out humbly*).

Mazzini. Will it be safe to have him in the house like that?

Guinness. Why didnt you shoot him, sir? If I'd known who he was, I'd have shot him myself. (*She goes out*).

Mrs Hushabye. Do sit down, everybody. (*She sits down on the sofa*).

They all move except Ellie. Mazzini resumes his seat. Randall sits down in the window-seat near the starboard door, again making a pendulum of his poker, and studying it as Galileo might have done. Hector sits on his left, in the middle. Mangan, forgotten, sits in the port corner. Lady Utterword takes the big chair. Captain Shotover goes into the pantry in deep abstraction. They all look after him; and Lady Utterword coughs consciously.

Mrs Hushabye. So Billy Dunn was poor nurse's little romance. I knew there had been somebody.

Randall. They will fight their battles over again and enjoy themselves immensely.

Lady Utterword (*irritably*) You are not married; and you know nothing about it, Randall. Hold your tongue.

Randall. Tyrant!

Mrs Hushabye. Well, we have had a very exciting evening. Everything will be an anticlimax after it. We'd better all go to bed.

Randall. Another burglar may turn up.

Mazzini. Oh, impossible! I hope not.

Randall. Why not? There is more than one burglar in England.

Mrs Hushabye. What do you say, Alf?

Mangan (*huffily*) Oh, I dont matter. I'm forgotten. The burglar has put my nose out of joint. Shove me into a corner and have done with me.

Mrs Hushabye (*jumping up mischievously, and going to him*) Would you like a walk on the heath, Alfred? With me?

Ellie. Go, Mr Mangan. It will do you good. Hesione will soothe you.

Mrs Hushabye (*slipping her arm under his and pulling him upright*) Come, Alfred. There is a moon: it's like the night in Tristan and Isolde. (*She caresses his arm and draws him to the port garden door*).

Mangan (*writhing but yielding*) How you can have the face—the heart— (*He breaks down and is heard sobbing as she takes him out*).

Lady Utterword. What an extraordinary way to behave! What is the matter with the man?

Ellie (*in a strangely calm voice, staring into an imaginary distance*) His heart is breaking: that is all. (*The Captain appears at the pantry door, listening*). It is a curious sensation: the sort of pain that goes mercifully beyond our powers of feeling. When your heart is broken, your boats are burned: nothing matters any more. It is the end of happiness and the beginning of peace.

Lady Utterword (suddenly rising in a rage, to the astonishment of the rest) How dare you?

Hector. Good heavens! Whats the matter?

Randall (in a warning whisper) Tch—tch—tch! Steady.

Ellie (surprised and haughty) I was not addressing you particularly, Lady Utterword. And I am not accustomed to be asked how dare I.

Lady Utterword. Of course not. Anyone can see how badly you have been brought up.

Mazzini. Oh, I hope not, Lady Utterword. Really!

Lady Utterword. I know very well what you meant. The impudence!

Ellie. What on earth do you mean?

Captain Shotover (advancing to the table) She means that her heart will not break. She has been longing all her life for someone to break it. At last she has become afraid she has none to break.

Lady Utterword (flinging herself on her knees and throwing her arms round him) Papa: dont say you think Ive no heart.

Captain Shotover (raising her with grim tenderness) If you had no heart how could you want to have it broken, child?

Hector (rising with a bound) Lady Utterword: you are not to be trusted. You have made a scene. (*He runs out into the garden through the starboard door*).

Lady Utterword. Oh! Hector, Hector! (*She runs out after him*).

Randall. Only nerves, I assure you. (*He rises and follows her, waving the poker in his agitation*). Ariadne! Ariadne! For God's sake be careful. You will— (*He is gone*).

Mazzini (rising) How distressing! Can I do anything, I wonder?

Captain Shotover (promptly taking his chair and setting to work at the drawing-board) No. Go to bed. Goodnight.

Mazzini (bewildered) Oh! Perhaps you are right.

Ellie. Goodnight, dearest. (*She kisses him*).

Mazzini. Goodnight, love. (*He makes for the door, but turns aside to the bookshelves*). I'll just take a book. (*He takes one*). Goodnight. (*He goes out, leaving Ellie alone with the Captain*).

The Captain is intent on his drawing. Ellie, standing sentry over his chair, contemplates him for a moment.

Ellie. Does nothing ever disturb you, Captain Shotover?

Captain Shotover. Ive stood on the bridge for eighteen hours in a typhoon. Life here is stormier; but I can stand it.

Ellie. Do you think I ought to marry Mr Mangan?

Captain Shotover (*never looking up*) One rock is as good as another to be wrecked on.

Ellie. I am not in love with him.

Captain Shotover. Who said you were?

Ellie. You are not surprised?

Captain Shotover. Surprised! At m y age!

Ellie. It seems to me quite fair. He wants me for one thing: I want him for another.

Captain Shotover. Money?

Ellie. Yes.

Captain Shotover. Well, one turns the cheek: the other kisses it. One provides the cash: the other spends it.

Ellie. Who will have the best of the bargain, I wonder?

Captain Shotover. You. These fellows live in an office all day. You will have to put up with him from dinner to breakfast but you will both be asleep most of that time. All day you will be quit of him; and you will be shopping with his money. If that is too much for you, marry a seafaring man: you will be bothered with him only three weeks in the year, perhaps.

Ellie. That would be best of all, I suppose.

Captain Shotover. It's a dangerous thing to be married right up to the hilt, like my daughter's husband. The man is at home all day, like a damned soul in hell.

Ellie. I never thought of that before.

Captain Shotover. If youre marrying for business, you cant be too businesslike.

Ellie. Why do women always want other women's husbands?

Captain Shotover. Why do horse-thieves prefer a horse that is broken-in to one that is wild?

Ellie (with a short laugh) I suppose so. What a vile world it is!

Captain Shotover. It doesnt concern me. I'm nearly out of it.

Ellie. And I'm only just beginning.

Captain Shotover. Yes; so look ahead.

Ellie. Well, I think I am being very prudent.

Captain Shotover. I didnt say prudent. I said look ahead.

Ellie. Whats the difference?

Captain Shotover. It's prudent to gain the whole world and lose your own soul. But dont forget that your soul sticks to you if you stick to it; but the world has a way of slipping through your fingers.

Ellie (wearily, leaving him and beginning to wander restlessly about the room) I'm sorry, Captain Shotover; but it's no use talking like that to me. Old-fashioned people are no use to me. Old-fashioned people think you can have a soul without money. They think the less money you have, the more soul you have. Young people nowadays know better. A soul is a very expensive thing to keep: much more so than a motor car.

Captain Shotover. Is it? How much does your soul eat?

Ellie. Oh, a lot. It eats music and pictures and books and mountains and lakes and beautiful things to wear and nice people to be with. In this country you cant have them without lots of money: that is why our souls are so horribly starved.

Captain Shotover. Mangan's soul lives on pigs' food.

Ellie. Yes: money is thrown away on him. I suppose his soul was starved when he was young. But it will not be thrown away on me. It is just because I want to save my soul that I am marrying for money. All the women who are not fools do.

Captain Shotover. There are other ways of getting money. Why dont you steal it?

Ellie. Because I dont want to go to prison.

Captain Shotover. Is that the only reason? Are you quite sure honesty has nothing to do with it?

Ellie. Oh, you are very old-fashioned, Captain. Does any modern girl believe that the legal and illegal ways of getting money are the honest and dishonest ways? Mangan robbed my father and my father's friends. I should rob all the money back from Mangan if the police would let me. As they wont, I must get it back by marrying him.

Captain Shotover. I cant argue: I'm too old: my mind is made up and finished. All I can tell you is that, old-fashioned or new-fashioned, if you sell yourself, you deal your soul a blow that all the books and pictures and concerts and scenery in the world wont heal. (*He gets up suddenly and makes for the pantry*).

Ellie (*running after him and seizing him by the sleeve*) Then why did you sell yourself to the devil in Zanzibar?

Captain Shotover (*stopping, startled*) What?

Ellie. You shall not run away before you answer. I have found out that trick of yours. If you sold yourself, why shouldnt I?

Captain Shotover. I had to deal with men so degraded that they wouldnt obey me unless I swore at them and kicked them and beat them with my fists. Foolish people took young thieves off the streets; flung them into a training ship where they were taught to fear the cane instead of fearing God; and thought theyd made men and sailors of them by private subscription. I tricked these thieves into believing I'd sold myself to the devil. It saved my soul from the kicking and swearing that was damning me by inches.

Ellie (*releasing him*) I shall pretend to sell myself to Boss Mangan to save my soul from the poverty that is damning m e by inches.

Captain Shotover. Riches will damn you ten times deeper. Riches wont save even your body.

Ellie. Old-fashioned again. We know now that the soul is the body, and the body the soul. They tell us they are different because they want to persuade us that we can keep our souls if we let them make slaves of our bodies. I am afraid you are no use to me, Captain.

Captain Shotover. What did you expect? A Savior, eh? Are you old-fashioned enough to believe in that?

Ellie. No. But I thought you were very wise, and might help me. Now I have found you out. You pretend to be busy, and think of fine things to say, and run in and out to surprise people by saying them, and get away before they can answer you.

Captain Shotover. It confuses me to be answered. It discourages me. I cannot bear men and women. I h a v e to run away. I must run away now. (*He tries to*).

Ellie (*again seizing his arm*) You shall not run away from me. I can hypnotize you. You are the only person in the house I can say what I like to. I know you are fond of me. Sit down. (*She draws him to the sofa*).

Captain Shotover (*yielding*) Take care: I am in my dotage. Old men are dangerous: it doesnt matter to them what is going to happen to the world.

They sit side by side on the sofa. She leans affectionately against him with her head on his shoulder and her eyes half closed.

Ellie (*dreamily*) I should have thought nothing else mattered to old men. They cant be very interested in what is going to happen to themselves.

Captain Shotover. A man's interest in the world is only the overflow from his interest in himself. When you are a child your vessel is not yet full; so you care for nothing but your own affairs. When you grow up, your vessel overflows; and you are a politician, a philosopher, or an explorer and adventurer. In old age the vessel dries up: there is no overflow: you are a child again. I can give you the memories of my ancient wisdom: mere scraps and leavings; but I no longer really care for anything but my own little wants and hobbies. I sit here working out my old ideas as a means of destroying my fellow-creatures. I see my daughters and their men living foolish lives of romance and sentiment and snobbery. I see you, the younger generation, turning from their romance and sentiment and snobbery to money and comfort and hard common sense. I was ten times happier on the bridge in the typhoon, or frozen into Arctic ice for months in darkness, than you or they have ever been. You are looking for a rich husband. At your age I looked for hardship, danger, horror, and death, that I might feel the life in me more intensely. I did not let the fear of death govern my life; and my reward was, I had my life. You are going to let the fear of poverty govern your life; and your reward will be that you will eat, but you will not live.

Ellie (sitting up impatiently) But what can I do? I am not a sea captain: I cant stand on bridges in typhoons, or go slaughtering seals and whales in Greenland's icy mountains. They wont let women be captains. Do you want me to be a stewardess?

Captain Shotover. There are worse lives. The stewardesses could come ashore if they liked; but they sail and sail and sail.

Ellie. What could they do ashore but marry for money? I dont want to be a stewardess: I am too bad a sailor. Think of something else for me.

Captain Shotover. I cant think so long and continuously. I am too old. I must go in and out. (*He tries to rise*).

Ellie (pulling him back) You shall not. You are happy here, arnt you?

Captain Shotover. I tell you it's dangerous to keep me. I cant keep awake and alert.

Ellie. What do you run away for? To sleep?

Captain Shotover. No. To get a glass of rum.

Ellie (*frightfully disillusioned*) Is t h a t it? How disgusting! Do you like being drunk?

Captain Shotover. No: I dread being drunk more than anything in the world. To be drunk means to have dreams; to go soft; to be easily pleased and deceived; to fall into the clutches of women. Drink does that for you when you are young. But when you are old: very very old, like me, the dreams come by themselves. You dont know how terrible that is: you are young: you sleep at night only, and sleep soundly. But later on you will sleep in the afternoon. Later still you will sleep even in the morning; and you will awake tired, tired of life. You will never be free from dozing and dreams: the dreams will steal upon your work every ten minutes unless you can awaken yourself with rum. I drink now to keep sober; but the dreams are conquering: rum is not what it was: I have had ten glasses since you came; and it might be so much water. Go get me another: Guinness knows where it is. You had better see for yourself the horror of an old man drinking.

Ellie. You shall not drink. Dream. I like you to dream. You must never be in the real world when we talk together.

Captain Shotover. I am too weary to resist or too weak. I am in my second childhood. I do not see you as you really are. I cant remember what I really am. I feel nothing but the accursed happiness I have dreaded all my life long: the happiness that comes as life goes, the happiness of yielding and dreaming instead of resisting and doing, the sweetness of the fruit that is going rotten.

Ellie. You dread it almost as much as I used to dread losing my dreams and having to fight and do things. But that is all over for me: m y dreams are dashed to pieces. I should like to marry a very old, very rich man. I should like to marry you. I had much rather marry you than marry Mangan. Are you very rich?

Captain Shotover. No. Living from hand to mouth. And I

have a wife somewhere in Jamaica: a black one. My first wife. Unless she's dead.

Ellie. What a pity! I feel so happy with you. (*She takes his hand, almost unconsciously, and pats it*). I thought I should never feel happy again.

Captain Shotover. Why?

Ellie. Dont you know?

Captain Shotover. No.

Ellie. Heartbreak. I fell in love with Hector, and didnt know he was married.

Captain Shotover. Heartbreak? Are you one of those who are so sufficient to themselves that they are only happy when they are stripped of everything, even of hope?

Ellie (*gripping the hand*) It seems so; for I feel now as if there was nothing I could not do, because I want nothing.

Captain Shotover. Thats the only real strength. Thats genius. Thats better than rum.

Ellie (*throwing away his hand*) Rum! Why did you spoil it?

Hector and Randall come in from the garden through the starboard door.

Hector. I beg your pardon. We did not know there was anyone here.

Ellie (*rising*) That means that you want to tell Mr Randall the story about the tiger. Come, Captain: I want to talk to my father; and you had better come with me.

Captain Shotover (*rising*) Nonsense! the man is in bed.

Ellie. Aha! Ive caught you. My real father has gone to bed; but the father you gave me is in the kitchen. You knew quite well all along. Come. (*She draws him out into the garden with her through the port door*).

Hector. Thats an extraordinary girl. She has the Ancient Mariner on a string like a Pekinese dog.

Randall. Now that they have gone, shall we have a friendly chat?

Hector. You are in what is supposed to be my house. I am at your disposal.

Hector sits down in the draughtsman's chair, turning it to face Randall, who remains standing, leaning at his ease against the carpenter's bench.

Randall. I take it that we may be quite frank. I mean about Lady Utterword.

Hector. Y o u may. I have nothing to be frank about. I never met her until this afternoon.

Randall (straightening up) What! But you are her sister's husband.

Hector. Well, if you come to that, you are her husband's brother.

Randall. But you seem to be on intimate terms with her.

Hector. So do you.

Randall. Yes; but I a m on intimate terms with her. I have known her for years.

Hector. It took her years to get to the same point with you that she got to with me in five minutes, it seems.

Randall (vexed) Really, Ariadne is the limit. (*He moves away huffishly towards the windows*).

Hector (coolly) She is, as I remarked to Hesione, a very enterprising woman.

Randall (returning, much troubled) You see, Hushabye, you are what women consider a good-looking man.

Hector. I cultivated that appearance in the days of my vanity; and Hesione insists on my keeping it up. She makes me wear these ridiculous things (*indicating his Arab costume*) because she thinks me absurd in evening dress.

Randall. Still, you d o keep it up, old chap. Now, I assure you I have not an atom of jealousy in my disposition—

Hector. The question would seem to be rather whether your brother has any touch of that sort.

Randall. What! Hastings! Oh, dont trouble about Hastings. He has the gift of being able to work sixteen hours a day at the dullest detail, and actually likes it. That gets him to the top wherever he goes. As long as Ariadne takes care that he is fed regularly, he is only too thankful to anyone who will keep her in good humor for him.

Hector. And as she has all the Shotover fascination, there is plenty of competition for the job, eh?

Randall (*angrily*) She encourages them. Her conduct is perfectly scandalous. I assure you, my dear fellow, I havnt an atom of jealousy in my composition; but she makes herself the talk of every place she goes to by her thoughtlessness. It's nothing more: she doesnt really care for the men she keeps hanging about her; but how is the world to know that? It's not fair to Hastings. It's not fair to me.

Hector. Her theory is that her conduct is so correct—

Randall. Correct! She does nothing but make scenes from morning till night. You be careful, old chap. She will get you into trouble: that is, she would if she really cared for you.

Hector. Doesnt she?

Randall. Not a scrap. She may want your scalp to add to her collection; but her true affection has been engaged years ago. You had really better be careful.

Hector. Do you suffer much from this jealousy?

Randall. Jealousy! I jealous! My dear fellow, havnt I told you that there is not an atom of—

Hector. Yes. And Lady Utterword told me she never made scenes. Well, dont waste your jealousy on my moustache. Never waste jealousy on a real man: it is the imaginary hero that supplants us all in the long run. Besides, jealousy does not belong to your easy man-of-the-world pose, which you carry so well in other respects.

Randall. Really, Hushabye, I think a man may be allowed to be a gentleman without being accused of posing.

Hector. It is a pose like any other. In this house we know all the poses: our game is to find out the man under the pose. The man under your pose is apparently Ellie's favorite, Othello.

Randall. Some of your games in this house are damned annoying, let me tell you.

Hector. Yes: I have been their victim for many years. I used to writhe under them at first; but I became accustomed to them. At last I learned to play them.

Randall. If it's all the same to you, I had rather you didnt play them on me. You evidently dont quite understand my character, or my notions of good form.

Hector. Is it your notion of good form to give away Lady Utterword?

Randall (*a childishly plaintive note breaking into his huff*) I have not said a word against Lady Utterword. This is just the conspiracy over again.

Hector. What conspiracy?

Randall. You know very well, sir. A conspiracy to make me out to be pettish and jealous and childish and everything I am not. Everyone knows I am just the opposite.

Hector (*rising*) Something in the air of the house has upset you. It often does have that effect. (*He goes to the garden door and calls Lady Utterword with commanding emphasis*) Ariadne!

Lady Utterword (*at some distance*) Yes.

Randall. What are you calling her for? I want to speak—

Lady Utterword (*arriving breathless*) Yes. You really are a terribly commanding person. Whats the matter?

Hector. I do not know how to manage your friend Randall. No doubt you do.

Lady Utterword. Randall: have you been making yourself ridiculous, as usual? I can see it in your face. Really, you are the most pettish creature.

Randall. You know quite well, Ariadne, that I have not an ounce of pettishness in my disposition. I have made myself perfectly pleasant here. I have remained absolutely cool and imperturbable in the face of a burglar. Imperturbability is almost too strong a point of mine. But (*putting his foot down with a stamp, and walking angrily up and down the room*) I i n s i s t on being treated with a certain consideration. I will not allow Hushabye to take liberties with me. I will not stand your encouraging people as you do.

Hector. The man has a rooted delusion that he is your husband.

Lady Utterword. I know. He is jealous. As if he had any right to be! He compromises me everywhere. He makes scenes all over the place. Randall: I will not allow it. I simply will not allow it. You had no right to discuss me with Hector. I will not be discussed by men.

Hector. Be reasonable, Ariadne. Your fatal gift of beauty forces men to discuss you.

Lady Utterword. Oh indeed! what about y o u r fatal gift of beauty?

Hector. How can I help it?

Lady Utterword. You could cut off your moustache: I cant cut off my nose. I get my whole life messed up with people falling in love with me. And then Randall says I run after men.

Randall. I—

Lady Utterword. Yes you do: you said it just now. Why cant you think of something else than women? Napoleon was quite right when he said that women are the occupation of the idle man. Well, if ever there was an idle man on earth, his name is Randall Utterword.

Randall. Ariad—

Lady Utterword (*overwhelming him with a torrent of words*) Oh yes you are: it's no use denying it. What have you ever done? What good are you? You are as much trouble in the house as a child of three. You couldnt live without your valet.

Randall. This is—

Lady Utterword. Laziness! You are laziness incarnate. You are selfishness itself. You are the most uninteresting man on earth. You cant even gossip about anything but yourself and your grievances and your ailments and the people who have offended you. (*Turning to Hector*) Do you know what they call him, Hector?

Hector   ⎱ (*speaking*   ⎰ Please dont tell me.
Randall   ⎰ *together*)   ⎱ I'll not stand it—

Lady Utterword. Randall the Rotter: that is his name in good society.

Randall (*shouting*) I'll not bear it, I tell you. Will you listen to me, you infernal— (*He chokes*).

Lady Utterword. Well: go on. What were you going to call me? An infernal what? Which unpleasant animal is it to be this time?

Randall (*foaming*) There is no animal in the world so hateful as a woman can be. You are a maddening devil. Hushabye: you will not believe me when I tell you that I have loved this demon all my life; but God knows I have paid for it. (*He sits down in the draughtsman's chair, weeping*).

Lady Utterword (*standing over him with triumphant contempt*) Cry-baby!

Hector (*gravely, coming to him*) My friend: the Shotover sisters have two strange powers over men. They can make them love; and they can make them cry. Thank your stars that you are not married to one of them.

Lady Utterword (*haughtily*) And pray, Hector—

Hector (*suddenly catching her round the shoulders; swinging her right round him and away from Randall; and gripping her throat with the other hand*) Ariadne: if you attempt to start on me, I'll choke you: do you hear? The cat-and-mouse game with the other sex is a good game; but I can play your head off at it. (*He throws her, not at all gently, into the big chair, and proceeds, less fiercely but firmly*). It is true that Napoleon said that woman is the occupation of the idle man. But he added that she is the relaxation of the warrior. Well, *I* am the warrior. So take care.

Lady Utterword (*not in the least put out, and rather pleased by his violence*) My dear Hector: I have only done what you asked me to do.

Hector. How do you make that out, pray?

Lady Utterword. You called me in to manage Randall, didnt you? You said you couldnt manage him yourself.

Hector. Well, what if I did? I did not ask you to drive the man mad.

Lady Utterword. He isnt mad. Thats the way to manage him. If you were a mother, youd understand.

Hector. Mother! What are you up to now?

Lady Utterword. It's quite simple. When the children got nerves and were naughty, I smacked them just enough to give them a good cry and a healthy nervous shock. They went to sleep and were quite good afterwards. Well, I cant smack Randall: he is too big; so when he gets nerves and is naughty, I just rag him till he cries. He will be all right now. Look: he is half asleep already. (*Which is quite true*).

Randall (*waking up indignantly*) I'm not. You are most cruel, Ariadne. (*Sentimentally*) But I suppose I must forgive you, as usual. (*He checks himself in the act of yawning*).

Lady Utterword (*to Hector*) Is the explanation satisfactory, dread warrior?

Hector. Some day I shall kill you, if you go too far. I thought you were a fool.

Lady Utterword (*laughing*) Everybody does, at first. But I am not such a fool as I look. (*She rises complacently*). Now, Randall: go to bed. You will be a good boy in the morning.

Randall (*only very faintly rebellious*) I'll go to bed when I like. It isnt ten yet.

Lady Utterword. It is long past ten. See that he goes to bed at once, Hector. (*She goes into the garden*).

Hector. Is there any slavery on earth viler than this slavery of men to women?

Randall (*rising resolutely*) I'll not speak to her tomorrow.

I'll not speak to her for another week. I'll give her s u c h a
lesson. I'll go straight to bed without bidding her goodnight.
(*He makes for the door leading to the hall*).

Hector. You are under a spell, man. Old Shotover sold himself to the devil in Zanzibar. The devil gave him a black witch
for a wife; and these two demon daughters are their mystical
progeny. I am tied to Hesione's apron-string; but I'm her husband; and if I did go stark staring mad about her, at least we
became man and wife. But why should y o u let yourself be
dragged about and beaten by Ariadne as a toy donkey is
dragged about and beaten by a child? What do you get by it?
Are you her lover?

Randall. You must not misunderstand me. In a higher sense
—in a Platonic sense—

Hector. Psha! Platonic sense! She makes you her servant;
and when pay-day comes round, she bilks you: that is what
you mean.

Randall (*feebly*) Well, if I dont mind, I dont see what
business it is of yours. Besides, I tell you I am going to punish
her. You shall see: *I* know how to deal with women. I'm really
very sleepy. Say goodnight to Mrs Hushabye for me, will you,
like a good chap. Goodnight. (*He hurries out*).

Hector. Poor wretch! Oh women! women! women! (*He lifts
his fists in invocation to heaven*). Fall. Fall and crush. (*He goes
out into the garden*).

ACT III

IN THE GARDEN, Hector, as he comes out through the glass door of the poop, finds Lady Utterword lying voluptuously in the hammock on the east side of the flagstaff, in the circle of light cast by the electric arc, which is like a moon in its opal globe. Beneath the head of the hammock, a campstool. On the other side of the flagstaff, on the long garden seat, Captain Shotover is asleep, with Ellie beside him, leaning affectionately against him on his right hand. On his left is a deck chair. Behind them in the gloom, Hesione is strolling about with Mangan. It is a fine still night, moonless.

Lady Utterword. What a lovely night! It seems made for us.

Hector. The night takes no interest in us. What are we to the night? (*He sits down moodily in the deck chair*).

Ellie (*dreamily, nestling against the Captain*) Its beauty soaks into my nerves. In the night there is peace for the old and hope for the young.

Hector. Is that remark your own?

Ellie. No. Only the last thing the Captain said before he went to sleep.

Captain Shotover. I'm not asleep.

Hector. Randall is. Also Mr Mazzini Dunn. Mangan too, probably.

Mangan. No.

Hector. Oh, you are there. I thought Hesione would have sent you to bed by this time.

Mrs Hushabye (*coming to the back of the garden seat, into the light, with Mangan*) I think I shall. He keeps telling me he has a presentiment that he is going to die. I never met a man so greedy for sympathy.

Mangan (*plaintively*) But I have a presentiment. I really have. And you wouldnt listen.

Mrs Hushabye. I was listening for something else. There was a sort of splendid drumming in the sky. Did none of you hear it? It came from a distance and then died away.

Mangan. I tell you it was a train.

Mrs Hushabye. And I tell you, Alf, there is no train at this hour. The last is nine forty-five.

Mangan. But a goods train.

Mrs Hushabye. Not on our little line. They tack a truck on to the passenger train. What can it have been, Hector?

Hector. Heaven's threatening growl of disgust at us useless futile creatures. (*Fiercely*) I tell you, one of two things must happen. Either out of that darkness some new creation will come to supplant us as we have supplanted the animals, or the heavens will fall in thunder and destroy us.

Lady Utterword (*in a cool instructive manner, wallowing comfortably in her hammock*) We have not supplanted the animals, Hector. Why do you ask heaven to destroy this house, which could be made quite comfortable if Hesione had any notion of how to live? Dont you know what is wrong with it?

Hector. We are wrong with it. There is no sense in us. We are useless, dangerous, and ought to be abolished.

Lady Utterword. Nonsense! Hastings told me the very first day he came here, nearly twenty-four years ago, what is wrong with the house.

Captain Shotover. What! The numskull said there was something wrong with my house!

Lady Utterword. I said Hastings said it; and he is not in the least a numskull.

Captain Shotover. Whats wrong with my house?

Lady Utterword. Just what is wrong with a ship, papa. Wasnt it clever of Hastings to see that?

Captain Shotover. The man's a fool. Theres nothing wrong with a ship.

Lady Utterword. Yes there is.

Mrs Hushabye. But what is it? Dont be aggravating, Addy.

Lady Utterword. Guess.

Hector. Demons. Daughters of the witch of Zanzibar. Demons.

Lady Utterword. Not a bit. I assure you, all this house needs to make it a sensible, healthy, pleasant house, with good appetites and sound sleep in it, is horses.

Mrs Hushabye. Horses! What rubbish!

Lady Utterword. Yes: horses. Why have we never been able to let this house? Because there are no proper stables. Go anywhere in England where there are natural, wholesome, contented, and really nice English people; and what do you always find? That the stables are the real centre of the household; and that if any visitor wants to play the piano the whole room has to be upset before it can be opened, there are so many things piled on it. I never lived until I learned to ride; and I shall never ride really well because I didnt begin as a child. There are only two classes in good society in England: the equestrian classes and the neurotic classes. It isnt mere convention: everybody can see that the people who hunt are the right people and the people who dont are the wrong ones.

Captain Shotover. There is some truth in this. My ship made a man of me; and a ship is the horse of the sea.

Lady Utterword. Exactly how Hastings explained your being a gentleman.

Captain Shotover. Not bad for a numskull. Bring the man here with you next time: I must talk to him.

Lady Utterword. Why is Randall such an obvious rotter? He is well bred; he has been at a public school and a university; he has been in the Foreign Office; he knows the best people and has lived all his life among them. Why is he so unsatisfactory, so contemptible? Why cant he get a valet to stay with him longer than a few months? Just because he is too lazy and pleasure-loving to hunt and shoot. He strums the piano, and sketches, and runs after married women, and reads literary books and poems. He actually plays the flute; but I never let him bring it into my house. If he would only— (*She is interrupted by the melancholy strains of a flute coming from an open window above. She raises herself indignantly in the hammock*). Randall: you have not gone to bed. Have you been listening? (*The flute replies pertly*):

How vulgar! Go to bed instantly, Randall: how dare you? (*The window is slammed down. She subsides*). How can anyone care for such a creature!

Mrs Hushabye. Addy: do you think Ellie ought to marry poor Alfred merely for his money?

Mangan (*much alarmed*) Whats that? Mrs Hushabye: are my affairs to be discussed like this before everybody?

Lady Utterword. I dont think Randall is listening now.

Mangan. Everybody is listening. It isnt right.

Mrs Hushabye. But in the dark, what does it matter? Ellie doesnt mind. Do you, Ellie?

Ellie. Not in the least. What is your opinion, Lady Utterword? You have so much good sense.

Mangan. But it isnt right. It— (*Mrs Hushabye puts her hand on his mouth*). Oh, very well.

Lady Utterword. How much money have you, Mr Mangan?

Mangan. Really— No: I cant stand this.

Lady Utterword. Nonsense, Mr Mangan! It all turns on your income, doesnt it?

Mangan. Well, if you come to that, how much money has she?

Ellie. None.

Lady Utterword. You are answered, Mr Mangan. And now, as you have made Miss Dunn throw her cards on the table, you cannot refuse to shew your own.

Mrs Hushabye. Come, Alf! out with it! How much?

Mangan (*baited out of all prudence*) Well, if you want to know, I have no money and never had any.

Mrs Hushabye. Alfred: you mustnt tell naughty stories.

Mangan. I'm not telling you stories. I'm telling you the raw truth.

Lady Utterword. Then what do you live on, Mr Mangan?

Mangan. Travelling expenses. And a trifle of commission.

Captain Shotover. What more have any of us but travelling expenses for our life's journey?

Mrs Hushabye. But you have factories and capital and things?

Mangan. People think I have. People think I'm an industrial Napoleon. Thats why Miss Ellie wants to marry me. But I tell you I have nothing.

Ellie. Do you mean that the factories are like Marcus's tigers? That they dont exist?

Mangan. They exist all right enough. But theyre not mine. They belong to syndicates and shareholders and all sorts of lazy good-for-nothing capitalists. I get money from such people to start the factories. I find people like Miss Dunn's father to work them, and keep a tight hand so as to make them pay. Of course I make them keep me going pretty well; but it's a dog's life; and I dont own anything.

Mrs Hushabye. Alfred, Alfred: you are making a poor mouth of it to get out of marrying Ellie.

Mangan. I'm telling the truth about my money for the first time in my life; and it's the first time my word has ever been doubted.

Lady Utterword. How sad! Why dont you go in for politics, Mr Mangan?

Mangan. Go in for politics! Where have you been living? I a m in politics.

Lady Utterword. I'm sure I beg your pardon. I never heard of you.

Mangan. Let me tell you, Lady Utterword, that the Prime Minister of this country asked me to join the Government without even going through the nonsense of an election, as the dictator of a great public department.

Lady Utterword. As a Conservative or a Liberal?

Mangan. No such nonsense. As a practical business man. (*They all burst out laughing*). What are you all laughing at?

Mrs Hushabye. Oh, Alfred, Alfred!

Ellie. You! who have to get my father to do everything for you!

Mrs Hushabye. You! who are afraid of your own workmen!

Hector. You! with whom three women have been playing cat and mouse all the evening!

Lady Utterword. You must have given an immense sum to the party funds, Mr Mangan.

Mangan. Not a penny out of my own pocket. The syndicate found the money: they knew how useful I should be to them in the Government.

Lady Utterword. This is most interesting and unexpected, Mr Mangan. And what have your administrative achievements been, so far?

Mangan. Achievements? Well, I dont know what you call achievements; but Ive jolly well put a stop to the games of the other fellows in the other departments. Every man of them thought he was going to save the country all by himself, and do me out of the credit and out of my chance of a title. I took good care that if they wouldnt let me do it they shouldnt do it themselves either. I may not know anything about my own machinery; but I know how to stick a ramrod into the other fellow's. And now they all look the biggest fools going.

Hector. And in heaven's name, what do you look like?

Mangan. I look like the fellow that was too clever for all the others, dont I? If that isnt a triumph of practical business, what is?

Hector. Is this England, or is it a madhouse?

Lady Utterword. Do you expect to save the country, Mr Mangan?

Mangan. Well, who else will? Will your Mr Randall save it?

Lady Utterword. Randall the rotter! Certainly not.

Mangan. Will your brother-in-law save it with his moustache and his fine talk?

Hector. Yes, if they will let me.

Mangan (sneering) Ah! Will they let you?

Hector. No. They prefer you.

Mangan. Very well then, as youre in a world where I'm appreciated and youre not, youd best be civil to me, hadnt you? Who else is there but me?

Lady Utterword. There is Hastings. Get rid of your ridiculous sham democracy; and give Hastings the necessary powers, and a good supply of bamboo to bring the British native to his senses: he will save the country with the greatest ease.

Captain Shotover. It had better be lost. Any fool can govern with a stick in his hand. I could govern that way. It is not God's way. The man is a numskull.

Lady Utterword. The man is worth all of you rolled into one. What do you say, Miss Dunn?

Ellie. I think my father would do very well if people did not put upon him and cheat him and despise him because he is so good.

Mangan (contemptuously) I think I see Mazzini Dunn getting into parliament or pushing his way into the Government. Weve not come to that yet, thank God! What do you say, Mrs Hushabye?

Mrs Hushabye. Oh, I say it matters very little which of you governs the country so long as we govern you.

Hector. We? Who is we, pray?

Mrs Hushabye. The devil's granddaughters, dear. The lovely women.

Hector (*raising his hands as before*) Fall, I say; and deliver us from the lures of Satan!

Ellie. There seems to be nothing real in the world except my father and Shakespear. Marcus's tigers are false; Mr Mangan's millions are false; there is nothing really strong and true about Hesione but her beautiful black hair; and Lady Utterword's is too pretty to be real. The one thing that was left to me was the Captain's seventh degree of concentration; and that turns out to be—

Captain Shotover. Rum.

Lady Utterword (*placidly*) A good deal of my hair is quite genuine. The Duchess of Dithering offered me fifty guineas for this (*touching her forehead*) under the impression that it was a transformation; but it is all natural except the color.

Mangan (*wildly*) Look here: I'm going to take off all my clothes. (*He begins tearing off his coat*).

Lady Utterword.		Mr Mangan!
Captain Shotover.	(*in consternation*)	Whats that?
Hector.		Ha! ha! Do. Do.
Ellie.		Please dont.

Mrs Hushabye (*catching his arm and stopping him*) Alfred: for shame! Are you mad?

Mangan. Shame! What shame is there in this house? Let's all strip stark naked. We may as well do the thing thoroughly when we're about it. Weve stripped ourselves morally naked: well, let us strip ourselves physically naked as well, and see how we like it. I tell you I cant bear this. I was brought up to be respectable. I dont mind the women dyeing their hair and the men drinking: it's human nature. But it's not human nature to tell everybody about it. Every time one of you opens your mouth I go like this (*he cowers as if to avoid a missile*) afraid of what will come next. How are we to have any self-respect if we dont keep it up that we're better than we really are?

Lady Utterword. I quite sympathize with you, Mr Mangan. I have been through it all; and I know by experience that men and women are delicate plants and must be cultivated under glass. Our family habit of throwing stones in all directions and letting the air in is not only unbearably rude, but positively dangerous. Still, there is no use catching physical colds as well as moral ones; so please keep your clothes on.

Mangan. I'll do as I like: not what you tell me. Am I a child or a grown man? I wont stand this mothering tyranny. I'll go back to the city, where I'm respected and made much of.

Mrs Hushabye. Goodbye, Alf. Think of us sometimes in the city. Think of Ellie's youth!

Ellie. Think of Hesione's eyes and hair!

Captain Shotover. Think of this garden in which you are not a dog barking to keep the truth out!

Hector. Think of Lady Utterword's beauty! her good sense! her style!

Lady Utterword. Flatterer. Think, Mr Mangan, whether you can really do any better for yourself elsewhere: that is the essential point, isnt it?

Mangan (*surrendering*) All right: all right. I'm done. Have it your own way. Only let me alone. I dont know whether I'm on my head or my heels when you all start on me like this. I'll stay. I'll marry her. I'll do anything for a quiet life. Are you satisfied now?

Ellie. No. I never really intended to make you marry me, Mr Mangan. Never in the depths of my soul. I only wanted to feel my strength: to know that you could not escape if I chose to take you.

Mangan (*indignantly*) What! Do you mean to say you are going to throw me over after my acting so handsome?

Lady Utterword. I should not be too hasty, Miss Dunn. You can throw Mr Mangan over at any time up to the last moment. Very few men in his position go bankrupt. You can live very comfortably on his reputation for immense wealth.

Ellie. I cannot commit bigamy, Lady Utterword.

Mrs Hushabye.		Bigamy! Whatever on earth are you talking about, Ellie?
Lady Utterword.	*(exclaiming all together)*	Bigamy! What do you mean, Miss Dunn?
Mangan.		Bigamy! Do you mean to say youre married already?
Hector.		Bigamy! This is some enigma.

Ellie. Only half an hour ago I became Captain Shotover's white wife.

Mrs Hushabye. Ellie! What nonsense! Where?

Ellie. In heaven, where all true marriages are made.

Lady Utterword. Really, Miss Dunn! Really, papa!

Mangan. He told me *I* was too old! And him a mummy!

Hector (quoting Shelley)

"Their altar the grassy earth outspread,
And their priest the muttering wind."

Ellie. Yes: I, Ellie Dunn, give my broken heart and my strong sound soul to its natural captain, my spiritual husband and second father.

She draws the Captain's arm through hers, and pats his hand. The Captain remains fast asleep.

Mrs Hushabye. Oh, thats very clever of you, pettikins. V e r y clever. Alfred: you could never have lived up to Ellie. You must be content with a little share of me.

Mangan (sniffing and wiping his eyes) It isnt kind— (*His emotion chokes him*).

Lady Utterword. You are well out of it, Mr Mangan. Miss Dunn is the most conceited young woman I have met since I came back to England.

Mrs Hushabye. Oh, Ellie isnt conceited. Are you, pettikins?

Ellie. I know my strength now, Hesione.

Mangan. Brazen, I call you. Brazen.

Mrs Hushabye. Tut tut, Alfred: dont be rude. Dont you feel how lovely this marriage night is, made in heaven? Arnt you happy, you and Hector? Open yor eyes: Addy and Ellie look beautiful enough to please the most fastidious man: we live and love and have not a care in the world. We women have managed all that for you. Why in the name of common sense do you go on as if you were two miserable wretches?

Captain Shotover. I tell you happiness is no good. You can be happy when you are only half alive. I am happier now I am half dead than ever I was in my prime. But there is no blessing on my happiness.

Ellie (her face lighting up) Life with a blessing! that is what I want. Now I know the real reason why I couldnt marry Mr Mangan: there would be no blessing on our marriage. There is a blessing on my broken heart. There is a blessing on your beauty, Hesione. There is a blessing on your father's spirit. Even on the lies of Marcus there is a blessing; but on Mr Mangan's money there is none.

Mangan. I dont understand a word of that.

Ellie. Neither do I. But I know it means something.

Mangan. Dont say there was any difficulty about the blessing. I was ready to get a bishop to marry us.

Mrs Hushabye. Isnt he a fool, pettikins?

Hector (fiercely) Do not scorn the man. We are all fools.

Mazzini, in pyjamas and a richly colored silk dressing-gown, comes from the house, on Lady Utterword's side.

Mrs Hushabye. Oh! here comes the only man who ever re sisted me. Whats the matter, Mr Dunn? Is the house on fire?

Mazzini. Oh no: nothing's the matter: but really it's impossible to go to sleep with such an interesting conversation going on under one's window, and on such a beautiful night too. I just had to come down and join you all. What has it all been about?

Mrs Hushabye. Oh, wonderful things, soldier of freedom.

Hector. For example, Mangan, as a practical business man

has tried to undress himself and has failed ignominiously; whilst you, as an idealist, have succeeded brilliantly.

Mazzini. I hope you dont mind my being like this, Mrs Hushabye. (*He sits down on the campstool*).

Mrs Hushabye. On the contrary, I could wish you always like that.

Lady Utterword. Your daughter's match is off, Mr Dunn. It seems that Mr Mangan, whom we all supposed to be a man of property, owns absolutely nothing.

Mazzini. Well of course I knew that, Lady Utterword. But if people believe in him and are always giving him money, whereas they dont believe in me and never give me any, how can I ask poor Ellie to depend on what I can do for her?

Mangan. Dont you run away with this idea that I have nothing. I—

Hector. Oh, dont explain. We understand. You have a couple of thousand pounds in exchequer bills, 50,000 shares worth tenpence a dozen, and half a dozen tabloids of cyanide of potassium to poison yourself with when you are found out. Thats the reality of your millions.

Mazzini. Oh no, no, no. He is quite honest: the businesses are genuine and perfectly legal.

Hector (*disgusted*) Yah! Not even a great swindler!

Mangan. So you think. But Ive been too many for some honest men, for all that.

Lady Utterword. There is no pleasing you, Mr Mangan. You are determined to be neither rich nor poor, honest nor dishonest.

Mangan. There you go again. Ever since I came into this silly house I have been made to look like a fool, though I'm as good a man in this house as in the city.

Ellie (*musically*) Yes: this silly house, this strangely happy house, this agonizing house, this house without foundations. I shall call it Heartbreak House.

Mrs Hushabye. Stop, Ellie; or I shall howl like an animal.

Mangan (breaks into a low snivelling)!!!

Mrs Hushabye. There! you have set Alfred off.

Ellie. I like him best when he is howling.

Captain Shotover. Silence! (*Mangan subsides into silence*). I say, let the heart break in silence.

Hector. Do you accept that name for your house?

Captain Shotover. It is not my house: it is only my kennel.

Hector. We have been too long here. We do not live in this house: we haunt it.

Lady Utterword (heart torn) It is dreadful to think how you have been here all these years while I have gone round the world. I escaped young; but it has drawn me back. It wants to break my heart too. But it shant. I have left you and it behind. It was silly of me to come back. I felt sentimental about papa and Hesione and the old place. I felt them calling to me.

Mazzini. But what a very natural and kindly and charming human feeling, Lady Utterword!

Lady Utterword. So I thought, Mr Dunn. But I know now that it was only the last of my influenza. I found that I was not remembered and not wanted.

Captain Shotover. You left because you did not want us. Was there no heartbreak in that for your father? You tore yourself up by the roots; and the ground healed up and brought forth fresh plants and forgot you. What right had you to come back and probe old wounds?

Mrs Hushabye. You were a complete stranger to me at first, Addy; but now I feel as if you had never been away.

Lady Utterword. Thank you, Hesione; but the influence is quite cured. The place may be Heartbreak House to you, Miss Dunn, and to this gentleman from the city who seems to have so little self-control; but to me it is only a very ill-regulated and rather untidy villa without any stables.

Hector. Inhabited by—?

Ellie. A crazy old sea captain and a young singer who adores him.

Mrs Hushabye. A sluttish female, trying to stave off a double chin and an elderly spread, vainly wooing a born soldier of freedom.

Mazzini. Oh, really, Mrs Hushabye—

Mangan. A member of His Majesty's Government that everybody sets down as a nincompoop: dont forget him, Lady Utterword.

Lady Utterword. And a very fascinating gentleman whose chief occupation is to be married to my sister.

Hector. All heartbroken imbeciles.

Mazzini. Oh no. Surely, if I may say so, rather a favorable specimen of what is best in our English culture. You are very charming people, most advanced, unprejudiced, frank, humane, unconventional, democratic, free-thinking, and everything that is delightful to thoughtful people.

Mrs Hushabye. You do us proud, Mazzini.

Mazzini. I am not flattering, really. Where else could I feel perfectly at ease in my pyjamas? I sometimes dream that I am in very distinguished society, and suddenly I have nothing on but my pyjamas! Sometimes I havnt even pyjamas. And I always feel overwhelmed with confusion. But here, I dont mind in the least: it seems quite natural.

Lady Utterword. An infallible sign that you are not now in really distinguished society, Mr Dunn. If you were in my house, you w o u l d feel embarrassed.

Mazzini. I shall take particular care to keep out of your house, Lady Utterword.

Lady Utterword. You will be quite wrong, Mr Dunn. I should make you very comfortable; and you would not have the trouble and anxiety of wondering whether you should wear your purple and gold or your green and crimson dressing-gown at dinner. You complicate life instead of simplifying it by doing these ridiculous things.

Ellie. Y o u r house is not Heartbreak House: is it, Lady Utterword?

Hector. Yet she breaks hearts, easy as her house is. That poor devil upstairs with his flute howls when she twists his heart, just as Mangan howls when my wife twists his.

Lady Utterword. That is because Randall has nothing to do but have his heart broken. It is a change from having his head shampooed. Catch anyone breaking Hastings' heart!

Captain Shotover. The numskull wins, after all.

Lady Utterword. I shall go back to my numskull with the greatest satisfaction when I am tired of you all, clever as you are.

Mangan (*huffily*) I never set up to be clever.

Lady Utterword. I forgot you, Mr Mangan.

Mangan. Well, I dont see that quite, either.

Lady Utterword. You may not be clever, Mr Mangan; but you are successful.

Mangan. But I dont want to be regarded merely as a successful man. I have an imagination like anyone else. I have a presentiment—

Mrs Hushabye. Oh, you are impossible, Alfred. Here I am devoting myself to you; and you think of nothing but your ridiculous presentiment. You bore me. Come and talk poetry to me under the stars. (*She drags him away into the darkness*).

Mangan (*tearfully, as he disappears*) Yes: it's all very well to make fun of me; but if you only knew—

Hector (*impatiently*) How is all this going to end?

Mazzini. It wont end, Mr Hushabye. Life doesnt end: it goes on.

Ellie. Oh, it cant go on for ever. I'm always expecting something. I dont know what it is; but life must come to a point sometime.

Lady Utterword. The point for a young woman of your age is a baby.

Hector. Yes, but, damn it, I have the same feeling; and *I* cant have a baby.

Lady Utterword. By deputy, Hector.

Hector. But I h a v e children. All that is over and done with for me: and yet I too feel that this cant last. We sit here talking, and leave everything to Mangan and to chance and to the devil. Think of the powers of destruction that Mangan and his mutual admiration gang wield! It's madness: it's like giving a torpedo to a badly brought up child to play at earthquakes with.

Mazzini. I know. I used often to think about that when I was young.

Hector. Think! Whats the good of thinking about it? Why didnt you do something?

Mazzini. But I did. I joined societies and made speeches and wrote pamphlets. That was all I could do. But, you know, though the people in the societies thought they knew more than Mangan, most of them wouldnt have joined if they had known as much. You see they had never had any money to handle or any men to manage. Every year I expected a revolution, or some frightful smash-up: it seemed impossible that we could blunder and muddle on any longer. But nothing happened, except, of course, the usual poverty and crime and drink that we are used to. Nothing ever does happen. It's amazing how well we get along, all things considered.

Lady Utterword. Perhaps somebody cleverer than you and Mr Mangan was at work all the time.

Mazzini. Perhaps so. Though I was brought up not to believe in anything, I often feel that there is a great deal to be said for the theory of an overruling Providence, after all.

Lady Utterword. Providence! I meant Hastings.

Mazzini. Oh, I beg your pardon, Lady Utterword.

Captain Shotover. Every drunken skipper trusts to Providence. But one of the ways of Providence with drunken skippers is to run them on the rocks.

Mazzini. Very true, no doubt, at sea. But in politics, I assure you, they only run into jellyfish. Nothing happens.

Captain Shotover. At sea nothing happens to the sea. Nothing happens to the sky. The sun comes up from the east and goes down to the west. The moon grows from a sickle to an arc lamp, and comes later and later until she is lost in the light as other things are lost in the darkness. After the typhoon, the flying-fish glitter in the sunshine like birds. It's amazing how t h e y get along, all things considered. Nothing happens, except something not worth mentioning.

Ellie. What is that, O Captain, my captain?

Captain Shotover (*savagely*) Nothing but the smash of the drunken skipper's ship on the rocks, the splintering of her rotten timbers, the tearing of her rusty plates, the drowning of the crew like rats in a trap.

Ellie. Moral: dont take rum.

Captain Shotover (*vehemently*) That is a lie, child. Let a man drink ten barrels of rum a day, he is not a drunken skipper until he is a drifting skipper. Whilst he can lay his course and stand on his bridge and steer it, he is no drunkard. It is the man who lies drinking in his bunk and trusts to Providence that I call the drunken skipper, though he drank nothing but the waters of the River Jordan.

Ellie. Splendid! And you havnt had a drop for an hour. You see you dont need it: your own spirit is not dead.

Captain Shotover. Echoes: nothing but echoes. The last shot was fired years ago.

Hector. And this ship that we are all in? This soul's prison we call England?

Captain Shotover. The captain is in his bunk, drinking bottled ditch-water; and the crew is gambling in the forecastle. She will strike and sink and split. Do you think the laws of God will be suspended in favor of England because you were born in it?

Hector. Well, I dont mean to be drowned like a rat in a trap. I still have the will to live. What am I to do?

Captain Shotover. Do? Nothing simpler. Learn your business as an Englishman.

Hector. And what may my business as an Englishman be, pray?

Captain Shotover. Navigation. Learn it and live; or leave it and be damned.

Ellie. Quiet, quiet: youll tire yourself.

Mazzini. I thought all that once, Captain; but I assure you nothing will happen.

A dull distant explosion is heard.

Hector (starting up) What was that?

Captain Shotover. Something happening. (*He blows his whistle*). Breakers ahead!

The light goes out.

Hector (furiously) Who put that light out? Who dared put that light out?

Nurse Guinness (running in from the house to the middle of the esplanade) I did, sir. The police have telephoned to say we'll be summoned if we dont put that light out: it can be seen for miles.

Hector. It shall be seen for a hundred miles. (*He dashes into the house*).

Nurse Guinness. The rectory is nothing but a heap of bricks, they say. Unless we can give the rector a bed he has nowhere to lay his head this night.

Captain Shotover. The Church is on the rocks, breaking up. I told him it would unless it headed for God's open sea.

Nurse Guinness. And you are all to go down to the cellars.

Captain Shotover. Go there yourself, you and all the crew. Batten down the hatches.

Nurse Guinness. And hide beside the coward I married! I'll go on the roof first. (*The lamp lights up again*). There! Mr Hushabye's turned it on again.

The Burglar (hurrying in and appealing to Nurse Guinness) Here: wheres the way to that gravel pit? The boot-boy says theres a cave in the gravel pit. Them cellars is no use. Wheres the gravel pit, Captain?

Nurse Guinness. Go straight on past the flagstaff until you fall into it and break your dirty neck. (*She pushes him contemptuously towards the flagstaff, and herself goes to the foot of the hammock and waits there, as it were by Ariadne's cradle*).

Another and louder explosion is heard. The burglar stops and stands trembling.

Ellie (rising) That was nearer.

Captain Shotover. The next one will get us. (*He rises*). Stand by, all hands, for judgment.

The Burglar. Oh my Lordy God! (*He rushes away frantically past the flagstaff into the gloom*).

Mrs Hushabye (emerging panting from the darkness) Who was that running away? (*She comes to Ellie*). Did you hear the explosions? And the sound in the sky: it's splendid: it's like an orchestra: it's like Beethoven.

Ellie. By thunder, Hesione: it i s Beethoven.

She and Hesione throw themselves into one another's arms in wild excitement. The light increases.

Mazzini (anxiously) The light is getting brighter.

Nurse Guinness (looking up at the house) It's Mr Hushabye turning on all the lights in the house and tearing down the curtains.

Randall (rushing in in his pyjamas, distractedly waving a flute) Ariadne: my soul, my precious, go down to the cellars: I beg and implore you, go down to the cellars!

Lady Utterword (quite composed in her hammock) The governor's wife in the cellars with the servants! Really, Randall!

Randall. But what shall I do if you are killed?

Lady Utterword. You will probably be killed, too, Randall. Now play your flute to shew that you are not afraid; and be good. Play us Keep the home fires burning.

Nurse Guinness (grimly) T h e y l l keep the home fires burning for us: them up there.

Randall (*having tried to play*) My lips are trembling. I cant get a sound.

Mazzini. I hope poor Mangan is safe.

Mrs Hushabye. He is hiding in the cave in the gravel pit.

Captain Shotover. My dynamite drew him there. It is the hand of God.

Hector (*returning from the house and striding across to his former place*) There is not half light enough. We should be blazing to the skies.

Ellie (*tense with excitement*) Set fire to the house, Marcus.

Mrs Hushabye. My house! No.

Hector. I thought of that; but it would not be ready in time.

Captain Shotover. The judgment has come. Courage will not save you; but it will shew that your souls are still alive.

Mrs Hushabye. Sh-sh! Listen: do you hear it now? It's magnificent.

They all turn away from the house and look up, listening.

Hector (*gravely*) Miss Dunn: you can do no good here. We of this house are only moths flying into the candle. You had better go down to the cellar.

Ellie (*scornfully*) I d o n t think.

Mazzini. Ellie, dear, there is no disgrace in going to the cellar. An officer would order his soldiers to take cover. Mr Hushabye is behaving like an amateur. Mangan and the burglar are acting very sensibly; and it is they who will survive.

Ellie. Let them. I shall behave like an amateur. But why should you run any risk?

Mazzini. Think of the risk those poor fellows up there are running!

Nurse Guinness. Think of t h e m, indeed, the murdering blackguards! What next?

A terrific explosion shakes the earth. They reel back into their seats, or clutch the nearest support. They hear the falling of the shattered glass from the windows.

Mazzini. Is anyone hurt?

Hector. Where did it fall?

Nurse Guinness (in hideous triumph) Right in the gravel pit: I seen it. Serve un right! I seen it. (*She runs away towards the gravel pit, laughing harshly*).

Hector. One husband gone.

Captain Shotover. Thirty pounds of good dynamite wasted.

Mazzini. Oh, poor Mangan!

Hector. Are you immortal that you need pity him? Our turn next.

They wait in silence and intense expectation. Hesione and Ellie hold each other's hand tight.

A distant explosion is heard.

Mrs Hushabye (relaxing her grip) Oh! they have passed us.

Lady Utterword. The danger is over, Randall. Go to bed.

Captain Shotover. Turn in, all hands. The ship is safe. (*He sits down and goes asleep*).

Ellie (disappointedly) Safe!

Hector (disgustedly) Yes, safe. And how damnably dull the world has become again suddenly! (*He sits down*).

Mazzini (sitting down) I was quite wrong, after all. It is we who have survived; and Mangan and the burglar—

Hector. —the two burglars—

Lady Utterword. —the two practical men of business—

Mazzini. —both gone. And the poor clergyman will have to get a new house.

Mrs Hushabye. But what a glorious experience! I hope theyll come again tomorrow night.

Ellie (radiant at the prospect) Oh, I hope so.

Randall at last succeeds in keeping the home fires burning on his flute.

MODERN LIBRARY GIANTS

A series of full-sized library editions of books that formerly were available only in cumbersome and expensive sets.
THE MODERN LIBRARY GIANTS REPRESENT A SELECTION OF THE WORLD'S GREATEST BOOKS

These volumes contain from 600 to 1,400 pages each

Interior by Melanie Kahane, A. I. D.

No modern library is complete
without THE AMERICAN
COLLEGE DICTIONARY